# THEY GAVE YOU A TITLE AND A PAYCHECK BUT WHAT YOU NEED MOST IS THIS BOOK

STEVEN SACK is a practicing attorney, author, lecturer, and radio host. He has written eighteen books on legal subjects, serves as a consultant for FindLaw.com, and hosts his own nationally syndicated radio show on workplace issues called *Steven Sack, The Employee's Lawyer* through the i.e. america radio broadcasting network. In this comprehensive guidebook, attorney Sack covers every aspect of your life on the job—from getting hired to leaving with all the benefits and pay you deserve. Use this book to:

- know the law, stop illegal harassment, and combat unfair work place practices

- collect the salary, overtime, or benefits you are entitled to

- take control of your job interview by knowing which questions prospective employers can legally ask, and which they can't

- find out how and when to resign from a job to your best advantage

- negotiate every aspect of your employment, from your starting salary to a severance package if you are fired

- bring a successful legal action against your employer—and win it.

*Please turn this page for praise for "The Employee's Lawyer" Steven Sack and his previous books.*

"Sack looks seemingly everywhere job discrimination might lurk and where special accommodations, if any, should be made."
**—New York Times**

"Sack offers tips that all workers should use to empower themselves. . . . If there's one message driving Sack through his work, it's 'know your rights.'"
**—Detroit News**

"Loaded with advice [and] peppered with interesting vignettes . . . turns a great deal of legal material into plain English that is easy to understand."
**—Denver Rocky Mountain News on Getting Fired**

"Get your hands on *Getting Fired* . . . [and] leave that company with more dignity and more money."
**—St. Louis Post-Dispatch**

"Salvaging your pride and your pocketbook is as easy as following this book. . . . A helpful guide through what could be, in less capable hands, a maze of legalese. . . . Run, don't walk, to the nearest bookstore."
**—Bellingham Business Journal (WA) on Getting Fired**

"Sack knows the law and what you can do. . . . His information is invaluable."
**—Rapport**

---

### ALSO BY STEVEN MITCHELL SACK

*The Salesperson's Legal Guide*
*Don't Get Taken: How to Avoid Everyday Consumer Rip-Offs*
*The Complete Legal Guide to Marriage, Divorce, Custody and Living Together*
*From Hiring to Firing: The Legal Survival Guide for Employers in the 90's*
*The Complete Collection of Legal Forms for Employers*
*The Lifetime Legal Guide*
*The Working Woman's Legal Survival Guide*
*Getting Fired*

# STEVEN MITCHELL SACK

# THE

# EMPLOYEE RIGHTS HANDBOOK

## *The Essential Guide for People on the Job*

### REVISED AND UPDATED

**WARNER BOOKS**

A Time Warner Company

PUBLISHER'S NOTE: This publication is designed to provide competent and reliable information regarding the subject matter covered. However, it is sold with the understanding that the author and publisher are not engaged in rendering legal or other professional advice. Laws and practices often vary from state to state and if legal or other expert assistance is required, the services of a professional should be sought. The author and publisher specifically disclaim any liability that is incurred from the use or application of the contents of this book.

Warner Books Edition
Copyright © 1991, 2000 by Steven Mitchell Sack
All rights reserved.

This Warner Books edition is published by arrangement with the author.
Warner Books, Inc., 1271 Avenue of the Americas, New York, NY 10020

Visit our Web site at www.twbookmark.com

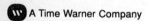 A Time Warner Company

Printed in the United States of America
First Warner Books Printing: October 2000
10  9  8  7  6  5  4  3  2  1

Library of Congress Cataloging-in-Publication Data

Sack, Steven Mitchell.
    The employee rights handbook / Steven Mitchell Sack.
        p.   cm.
    Includes index.
    ISBN 0-446-67326-9
    1. Labor laws and legislation—United States Popular works.
    2. Employee rights—United States Popular works.   I. Title.
KF3455.Z9S23   2000
344.7301—dc21                                                    99-33758
                                                                 CIP

*Book design by Charles Sutherland*
*Cover design by Jon Valk*

# ACKNOWLEDGMENTS

I would like to thank the following individuals for assisting me in the preparation of this book.

First, gratitude is extended to my literary agent, Alex Hoyt, for his capable efforts and talents in finding a great home at Warner Books for this revised second edition. I also thank Mel Parker, a former senior vice-president at Warner Books, for the interest he has shown in my work and career in general and this book in particular.

I also thank Sheryl Fletcher for her competent typing skills, my publicist, Donna Gould at Phoenix Media, for her assistance, and the previous efforts of the staff at Planned Television Arts, including Rick Frishman, Paul Schwartz, and Hillary Rivman, among others.

With respect to the first edition, thanks are given to my former agent, Bert Holtje, for his efforts in getting the book originally published and Robert Davidson III for his assistance in reviewing and drafting selected portions of the original manuscript. In the first edition, I am grateful to I. Gregg Van Wert of the National Association of Printers and Lithographers for permitting me to use extensive material from articles I furnished to NAPL as general labor counsel in *Printing Manager* magazine and from publications I have drafted for NAPL, including the *NAPL Employee Handbook* and the *Hiring and Firing Guide*. Without permission to reuse this material, this book could not have been written.

I also thank J. Robert Connor, editor in chief of *Graduating Engineer* magazine, for permitting me to include materials previously furnished in articles written for the magazine on the rights of pregnant workers and minorities (i.e., race discrimination). Kudos also go to Marilyn Stephens, executive director of the Manufacturers' Representatives Educational Research Foundation, for allowing me to reproduce text I previously drafted on litigation concerns in the *Operations Manual for Manufacturers' Representative Firms.*

Special thanks go to Henry Bergson, executive director of the National Electrical Manufacturers' Representatives Association (NEMRA), for permitting me to include a copy of the association's *Guidelines for Negotiating Agreements Between Sales Representatives and Manufacturers.*

I offer my warmest appreciation to friend and fellow attorney Stanley A. Spiegler, who taught me more about the practice of labor law than he could ever realize, and J. Clifford Curley, executive vice-president at i.e. america radio network, for his interest in and support of my work.

Thanks are given to my brother and law partner, Jonathan Scott Sack, Esq., for his love and assistance. Of course, personal gratitude is extended to Joan and Sidney Pollack, and Philip Sassower and family for their constant encouragement, and to my wife, Gwen, who provides the nourishment and family support to enable me to work such long hours "stress-free" and uninterrupted during my writing activities.

I also acknowledge Dr. Subhi Gulati, who literally saved my life; my mother, Judith; and my extended family and friends for their constant love and encouragement.

Gratitude is given to my two sons, Andrew and David, for future dreams.

As always, I wish to express my appreciation and gratitude to my father, Bernard, whose insights and dreams helped make this book a reality.

Finally, special thanks must be given to those legislators, lawyers, judges, and others who have enacted and enforce legislation to protect people in the workplace.

# CONTENTS

# AGREEMENTS, FORMS, AND SAMPLE LETTERS INCLUDED IN THIS BOOK

# AUTHOR'S NOTE

The information in this book is my attempt to reduce complex and confusing law to practical general legal strategies. These strategies are meant to serve as helpful guidelines and concepts to think about in all legal decisions affecting your job. They are not intended as legal advice per se, because laws vary considerably throughout the fifty states and the law can be interpreted differently depending on the particular facts of each case. Thus, it is important to consult experienced counsel regarding the applicability of any strategy or point of information contained herein.

Additionally, this book is sold with the understanding that the publisher is not engaged in rendering legal, accounting, or other professional service. If legal advice or other professional assistance is required, the services of a competent professional must always be sought.

Finally, fictitious names have been used throughout the work and any similarity to actual persons, places, or events is purely coincidental.

# PREFACE

This revised edition of *The Employee Rights Handbook,* like the original work, was written to save you money and aggravation.

I often compare a job to a romance. Companies woo applicants with promises of security, fulfillment, and riches. Then, when the honeymoon is over, even qualified people often find themselves being treated unfairly. Many employees are not promoted, despite doing good work, often because they are women, over forty, or belong to a minority. Many others are fired for no justifiable reason. Still others fail to receive anticipated financial benefits, including accrued vacation pay, overtime, commissions, earned bonuses, promised raises, or expenses.

You have the power to change that by reading this book. Years ago, the law favored employers when it came to resolving employment disputes. It used to be that employers could fire workers with or without cause with little fear of legal reprisal. But this kind of exploitation may be a thing of the past. Now, for example, federal and state rulings grant employees access to their personnel files, allow them to get their jobs back when they are fired in retaliation for tattling on abuses of authority—i.e., whistleblowing—and even allow them to collect damages if they are sexually harassed by a supervisor, even though the employer knew nothing about a supervisor's threats.

More and more terminated workers are successfully arguing and proving that company promises made at the time of the hiring interview are binding on the employer. Years ago, terminated employees would merely bow their heads and shuffle out the door after hearing they had been fired. Now most terminated workers are questioning these decisions and regularly negotiating better severance packages and other post-termination benefits.

When I wrote the first edition of *The Employee Rights Handbook,* I reported that in every industry, unfair discharge litigation had proliferated and the amount of money involved in settlements ran into millions of dollars annually. The *Wall Street Journal* confirmed in a 1987 article that more than one-third of the New England companies interviewed indicated they were involved in legal actions with terminated employees, and most cases were settled for cash payments ranging from $1,000 to $50,000—not including other benefits such as continued medical, dental, and life insurance coverage, office space, use of telephone, secretarial help, résumé preparation, and outplacement guidance while looking for a new job.

The growing trend to protect workers is probably due to the fact that the law has finally grasped the concept that a job is an integral part of a person's life. Even the millions of independent sales reps and agents in this country who derive compensation in the form of commissions have received a boost from laws recently passed in more than thirty-four states. These laws guarantee prompt payment of commissions upon termination or resignation and award up to triple damages, plus reasonable attorney fees and costs of litigation, from companies who fail to pay reps in a timely fashion or who fail to comply with the appropriate provisions of each applicable state law. From a lawyer's perspective, the creation of these and numerous other "pro-employee" laws such as the Age Discrimination in Employment Act, the Older Workers Benefit Protection Act, the Civil Rights Act of 1991, the Americans with Disabilities Act, and the Family and Medical Leave Act, to name just a few, was unthinkable when I started practicing labor and employment law in 1980.

The idea for writing *The Employee Rights Handbook* first began in the fall of 1984 when I was interviewed by the *Wall Street Journal* for an article about the rights of terminated workers. Dozens of terminated employees who read the article began calling me at my New York City office to determine if they had any legal rights after being fired. I began negotiating post-termination benefits for a large number of clients and was surprised to learn that cash settlements and other perks were obtained a large majority of the time through my intervention. This has convinced me that the vast majority of private employers are fearful of the repercussions of most firings and are anxious to explore amicable solutions to avoid additional legal expenses, bad publicity, and potential damages that sometimes arise.

I started counseling companies in the printing industry on how to deal effectively and fairly with employees and did extensive research on all aspects of employment law. This included researching hundreds of cases and articles. In the late 1980s I began writing *The Employee Rights Handbook,* which was published in 1992.

The success of the book exceeded my expectations. Tens of thousands of copies have been sold, and I have received many positive letters from readers throughout the United States thanking me for writing the book. Since the book was first published, I have appeared on literally hundreds of radio and television programs discussing various topics of interest in this field and have been interviewed by dozens of national and regional magazines and newspapers. This led to hosting my own nationally syndicated radio show *Steven Sack, the Employee's Lawyer,* which currently airs every Sunday from 2:00–5:00 P.M. through the i.e. america radio network.

This second, revised edition takes off where the original book ended. I have added new sections and updated information where the law changed. New case decisions, trends, and developments have been incorporated into the text wherever possible. The result, I believe, is an even more valuable and timely body of work on employee rights for your use.

People should be able to benefit from the book regardless of background, education, age, job experience, or work skills. *The Employee Rights Handbook* offers practical advice and hundreds of preventive steps to take to help you avoid many common problems. The tips and comments may prove to be invaluable. For example, you will learn how to be properly hired to reduce the chances of exploitation later. You will understand your on-the-job rights and how companies are obligated to deal fairly and in good faith with longtime workers. In many cases this prohibits employers from terminating workers merely to deny them an economic benefit, such as a pension, commission, bonus, or enhanced medical benefits, that has been earned or is about to become due.

The book will also instruct you on how to resign properly so you do not forfeit valuable benefits. Additionally, you will learn the correct steps to take when you are fired to protect your rights and increase the chances of obtaining severance compensation and other post-termination benefits. The material can reduce the odds of your being fired unfairly and give you ammunition to maximize claims if you are fired. For example, you will learn how to increase the odds of winning an unemployment or workers' compensation case.

Although the book was not meant to replace a lawyer, it will help you initially determine whether your problem requires a lawyer's assistance. If you currently have a lawyer, the information will help you make that lawyer work more effectively on your behalf, and it will enable you to make more intelligent choices and avoid being pressured into making decisions you may regret.

You will certainly become more aware of the legal consequences of your boss's actions. If litigation becomes necessary, your chances of success and the value of your claim may increase substantially because you will recognize potential exploitation and know what to do about it. I also suggest courses of action to take *before* consulting a lawyer; such advice may prove invaluable to your lawyer once he or she has been retained. Of course, you will discover that many of my suggestions can be followed without the help of a lawyer.

My goal in writing this book was to give you the practical information my clients receive at a fraction of the cost. My suggestion is that you read the applicable sections before making a decision or when you have a problem. That is what "preventive law" is all about.

I am a practicing labor and employment lawyer with more than twenty years of hands-on experience and am consulted by hundreds of individuals each year. To make the book as relevant and useful as possible, I focus my attention on key topics where my clients typically seek guidance. Consequently, the strategies contained in this book cover areas where people are commonly exploited and misinformed, such as:

- College students and those entering the job market for the first time who need to know what negotiating points to discuss, what to ask for, and how to protect themselves before being hired
- Seasoned workers experiencing on-the-job sexual harassment, pregnancy discrimination, invasion of privacy, defamation, and other problems
- Part-time workers not receiving proper overtime compensation, tips, or benefits
- Longtime workers suddenly fired for no apparent reason
- Employees denied expected benefits and compensation
- Individuals recently fired and denied reasonable severance, favorable job references, or unemployment benefits
- Sales reps and traditional nonunion employees who wish to learn how to protect their jobs and earnings
- Union employees and people generally interested in knowing all of their rights before working, while on the job, and after their employment relationship has ended

I wrote *The Employee Rights Handbook* to give you an edge and devoted all my energies to make the book as relevant and useful as possible. Throughout the book you will note the numerous questions to ask and points to consider to protect your rights. You should also review the sample letters and agreements to implement many of my suggestions. The glossary at the end of the book will help you understand the meaning of many legal terms and concepts and apply them properly. The appendix contains the addresses and telephone numbers of many federal, state, local, and private agencies to contact to facilitate your efforts.

The benefits of applying this information can be significant, as the following true case demonstrates. I once represented a longtime employee who worked a full year and was expecting a bonus of $22,500 to be paid on February 15 of the following year. The company had a policy of requiring workers to be employed on the date of payment in order to receive the bonus. My client was fired on February 10 for alleged misconduct due to an unauthorized absence taken the day before. The employer refused to pay the bonus or severance, and the client came to me for advice.

I advised him that what the company did was wrong and told him what to say. He immediately scheduled an appointment with a personnel director and explained that he had a valid excuse for missing work. He advised the employer that he properly and timely reported the absence, and that he had met with an experienced employment lawyer who advised that the company's policy of paying earned bonuses only for people still employed the following year was unfair and perhaps discriminatory. Although he was unable to get his job back, he did manage to negotiate a very generous severance package with my assistance, which included a favorable letter of reference, unemployment insurance benefits, and the expected bonus.

He told me later that other workers told him "to forget about it" before coming to see me. Obviously, he appreciated my advice.

That is the kind of assistance I hope you will derive from *The Employee Rights Handbook*. I am very proud that Warner Books chose to publish this book in its expanded and revised second edition. Now I am confident that new readers will benefit from this work to protect their rights.

No one should take a job expecting the worst. However, this book will help you recover money for your efforts when you have been wronged. I have reduced complicated court rulings, regulations, and labor laws into simple strategies you can understand and follow. For the millions of employees who think they have no rights in the working world, think again—you are about to learn that knowledge is power and that you have more rights in the workplace than you think!

Steven Mitchell Sack, Esq.
New York City

# PART I

# How to Be Hired Properly

People are exploited in many ways when they look for a job. Some are victimized by discriminatory advertisements and brochures during job recruitment. Others are asked illegal questions during the job interview. Still others rely on phony promises or are subjected to various forms of job misrepresentation.

This first chapter covers problems sometimes encountered before hiring and suggests steps that can be taken to avoid such problems. The information will assist you in discovering how to reduce your chances of being misled by a job offer or being abused during the hiring interview. For example, you will learn when it is illegal for a potential employer to ask you to submit to a lie-detector or drug test. You will understand just how far a potential employer can go in obtaining private credit and background information to verify your job qualifications. Additionally, you will learn answers to such questions as: Do you have the right to review and respond to inaccurate information discovered during the hiring process? Can you rely on statements of job security and other promises before you begin working? Are such promises binding? What effect, if any, do disclaimers have in employment applications, job descriptions, and letter offers?

This chapter also offers strategies to help you learn how to properly investigate an employer before accepting a job. Many individuals rush too quickly into jobs they know nothing about, often after resigning from a good job. They then discover that the new job is not what they expected in terms of remuneration or job duties. This chapter reexamines ways to investigate potential employers and get answers to simple questions so this may not happen to you.

The second chapter in this section discusses how to be hired properly. The hiring phase is probably the most important part of the employment relationship. During this phase you can increase your job security, acquire additional compensation and benefits, reduce misunderstandings, and protect your rights. Unfortunately, most workers do not understand or know how to accomplish this. They accept work without clearly defining the terms of their employment or negotiating for additional terms. Others forget to ask for a written contract; they shake hands with the new employer and assume that everything will go smoothly. Later when problems develop, they learn that their failure to negotiate properly has placed them at a serious legal disadvantage.

In this second chapter you will gain valuable information on how to negotiate for a job. You will discover why it is best to obtain a written contract and how to protect yourself when you don't receive one. I have provided a detailed checklist of key negotiating points to ask and insist upon, whatever job you are seeking. You will also learn how to clarify confusing points regarding bonuses, advances, and other compensation terms. Sample employment contracts and letter agreements are included for your review and analysis.

The chapter also contains strategies pertaining to points to avoid in any agreement. These include discussion regarding restrictive covenants (also known as covenants not to compete) and other onerous contract provisions. Finally, the chapter stresses the right questions to ask and correct steps to take before accepting any job.

# CHAPTER 1

# Avoiding Prehiring Abuses

Most employers train and advise staff in charge of hiring applicants to correctly design advertisements and brochures, screen people carefully, avoid misrepresenting any job, fill a vacancy, and conduct the hiring interview legally to avoid charges of discrimination. Staff members are also taught how to properly investigate a candidate's references and statements on the employment application to avoid charges of defamation and invasion of privacy. Unfortunately, however, some employers do not follow the law.

## Illegal Advertisements and Brochures

The prospective employee's first exposure to a company sometimes begins after reading an advertisement or brochure. Applicants should be concerned with two potential forms of exploitation in this area.

First, employers may use descriptions in ads and brochures implying that the job is secure. Words often used include "long-term growth," "permanent," "secure," and "career path." Such words may create an inference that the employer is offering a job that cannot be terminated except for notice or cause. However, most employers have no intention of giving workers additional job security despite such words in ads and brochures. (You will learn in the next chapter that the issue of job security is a point that should be negotiated and confirmed at the hiring interview so you know what kind of job protection, if any, you will be receiving.)

Second, employers often draft advertisements and brochures that fail to comply with various federal and state discrimination laws. For example, employers are prohibited from publishing advertisements indicating any preference, limitation, specification, or discrimination based on age. The U.S. Department of Labor has published an "Interpretive Bulletin" stipulating that help-wanted notices containing phrases such as "age 25 to 35 preferred," "recent college graduate," "sales trainee, any recent degree," "sales executive, 2–4 yrs. out of college," and others of a similar nature illegally discriminate against the employment of older persons when used in relation to a specific job.

Such laws apply equally to help-wanted advertisements that favor men over women, whites over blacks, or any other class of people to the detriment of protected minorities.

Proper advertisements list the job title and division in which the position is available, hours of work, salary and benefits, job duties and responsibilities, qualifications, and the deadline for applying. Typically, such ads contain the manner of a reply (i.e., by telephone, in person, or through the mail). They also usually contain an EEO statement so that all applicants are notified that the employer does not discriminate on the basis of race, color, creed, or age.

---

**STRATEGY:** *If you read such an ad and believe it discriminates by denying you access to any job interview, contact your nearest Department of Consumer Affairs office, Equal Employment Opportunity Commission office, division of human rights office, or the state attorney general's office. You may be able to file charges and obtain damages or force the employer to rewrite the ad as a result.*

---

## Employment Applications and Applicant Screening

Proper screening procedures begin with an accurate, detailed job description so that applicants know what type of job is being offered. Generally, candidates are requested to complete a formal application form pertaining to the candidate's educational background, work experience, references, and other pertinent information.

Many employers require candidates to sign lengthy employment applications. Be aware that most employment applications are used to undercut job security, reduce an employer's exposure to invasion of privacy lawsuits when investigating your past employment and credit information, and give the employer added grounds for immediate termination when false statements contained in the application are discovered.

The following language was taken from an employment application I reviewed for a client:

I acknowledge that I have given (name of company) the right to make a thorough investigation of my past employment, education, and activities without liability, and understand that any false answer, statement, or implication made by me in my employment application or at any job interview shall be considered grounds for my immediate discharge.

If hired, I agree to conform to the rules and regulations of (name of company) in all respects. I understand that my employment with and compensation from (name of company) can be terminated at any time without notice or cause at the option of either of us. I also acknowledge that no representations or promises regarding continued employment for any specified period of time have been made to me during job discussions.

Just as I am free to resign any time without notice, so may (name of company) terminate me at any time with or without cause and with or without notice. Upon my resignation or termination, I agree to return all company property in my possession or under my control at the company's request.

Most employment applications typically contain a space for the applicant's signature and date, particularly when disclaimers similar to the above are included. Be aware that if you do not allow the potential employer to investigate the private facts of your life or if you refuse to sign such an application, you will probably not be considered for the job. Employers can insist on this requirement, and it is legal in most situations.

However, always review employment applications before signing them. Question ambiguous or misleading language. Some employers discriminate against certain applicants when only they, and not others, are required to fill out formal applications. And, just as some employers are guilty of asking illegal hiring questions at the formal interview, many employment applications contain illegal inquiries in personal areas involving your age, citizenship, disabilities, credit and garnishment history, arrest records, and other private matters. The following section will familiarize you with the kinds of questions that are illegal and must never be asked of you either directly at an interview or on a job application form.

Recognize that particular clauses in the application can and may be used against you at a later date. That is why you should request a copy of the employment application after you have signed it. This can minimize a frequent problem that arises when the application becomes a part of a job dispute or firing but you cannot locate (and the employer won't give you) the application in question.

Finally, be careful not to embellish your past work experience and qualifications. Most employers thoroughly investigate all statements made on job applications these days. Material misstatements are usually dealt with by immediate discharge when discovered, no matter how long or successfully the person has worked for the company.

## Illegal Questions at the Hiring Interview

In the past, employers could ask almost any question they wanted of an applicant or employee. Questions could be asked about marital status, past arrests, alcohol and drug use, credit history, childbearing plans, or age. Now such questions are illegal.

The law has taken great strides to protect female applicants in this area. Questions pertaining to child care, marital status (for example, Who will look after your child if you are hired? Do you have children? What form of birth control, if any, do you use? If you became pregnant while working, would you continue to work? Are you married? Does your husband support your decision to work?), and related matters are illegal.

Generally, employers may ask questions to learn about a candidate's motivation and personality. Such questions can relate to former job responsibilities and outside interests. However, inquiries into an applicant's race, color, age, gender, religion, and national origin that further discriminatory purposes are illegal under Title VII of the Civil Rights Act of 1964, as amended. This law applies to private employers, employment agencies, labor organizations, and training programs.

Additionally, each state has its own discrimination laws, which often go even further in protecting the rights of applicants during job interviews. Companies must conduct preemployment interviews properly to avoid liability, since innocent questions can often cause employers to face costly and time-consuming charges of discrimination filed with the federal Equal Employment Opportunity Commission and with various other human rights agencies, the Civil Liberties Union, and the state attorney general's office. If discrimination is found, an applicant may be awarded significant damages, including a job offer, attorney costs, and other benefits. Following enactment of the Civil Rights Act of 1991, successful claimants may also demand jury trials and receive compensatory damages (i.e., money paid for emotional pain and suffering) of up to $300,000, depending on the employer's size, and punitive damages, plus legal fees and money for expert witnesses who testify at the trial.

One recent case illustrates the legal exposure resulting from sloppy preemployment interviewing techniques. The applicant interviewed for a stocker's job at Wal-Mart. The manager asked the job applicant, who had lost part of his arm in an automobile accident, "What current or past medical problems might limit your ability to do the job?" After the applicant was not hired for the position, he filed a charge of disability discrimination with a local EEOC office pursuant to the Americans with Disabilities Act (ADA).

After the EEOC subsequently filed a federal court action on the applicant's behalf, a federal jury reportedly awarded the applicant $157,500. The jury rejected Wal-Mart's claim that it refused to hire him because of his rude demeanor and noted that the manager failed to recognize that the question asked of the applicant, although once legal, was now not permitted under the ADA. Furthermore, the jury noted that rather than inquire about the applicant's medical condition, the personnel manager should have given the candidate a job description and asked whether he could perform the essential functions of the job.

Another job candidate was awarded $15,000 in compensatory damages and $30,000 in punitive damages by the EEOC from an employer who asked an improper question during a job interview and failed to hire the applicant as a result of her answer.

The table on pages 9–14 gives you a better understanding of the kinds of questions that are illegal under federal Equal Employment Opportunity Commission guidelines and state regulations. This chart should be used only as a guide, since some questions that are indicated as being illegal can be asked in certain situations (for example, where the applicant is applying for a security-sensitive job). Thus, the potential illegality of such questions must always be examined in the context in which they are asked.

# Interview Questions and the Law

| SUBJECT | LEGAL | ILLEGAL |
|---------|-------|---------|
| Name | What is your full name? Have you ever worked under a different name? If so, what name? What is the name of your parent or guardian? *(but only in the case of a minor job applicant)* What is your maiden name? *(but only to check prior employment or education)* | Have you ever changed your name by court order or other means? |
| Residence | What is your address? How long have you been a resident of this state? of this city? What is your phone number? | Do you rent or own your home? How long have you lived in the United States? Do you live with someone? If so, what is your relationship with that person? Do you live in a foreign country? |
| Color | | What is your skin coloring? |

| SUBJECT | LEGAL | ILLEGAL |
|---------|-------|---------|
| National origin | | What is your ancestry? place of birth? What is your mother's native language? What is your spouse's nationality? What is your maiden name? |
| Citizenship | Are you a citizen of the U.S.? If not, do you intend to become one? Do you have a legal right to be employed in this country? | Of what country are you a citizen? Are your parents or spouse naturalized or native-born citizens? When did they acquire citizenship? Are you a native-born citizen? |
| Age | Are you old enough to work? Are you between eighteen and sixty-five years of age? If not, state your age. | How old are you? What is your date of birth? Why did you decide to seek employment at your age? |
| Religion | | What is your religion? Are you available to work on the Sabbath? What religious holidays do you observe? What church do you attend? |

| Marital status | What is your marital status? |
| --- | --- |
| | Are you dating anyone? |
| | Are you married, single, divorced, separated, engaged, or widowed? |
| | Which is more important to you, a family or a career? |
| | If you are single, are you living with anyone? |
| | If you have children, what are their ages? |
| | What would you do if your spouse was required to transfer out of state? |
| | Would you take time off under the Family and Medical Leave Act? |
| | Do you feel capable of supervising men? |
| | Where does your spouse work? |
| | What does your spouse do? |
| | When do you plan to marry? |
| | Do you plan on having children? |
| | Who will care for the children while you work? |
| | What is your spouse's health insurance coverage? |
| | How much does your spouse earn? |
| | What is your view on ERA? |
| | Are you a feminist? |

| SUBJECT | LEGAL | ILLEGAL |
|---|---|---|
| Marital status | | Do you advocate the use of birth control or family planning? |
| | | Are you the head of the household? |
| | | Are you the principal wage earner? |
| | | Should we call you Mr, Mrs., Miss, or Ms.? |
| Disability | Do you currently use illegal drugs? | What medications are you currently taking? |
| | Have you ever been convicted for driving under the influence? | Have you ever been treated for drug use? |
| | Would you submit to a company-paid physical or provide a doctor's certificate of health after being offered the job? | How often did you use drugs in the past? |
| | | Are you an alcoholic? |
| | | How much and how frequently do you drink? |
| | | Do you have a disability that would interfere with your ability to perform the job? |
| | | Have you ever filed for workers' compensation benefits? |
| | | Have you ever been injured on the job? |
| | | Do you have AIDS? |
| | | Do you have cancer? |
| | | Have you ever been treated for mental health problems? |

| Category | | |
|---|---|---|
| | Can you lift heavy objects with or without reasonable accommodations? *(but only if the job directly requires this)* | Have you ever been unable to handle work-related stress?<br>How many sick days were you out last year? Why were you sick so often?<br>Have you ever been compensated for injuries? |
| Job requirements | | |
| Credit | If hired, would you allow us to order a credit report to confirm statements made on your employment application (provided you receive a copy)? | Do you have any credit problems?<br>Have you recently filed for personal bankruptcy?<br>Is your salary presently subject to legal attachment or wage garnishment? |
| Arrest record | Have you ever been convicted of a felony within the past seven years?<br>Do you have a valid driver's license? | Have you ever been arrested?<br>Have you ever pled guilty to a crime?<br>Have you ever been in trouble with the law? |

| SUBJECT | LEGAL | ILLEGAL |
|---------|-------|---------|
| Child-care responsibilities | Is there any reason that you will not be able to come to work every day, on time? (*only if asked of all applicants*) | Do you have any young children at home? Do you have a baby-sitter? How old are your children? |
| Language | Do you speak a foreign language? If so, which one? | What is your native tongue? How did you acquire the ability to read, write, and speak a foreign language? |
| Relatives | Names of relatives already employed by this company. | Names, addresses, age, and other pertinent information concerning your spouse, children, or relatives not employed by the company. What type of work does your mother/father do? |
| Organizations | List all organizations in which your membership is relevant to this job. | List all clubs, societies, and lodges to which you belong. |

The table demonstrates just how often job applicants are exploited in this area (since many illegal questions are typically regarded as routine).

You should also be aware that illegality sometimes arises when employers:

- Ask applicants for photographs before hiring
- Ask applicants for references from clergy before hiring
- Ask questions of females that are not asked of males
- Ask questions about the applicant's military service in countries other than the United States
- Ask questions about the applicant's military record or type of discharge

According to the Older Workers Benefit Protection Act, employers are forbidden from discussing or asking any questions pertaining to a person's age. Thus, if you are an older (i.e., over forty) job applicant and are told that you "lack formal education credits," "are overqualified," "are overspecialized," or that the company is "looking to hire someone with a more recent college degree," speak to a labor lawyer if you are denied a job. Recent cases demonstrate it may be illegal for a company to refuse to hire an older applicant by arguing that being *over*qualified for a position means that the applicant is *un*qualified for the position. (Simply showing that a younger individual was hired over a qualified older applicant does not prove age discrimination if the employer can show that the decision was based on an honest evaluation of the candidate's qualifications; e.g., that the prospective employee would be bored or likely to leave upon finding a better job, or both.)

Employers are not permitted to ask questions about past arrests, since these often end in acquittal, dismissal, withdrawal of charges, or overturning of the conviction.

The federal Fair Credit Reporting Act places certain restrictions on the use of credit reports and investigative consumer reports by employers. Under this law, employers are forbidden to use credit reports (defined as summaries of a person's credit history) for hiring or employment decisions. The same is true for investigative consumer reports (defined as descriptions of a person's creditworthiness and general reputation in her community based on interviews with coworkers, friends, and neighbors).

As a result of a revision to this law, employers cannot obtain any report without your permission. If your consent is obtained and a report is made, you have the right to receive a copy, including the name and address of the credit agency supplying it, together with a written description of your rights under the act.

When any adverse action is taken, such as your not being hired, you are entitled to receive notice of such adverse action, the name, address, and telephone number of the consumer reporting agency that provided the report to the employer (which includes an 800 number if one is available), *and* a written statement by the employer indicating that such information was not used in any way in the adverse action. Information also given with this is a statement that you can obtain a free copy of the report within sixty days of the notice and your right to dispute the accuracy or completeness of the report with the consumer reporting agency. The law also requires that the employer notify the credit reporting agency before receiving the report that it got your permission, provided you with the required notice, will not use the information to violate federal or state discrimination laws, and will not use the information to make any adverse action.

---

**STRATEGY:** *As a result of the law's requirements, speak to a knowledgeable employment lawyer immediately if you believe your rights have been violated in this area.*

---

Be aware that employers sometimes design medical history forms that contain discriminatory questions. If you are asked discriminatory questions on a medical form or during a physical exam, you have the right to refuse to answer such questions.

Thus, be sure to review all employment applications and forms to determine whether they contain discriminatory questions and be aware of improper questions during the interview. If you feel that a question is discriminatory, point this out to the interviewer. Be tactful. Explain that you believe the question is illegal and that you decline to answer it for that reason.

Some employers will appreciate your candor and may be impressed by your knowledge of the law. Others may feel you are a threat and may decline to offer you the job. However, if you feel you were denied a job based on a refusal to answer discriminatory questions, contact an appropriate agency to protect your rights. This includes a regional office of the division of human rights in your state, a local chapter of the Civil Liberties Union, or a regional office of the Equal Employment Opportunity Commission. If you work for a company with fewer than fifteen employees, you should probably first contact a state or local antidiscrimination agency, since federal law generally applies to companies with fifteen or more employees.

If you believe you were victimized, document your complaint by writing a letter similar to the one on page 18. Follow up the letter by contacting the agency to confirm that action is being taken to protect your rights. Speak to a lawyer to determine your options if you are not satisfied with the progress of the investigation. You should also consider filing a formal discrimination lawsuit through a private attorney (after an investigation by a state agency or the EEOC) if you were denied a job by refusing to answer discriminatory questions or furnishing answers to illegal questions. Sometimes it is not necessary to hire a lawyer, because a state agency or EEOC will sue on your behalf.

---

**STRATEGY:** *Some applicants innocently provide illegal information. Employers are trained to circumvent the law at an interview by* *asking the applicant a general question such as "Tell us about yourself." The applicant then volunteers personal information the employer has no right to hear, such as "Well, I'm married to a teacher, we have two young children, and I desire a position with your firm because I'm bored of being a housewife and want to wait several years before having more children." Try to limit what you say and avoid volunteering personal information at an interview where possible.*

*Recognize that discriminatory questions are often asked after the formal interview has concluded (for example, during lunch after the interview but before the decision to hire has been made). Answers to such questions may not be considered in the hiring process, and the ramifications of asking illegal questions in such informal settings are just as serious as when they are asked during a formal interview.*

## Sample Letter to Protest Illegal Interview Questions

Your Name
Address
Telephone Number
Date

Name of Official
Title
Name of Agency
Address

Dear (Name of Official),

This letter is a formal protest against certain hiring practices of (name of employer), which I believe are illegal.

On (date) I was interviewed by (name and title of employee) for the position of (specify). The interview took place at (specify). During the interview, (name of employee) asked the following questions, which I believe were illegal under federal and state law: (specify).

I explained to the interviewer that such questions were improper and refused to answer them. The interviewer told me such questions were routinely asked of all job candidates and that the interview would be terminated immediately if I chose not to answer them.

The interviewer then told me I had "an attitude problem" and that the position was no longer available. Based on this, I believe I have been victimized by discrimination, since I am highly qualified for the job in question and was never given an adequate opportunity to display my qualifications.

I authorize you to investigate this matter on my behalf if it is determined that my charges have merit. You may also institute legal proceedings if appropriate. I am available to meet with you at your office at a mutually convenient date to furnish you with additional details and can be reached at (home address and telephone number).

Thank you for your cooperation and attention in this matter.

Very truly yours,
Your Name

*Sent certified mail, return receipt requested.*

## Job Misrepresentation and Phony Employment Schemes

People are often exposed to phony advertisements and employment schemes promising large income for part-time work or offering jobs with unlimited earning potential. The following is an example of a typical ad.

OVER $1000 PER WEEK possible by working at home. Manage your own time—no prior experience necessary.

Newspapers are filled with ads for such jobs. However, the vast majority of these ads are misleading. Applicants sometimes travel great distances (at their own expense) to apply. They then learn that a large amount of some product (for example, $10,000 worth) must be purchased in order to sell for the company and be hired!

As a general rule, be skeptical of work-at-home employment ads. Many ads turn out to be envelope-stuffing pyramid schemes requiring people to purchase introductory mailing lists. These lists actually cost you more than you can possibly earn from work-at-home activities.

Always beware of companies you can't communicate with by telephone, especially those that only list a post office box address. This is because there may be no one to reach when you have questions about the work or have not received agreed-upon payments.

It is also a good idea to understand how much money and time you will be required to expend to get started and whether the job requires special training or skills. Inquire about refund policies. Once a product is completed by you, who is required to sell it?

Most important, never commence work at home until you understand the amount of compensation and how often you will be paid. Avoid working for long periods of time without being paid; demand to receive payment on a regular basis (never less than once a month). That way you can cut your losses if the company misses a payment.

Finally, if you are buying a work-at-home franchise, demand to review all the written documents concerning the venture, including the prospectus, before you invest. Speak to your lawyer, accountant, and similar franchise owners for advice whenever possible.

Job offers that require people to buy a product before working are not the only common illegal employment scheme. Applicants are sometimes misled by interviewers who oversell by making exaggerated guaranteed-earnings claims. For example, applicants are told, "If you come to work for us, you will make $100,000 in commission this year, based on what our other salespeople make." People then accept the job based on such representations, not realizing that the statements may be illegal. This is because, according to the Federal Trade Commission, a promise of earnings that exceed the average net earnings of other employees or sales reps is an unfair and deceptive trade practice.

---

**STRATEGY:** *Always be on the alert when a potential employer makes claims regarding guaranteed earnings. You have the right to see copies of the wage statements (for example, W-2s or 1099s) of other employees of the company to confirm such claims. If the employer tells you such information is confidential, tell him or her to remove the names of the employees. If the employer refuses to do this or cannot provide ample factual information to support such claims, think twice before accepting the job.*

---

To avoid misleading potential employees, prudent employers hedge by using the following types of phrases when advising applicants of potential earnings. "It is possible you may make $100,000 this year, since three out of eight sales reps achieved that figure last year," or "Although not typical, we have had employees who earned as much as $100,000 in a given year."

Some employers also misrepresent the amount and quality of assistance to be rendered. The law is violated when false promises of support are made or when other material terms (for example, exclusive sales territories) are offered that do not exist.

---

**STRATEGY:** *To protect yourself in this area, always speak directly to the people who will supposedly assist you. Find out what their functions and duties are and how long they have worked for the employer. Talking to people directly will help you form a "gut" opinion and make it easier to determine when false claims have been made.*

---

If you believe you have been victimized by an employment scheme or a work-at-home advertisement, you have many options. Obviously, you can contact a lawyer or Legal Aid service to protect your rights and take action on your behalf. Such action could include filing a private lawsuit based on fraud and misrepresentation. Some lawsuits even allow you to sue the officers of an employer in their individual capacities.

You can also contact the nearest regional office of the Federal Trade Commission, the Better Business Bureau, or the U.S. Postal Service. Numerous federal and state laws have been enacted, including the Uniform Deceptive Trade Practices Act, the Racketeer Influenced and Corrupt Organizations Act (RICO), and other labor statutes, to prevent employers from engaging in a variety of phony employment schemes or using the mails to further such schemes.

For example, the Federal Trade Commission has the authority to investigate claims and impose cease and desist orders prohibiting the continuation of illegal activity by phony employers. Each state's attorney general's office maintains a division for labor fraud and other related deceptive employment practices. In certain cases the U.S. Postal Service can be of great assistance by issuing a court order preventing employers from using the mails or receiving mail.

---

**STRATEGY:** *Whenever you are in doubt about a particular employer or an individual representing the employer, contact your local Better Business Bureau. Most Better Business Bureaus maintain lists of employers and individuals accused of engaging in phony employment-related practices. Obtaining such information before accepting employment or participating in a dubious venture can save you a great deal of aggravation and expense down the road.*

---

Try to recognize phony employment schemes and advertisements before problems develop, and take immediate action when appropriate.

## Abuses by Employment Agencies, Search Firms, or Career Counselors

In your anxiousness to find a job, you may risk being exploited by unscrupulous persons or organizations promising to help you find employment. The required placement fee may be exorbitant, you may pay nonrefundable fees for so-called leads that do not lead to employment, you may be asked illegal discriminatory questions at the initial interview, or you may be told that you must register in prescribed training for which the agency gets a fee.

How can you avoid such skulduggery? Here are a few of the ways you can protect yourself from unethical or illegal employment practices.

**1. Know whom you are dealing with.** The main purpose of an employment agency is to find a job for you. Career counselors and search firms offer additional services such as résumé and letter preparation and training in interview techniques, as well as providing job-opening leads. Career counselors do not, however, obtain jobs for applicants.

**2. Understand the terms of the arrangement.** Ask the following questions before you agree to be represented by an employment agency, search firm, or career counselor:

- Is the firm licensed? (In some states, employment agencies are licensed and regulated by the Department of Consumer Affairs. To obtain a license, the agency must fill out a detailed application, post a performance bond, maintain accurate financial records, and avoid engaging in illegal acts. Career counselors and search firms generally are not required to be licensed to conduct business.)

- What are the precise services the firm or individual will render?
- What is required of the job applicant (prepare a résumé, buy interviewing attire, etc.)?
- When will the firm or individual earn its fee: when you are offered a job by an acceptable employer, when you accept the job, or when you have worked a minimum amount of time?
- What is the maximum fee to be charged?
- Who will pay for the fee, you or the employer? When is it payable?
- What happens if you decide not to accept a job that is offered?
- Is a deposit required once a job is accepted?
- Will you receive a detailed description of each potential employer before you go on an interview, including the name, address, kind of work to be performed, title, amount of wages or compensation, hours, and whether the work is temporary or permanent?
- Will the agency investigate whether the potential employer has defaulted in the payment of salaries to others during the past five years?
- What happens to the fee if you resign or are fired within a short period of time?
- Will the agency help you obtain another job if you are terminated?
- Does the agency have the right to represent you on an exclusive basis?
- What happens to the fee if you become disabled and cannot work?

**3. Confirm everything in writing.** While the law says an oral contract is just as binding as a written contract, oral contracts are often difficult to prove. Thus, reduce the arrangement to writing. If you have questions, don't sign a contract until you understand what it will mean to you. If the contract is long and complicated, you may need the advice of a lawyer before signing.

**4. Don't pay money in advance of results.** While it is illegal for employment agencies to charge fees *before* they have found a job for you, career counselors and search firms are allowed to charge up-front fees. Resist such requests, because all too often, promised services are not received.

**5. Know in advance what is prohibited.** Check with your local library, bar association, or Better Business Bureau for a description of what employment agencies, career counselors, and search firms are allowed to do and what prohibitions exist. For example, under the laws in many states, it is illegal for an employment agency to:

- Induce you to terminate your job so the agency can obtain new employment for you
- Publish false or misleading ads
- Advertise in newspapers without providing the name and address of the agency
- Send you to an employer without obtaining a job order from the employer
- Require you to subscribe to publications, pay for advertising or mailing costs, enroll in special courses, or pay for additional services
- Charge a placement fee when the agency represents that it was a fee-paid job
- Discriminate on the basis of gender, age, or race
- Require you to complete application forms that obtain different information from male and female applicants
- Make false representations or promises

**6. Seek immediate relief if you have been exploited.** Don't procrastinate if an employment agency or career service takes advantage of you. The longer you wait, the harder it may be to prove your case and collect damages. If you believe you have been exploited, send a letter to the firm to document your protest. The letter should state the reasons for your dissatisfaction and the manner in which you would like the problem resolved. The letter below illustrates this. If the financial exploitation is significant, contact a lawyer immediately. In any event, if your problem is not resolved amicably, contact your local Department of Consumer Affairs or Better Business Bureau, outlining your complaint in writing, as shown in the example on page 27. In many states these agencies have the power to investigate charges and take action, including revoking licenses, when wrongdoing is proved. If you are still dissatisfied with the outcome, you can consider suing in small-claims court or through formal litigation.

## Sample Complaint Letter to Job-Search Firm

Your Name
Address
Telephone Number
Date

Name of Officer
Name of Firm
Address

Dear (Name of Officer),

On (date) I responded to an advertisement your firm ran in (name of newspaper or magazine). The ad specifically promised that your firm could find a job for me as a salesperson in the cosmetics industry. The ad stated that a ($X) advance was fully refundable in the event I could not obtain a job paying more than $20,000 per year.

Per your request, and after several telephone conversations, I sent you a check for ($X), which was cashed. That was four months ago.

Since that time I have received one letter from you dated (specify), which states you are reviewing my employment history.

In view of the fact that you have not obtained full-time employment on my behalf, I hereby demand the return of ($X), per our agreement.

If I do not receive the money within 14 days from the date of this letter, be assured that I shall contact the Department of Consumer Affairs, Better Business Bureau, the frauds division of the attorney general's office, and my lawyer to commence a formal investigation.

Hopefully this can be avoided and I thank you for your immediate cooperation in this matter.

Very truly yours,
Your Name

*Sent certified mail, return receipt requested.*

## Follow-up Letter to Department of Consumer Affairs (or appropriate agency)

Your Name
Address
Telephone Number
Date

Commissioner
Department of Consumer Affairs
Address

Re: Formal complaint against ABC Employment Agency, license #XXXXX

Dear Commissioner,

I hereby make a formal complaint against (name of firm). I believe the firm has committed the following illegal acts: (specify).

The facts on which I base my allegations are as follows: (state the facts in detail).

On (date) I sent the agency a formal demand letter requesting the return of my deposit. This letter was sent by certified mail, was received by the firm, yet I have received no response. I enclose a copy of the letter for your review together with all pertinent documentation from my files.

I request that you convene a formal investigation regarding this matter. Feel free to contact me at the above address if you need further assistance or information.

Thank you for your cooperation and attention.

Very truly yours,
Your Name

*Sent certified mail, return receipt requested.*
cc: the employment agency, your lawyer, Better Business Bureau, and the frauds division of the state attorney general's office

## Unfair Job Requirements

Are you a member of a protected minority (for example, black, female, person over forty) who has been barred from applying for a job on the basis of your education or skills? If so, is the education or skills requirement specified in the ad, recruiting brochure, or employment opportunity notice really necessary to do the job properly? If not, you may have a valid discrimination claim.

When employers set a higher requirement than is needed for a job just to attract a different kind of applicant, they sometimes inadvertently discriminate against a particular class of applicant; *this is illegal.*

For example, in the case of *United States v. Georgia Power Company*, the requirements of a high school diploma and aptitude test scores by the employer raised a question as to whether such requirements were really related to successful job performance. The diploma requirement was found to be unlawful, since it did not measure an individual's ability to do the job. In fact, the court determined that since blacks, as opposed to whites, were more likely not to have completed high school in Georgia in the late 1960s and early 1970s, such a requirement essentially excluded them from working for the company.

Thus, if you are a member of a protected minority and believe you are being unfairly excluded from applying for employment due to unfair job requirements, you may wish to speak to a representative from a regional office of the federal Equal Employment Opportunity Commission or state division of human rights.

## Disabled Applicants

Due to the enactment of the ADA, employers must be certain that recruitment and job application procedures do not discriminate against qualified job applicants based on their disabilities. Many knowledgeable companies have written their ads so that the following (or similar) words are present: "Our company is an Equal Opportunity Employer and does not discriminate on the basis of a physical or mental handicap."

Employers are required to take reasonable steps to accommodate the needs of handicapped workers under federal and state law. Persons with disabilities cannot be disqualified from applying because of the inability to perform nonessential or marginal functions of the job; proper language in job advertisements can demonstrate a company's desire to comply with the law and not initially exclude qualified but disabled applicants from the potential job pool.

Under the ADA, an employer may deny a job to an individual with a disability if the individual fails to meet a selected criterion under the act. However, it is unlawful to exclude applicants with disabilities and fail to hire them if the criterion can be satisfied by the applicant with a reasonable accommodation by the employer. According to the Senate Labor and Human Resources Committee, which was responsible for drafting the bill, if an employer has an opening for a typist and two persons apply for the job, one being an individual with a disability who types fifty words per minute and the other being an individual without a disability who types seventy-five words per minute, the employer is permitted to choose the applicant with the higher typing speed.

On the other hand, if one of the two applicants has a hearing impairment and requires a telephone headset with an amplifier and the other applicant has no disability, but both have the same typing speed, the employer is not permitted to choose the individual without a disability because of the requirement to provide the needed reasonable accommodation.

A disabled applicant can only be rejected if the person cannot perform essential job functions, even with reasonable accommodation. You cannot be disqualified because of an inability to perform nonessential or marginal functions of the job. The following is a good summary of rules to remember in this area:

1. Employers must avoid disability-related questions in interviews or questions about your ability to perform specific job-related tasks or requirements.
2. Employers cannot inquire what kind of accommodation the person needs in order to perform the job properly if hired.
3. A medical exam can only be requested after hiring and provided it is a condition of employment for all entering employees in that position.

The Philadelphia law firm of Blank, Rome, Comisky & Mc-Cauley suggests the following steps for employers to comply with the ADA:

- Develop job descriptions in order to determine if an individual is "qualified."
- Examine employment applications to make sure that language is nondiscriminatory.
- Examine employment tests and other selection criteria to make sure that those with disabilities are not screened out.
- Examine preemployment drug-testing procedures to make sure that they do not eliminate applicants because of prescription drugs taken for a medical reason.
- Reevaluate medical exam procedures so that exams are performed only after an offer of employment is made and confidentiality of examination results is maintained.
- Evaluate your workforce in order to accommodate those who have identified themselves as disabled.
- Train the workforce to deal with disabled coworkers.
- Reconsider your safety programs to include the disabled.
- Reconsider and revise personnel policies to make them more neutral, as well as fair to the company. For example, the ADA doesn't entitle those with disabilities to more paid leave than other employees.
- Prepare and post ADA notices throughout your company.
- Develop contacts among organizations for the disabled.
- Prepare reasonable accommodation options.
- Prepare both work and other areas such as rest rooms and lunchrooms to accommodate the disabled.
- Review performance appraisals to be sure they are neutral, and that they allow for documenting all negative as well as positive incidents.
- Consider a peer review panel to give feedback on employment practices and decisions.
- Document all efforts to accommodate applicants and employees who are disabled.
- Review contracts with employment agencies, unions, etc., and review all insurance plans to be sure they are nondiscriminatory.

## Immigration Checks

The Immigration Reform and Control Act of 1986 (IRCA) states that employers should hire only U.S. citizens and aliens who are authorized to work in the United States. The law requires every employer to verify the employment eligibility of every worker hired to avoid civil fines and criminal penalties for failure to comply with the law's record-keeping requirements. Companies must follow fixed guidelines regardless of company size or the number of employees being hired. The Immigration and Naturalization Service (INS) has developed a form (I-9) that employers must complete and retain in order to verify employment eligibility for all employees.

Essentially, employers have five verification obligations:

1. Employees must be instructed to fill out their portion of Form I-9 when they begin work.
2. Employers must check documents establishing employees' identity and eligibility to work.
3. Employers must properly complete the remaining portion of Form I-9.
4. Employers must retain the form for at least three years or until one year after a person leaves employment, whichever is later.
5. Employers must present the form for inspection to INS or Department of Labor officials upon request after three days' advance notice.

All companies must verify the identity and work authorization of every person hired. Evidence must be examined, collected, and saved by the employer to refute charges that it knew it was hiring an unauthorized alien.

Form I-9 must be completed and attested to by the new employee at the time of hiring; the company must review all documentation and submit the form within three business days of the hiring. The applicant has twenty-one additional business days to furnish documents that are lost or not yet processed. Copies of the INS form may be obtained from any district INS office and photocopied for future use by other applicants.

All completed I-9 forms must be saved for at least three years after the hiring, or for one year after the person is terminated, whichever occurs later; these rules apply to temporary workers and independent contractors as well. However, companies are not obligated to verify employment eligibility for people working as employees for such independent contractors.

Employers failing to follow the law are currently liable for fines ranging from $250 to $2,000 for each unauthorized alien hiring for a first offense; $2,000 to $5,000 for each unauthorized alien for a second offense; and $3,000 to $10,000 for each unauthorized alien for subsequent offenses. The law also imposes criminal penalties against companies and their principal officers up to $3,000 for each unauthorized alien with respect to whom a violation occurs, or imprisonment for not more than six months, or both.

## Acceptable Documents for Immigration Control and Reform Act

**List A: Documents that establish both identity and employment eligibility**

1. U.S. passport (unexpired or expired)
2. Certificate of U.S. Citizenship (INS Form N-560 or N-561)
3. Certificate of Naturalization (INS Form N-550 or N-570)
4. Unexpired foreign passport with I-551 stamp or attached INS Form I-94 indicating unexpired employment authorization
5. Alien Registration Receipt Card with photograph (INS Form I-151 or I-551)

6. Unexpired Temporary Resident Card (INS Form I-668)
7. Employment Authorization Card (INS Form I-688)
8. Unexpired Reentry Permit (INS Form I-327)
9. Unexpired Refugee Travel Document (INS Form I-571)
10. Unexpired Employment Authorization Document issued by the INS which contains a photograph (INS Form I-688B)

**List B: Documents that establish identity**

1. Driver's license or ID card issued by a U.S. state or outlying possession provided it contains a photograph or information such as name, date of birth, gender, height, eye color, and address
2. ID card issued by federal, state, or local government agencies or entities provided it contains a photograph or information such as name, date of birth, gender, height, eye color, and address
3. School ID card with a photograph
4. Voter's registration card
5. U.S. military card or draft record
6. Military dependent's ID card
7. U.S. Coast Guard Merchant Mariner card
8. Native American tribal document
9. Driver's license issued by a Canadian government authority

For persons under age eighteen who are unable to present a document listed above:

10. School record or report card
11. Clinic, doctor, or hospital record
12. Day-care or nursery school record

**List C: Documents that establish employment eligibility**

1. U.S. Social Security card issued by the Social Security Administration (other than a card stating that it is not valid for employment)

2. Certification of Birth Abroad issued by the Department of State (Form FS-545 or Form DS-1350)
3. Original or certified copy of a birth certificate issued by a state, county, municipal authority, or outlying possession of the United States bearing an official seal
4. Native American tribal document
5. U.S. Citizen ID Card (INS Form I-197)
6. ID Card for use of Resident Citizen in the United States (INS Form I-197)
7. Unexpired employment authorization document issued by the INS (other than those listed in List A)

---

**STRATEGY:** *Speak to an employment attorney or contact a regional office of the EEOC or state discrimination agency if you believe that, although you are a U.S. citizen, you were denied a job because of a foreign accent, are foreign born, or were required to take a fluency exam or other tests not given to native-born applicants. Although the company may be acting properly pursuant to the IRCA, it may nonetheless be violating your Title VII discrimination rights pursuant to the Civil Rights Act of 1964, as amended.*

---

## English-Only Rules

With more foreign-born employees entering the workforce, a wave of English-only regulations has been spreading among companies throughout the United States. Some of these regulations are very restrictive (only English may be spoken on company premises); others are fairly loose (only English may be spoken when customers are present); and many more are merely the verbal equivalents of informal company policy.

The Equal Employment Opportunity Commission has published strict guidelines relating to English-only rules. Therefore, the commission will presume that such a rule violates Title VII and will closely scrutinize it.

Depending on the circumstances, it may be permissible to regulate use of a foreign language in cases where groups of employees are performing hazardous tasks and fast and precise communication among all of them is essential. The burden of proving such a compelling business necessity falls to the employer.

Cases indicate that federal courts are less likely to follow the EEOC's position provided an employer can prove that its policy is evenhanded and supported by clear business justification. However, the EEOC has taken the position that virtually all English-only rules are repugnant and create an atmosphere of inferiority, isolation, and intimidation based on national origin.

According to the August 1997 issue of the newsletter *You and the Law,* the following summarizes EEOC policy in this area:

- English-only rules applied at all times (including lunch hours and breaks) are presumed to violate Title VII and will be scrutinized closely.
- English-only rules that apply only at certain times may be lawful if the employer can show they are justified by business necessity.
- If a limited English-only rule is adopted for business necessity, the employer should inform all employees of the rule, explain the circumstances under which English is required, and make sure employees are aware of the repercussions of violating the rule.
- If an employer fails to provide notice of the rule, including the consequences for violating it, taking adverse action against an employee for violating the rule constitutes national-origin discrimination.
- An English-only rule applied only to a particular group violates Title VII as unlawful disparate treatment.

- English-only rules, whether applied at all times or only at certain times, may create a hostile work environment that could constitute unlawful harassment under Title VII.
- If a job applicant is not hired because of an accent or manner of speaking, the employer must show that the accent interfered materially with the person's ability to perform the job.

Speak to an employment attorney or contact your regional office of the EEOC for advice and guidance if you believe you are a victim in this area.

---

**STRATEGY:** _When a qualified U.S. citizen applies for any position, that person must be given preference over a qualified alien, even if the U.S. citizen is less qualified._

---

## Applicant References

The majority of states limit an employer's ability to make preemployment inquiries regarding criminal arrests and convictions more than ten years before and restrict the use of such information. However, many employers conduct thorough background checks of applicants before hiring. In fact, when companies fail to investigate an applicant's background and they hire a person unfit for the position who causes harm or injury to another, they are sometimes liable under a legal theory referred to as negligent hiring and retention.

Under this negligent-hiring doctrine, in most jurisdictions, employers have a duty of reasonable care in hiring individuals who, because of employment, may pose a threat of injury to fellow employees and members of the public. Negligent-hiring claims have been made against employers for murders, rapes, sexual assaults, physical assaults, personal injuries, and property losses allegedly committed or caused by an unfit employee. In one case a McDonald's worker in Colorado, while on the job, sexually assaulted a three-year-old boy. The fast-food restaurant had hired the man without a complete background check, which would have shown a history of sexually assaulting children. The family sued and a jury reportedly awarded the victim $210,000.

However, liability may not be found under the negligent-hiring theory in cases where the employee's acts are not foreseeable and where the preemployment investigation of an employee's qualifications did not give rise to actual or constructive knowledge of a potential problem. For example, a union was held not liable for recommending the hiring of a cruise ship employee who committed a sexual assault upon another seaman while both men were vacationing onshore after working together on the cruise ship, because evidence of a propensity for aggressive behavior did not show up in the union's standard preemployment investigation of the perpetrator.

Employers may be liable to the applicant and employee under legal claims (including defamation, intentional infliction of emotional distress, and violations of the implied covenant of good faith and fair dealing) when references are not investigated properly or are leaked to nonessential third parties. (Libel suits filed by discharged employees and job applicants now account for approximately one-third of all defamation actions, and the average winning verdict exceeds $100,000 for such cases.)

For example, in one case a man terminated from an insurance company discovered that his former boss, in reference checks, had called him "untrustworthy, disruptive, paranoid, hostile, irrational, a classic sociopath." He sued and a jury decided those characterizations were out of line, a mistake that cost the company $1.9 million.

Such cases typify the legal dilemma employers face with reference checks. When hiring, if they miss a potential problem, some courts find them negligent. But when giving references, if they say too much, they may be liable for defaming former workers. Thus, employers must be familiar with local, state, and federal laws in this area.

Be aware that you may have rights in the event that harmful confidential information (for example, credit references) is communicated to nonessential third parties to your detriment. For more information and strategies on this subject, consult the section in Chapter 7 that discusses defamatory job references.

## Investigation of Bankruptcy Records

Can an applicant be denied a job because he or she has gone bankrupt? According to the Bankruptcy Code, no private employer may terminate the employment of, or discriminate with respect to employment against, an individual who is or has been a debtor or bankrupt under the Bankruptcy Act, or an individual associated with such debtor or bankrupt, solely because such debtor or bankrupt is or has been a debtor or bankrupt under the Bankruptcy Act, has been insolvent before the grant or denial of a discharge, or has not paid a debt that is dischargeable in a case under the Bankruptcy Act.

When considering minority candidates, case law and the Equal Employment Opportunity Commission advise against refusing to hire based on poor credit rating, because minorities often have more difficulty paying their bills. In fact, the EEOC has ruled that it is illegal to refuse to hire minority applicants (particularly Afro-Americans) with a poor credit rating, since minorities are more likely to be unable to pay their bills and such a policy effectively excludes a class of applicant from the job market.

In the majority of states and under the federal Consumer Credit Protection Act, it is illegal for a company to fire a person being sued for the nonpayment of a debt or when the company is instructed to cooperate in the collection of a portion of the person's wages through garnishment proceedings for any one indebtedness. Enforcement of this federal law is tough—violations are punishable by a fine of up to $1,000 and imprisonment for up to one year. Discharge for garnishment for more than one indebtedness is not prohibited, however, but such a policy may be restricted by Title VII of the Civil Rights Act of 1964 when it has a disproportionate effect on minority workers. And, since many states have even more strict laws on the books in this area (i.e., some states prohibit garnishment altogether or garnishment of pensions, while others only allow garnishment on delinquent spouse- or child-support arrears) and problems often ensue when employers receive multiple garnishment orders (which one to pay first?), always check your state's law.

## Preemployment Drug and Alcohol Testing

Experts suggest that as many as 25 percent of the major corporations in the United States now engage in drug screening before hiring new employees; such tests are on the rise, particularly in high-technology and security-conscious industries.

Drug tests have generally been upheld as legal, particularly with respect to job applicants (as opposed to employees who are asked to submit to random tests as a requisite for continued employment). Applicants have fewer rights to protest such tests than employees. The reason is that drug tests are generally not viewed as violating people's privacy rights, since applicants are told in advance that they must take and pass the test to get the job and that all applicants must submit to such tests even to be considered for employment.

However, the right to test does not give potential employers the right to handle test results carelessly. Unwarranted disclosure of this information can result in huge damages, so be aware that you have rights in this area. You may also have rights in the event you are refused a job because you allegedly failed a test and it is determined later that there was a mistake in the test results (in other words, that the test results were really negative).

Speak to a lawyer immediately if you are denied employment for allegedly failing a drug test when you know this cannot be so, if you are fired shortly after accepting employment for allegedly failing a test, or if the results of a failed test are conveyed to nonessential third parties, causing you humiliation and embarrassment. (Chapter 4 in Part II, dealing with on-the-job rights of employees, covers the legality and strategies of drug and alcohol tests for workers in more detail.)

Drug and alcohol tests of job applicants are neither encouraged nor prohibited by the Americans with Disabilities Act (ADA), and the results of such tests may be used as a basis for disciplinary action. The reason is that an employer does not have to hire an applicant who poses a direct threat to the health or safety of himself/herself or others. In determining whether an individual poses such a threat, the nature and severity of the potential harm, duration of the risk, and the likelihood and immediacy that potential harm will occur are all factors to consider.

An employee or applicant who is currently engaging in illegal drug use is not protected under federal ADA law. Nor is a current alcoholic whose employment presents a threat to the safety of others.

## Lie-Detector and Other Preemployment Tests

The federal Polygraph Protection Act of 1988 forbids employers to give any job applicant a lie-detector test or agree to submit to such a test in order to be hired. This law also forbids the use of such tests in all states that previously allowed them and prohibits the use of lie detectors in all preemployment screening.

Many states have enacted strong laws protecting job applicants from stress tests, psychological evaluator tests, and other honesty tests. In other states the trend is to eliminate or strongly discourage the use of such tests. To be safe in this area, you are strongly advised to speak to a knowledgeable attorney who can advise you on the current status of such laws in your state. Additionally, all tests presently being used should be carefully reviewed, since such tests must comply with existing federal and state law.

---

**STRATEGY:** *If you are asked to submit to such a test as a condition of being offered a job and believe that the test is unfair, harmful, or distasteful, it may be a good idea to investigate the particular law in your state before acting in this area. Even if such tests are legal, they may be discriminatory by causing a different effect, positive or negative, on any race, gender, or ethnic group when compared with another group. Any tests that cannot work as well with minorities as with other groups are illegal under EEOC guidelines. Thus, investigate whether inherent discrimination problems exist with such tests so that all tests given do not contain hidden bias or unfairly penalize one group over another.*

---

## Tips to Avoid Being Hired by a Deceitful Employer

No matter what type of job you are considering, you should investigate the potential employer even if you desperately need the job. This should always be done before accepting employment. Typical information you would like to learn are facts regarding the employer's business reputation, credit rating, financial status, rate of employee turnover, morale problems with workers, whether the company has been involved in any employee-related lawsuits recently (and if so, did the employee win or lose?), and commitments to the community in which the company is located.

For example, if you are being hired to replace someone in an important position, try to obtain the name of the person you might be replacing and find out why the individual is no longer there. Better still, by speaking to that person you could learn valuable information to influence your decision. Many applicants who follow this advice discover that the individual decided to resign because he or she was being harassed on the job by a supervisor, the job was long and tedious, or promised commissions, bonuses, raises, and promotions were not given.

It is particularly important to do your homework when you are being offered an important position that includes long-term employment, stock options, profit sharing, and other valuable financial benefits. Such an investigation should be made to assess the chances that the employer has sufficient assets to pay these benefits or that the employer will still be in business when you retire.

Most lawyers and accountants who represent successful business clients obtain the following kinds of financial information from credit reporting agencies (such as Dunn & Bradstreet) and the banks with whom the company does its business. The following list of questions is a good starting point in this area:

1. What is the legal form of the employer? Is it a corporation, an S corporation, a partnership, or a sole proprietorship? (You should know the legal distinctions among these terms for additional protection.)
2. What are the names of the principal shareholders or partners?
3. What is the financial history of the employer? Is it a recently established business, or has it been in existence for a while? (Many new businesses fail within the first few years, hurting employees in the process by firing them suddenly and not paying adequate severance benefits. I always instruct clients wishing to join nonestablished employers to proceed with caution.)
4. With whom does the employer maintain banking relations? For how long has it done so? What is the average balance on deposit? Does the employer have a line of credit? If so, for how much?
5. How many people work for the company? Do any of them belong to a union? Is the employer opposed to union participation? Could you join a union? What additional bene-

fits would you receive if you joined a union? Has the employer recently been involved in any litigation with any of its employees? What was the lawsuit about? Did the employer win? What was the effect on employee morale? What is the rate of employee turnover?

6. Does the employer offer generous benefits? These include such items as liberal sick day and vacation policies, paid maternity and paternity leaves, etc., and will be discussed in greater detail in the next chapter.

7. Has the employer filed a recent financial statement? Was it a certified statement? (Certified financial statements are usually more accurate and verifiable than regular financial statements.) What are the company's assets and liabilities? Does it have an unusually high late-paying accounts receivables problem? (This might indicate a cash flow problem and potential bankruptcy situation if the receivables aren't paid.)

8. What are the employer's assets? Does it own real estate, patents, inventions, licenses, and other tangible assets?

9. What does the latest balance sheet reveal? This is an important document. It shows the employer's financial status on the last date of the reported fiscal year. For example, you can learn what the employer owns in terms of cash, marketable securities, accounts receivable, inventory, and property and equipment. The balance sheet will also indicate money owed for unpaid bills and taxes, loan repayments to banks, bondholders, and other lenders. You may also be able to determine the amount of the employer's working capital, costs of doing business, and other pertinent information. If you are being hired for an important position and are given stock or stock options, be sure that you obtain copies of such documents for the current year and several past years of the employer's operations.

10. What are the liabilities of the employer? Are there any outstanding encumbrances, judgments, or liens?

11. Has the business been sold recently? Did the new owners assume the liabilities or just purchase the assets? This is important. Suppose you are owed bonuses which the old employer refuses to pay. The new owners may be able to step away from this obligation if they only purchased the company's assets and not its liabilities.
12. Who administers the employer's pension plan? Is it a reliable company?

You should never accept a new job blindly, particularly when a high salary and other substantial benefits are offered. Negotiating a job is a two-way street. The employer spends much time and expense verifying the personal background, job qualifications, and prior references of job applicants. You should try to gather as much information as possible on the employer's history, management style, and financial stability as well. In certain instances, what you learn may give you second thoughts—you may come to suspect that you will not be promoted properly or even that the company may not be around in the future.

Thus, try to gather as much information as possible before making your decision. Talk to fellow workers; listen to what they say. Many are accessible and honest and will give you a true picture of the way the employer really runs its business (as opposed to what you're told at the interview).

Better still, speak to friends and business associates in the industry to learn more about the employer's business reputation. For example, if you learn names of customers, suppliers, or distributors of the employer, it may be a good idea to inquire discreetly to learn their opinions about the company. What you learn may surprise you. The same is true for reputable employment agencies who have dealt with the employer in the past and can tell you about the company's reputation and business methods. Finally, if you are about to work for a large company, you may be able to locate written information in the business press. Check the microfiche files in a good library for articles in leading business publications.

Remember, ask questions and do your homework. You may learn information that will save you money and aggravation in the future.

## CHAPTER 2

# Negotiating the Job

Smart applicants never accept employment until they have carefully discussed and clarified all key terms, conditions, and responsibilities of the job up front, no matter what type of job is being offered. You risk being exploited when you fail to do so. When key terms (including the compensation arrangement and benefits package) are not agreed on before the hiring, the law will not generally impute such rights and you cannot force an employer to give valuable benefits not promised before the start date after you begin working.

Never be afraid to negotiate. Remember that a successful job negotiation is one of give and take. Obviously, the more points you insist on, the more benefits and protections you will obtain. Be aware, however, that certain employer policies may not be negotiable. While salary, title, duties, authority, and such are fair game for negotiation, fringe benefit, profit-sharing, and pension programs are usually fixed and not open to negotiation. Reviewing your prospective employer's employee handbook or personnel manual will give you a good idea of where the flexibilities and inflexibilities are. Types of negotiations and strategies you can use are discussed in the following pages.

Most well-run companies respect applicants who thoroughly negotiate their jobs. Thus, use the following checklist of negotiating points wisely. Even if you cannot negotiate many of the points cited below, you can minimize disappointment and confusion by knowing what to expect after you begin working. Thorough negotiations can also reduce potential litigation claims arising from breach of contract, wrongful discharge, and other legal problems that frequently arise during and after the employment relationship has ended.

Finally, do not expect to get everything you request. However, by understanding the nature of successful job negotiations and the many options that are available, you can receive additional benefits and protection merely by recognizing what to ask for.

## Checklist of Key Negotiating Points to Cover During the Hiring Interview

The following checklist is divided into three main sections: The Job; Job Security; and Salary and Benefits. Where appropriate, detailed "strategies" have been inserted into the checklist for further information. (Additional negotiating points for salespeople and others who earn commissions are provided in Chapter 9.)

### THE JOB

1. *Job description.* (Understand the nature of the job being offered.)
2. What is your *title*?
3. What will be your *job functions*? Will you report to a superior? If so, who?
4. When are you expected to *begin working* (start date)?
5. What is your *employment status*?

a. Are you considered a regular full-time employee eligible for all employer-provided fringe benefits (as opposed to a part-time or exempt employee paid on an hourly basis with limited fringe benefits)?

b. Are you considered an employee or an independent contractor? (As an independent contractor, you may be required to pay all federal, state, and local withholding taxes, Social Security, and other taxes. However, there are certain advantages to being hired as an independent contractor which will be discussed later in this chapter.)

c. Are you being hired as a consultant? If so, can you work for other companies, have outside work and sidelines, etc.? This, too, will be discussed later in the chapter.

## JOB SECURITY

1. Will you be given *job security* (as opposed to merely being "hired at will," which gives the employer the right to fire you at any time with or without notice and with or without cause)?
2. If so, what kind of job security is being offered?

---

**STRATEGY 1:** *Your objective in negotiating for job security is to avoid being fired suddenly at the employer's discretion.*

---

The best job security to obtain is to be employed for a definite term—for example, two years. This means that the employer cannot fire you prior to the expiration of that term except for a compelling reason—that is, for cause. (Most employers are reluctant to hire people for a definite term because it reduces their ability to fire employees at any time.) Thus, always ask for a definite term when being hired. Use your discretion as to the amount of job security you request. Your request can range from six months to several years. Tell the employer you want an X-year contract; the employer will know what you mean.

---

**STRATEGY 2:** *If the employer refuses to hire you for a definite term, ask for a guarantee that you cannot be fired except for cause or* *as long as you achieve certain goals (for example, a minimum sales quota if you are being hired as a salesperson). This request can give you needed protection without locking the employer into a time frame.*

---

**STRATEGY 3:** *If this request is refused, ask to be guaranteed a written warning within a definite period of time (for example, thirty days to cure alleged deficient performance) before being fired. This will protect you from a sudden firing, and some employers will accept this. Or you can ask for a written notice of termination (for example, thirty days before the contract will end) before the effective termination date so that you can plan ahead and look for other employment while still collecting a paycheck.*

---

**STRATEGY 4:** *If the employer refuses #3, request pay in lieu of notice in the event you are fired without warning; for example, ask to receive two weeks' additional pay at your current salary level in the event you are fired suddenly. (This is in addition to severance pay, more fully discussed below.)*

---

**STRATEGY 5:** *Be sure you understand if you are being hired for a probationary period. Some employers establish a probationary period (for example, the first 90 days of employment) ranging from 30 to 120 days to evaluate an employee's performance. If you are hired for a probationary period but are fired before the end of the period, you may be entitled to receive salary and other benefits until the end of the probationary period in certain situations.*

---

### SALARY AND BENEFITS

1. What is your *base salary*, and when is it payable? Understand all deductions from your paycheck.

2. When does the pay period start and end?
3. If payday falls on a holiday, when are paychecks distributed?
4. Is *overtime* offered? If so, at what rate? Is there a seniority basis for offering overtime (e.g., a policy that overtime is first offered to longtime workers)? Most states, in addition to federal law, require that overtime must be paid whenever a part-time or hourly employee works in excess of forty hours per week. Special employees working in government contracting or subcontracting work may also be required to be paid overtime if they work more than eight hours on any given day. Discuss this if relevant.
5. Will you be required to outlay *expenses*? If so, are expenses reimbursable? Be sure you know the kind and amount of expenses that are. Be sure you understand the kind of documentation to be supplied to the employer for reimbursement and how long you must wait before reimbursement.
6. Are you entitled to *commissions*? If so, understand how commissions are earned, the commission rate, and when commissions are paid. (See Chapter 9.)
7. Are you to receive a *bonus*? If so, how is it calculated, and when is it paid? Is the bonus gratuitous (in other words, merely paid at the employer's whim and discretion in an amount determined solely by the employer), or is it enforceable by contract with a verifiable sum linked to some specific formula (profits, revenue, output, etc.)?

Many people fail to understand their rights regarding bonuses and are later disappointed or exploited. For example, while some people work a full year counting on a bonus and don't receive it, others receive bonuses that are not even closely related to what they were expecting. But that is not the worst problem that frequently arises. Employers sometimes fire individuals after the bonus has technically been earned (at the end of the year) but before it is distributed (on February 15 of the following year). They then tell the ex-employee that he or she must be working for the company at the time the bonus is paid in order to collect!

These common abuses can be avoided by understanding and negotiating the following.

---

**STRATEGY 1:** *Request a verifiable bonus that is not subject to the employer's discretion. Specify the amount, when it will be paid, and that there are to be no strings or conditions attached. In other words, treat the bonus as part of your salary package; this will increase your legal rights in the event you are not paid.*

---

**STRATEGY 2:** *Request a* pro rata *bonus in the event you resign or are fired prior to the bonus being paid. For example, if the bonus is computed on sales volume and you work a full year and resign or are fired on December 1 of that year, you should be able to receive eleven-twelfths of the expected bonus. Many employers will accept this provided you give ample notice before the resignation and you are not fired for misconduct (that is, for cause).*

---

**STRATEGY 3:** *Avoid allowing the employer the right to arbitrarily determine when and if a bonus will be paid and in what amount. This arrangement is considered a gratuitous bonus, which may not be enforceable by contract. When an employer controls the timing, amount, and whether or not to pay a bonus at all, or states that the money is paid in appreciation for continuous, efficient, or satisfactory service, employees have a weaker chance to recover an expected bonus from the employer when they are not paid.*

---

**STRATEGY 4:** *Resist arrangements that require you to be on the job after a bonus is earned in order to receive it. If the employer insists on this condition, negotiate the right to receive a bonus if* *you are fired due to a business reorganization, layoff, or any reason other than gross misconduct.*

---

**STRATEGY 5:** *Get it in writing. Verbal promises to pay bonuses are not always enforceable. Confirm your understanding in writing for additional protection. (You will learn how to do this effectively later in this chapter.)*

---

**STRATEGY 6:** *Are additional services required in order to earn the bonus? If so, promises to pay a bonus for work, labor, or services already completed at the time the promise is made may not be valid.*

---

**STRATEGY 7:** *Try to link the bonus to some verifiable formula (for example, gross profits or sales volume). Such an arrangement can give you extra legal protection; in the event you are not paid a correct amount, you would be able to verify the bonus from the company's books and records. In fact, if a bonus-enforceable-by-contract arrangement could be proved in court, you would have the right to inspect the employer's books and records in a lawsuit.*

---

Many employers are reluctant to base bonuses on verifiable components because they are aware of the vulnerability to exposure in a lawsuit. However, you should leave nothing up to chance when negotiating a bonus. You want to know precisely how the bonus is to be earned and steps to take (for example, the right to be given company records for review) in the event you are not paid what you believe you are owed. Insist on nothing less.

8. What *fringe benefits* will you receive?

Most employees fail to properly negotiate extra compensation in the form of fringe benefits. Many forms of fringe benefits are even more valuable than salary because they are nontaxable.

Don't forget to ask for fringe benefits during the negotiating process.

The following detailed summary of fringe benefits will be helpful in this area.

**Insurance benefits.** These include basic group term life insurance, basic accidental death and dismemberment coverage, optional group term life insurance, dependent term life insurance, optional accidental death and dismemberment insurance, business travel accident insurance, weekly income accident and sickness plans, illness payment plans, short- and long-term disability insurance plans, medical benefit plans, dental benefit plans, and legal benefit plans.

This list is not meant to be all-inclusive. Rather, it gives you an idea about the kinds of benefits that are available. However, most insurance benefits are not negotiable, since employers must offer them to all employees so as not to be liable for charges of discrimination.

**Other benefits.** These can include the use of an automobile, free parking, car insurance, gasoline allowance, death benefits, prepaid legal services, credit cards, and loans at reduced rates of interest with favorable repayment schedules. Be sure you know all the elements of your benefit package, and don't be afraid to negotiate extra benefits when appropriate.

**Pensions and profit-sharing plans.** Are you entitled to additional compensation in the form of defined benefit, profit-sharing, money purchase, and pension plans? Other benefits you should be aware of are Social Security benefits, Individual Retirement Accounts (IRAs), 401(k) plans, thrift plans, stock bonus plans, and employee stock ownership plans (ESOPs).

All of these plans are extra financial perks to help you accumulate additional revenue for financial security and your retirement. Be sure you understand what benefits the employer offers in this area and what contributions will be made on your behalf. Other questions to ask:

- Are you required to contribute matching sums of money? If so, how much will this cost you? Can you increase or decrease matching contributions at your discretion? If so, is notice required and how much?
- Does the investment accumulate tax-free?
- Can the money be taken prior to your retirement? If so, is there a penalty?
- What happens if you resign or are fired for cause? Is the money forfeited?
- What happens if the company is sold or goes bankrupt? Is the money protected?
- Who administers the plan benefits? How can you be sure that there are no funding liabilities—in other words, how can you be sure that monies will be set aside as promised? Are the plan benefits invested in such a manner as to preclude large losses?
- If as a result of an acquisition through the purchase of the company you are laid off, how will COBRA and ERISA laws apply? ERISA (Employee Retirement Income Security Act) as modified by COBRA (Consolidated Omnibus Budget Reconciliation Act of 1986) is a federal law designed to protect you and your beneficiaries' pension and other benefit rights when you are laid off. Note that ERISA does not apply to employment by churches or federal, state, or local governments, or by companies with twenty or fewer employees, and may not apply if it can be proved that your termination was for gross misconduct. However, in most situations, these laws ensure that money previously set aside on your behalf will be given to you, regardless of internal changes or organizational restructuring in your company.

All of these points and many more should be explored and explained to your satisfaction. Since these financial benefits can account for a large part of additional compensation, never overlook their importance. Always negotiate to receive the maximum amount of benefits available.

**Raises and job advancement.** Are periodic raises given? What is the procedure for merit raises and job advancement?

---

**STRATEGY:** *Employees are sometimes disappointed by the size of annual or periodic merit increases or the speed of job advancement. To avoid problems in this area, be sure you know if such increases are determined by one person's subjective decision. If they are, request the right to appeal this person's decision and discuss how this may be accomplished.*

---

**Relocation expenses.** This is money often paid to employees who are required to relocate. Points to discuss and negotiate include questions like these: How much relocation pay will be given? When is it payable, and who will pay for it? Are taxes taken out of the payments? Be sure to determine whether you need to furnish supporting documentation (copies of bills for legal fees incurred in a house closing, etc.) in order to receive reimbursement. Also ask what arrangements will be made if you resign or are terminated within a short period of time.

---

**STRATEGY:** *Do not allow the employer to unilaterally cancel relocation expenses if the job doesn't work out, because you may have relocated yourself and your family thousands of miles at great expense with no protection. If you are planning to relocate to a distant location, always receive assurances in writing that relocation expenses will be paid regardless of how long you work for the company.*

---

**Severance pay.** Does the employer have a definite stated policy regarding severance (e.g., two weeks of severance for each year of employment)?

Inquire whether severance is paid if you resign as opposed to being fired. Some companies do not pay severance upon resignation and do not pay severance when the termination is for cause.

**Vacation pay.** How much vacation pay you get often depends on your salary grade, type of job offered, and how well you negotiate.

Be sure you understand how vacation pay is computed and other important matters regarding the granting of vacation time. Consider the following as starting points:

- Must vacation days be used in the year they are granted, or can they be carried over to the next year? If they can't, can a prorated share (e.g., one-half the days) be carried over?
- How long must you work in order to be qualified?
- Does the amount of vacation time increase depending on the number of years with the company (e.g., two weeks of vacation pay for the first five years, increasing to three weeks of paid vacation from years six to ten)?
- Must vacation days be taken all at once, or can they be staggered? If so, how?
- How much notice are you required to give before you can take vacations?
- Are there times during peak seasonal demands when requests will not be granted?
- If you leave or are terminated, will you be paid for all unused vacation time?

This last point should be considered carefully. Employees frequently leave their jobs expecting to receive large payments for unused vacation (carried over for several years) but are denied payment in this regard. Some states, including California, require companies to pay accrued vacation pay in all circumstances, even when the employee is fired for cause. Thus, check with the department of labor in your state or speak to competent legal counsel.

**Personal days.** Personal days give you a chance to attend to personal business, religious observances, or special occasions. Some companies add them to vacation time with pay. Others only allow personal days without pay. In addition, inquire about absences due to medical and dental appointments, bereavement pay, military leave, paternity leave, appearance in court, and jury duty.

**Personal leaves.** Employers are not required by law to allow employees paid personal leaves of absence, but must apply such practices consistently to all employees if they do. If you are considering taking an extended leave, what about the continuation of medical benefits during this period? Ask whether medical and other benefits terminate at the end of the month when the leave becomes effective. Can you keep those benefits in effect during the absence period by continuing to pay your payroll deductions?

Be aware that federal law prohibits companies from requiring employees to work an extended period of time (such as twelve months) before being allowed to take unpaid personal leaves. The Equal Employment Opportunity Commission has ruled that not allowing unpaid leave has a disparate impact on women who desire to nurse their newborn children and may violate the federal Family and Medical Leave Act (FMLA).

**Disability leave.** If you will be a full-time employee, you may be entitled to disability leave should you become unable to work due to a nonoccupational illness.

Note: A company cannot treat pregnancy-related disability or maternity leave differently than it treats other forms of disability leaves of absence. This is explained in greater detail in Chapter 5.

**Disability.** What happens in the event you are disabled? Can you receive salary and other benefits for a predetermined period of time? Understand the meanings of temporary disability and permanent disability and know what ramifications will ensue in the event of such disability.

## OTHER MATTERS OF CONCERN

In addition to financial benefits, job security, and duties, there are many other matters to discuss at the hiring interview. The following checklist will cover concerns often enunciated by the employer (which may or may not be relevant depending upon your particular situation).

1. Are you required to protect confidential information and trade secrets acquired while working for the company? If so, agree how this can be accomplished.
2. Can you have side ventures in a noncompeting business, or must you work exclusively for the company on a full-time basis?
3. Who owns inventions and processes created by you during employment?
4. Will disputes be resolved by litigation or binding arbitration? Can the prevailing party recover attorney fees and court costs from the losing party?
5. To perform your job better and reduce misunderstandings, it is also wise to receive information regarding the following policies:

- Time clock regulations
- Rest periods
- Absences
- Safety and accident prevention
- Authorized use of telephones
- Reporting complaints
- Making suggestions

- Resolving disputes
- Personal appearance rules
- Solicitation rules
- Conflict of interest and code of ethic rules

6. Does the company require you to sign a contract containing a restrictive covenant prohibiting you from working for a competitor or calling on customers previously solicited during your employ? If so, does the company require all new employees to sign similar contracts?

Restrictive covenants are provisions in employment agreements that prohibit a person from directly competing or working for a competitor after leaving his or her employer. The effect of such clauses varies greatly. For example, they can:

- Restrict an employee from working for a competitor of the former employer
- Restrict an employee from starting a business or forming a venture with others that competes against the former employer
- Restrict an employee from contacting or soliciting former or current customers or employees of the employer
- Restrict an employee from using confidential knowledge, trade secrets, and other privileged information learned while working for the former employer
- Restrict an employee from any of the above in both geographic and time limitations

The above points are illustrated by the following clauses taken from employment agreements:

For a period of one (1) year following the termination of your employment for any reason, it is agreed that you will not contact or solicit any person, firm, association, or corporation to which you sold products of the Company during the year preceding the termination of your employment.

Upon termination of the Doctor's employment under this Agreement for any reason, the Doctor shall not engage in the practice of neurology or open his own office for the practice of neurology or associate himself with other physicians within a five (5) mile radius of the office of the Corporation or a five mile radius of any hospital for which the Doctor has worked on behalf of the Corporation for a period of one (1) year after the effective date of termination.

In consideration of compensation paid to me as an employee, I hereby recognize as the exclusive property of the employer and agree to assign, transfer and convey to the employer, every invention, discovery, concept, idea, process, method and technique which I become acquainted with as a result or consequence of my employment and agree to execute all documents requested by the employer to evidence its ownership thereof.

You may be surprised to learn, however, that such clauses are not always enforceable. Although every case is different, judges have been taking dimmer views of such attempts to restrict an employee's livelihood. Consult Chapter 7 for more information about the weight such clauses can carry once you are fired or resign.

Whether or not such covenants are legal, however, defending lawsuits involving restrictive covenants is time-consuming and expensive, so you should avoid signing such agreements in the first place. Many employers have a tendency to "hang" such a clause over individuals by threatening to institute legal action after a person's resignation or termination. This can discourage you from contacting prospective employers and customers in your industry and trade or establishing your own business. Thus, consider the following strategies for help in this area.

**STRATEGY 1:** *Carefully review and resist signing contracts containing restrictive covenants. An employee who works without an employment contract and who leaves without taking any trade secrets has total freedom to work elsewhere in the same industry. This generally includes the right to solicit the ex-employer's customers. However, you may be subjecting yourself to a lawsuit (even when no valid grounds exist) by signing an agreement containing such a clause.*

*Always read your employment contract carefully before signing it. What does the restrictive covenant say? For example, does it prohibit you from working for a competitor or calling on customers you previously sold for the company for an excessive period (e.g., two years)? If so, make the employer aware of this. Negotiate to reduce the covenant to a reasonable period you can live with (e.g., three months) and insist on the right to receive continued salary and other benefits while the restrictive covenant is in effect. Remember, everything is negotiable before you sign on the bottom line. Once the agreement is signed, however, you may be bound by its terms.*

**STRATEGY 2:** *Always obtain a copy of the agreement after it is signed. Many people forget to do this. After they resign or are discharged and receive a formal demand requesting them to refrain from certain acts (usually in the form of a written cease and desist letter), they cannot locate the agreement containing the restrictive provision. This places them at a disadvantage. For example, they may be unable to obtain an accurate opinion from a lawyer if he or she cannot review the contract or may be forced to spend unnecessary legal fees trying to obtain a copy from the employer. Thus, request a copy of all documents that you sign, and store them in a safe place for later review.*

## Confirming These Points in Writing

Once you and the company have agreed to key terms, it is essential to confirm the deal *in writing*. Legal disputes often arise when people are hired on a handshake. A handshake, or oral agreement, indicates only that the parties came to some form of agreement; it does not say what the agreement was. Failure to spell out important terms often leads to misunderstandings and disputes. Even when key terms are discussed, the same spoken words that are agreed upon have different meanings from the employee's and company's perspective. Written words limit this sort of misunderstanding.

Although a written contract cannot guarantee you will be satisfied with the company's performance, it can provide additional remedies in the event of the employer's nonperformance. Once the agreement is signed, the law presumes that the parties incorporated their intentions into the contract. The instrument "speaks for itself," and courts will not hear testimony about understandings or discussions before the contract was signed unless the information is necessary to interpret ambiguous terms or establish particular trade customs.

Additionally, be aware that clauses in written contracts can give you negotiating strength. For example, some employment contracts state that terms cannot be changed without the written consent of both parties. If such a clause was included in your contract and an employer attempted to reduce your salary or other benefits, this could not be done without your written approval.

Written contracts also protect employees who are fired in a manner prohibited by the contract. The following is an example of a situation that could occur.

Andrew received a one-year contract to work as an advertising executive. The contract stated that it would be automatically renewed for an additional year if notice of termination was not received at least ninety days prior to the expiration of the first year. Andrew's company gave him notice that the contract would not be renewed one week prior to the start of the next year. Andrew sued for damages; the court ruled that he was entitled to additional compensation because the employer failed to abide by the terms of the agreement.

Working on a handshake for an indefinite period of time is risky. In most states the law says that if you are hired without a written contract and for a nonspecific period of time, you are "hired at will." This means that, subject to various exceptions outlined in later chapters of this book, your employer can fire you at any time without notice and without cause.

The at-will doctrine developed in the 1800s during the transition from the master-servant relationship of employment to the application of contract law. The legal concept was "mutuality of obligation." It was reasoned that if an employee could quit his job without notice, the employer also had the right to terminate an employee for any reason or for no reason.

A number of states have recognized the inequality of power between the employee and the employer and have found ways to modify the at-will doctrine. This is discussed later in the book.

Due to the unfairness of the at-will doctrine, which affects hundreds of thousands of employees each year, many more people are no longer accepting being hired on a handshake. Instead, they are recognizing that they can be better protected by including favorable clauses in clearly drafted contracts and are insisting on receiving written agreements whenever they accept a job.

A good employment contract should describe in specific detail all important aspects of your employment, such as term of the contract, duties, authority and responsibility, job description and title, compensation and reimbursement, benefits, termination, and methods for resolving disputes, such as arbitration, mediation, and more.

There are three purposes for every written contract. First, the act of writing helps ensure that both parties to the contract understand and agree to its terms. Second, the written word provides a reminder to both parties of the terms of the agreement. Third, the written, signed, and witnessed contract can serve as evidence if legal action is required to enforce the terms. Each employment contract must be drafted to meet specific situations, needs, and understandings for both the employee and the employer.

Everything in the contract should be very specific. Anything that is vague or open for later negotiation creates a potential misunderstanding and may fail to carry weight in a court of law. So be sure to cover everything that is important to you, and be sure that all understandings based on your discussions and negotiations are included in the written words of the contract. Consider, for example:

- Compensation: salary, salary increases, bonus program and requirements, profit sharing, etc.
- Job description: statement of job duties, authorities, responsibilities, title, etc.
- Terms of employment: contract period and provision for renewal, at-will, etc.
- Fringe benefits: pension plan (and when vested), life and health insurance, savings plan, company contribution, etc.
- Vacation time: number of days, when earned, carryover, etc.
- Sick leave: number of days, conditions for allowance, salary and benefits continuance during extended health-based absences, etc.
- Arbitration: provision for arbitration or mediation in the event of unreconcilable disagreements affecting the basis of a term in the employment agreement.
- Termination/resignation: terms leading to employment termination or allowing no-fault resignation, with terms for payment and continuation of benefits upon leaving the company's employment, etc.
- Special provisions: office facilities, parking space, dining room rights, recreational facilities, health maintenance programs, medical examinations, company car or equivalent, bonding, liability coverage (and indemnification), etc.

Don't stop here, however. Consider all of the things that are important to you related to the job, its benefits, its responsibilities, and its expectations, both positive and potentially negative. Consider what will happen if the economic fortunes of the company fade. What if your job or department is abolished? What if the firm is taken over by another firm? Will you, as the newest employee, be the first to be laid off? Or do you have employment protection? If not, are there protections for termination payments if you are asked or invited to leave?

Following are several examples of employment contracts often given to new employees. Since these agreements are included for illustrative purposes only, do not use them without first consulting with an employment attorney.

---

**STRATEGY:** *Note the difference in style with these agreements. The sample employment agreement drafted in letter form (page 82) is written in "plain English" in contrast to "legalese." Some states now require that all contracts be written in language that is clearly understood by those not trained in the legal profession.*

---

Whenever you obtain an employment contract or any business document, read it carefully. Question all ambiguous and confusing language. Consult a lawyer if you do not understand the meaning of any terms. Remember that contracts prepared by employers usually contain clauses that work to your disadvantage. Thus, you should review the agreement thoroughly before signing.

When written agreements are used, be sure that all changes, strike-outs, and erasures are initialed by both parties and that all blanks are filled in. If additions are necessary, include them in a space provided or attach them to the contract itself. Then note on the contract that addenda have been added and accepted by both parties. This prevents questions from arising if addenda are lost or separated, because it is difficult to prove there were any without mention in the body of the contract.

Also be sure that the contract is signed by a bona fide officer who has the legal authority to bind the employer to important terms. Finally, always obtain a signed copy of the executed agreement for your files and keep it in a safe place where you store other valuable documents.

## Sample Employment Agreement

EMPLOYMENT AGREEMENT, entered into and effective as of [date] between [name of company] (the "Company") and [name of employee] (the "Employee")

**1. Employment, Duties, and Acceptance**

1.1 Company hereby employs Employee for the Term (as defined in Section 2 hereof) to render exclusive and full-time services in an executive capacity to Company and to the subsidiaries of Company engaged in the business of [specify] and in connection therewith to devote his best efforts to the affairs of the Company and to perform such duties as Employee shall reasonably be directed to perform by officers of the Company.

1.2 Employee hereby accepts such employment and agrees to render such services. Employee agrees to render such services at Company's offices located in the [specify location] area, but Employee will travel on temporary trips to such other place or places as may be required from time to time to perform his duties hereunder. During the Term hereof, Employee will not render any services for others, or for Employee's own account, including any services to any supplier or significant customer of Company.

**2. Term of Employment**

2.1 The term of Employee's employment pursuant to this Agreement (the "Term") shall begin on the date hereof, and shall end on [specify], subject to the provisions of Article 4 of this Agreement providing for earlier termination of Employee's employment in certain circumstances.

## 3. Compensation

3.1 As compensation for all services to be rendered pursuant to this Agreement to or at the request of Company, Company agrees to pay Employee a salary at the rate of [$X] per annum.

The Salary set forth hereinabove shall be payable in accordance with the regular payroll practices of the Company. All payments hereunder shall be subject to the provisions of Article 4 hereof.

3.2 Company shall pay or reimburse Employee for all necessary and reasonable expenses incurred or paid by Employee in connection with the performance of services under this Agreement upon presentation of expense statements or vouchers or such other supporting information as it from time to time requests evidencing the nature of such expense, and, if appropriate, the payment thereof by Employee, and otherwise in accordance with Company procedures from time to time in effect.

3.3 During the Term, Employee shall be entitled to participate in any group insurance, qualified pension, hospitalization, medical health and accident, disability, or similar plan or program of the Company now existing or hereafter established to the extent that he is eligible under the general provisions thereof. Notwithstanding anything herein to the contrary, however, Company shall have the right to amend or terminate any such plans or programs.

## 4. Termination

4.1 Disability. If Employee shall be prevented from performing Employee's usual duties for a period of 3 consecutive months, or for shorter periods aggregating more than 4 months in any 12-month period by reason of physical or mental disability, total or partial (herein referred to as "disability"), Company shall nevertheless continue to pay full salary up to and including the last day of the third consecutive month of disability, or the day on which the shorter periods of disability shall have equaled a total of 4 months, but Company may at any time or times on or after such last day (but before the termination of such disability) elect to terminate this Agreement upon written notice to employee, effective on such 1st day, without further obligation or liability to Employee, except for any compensation set forth in Article 3 hereof to Employee during the remaining period of disability.

4.2 Death. In the event of Employee's death during the Term, this Agreement shall automatically terminate, except that (a) Employee's estate shall be entitled to receive the compensation provided for hereunder to the last day of the month in which Employee's death occurs; and (b) such termination shall not affect any amounts payable as insurance or other death benefits under any plans or arrangements then in force or effect with respect to Employee.

4.3 Specified Cause. Company may at any time during the Term, by notice, terminate the employment of Employee for malfeasance, misfeasance, or nonfeasance in connection with the performance of Employee's duties, the cause to be specified in the notice of termination. Without limiting the generality of the foregoing, the following acts during the Term shall constitute grounds for immediate termination of employment hereunder:

4.3.1 Any willful and intentional act having the effect of injuring the reputation, business, or business relationships of Company or its affiliates;

4.3.2 Conviction of or entering a plea of *nolo contendere* to a charge of a felony or a misdemeanor involving moral turpitude;

4.3.3 Material breach of covenants contained in this Agreement; and

4.3.4 Repeated or continuous failure, neglect, or refusal to perform Employee's duties hereunder.

## 5. Protection of Confidential Information

5.1 In view of the fact that Employee's work as an employee of Company will bring Employee into close contact with many confidential affairs of the Company and its affiliates, including matters of a business nature, such as information about costs, profits, markets, sales, and any other information not readily available to the public, and plans for future developments, Employee agrees:

5.1.1 To keep secret all confidential matters of Company and its affiliates and not to disclose them to anyone outside of Company, either during or after Employee's employment with Company, except with Company's written consent; and

5.1.2 To deliver promptly to Company on termination of Employee's employment by Company, or at any time Company may so request, all memoranda, notes, records, reports, and other documents (and all copies thereof) relating to Company's and its affiliates' businesses which Employee may then possess or have under the Employee's control.

## 6. Ownership of Results of Services

6.1 Company shall own, and Employee hereby transfers and assigns to it, all rights of every kind and character throughout the work, in perpetuity, in and to any material and/or ideas written, suggested, or submitted by Employee hereunder and all other results and proceeds of Employee's services hereunder, whether the same consists of literary, dramatic, mechanical, or any other form of works, themes, ideas, creations, products, or compositions. Employee agrees to execute and deliver to Company such assignments or other instruments as Company may require from time to time to evidence its ownership of the results and proceeds of Employee's services.

## 7. Notices

7.1 All notices, requests, consents, and other communications required or permitted to be given hereunder shall be in writing and shall be deemed to have been duly given if delivered personally or sent by prepaid telegram, or mailed first-class, postage prepaid, as follows:

If to Employee: address

If to Company: address

With copies to: address

or as such other addresses as either party may specify by written notice to the other as provided in this Section 7.1.

## 8. General

8.1 It is acknowledged that the rights of Company under this Agreement are of a special, unique, and intellectual character which gives them a peculiar value, and that a breach of any provision of this Agreement (particularly, but not limited to, the exclusivity provisions hereof and the provisions of Article 5 hereof) will cause Company irreparable injury and damage which cannot be reasonably or adequately compensated in damages in an action at law. Accordingly, without limiting any right or remedy which Company may have in the premises, Employee specifically agrees that Company shall be entitled to seek injunctive relief to enforce and protect its rights under this Agreement.

8.2 This Agreement sets forth the entire agreement and understanding of the parties hereto, and supersedes all prior agreements, arrangements, and understandings. Nothing herein contained shall be construed so as to require the commission of any act contrary to law, and wherever there is any conflict between any provision of this Agreement and any present or future statute, law, ordinance, or regulation, the latter shall prevail, but in such event the provision of this Agreement affected shall be curtailed and limited only to the extent necessary to bring it within legal requirements. Without limiting the generality of the foregoing, in the event that any compensation or other monies payable hereunder shall be in excess of the amount permitted by any such statute, law, ordinance, or regulation, payment of the maximum amount allowed thereby shall constitute full compliance by Company with the payment requirements of this Agreement.

8.3 No representation, promise, or inducement has been made by either party that is not embodied in this Agreement, and neither party shall be bound by or liable for any alleged representation, promise, or inducement not so set forth. The section headings contained herein are for reference purposes only and shall not in any way affect the meaning or interpretation of this Agreement.

8.4 The provisions of this Agreement shall inure to the benefit of the parties hereto, their heirs, legal representatives, successors, and assigns. This Agreement, and Employee's rights and obligations hereunder, may not be assigned by Employee. Company may assign its rights, together with its obligations, hereunder in connection with any sale, transfer, or other disposition of all or substantially all of its business and assets. Company may also assign this Agreement to any affiliate of Company; provided, however, that no such assignment shall (unless Employee shall so agree in writing) release Company of liability directly to Employee for the due performance of all of the terms, covenants, and conditions of this Agreement to be complied with and performed by Company. The term "affiliate," as used in this agreement, shall mean any corporation, firm, partnership, or other entity controlling, controlled by, or under common control with Company. The term "control" (including "controlling," "controlled by," and "under common control with"), as used in the preceding sentence, shall be deemed to mean the possession, directly or indirectly, of the power to direct or cause the direction of the management and policies of such corporation, firm, partnership, or other entity, whether through ownership of voting securities or by contract or otherwise.

8.5 This Agreement may be amended, modified, superseded, canceled, renewed, or extended, and the terms or covenants hereof may be waived, only by a written instrument executed by both of the parties hereto, or in the case of a waiver, by the party waiving compliance. The failure of either party at any time or times to require performance of any provisions hereof shall in no manner affect the right at a later time to enforce the same. No waiver by either party of the breach of any term or covenant contained in this Agreement, whether by conduct or otherwise, in any one or more instances, shall be deemed to be, or construed as, a further or continuing waiver of any such breach, or a waiver of the breach of any other term or covenant contained in this Agreement.

8.6 This Agreement shall be governed by and construed according to the laws of the State of [specify state] applicable to agreements to be wholly performed therein.

IN WITNESS WHEREOF, the parties hereto have duly executed this Agreement as of the date first above written.

Name of Company       Name of Employee
By:       Date:
Title:
Date:


## Sample Employment Agreement

**(Typically given to executives with a definite term of employment)**

Employment Agreement dated as of [specify], by and between [name of company], a [specify state] corporation with its principal place of business at [specify address] (the "Company"), and [name of employee] (the "Employee").

WHEREAS, effective January 1, 1998, the Company and the Employee entered into an employment agreement, which agreement terminated December 31, 2000; and

WHEREAS, the Company desires to continue to employ the Employee, and the Employee desires to continue his employment with the Company; and

WHEREAS, the Company and the Employee wish to set forth the terms and conditions of the Employee's employment with the Company.

NOW, THEREFORE, in consideration of the mutual promises, warranties, and covenants set forth below, the parties hereto, intending to be legally bound, hereby agree as follows:

**1. Employment.** Effective as of the commencement date described in Section 2 below, the Company employs the Employee and the Employee accepts employment by the Company upon the terms and conditions hereafter set forth.

**2. Term of Employment.** The employment of the Employee under this Agreement shall commence as of January 1, 2001, and terminate on December 31, 2003. Thereafter, this Agreement shall be extended automatically for successive terms of one (1) year unless (i) the Company or the Employee shall give written notice of termination to the other party hereto at least sixty (60) days prior to the termination of the initial term of employment hereunder or any renewal term thereof, or (ii) unless earlier terminated as herein provided. The initial term of this Agreement and any renewal term thereof are hereinafter collectively referred to as the "Employment Period."

**3. Scope of Duties.** During the Employment Period, the Employee shall be employed as [specify] as well as such other duties and responsibilities which may be assigned to him by a Company manager or official. The Employee shall perform such service in good faith and comply with all rules, regulations, and policies established or issued by the Company.

**4. Extent of Service.** The Employee shall devote his entire time, attention, and energies to the business of the Company, and shall not during the Employment period engage in any other business activity which in the judgment of the Company conflicts with the duties of the Employee hereunder.

**5. Compensation.** In consideration of the services rendered by the Employee hereunder, the Company shall pay the Employee an aggregate base salary of [specify] per annum (the "Base Salary"), payable weekly. In addition to the Base Salary, the Employee shall also be paid [specify]. The Employee shall also be entitled to (i) the use of an automobile provided by the Company and (ii) medical, life insurance, disability, and other such benefits which the Company may from time to time make available generally to its employees in accordance with the terms of such benefit and welfare plans.

**6. Business Expenses.** During the Employment period, the Company shall reimburse the Employee for all reasonable and necessary travel expenses and other disbursements incurred by him for or on behalf of the Company in the performance of his duties hereunder (hereinafter referred to as "Business Expenses") upon presentation by the Employee to the Company of appropriate expense reports.

**7. Death.** If the Employee dies during the Employment Period, his employment hereunder shall be deemed to terminate as of the last day of the month during which his death occurs. Upon the death of the Employee, neither the Employee nor his beneficiaries or estate shall have any further rights or claims against the Company, except the right to receive:

A. The unpaid portion of the Base Salary, computed on a *pro rata* basis to the date of termination;

B. Any earned but unpaid commissions or other sales incentives;

C. Unused personal and vacation days to which the Employee is entitled in accordance with Company policy;

D. Reimbursement for any unpaid business expenses; and

E. Life insurance and other post-termination benefits in accordance with the Company welfare and benefit plans.

**8. Termination for Cause.** Upon furnishing of notice to the Employee, the Company may terminate the employment of the Employee for cause at any time during the Employment Period by reason of the Employee's (i) neglect of his duties hereunder, (ii) breach of or negligence with respect to his obligations under this Agreement, (iii) engaging in misconduct injurious to the Company, or (iv) the Employee's commission of an act constituting common law fraud or a felony. If the Employee's employment is terminated by the Company for cause as herein defined, his Base Salary and his eligibility for all other benefits provided by the Company shall cease as of his termination date, after which time the Company shall have no other further liability or obligation of any kind to the Employee under this Agreement, except the Employee shall have the right to receive:

A. The unpaid portion of the Base Salary, computed on a *pro rata* basis to the date of termination;

B. Reimbursement for any unpaid business expenses;

C. Any earned but unpaid commissions or other sales incentives;

D. Unused personal and vacation days to which the Employee is entitled in accordance with Company policy; and

E. Any post-termination benefits in accordance with the company welfare and benefit plans.

**9. Employee Acknowledgments.** Employee recognizes and acknowledges that in the course of Employee's employment it will be necessary for Employee to acquire information which could include, in whole or in part, information concerning the Company's sales, sales volume, sales methods, sales proposals, customers and prospective customers, suppliers and prospective suppliers, identity, practices, and procedures of key purchasing and other personnel in the employ of customers and prospective customers and suppliers and prospective suppliers, amount or kind of customers' purchases from the Company, research reports, the Company's computer program, system documentation, special hardware, related software development, the Company's manuals, methods, ideas, improvements, or other confidential or proprietary information belonging to the Company or relating to the Company's affairs (collectively referred to herein as "Confidential Information") and that such information is the property of the Company.

Employee further agrees that the use, misappropriation, or disclosure of the Confidential Information would constitute a breach of trust and could cause irreparable injury to the Company, and it is essential to the protection of the Company's goodwill and to the maintenance of the Company's competitive position that the Confidential Information be kept secret and the Employee agrees not to disclose the Confidential Information to others or use the Confidential Information to Employee's own advantage or the advantage of others.

Employee further recognizes and acknowledges that it is essential for the proper protection of the business of the Company that Employee be restrained from soliciting or inducing any employee of the Company to leave the employ of the Company, or hiring or attempting to hire any employee of the Company.

**10. Nondisclosure of Confidential Information.** Employee shall hold and safeguard the Confidential Information in trust for the Company, its successors and assigns, and shall not, without the prior written consent of the Company, misappropriate or disclose or make available to anyone for use outside the Company organization at any time, either during his employment with the Company or subsequent to the termination of his employment with the Company for any reason, including, without limitation, termination by the Company for cause or without cause, any of the Confidential Information, whether or not developed by Employee, except as required in the performance of Employee's duties to the Company.

**11. Return of Materials.** Upon the termination of Employee's employment with the Company for any reason, including, without limitation, termination by the Company for cause or without cause, Employee shall promptly deliver to the Company all correspondence, manuals, orders, letters, notes, notebooks, reports, programs, proposals, and any documents and copies concerning the Company's customers or concerning products or processes used by the Company and, without limiting the foregoing, will promptly deliver to the Company any and all other documents or material containing or constituting Confidential Information.

**12. Nonsolicitation of Customers and Suppliers.** Employee shall not during his time of employment with the Company, directly or indirectly, solicit the trade of, or do business with, any customer or prospective customer, or supplier or prospective supplier of the Company for any business purpose other than for the benefit of the Company. Employee further acknowledges that, in consideration of the promises contained in the Agreement and to induce the company to enter into this Agreement, he shall not for one (1) year following the termination of his employment with the Company, including, without limitation, termination by the Company for cause or without cause, directly or indirectly, solicit the trade of, or do business with, any person or entity whatsoever who or which is or was a customer or supplier of the Company in any of the territory or territories assigned to the Employee during the Employment Period, with respect to products of the same or similar kind as those presently or in the future distributed by the Company.

**13. Nonsolicitation of Employees.** The Employee shall not during his employment with the Company and for one (1) year following termination of Employee's employment with the Company, including, without limitation, termination by the Company for cause or without cause, directly or indirectly, solicit or induce, or attempt to solicit or induce, any employee, current or future, of the Company to leave the Company for any reason whatsoever, or hire any current or future employee of the Company.

**14. Advice of Counsel/Restrictive Covenants.** The Employee has had the opportunity to consult with independent counsel and understands the nature of and the burdens imposed by the restrictive covenants contained in this Agreement. The Employee represents and acknowledges that such covenants are reasonable, enforceable, and proper in duration, scope, and effect. Moreover, Employee represents and warrants that his experience and capabilities are such that the restrictive covenants set forth herein will not prevent him from earning his livelihood and that Employee will be fully able to earn an adequate livelihood for himself and his dependents if any of such provisions should be specifically enforced against Employee.

**15. Authorization to Modify Restrictions.** The Employee acknowledges that the remedies at law for any breach by Employee of the provisions of the restrictive covenants will be inadequate and that the Company shall be entitled to injunctive relief against the Employee in the event of any such breach, in addition to any other remedy and damage available. The Employee acknowledges that the restrictions contained herein are reasonable, but agrees that if any court of competent jurisdiction shall hold such restrictions unreasonable as to time, geographic area, activities, or otherwise, such restrictions shall be deemed to be reduced to the extent necessary in the opinion of such court to make them reasonable.

**16. No Prior Agreements.** Employee represents and warrants that he is not a party to or otherwise subject to or bound by the terms of any contract, agreement, or understanding which in any manner would limit or otherwise affect his ability to perform his obligations hereunder, including, without limitation, any contract, agreement, or understanding containing terms and provisions similar in any manner to those contained in Section 12 hereof. Employee further represents and warrants that his employment with the Company will not require the disclosure or use of any Confidential Information.

**17. Covenants of the Essence.** The covenants of the Employee set forth herein are of the essence of this Agreement; they shall be construed as independent of any other provision in this Agreement, and the existence of any claim or cause of action of the Employee against the Company, whether predicated on this Agreement or not, shall not constitute a defense to the enforcement by the Company of these covenants.

**18. Tolling Period.** If it should become desirable or necessary for the Company to seek compliance with the restrictive covenants by judicial proceedings, the period during which the Employee will not engage in the activities prohibited by Sections 12 and 13 hereof shall be extended to the first anniversary of the date of the judicial order requiring such compliance.

**19. Arbitration.** The parties expressly agree that all disputes or controversies arising out of this Agreement, its performance, or the alleged breach thereof, if not disposed of by agreement, shall be resolved by arbitration in accordance with this section. Either party must demand such arbitration only within nine (9) months after the controversy arises by sending a notice of demand to arbitrate to the American Arbitration Association (the "Association"), with a copy thereof to the other party. The dispute shall then be arbitrated by a three-arbitrator panel pursuant to the commercial Rules of the Association at the Association office in [specify state/place]. In the disposition of the dispute, the arbitrators shall be governed by the express terms of this Agreement and otherwise by the laws of the State of [specify] which shall govern the interpretation of the Agreement. The decision of the arbitrators shall be final and conclusive on the parties and shall be a bar to any suit, action, or proceeding instituted in any federal, state, or local court or before any administrative tribunal. Notwithstanding the foregoing, judgment on any award by the arbitrators may be entered in any court of competent jurisdiction. This arbitration provision shall survive any expiration or termination of the Agreement.

**20. Notices.** Any notice required or permitted to be given under this Agreement shall be sufficient if in writing, personally delivered, mailed, or telecopied, if to the Employee, to the Employee's residence as contained in Company records, and if to the Company, to its principal place of business set forth in the first paragraph of this Agreement.

**21. Assignment.** This Agreement is personal in its nature and the Employee shall not without the prior written consent of the Company assign or transfer this Agreement or any rights, duties, or obligations hereunder.

**22. Entire Agreement.** This Agreement constitutes the full and complete understanding and agreement of the parties hereto with respect to any employment of the Employee by the Company and supersedes all prior agreements and understanding with respect to the subject matter hereof, whether written or oral. This Agreement may not be changed orally, but only by an agreement in writing signed by the party against whom enforcement of any waiver, change, modification, or discharge is sought.

**23. Governing Law.** This Agreement shall be governed by, and construed in accordance with, the laws of the State of [specify].

**24. Remedies.** All remedies hereunder are cumulative, are in addition to any other remedies provided by law, and may be exercised concurrently or separately, and the exercise of any one remedy shall not be deemed to be an election of such remedy or to preclude the exercise of any other remedy. No failure or delay in exercising any right or remedy shall operate as a waiver thereof or modify the terms of this Agreement.

IN WITNESS WHEREOF, the parties have executed this Agreement as of the date first above written.

Name of Company        Name of Employee
By:

## Sample Employment Agreement, Letter Version

Date

Name of Employee
Address

Dear [Name of Employee]:

This letter confirms that [name of company] (the "Company") has hired you as its [specify title]. In consideration thereto, you agree to be employed under the following terms and conditions:

1. You agree to work full-time and use your best efforts while rendering services for the Company. As our [specify title], you will be responsible for: [specify in detail].

2. You will make no representations, warranties, or commitments binding the Company without our prior consent nor do you have any authority to sign any documents or incur any indebtedness on the Company's behalf.

3. You shall assume responsibility for all samples, sales literature, and other materials delivered to you and you shall return same immediately upon the direction of the Company.

4. THE COMPANY EMPLOYS YOU AT WILL AND MAY TERMINATE YOUR EMPLOYMENT AT ANY TIME, WITHOUT PRIOR NOTICE, WITH OR WITHOUT CAUSE. LIKEWISE, YOU ARE FREE TO RESIGN AS OUR [specify title] AT ANY TIME, WITH OR WITHOUT NOTICE.

5. The Company shall pay you a salary of [specify $X] per [specify] as consideration for all services to be rendered pursuant to this Agreement. In addition, the Company shall provide you with health insurance coverage for you and your family, and you will be eligible to participate in the Company pension plan. You will also receive two (2) weeks paid vacation each year, provided you give the Company appropriate notice, and the Company reserves the right to schedule your vacation(s) so as not to conflict with its normal business operations.

6. You shall also be paid for absences due to illness up to a

maximum of two (2) weeks per year, provided you submit a doctor's authorization indicating the reason for extended illness and the treatment received.

7. The Company shall also provide you time off with pay for the following holidays: [specify].

8. You agree and represent that you owe the Company the highest duty of loyalty. This means that you will never make secret profits at the Company's expense, will not accept kickbacks or special favors from customers or manufacturers, and will protect Company property.

9. While acting as an employee for the Company, you will not, directly or indirectly, own an interest in, operate, control, or be connected as an employee, agent, independent contractor, partner, shareholder, or principal in any company which markets products, goods, or services which directly or indirectly compete with the business of the Company.

10. All lists and other records relating to the customers of the Company, whether prepared by you or given to you by the Company during the term of this Agreement, are the property of the Company and shall be returned immediately upon termination or resignation of your employment.

11. You further agree that for a period of six (6) months following the termination or resignation of your employment, you shall not work for, own an interest in, or be connected with as an employee, stockholder, or partner, any company which directly or indirectly competes with the business of the Company.

12. There shall be no change, amendment, or modification of this Agreement unless it is reduced to writing and signed by both parties. This Agreement cancels and supercedes all prior agreements and understandings.

13. If any provision of this Agreement is held by a court of competent jurisdiction to be invalid or unenforceable, the remainder of the Agreement shall remain in full force and shall in no way be impaired.

Your signature in the lower right corner of this Agreement will indicate the acceptance of the terms and conditions herein stated.

Sincerely yours,

By: Name and Title
Name of Company

I, [name of employee], the Employee stated herein, have read the above Agreement, understand and agree with its terms, and have received a copy.

Name of Employee

## Turning an Oral Contract into a Written Agreement

A formal agreement similar to the above is not always required to serve your purposes; in some cases an oral contract confirmed in writing can be an acceptable substitute. Before I describe how this may be accomplished, a few words about oral contracts are appropriate. An oral contract is a verbal agreement between the employee and the company defining their working relationship. Such contacts may be binding when the duties, compensation, and terms of employment are agreed to by both parties.

There are certain types of contracts that must be in writing to be legally binding. The rule requiring this is called the statute of frauds. While there are a number of items covered in the statute of frauds, the one of direct interest to you regarding employment states that any contract agreement that will require more than a year to complete must be in writing. Each state has its own version of the statute of frauds, and various courts interpret its provisions differently. However, remember that most courts do not support indefinite employment agreements based on an oral contract, because employment could be terminated at any time prior to the elapse of a year. Thus, to ensure enforceability of a working arrangement in excess of one year, you must include such an arrangement in writing.

Many workers have oral agreements simply because their companies refuse to give them a written contract. In fact, companies like to operate under oral agreements because there is no written evidence to indicate what terms were discussed and accepted by both parties when they entered into the employment arrangement. If disputes arise, it is more difficult for the employee to *prove* that the company failed to abide by the terms of the agreement. For example, if a bonus totaling $10,000 to be paid was accepted orally, a dishonest employer could deny this by stating that a gratuitous bonus arrangement had been accepted that was substantially less than $10,000. The employee would then have to prove that both parties had agreed upon the higher bonus figure.

When a legal dispute arises concerning the terms of an oral contract, a court will resolve the problem by examining all the evidence that the employee and company offer and weighing the testimony to determine who is telling the truth. Thus, to avoid problems, all employees should try to obtain a written contract to clarify their rights. However, if your company refuses to sign a written agreement, there are ways to protect yourself if you have an oral contract. Your chief concern should be directed toward obtaining written evidence that indicates the accepted terms, including information that defines your compensation, additional benefits, job security concerns, notice of termination requirements, and other considerations.

If your company refuses to sign a written agreement, it is advisable to write a letter whenever you reach an oral agreement relating to your job. Whatever deal is agreed upon, a letter should be drafted similar to the following.

## Sample Letter Confirming an Oral Agreement

Your Name
Address
Telephone Number
Date

Name of Corporate Officer
Title
Name of Employer
Address

Dear (Name of Officer),

I enjoyed meeting you on (date). This letter confirms that I agree to be employed by (name of company) as a (specify job title or position) for an initial term of one (1) year commencing on February 10, 2002, and terminating on February 9, 2003.

As compensation for my services, I agree to accept an annual salary of $40,000 payable in equal weekly installments in the sum of (specify). Additionally, I shall receive this reimbursement by a separate check within two (2) weeks of my presentation of appropriate vouchers and records.

This agreement cannot be shortened or modified without the express written consent of both parties. Additionally, in the event notice of termination is not received no later than one (1) month prior to the expiration of the original term, this agreement shall be automatically renewed, under the same terms and conditions, for an additional one (1) year period.

Upon termination of this agreement for any reason, I shall be entitled to receive my bonus and salary for the remaining period of the quarter in which my termination occurs.

If any terms of this letter are ambiguous or incorrect, please reply within (specify) days from your receipt hereof. Otherwise, this letter shall set forth our entire understanding in this matter.

I look forward to working for (name of company).

Very truly yours,
Name of Employee

*Sent certified mail, return receipt requested.*

After being hired, *always* write a letter similar to the above confirming the points you and the company agreed upon if you cannot obtain a written contract. Be aware that in many instances the letter you write to the company can serve in place of a formal employment contract. You may find that your letter holds you to your stated understanding of the employment terms, so be very careful, specific, and accurate in your wording. If the company replies in agreement, particularly if it replies in writing, or does not argue with your stated understanding, a court may rule that these terms are also binding on the company. Another way that a company may be bound to certain terms of employment is through statements published in their employee handbook or personnel manual. This aspect is discussed in detail in Chapter 6.

Write the letter with precision, since ambiguous terms are resolved against the letter writer. Be sure to keep a copy of the letter for your own records and save the certified mail receipt. If at a later date the terms of the oral agreement are changed (for instance, additional compensation is paid to you or your duties are expanded), write another letter specifying the new arrangement that has been reached. Keep a copy of this letter and all correspondence sent to and received from your company for your protection.

# PART II

# How to Protect Your On-the-Job Rights

Most employees are unaware of the numerous rights that exist in the workplace. These rights are frequently violated by executives, security personnel, private investigators, and owners of businesses that hire them, and the law allows people to recover damages when employees, agents, and their companies act improperly.

This section of the book covers your rights on the job. Chapter 3 is devoted to employee benefits. It discusses a variety of subjects including overtime, equal pay, and union rights of employees. Chapter 4 discusses privacy and other basic freedoms of employees. This includes searches, interrogations, wiretapping, eavesdropping, and other forms of surveillance that are often perpetrated on employees. It also discusses such diverse subjects as a person's right to work in a smoke-free environment, federal legislation dealing with the right to be warned of a mass layoff sixty days prior to a plant closing, and whether employees can have access to their personnel records.

You will also learn about your rights regarding lie-detector tests, voice-stress analyzers, psychological-stress evaluators, and other tests, and whether or not you can lawfully refuse to submit to such tests while working. AIDS, drug, and alcohol testing will also be discussed so you will know your rights in this area.

Finally, you will learn how workers are protected under the Occupational Safety and Health Act (OSHA), a law that requires all employers to provide a safe and healthful workplace.

Chapter 5 is devoted to how workers can protect themselves from discrimination. In this chapter you will learn what constitutes age, gender, race, handicap, and religious discrimination and how to enforce your rights and protect yourself if you are a victim in this area. For example, if you are being forced to work in a hostile and offensive environment (if, for example, you are the victim of sexual harassment), you will learn how to prove your claim by sending letters to document such exploitation.

You will also learn how to file a formal complaint with the Equal Employment Opportunity Commission or other appropriate agency to start the ball rolling. Additionally, the chapter provides strategies to help you win your case. More than 100,000 charges of on-the-job discrimination are filed with various agencies each year; the chapter will help you know when you are being victimized, how to fight back, and how to successfully prove your case and collect damages when you are being treated unfairly.

# CHAPTER 3

# Employee Benefits

Being properly hired is only the first step in the employment relationship. It is also important to know your rights in the event that problems develop on the job. For example, recent changes in the law regarding overtime, COBRA, medical, ERISA, equal pay, and financial benefits are protecting workers throughout the United States.

The first section in this chapter discusses union rights of employees. Although much of the information and strategies discussed in the book pertain to nonunion employees, a brief explanation of the genesis of your on-the-job rights as a union member are included here.

## Union Rights of Employees

To understand your rights under modern labor law, it helps to understand the source of the laws and regulations that serve to protect workers who belong to unions. Labor law as we know it today began in 1935 with the Wagner Act, created by Congress to protect union members from the excesses of employers. The three main objectives of the Wagner Act were to end labor conflict (including conflict among labor unions themselves), to create a system for fair collective bargaining, and to create a concept to identify unfair labor practices. The National Labor Relations Board (NLRB) was created to interpret and enforce the Wagner Act.

The NLRB acts as a court, hearing disputes related to labor law. It oversees labor-union representation elections and union representation, and it determines or defines appropriate bargaining units. By definition, the NLRB enters the picture when employees seek to protect themselves by "concerted action" for "mutual aid and protection."

In 1947 the Taft-Hartley Act was passed by Congress to protect employers from the excesses of unions. The act outlawed the closed shop, in which an employer would agree to hire only union members, but allowed what is called an agency shop. In an agency shop a person coming to work for a unionized shop does not have to join the union but must within a certain time start paying union dues. While federal law allows the agency shop, state right-to-work laws can outlaw them.

The Taft-Hartley Act added to labor law prohibitions against union coercion, unreasonable union dues, and featherbedding. It also allowed the president of the United States to stop a strike that endangered health or safety. The eighty-day cooling-off period was another result of the Taft-Hartley Act.

The next step in labor law was the Landrum-Griffin Act of 1959, which was enacted for the purpose of protecting union members from the unions themselves. Most notable in the act was what is known as a Bill of Rights for union members. Elements of this act guaranteed union members that they would receive equal treatment, could criticize the union (free speech and assembly), and could sue the union. It provided for fair union discipline hearings, fair and open elections, review of union financial information, and fair representation.

A labor union is an organization of working people who collectively negotiate (or attempt to negotiate) benefits, better working conditions, grievances, and employment contracts for its members. The federal Taft-Hartley Act allows certain classes of workers to band together, form, and join unions. Supervisors, managers, executives, and some government employees cannot be union members because "blue-collar" (nonmanagement) working-class status is often required for membership.

If you belong to a union, much of your protection as a union member derives from the powers and actions of the National Labor Relations Board together with the U.S. Department of Labor and state law. For example, if you believe that your union is not zealously representing your interests, or has engaged in an unfair or illegal labor practice, it may be necessary to file a grievance against your union through a local office of the NLRB. Federal law is more powerful than state law with regard to minimum legal requirements. States, however, can have even more restrictive laws.

Under the federal National Labor Relations Act and state laws, employers are forbidden from penalizing workers who decide collectively to discuss common grievances and form and participate in a labor union. Workers cannot be disciplined, demoted, reassigned, fired, threatened, or treated poorly as a result of union involvement. Neither can employers offer nonunion workers more benefits or better working conditions than union workers. Speak to a labor lawyer to protect your rights if this is the case.

In certain situations, such as when an employer has entered into a comprehensive collective bargaining agreement with a union permitting the union to act as spokesperson for all workers of the company, you may be forced to belong to a union even if you do not want to participate in union activities. This means that union dues may be automatically deducted from your paycheck, and there is little you can legally do about it. However, in some states, people are permitted to work at companies without being required to participate in union activities or be affiliated with a union.

There are several advantages and disadvantages in belonging to a union. For example, employers are bound to follow rules concerning discharge procedures in collective bargaining agreements previously negotiated and ratified by a union. In such agreements employers are sometimes forbidden from terminating union workers except in situations involving worker misconduct or serious offenses. If a union worker is fired wrongly or under circumstances suggesting that the employer acted improperly, the union should schedule an arbitration proceeding or grievance procedure without delay so that an impartial arbitrator can hear the case and hopefully reinstate the terminated worker (and order back pay and other lost benefits in appropriate circumstances).

---

**STRATEGY:** *If you are a union member and are treated unfairly while working, denied expected benefits, or fired from a job, immediately speak to a lawyer hired by the union or a private lawyer to discuss your rights. The specifics of your work relationship are spelled out in the collective bargaining agreement. Most agreements allow you to discuss a problem with a designated union representative, who will then communicate the matter to union officials. If the union determines that your grievance is sound, the union should guide you through the complaint process.*

*Most collective bargaining agreements provide little or no severance pay and other post-termination benefits for terminated union workers. This differs from nonunion employees, who may be able to receive large severance packages after having worked for an employer for many years and been discharged through no fault of their own, such as for a job elimination or company reorganization.*

---

When a union is organizing a strike, an employer may be able to keep workers off the premises legally (known as a lockout) in an attempt to force the union to back down. Union workers may not receive any pay during a lockout, and sometimes the employer does not have to rehire workers if they were permanently replaced while on strike. Some unions provide short-term strike funds to workers who are forced to go out on strike. Under federal law, the obligation to rehire union workers who were replaced often depends on whether the employer acted properly before the strike. For example, if the employer engaged in an unfair labor practice that caused the strike (e.g., failing to provide a safe work environment), the employer may be legally required to rehire its original union workers. Rules concerning the circumstances permitting union workers to legally strike (e.g., to protest unsafe working conditions) are spelled out in the National Labor Relations Act.

Remember, if your complaint involves an employer, your relief will come from the NLRB. Unfortunately, if you have a complaint against a small company, the NLRB will not act. And the law does not apply to state or local government jobs. However, if your complaint is against a union (or your union), it must go through the NLRB or the Department of Labor, but a safety complaint would be filed with OSHA (Occupational Safety and Health Administration).

Regardless of your union or nonunion status, Title VII of the Civil Rights Act of 1964 is the basis of the EEOC (Equal Employment Opportunity Commission), to which you can appeal if you are being discriminated against because of your race, color, religion, gender, or national origin. Through the EEOC, you can sue an employer who discriminates if the employer has at least fifteen employees for at least twenty weeks out of the year. You cannot, however, sue a religious organization for religious discrimination, but you can sue federal, state, and local governments, as well as labor unions and employment agencies. Strategies to prove and win discrimination cases are discussed in Chapter 5.

## Part-Time Employees

Part-time workers must typically comply with the same company rules, policies, and procedures as full-time employees, including working regular stated hours. Most states define part-time workers as those who are employed on jobs with fewer than thirty hours per week. Most part-time workers are paid on an hourly basis and are not entitled to company benefits, such as extended vacations, company pension and profit-sharing plans, health insurance, and other benefits. Some states grant coverage to employees who work more than a stated number of hours (e.g., twenty-five) per week. Under federal ERISA law, employees who generally work one thousand hours in a pension plan year must be included in all appropriate company pension plans that are offered to other similar workers.

---

**STRATEGY:** *Contact the nearest office of your state's department of labor to learn about all benefits that must be offered to you as a part-time worker. In some states part-time workers must have paid overtime, vacations, lunch breaks, and coffee breaks like regular workers. Be certain you understand what benefits are or are not available before accepting a job to be sure the company complies with all appropriate benefits laws. If, for example, you do not qualify for medical benefits, inquire how much extra it would cost to be included in such coverage. You may also learn that the company will offer prorated fringe benefits, including shorter paid vacations, sick leave, and life insurance, just by asking. Point out to the prospective employer that by offering you and similar part-timers prorated benefits, the company may qualify for cheaper group HMO and medical insurance rates.*

---

Under the federal Equal Pay Act, part-time workers and temporary employees are not subject to strict rules that men and women doing the same job must be paid equally. And many companies not wishing to offer benefits required to be offered to employees under the federal Family and Medical Leave Act (FMLA) are exempt from that law when they employ a sufficient number of temporary, contract employees or part-time workers (defined in the act as those who work twenty-five or fewer hours a week) to reduce the number of full-time employees to fewer than fifty.

However, when companies use temporaries to supplement full-time personnel, the practice has been successfully attacked by unions on the grounds that bargaining-unit employees are deprived of job opportunities and overtime.

As a part-time worker, you may be terminated for poor performance and are subject to the company's work rules and requirements like other workers. Your paycheck will reflect payroll deductions and taxes. All legal obligations owed by the company to its workforce, such as complying with safety (OSHA) rules and regulations, not making promises it does not intend to keep, and avoiding discriminatory acts, apply to you as well.

---

**STRATEGY:** *Negotiate the right to convert into a full-time position if your work skills are satisfactory or if the employer's needs or your needs change. Don't forget to discuss this with management where appropriate. Additionally, inquire if the employer will allow you and someone else to share a job that requires forty or more hours of work per week. Some companies are offering job shares where circumstances warrant. The advantage of a job share is that these employees often obtain prorated shares of benefits normally available only to full-time workers. They also work flexible hours and have the opportunity to take time off during the workweek to meet family obligations, such as child care, or pursue other interests. Inquire if the employer has a job-share plan in effect.*

---

## Leased and Temporary Employees

Leased and temporary employees work for the service firm supplying workers to the client company. Although they report directly to an employer, they receive their paychecks and benefits from the company leasing their services. Leased employees typically do not work at one job site for more than a fixed period (e.g., one year). Once a particular job is finished, they are then assigned to work at another company.

Although the Department of Labor reports that the use of temporary workers has surged 400 percent since 1982, statistics provided by *USA Today* reveal that temps earn an average 40 percent less per hour than full-time workers. Even though the vast majority (80 percent) work thirty-five hours a week, most do not have health benefits, pensions, and life insurance, and most temps are women. This has caused some commentators to point out that when you are a temp you are treated at a lower status despite the advantages of a flexible work schedule.

Although leased employees are obligated to conduct themselves in accordance with the work rules and regulations stipulated by the company for which services are being provided, they must ultimately answer to the leasing company hiring them. When a dispute arises, such as whether unemployment insurance is available after a layoff or firing, the issue may depend on the rights and remedies available against the leasing company and not the client.

All applicants applying for work as leased employees should know the ramifications of their status before accepting employment. At a minimum, get answers to the following questions:

- Which company will pay me?
- Can I collect overtime for my efforts? If so, how do I go about this?
- To whom do I look for instructions about when, where, and how work is to be performed?
- Who controls my work schedule?
- Under what circumstances may I be dismissed?
- Who furnishes the tools and equipment used by me for the job?
- How do we resolve problems I may have with the client?
- Am I prohibited from working directly for the client company (such as being required to sign a restrictive covenant in an employment contract) if they like my skills and work performance?

- Do I have a say in my assignments?
- How often do I have to report back to the leasing company?
- What are my benefits, and who pays for these benefits?

Although employee leasing is being used more these days, critics contend that employees suffer by not receiving commensurate benefits from the company leasing their services. Thus, it is critical to negotiate a fair hourly rate or weekly salary as well as obtain equivalent benefits that would be available if you worked for a company as a regular employee.

The relationship of a leased or temporary worker to his employer has unique ramifications with respect to workers' compensation, unemployment insurance benefits, and tax matters. In some states a person who is employed by a leasing company is also considered to be in the special employ of the client company despite the fact that the leasing employer is responsible for the payment of wages, has the power to hire and fire, has an interest in the work performed by the employee, maintains workers' compensation for the employee, and provides some of the employee's equipment. This means, for example, that if you are injured while working for the client company, you may be covered under workers' compensation and cannot institute a private negligence lawsuit.

However, if the client company approved your hiring and possessed the right of control, an employer/employee relationship might be found, making the client responsible for any discriminatory acts (including sexual harassment) perpetrated against you on the job site. The same is true if you desire to take time off to care for a newborn or an adopted child, an elderly parent, or a sick spouse under the federal Family and Medical Leave Act (FMLA).

Under what conditions will companies using temporary labor be required to comply with the FMLA? Generally, where two or more businesses exercise some control over the work or working conditions of the employee, a joint relationship may be found to exist. Once this occurs, the client as the secondary employer may have the obligation to comply with the FMLA and cannot discriminate against you if you seek to exercise your rights under this law.

---

**STRATEGY:** *If you are a leased or a temporary employee, speak to a lawyer immediately if you believe your rights are being violated. This may include, for example, being a victim of gender, race, age, or disability discrimination, or being denied unemployment insurance benefits or workers' compensation coverage after an accident.*

---

## Statutory Employees

Many people who work at home or who are paid on a commission basis (such as life insurance agents or salespeople) are classified by the IRS as statutory employees. The fact that you may work out of your home with little or no direction or control from an employer and are paid commissions for services rendered does not matter for tax purposes. If you are a statutory employee, your commissions or pay will be subject to the same tax withholding requirements as other employees. Speak to your accountant or professional adviser for more information on this subject, such as to determine if you are a statutory *nonemployee* not subject to withholding requirements. (Licensed real estate agents and direct sellers such as door-to-door salespeople are considered statutory nonemployees.)

## Employee Versus Independent Contractor Status

The IRS generally opposes independent status because companies who retain independents don't have to withhold income or employment taxes. Since a contractor can manipulate earnings by claiming all business-related expenses on Schedule C (where expenses offset gross business income), the IRS believes that many dollars of compensation go unreported. Additionally, if you are an independent contractor who is injured while working, you are not bound to collecting workers' compensation damages for your injuries. This is advantageous, since the awards are typically larger for claimants who commence private lawsuits for injuries than for those who receive workers' compensation benefits.

As an independent contractor, however, you are not permitted to file for unemployment benefits after a job has ended or you are terminated unless it is determined at the unemployment hearing that you are legally an employee. You probably cannot avail yourself of employer-provided disability and health insurance plans and may have to establish your own retirement and pension plans. Since you will receive an IRS Form 1099 and not a W-2 form with deductions withheld, you are responsible to pay all applicable Social Security, unemployment insurance, state and local income taxes, and workers' compensation insurance benefits for any people you employ. Under the laws of many states, you will probably have a more difficult time asserting discrimination claims. Furthermore, you cannot assert claims for overtime, since wage and hour laws apply only to employees. (In a recent ruling, however, the 9th U.S. Circuit Court of Appeals rejected Microsoft's attempt to withhold benefits from workers it said were freelancers rather than employees. The court stated that the practice of hiring temporary employees or independent contractors as a means of avoiding payment of certain employee benefits was troubling. Microsoft has appealed the decision.)

No precise legal definition of an independent contractor exists, and each state has its own laws to determine whether an individual is an employee or an independent contractor. When the courts attempt to determine the difference, they analyze the facts of each particular case. Significant factors courts look for when making this distinction are:

1. The company's right of control over the worker
2. Whether the individual works exclusively for the company or is permitted to work for others at the same time
3. Whether the parties have a written agreement that defines the status of the worker and states she is not considered an employee for the purposes of the Federal Contributions Act and the Federal Unemployment Tax Act and that the individual must pay all self-employment and federal income tax
4. Whether the individual controls her own work schedule and the number of working hours
5. Whether the individual operates from her own place of business (or pays rent if an office is provided) and supplies her own stationery and business cards not at the company's expense

Typically, employees undertake to achieve an agreed result and to accept an employer's directions as to the manner in which the result is accomplished, while independent contractors agree to achieve a certain result but are not subject to the orders of the employer as to the means that were used. In each case, the court looks at the specific facts in making its determination. For instructive purposes, the company's right of control is best explained by the use of examples. Courts have found workers to be employees if companies:

- Have the right to supervise details of the operation
- Require salespeople to collect accounts on its behalf
- Provide workers with an office, company equipment, company car, and/or reimbursement for some or all expenses
- Require workers to call on particular customers
- Deduct income and FICA taxes from their wages or salary
- Provide workers with insurance and workers' compensation benefits

- Restrict their ability to work for other companies or jobs and require full-time efforts

This list is not meant to be all-inclusive, but rather to help you determine what classification you fall under. Since the law is quite unsettled, the IRS follows a summary of rules used to determine proper status. According to the IRS, an employer-employee relationship for tax purposes exists when the person for whom the services are performed has the right to control and direct the individual who performs the services, not only as to the result to be accomplished by the work but also as to the details and means by which the result is accomplished. In this connection it is not necessary that the employer actually direct or control the manner in which services are performed; it is sufficient if the firm had the *right* to do so. The designation or description of the relationship of the parties in a written agreement other than that of an employer and employee is immaterial if such a relationship exists, and the IRS will disregard other designations (such as being called a partner, agent, consultant, or independent contractor) in the agreement.

On pages 104–5 you will find a summary of rules used by the IRS to determine proper status. Courts do consider other relevant facts and circumstances not contained in the list and may overrule initial IRS and state tax determinations where warranted.

---

**STRATEGY:** *The odds of finding employee status become lower when you form a corporation and receive compensation from your corporation. The IRS is also impressed when you or your corporation works for several companies and not just one.*

*When an initial determination is made by the IRS finding employee status, costly damages, penalties, and interest can ensue to you and the company hiring you. Speak to a competent lawyer or accountant immediately upon receiving an initial IRS or state taxing agency notice of determination or request for facts. Competent tax advice and guidance are crucial in this area.*

---

## STEPS TO TAKE TO AVOID PROBLEMS

If you are not a statutory or common law employee (which includes leased employees, part-time workers, and temporaries), you are legally considered to be an independent contractor. This is so even if you call yourself a consultant or subcontractor. As an independent contractor, it is crucial to discuss all the terms and conditions of your working relationship with a company or individual. This must be done before commencing work, no matter what your trade or profession. All key terms of the relationship, including the services to be rendered, payment, stages of payment, whether expenses are to be reimbursed (and to what extent), and the length (also known as the term) of the arrangement, should be understood and agreed upon to reduce misunderstandings.

## SUMMARY OF IRS RULES TO DETERMINE EMPLOYEE VERSUS INDEPENDENT CONTRACTOR STATUS

Many of these rules are followed by the IRS when determining employee or independent contractor status. Speak to an accountant or other professional for more advice.

1. Instructions. Employees generally follow instructions about when, where, and how work is to be performed; contractors establish their own hours and have no instructions regarding how the job should be completed.
2. Training. Employees typically receive training via classes and meetings regarding how services are to be performed; contractors generally establish their own procedures and receive no training.
3. Services performed personally. Services are typically performed personally by the employee; contractors may utilize others to perform job tasks and duties.
4. Supervision. Most employees are supervised by a foreman

or representative of the employer; contractors generally are not.

5. Set hours of work. An employee's hours and days are set by the employer; contractors dictate their own time and are often retained to complete one particular job.

6. Full time required. An employee typically works for only one employer; contractors may have several jobs or work for others at the same time.

7. Work on premises. Employees work on the premises of an employer or on a route or site designated by the employer; contractors typically work from their own premises and pay rent for their own premises.

8. Manner of payment. Employees are generally paid in regular amounts at stated intervals; contractors are paid upon the completion of the job or project, in a lump sum or other arrangement (such as on a commission basis).

9. Furnishing of tools and materials. Employees are usually furnished tools and materials by employers; contractors typically furnish and pay for their own tools, materials, and expenses.

10. Profit. Employees generally receive no direct profit or loss from work performed, while contractors do.

11. Job security. Employees may be discharged or quit at any time without incurring liability; contractors are typically discharged after a job is completed and are legally obligated to complete a particular job to avoid liability.

## Equal Pay

Wage disparities unfortunately still exist in American society. It has been reported that the typical American workingwoman is paid 74 cents for each $1 earned by a man. The largest gap is with black and Hispanic women, who, according to U.S. Census figures, earn 64.2 percent and 53.4 percent, respectively, of what men do.

The federal Equal Pay Act (EPA) prohibits covered employers with two or more employees from paying unequal wages to male and female employees who perform substantially the same jobs. For example, a major university was ordered to pay 117 women an award of $1.3 million after a federal court judge ruled that the university paid less money to women on the faculty than to men in comparable posts.

While the EPA and the Civil Rights Act of 1964 both prohibit sex discrimination in the workplace, the EPA applies only to wage inequities between the genders. Under the Equal Pay Act, employers are barred from paying women less than men if they are working on jobs that require equal skill, effort, and responsibility and if those jobs are performed under similar working conditions. This includes everyone from hourly workers to salaried employees engaged in executive, administrative, and professional functions, such as teachers. The courts have held that the jobs need not be identical, only "substantially equal." Further, an employer may not retaliate against a female worker, such as by firing her, because an EPA charge was initiated.

Fringe benefits are included in the definition of wages under the law. Thus, employers may not differentiate with items such as bonuses, expense accounts, profit-sharing plans, or leave benefits. Under EPA, it is not a defense to a charge of illegality that the costs of such benefits are greater with respect to women than to men, since the law is designed to ensure that women do not receive lower salaries and benefits than their male counterparts.

There are loopholes in the law, however. Employers may pay different wages if there is a bona fide preestablished seniority system, a merit system, or a system that measures earnings by quantity or quality of production. Differential pay is also permitted when the jobs are different or are based on a legitimate factor other than gender.

For example, a company began operations in 1985. Initially,

eleven production assistants were hired, all male. Many of them are still employed by the company. In 2002 the company expanded and hired ten more production assistants, six of whom were women. Although all production assistants perform the same job, many of the older male workers receive greater hourly pay rates because of their seniority and number of years with the company. This is legal.

Determining if a job is different is not always clear-cut. A major problem arises when two jobs are similar but one includes extra duties. Although it is legal to give higher pay for the job with more responsibilities, a judge will scrutinize if the greater-paying jobs are given only to males at a particular company. This is often the case and may be illegal depending on the facts.

A female worker may seek damages in federal or state court or through the EEOC and may obtain a trial by jury when asserting an EPA violation. Successful litigants are entitled to recover retroactive back pay, liquidated damages, reasonable attorney fees, and costs. If willful violations (defined as reckless disregard for the law) are found, double back pay may be awarded. Employers are obligated to maintain and save records documenting wages and benefits paid to all employees. Once a complainant shows that she is working in the same place, is doing equal work under similar working conditions, and is paid less than employees of the opposite sex, the burden shifts to the employer to show an affirmative defense that any wage differential is justified by a permitted exception. Practices that perpetrate past sex discrimination are not accepted as valid affirmative defenses.

If a violation is present, you can sue the employer privately instead of filing a charge of sex discrimination, such as failing to promote you or firing you. Any other form of sex discrimination must be filed under Title VII or various state discrimination laws.

To avoid charges of EPA violations, employers are instructed to prepare precise job descriptions that demonstrate different duties and job responsibilities for different pay. When offering jobs with different salaries and benefits, companies are instructed to assign those higher-paying jobs on the basis of such factors as technical skills, additional education, work experience, and knowledge required, rather than gender.

---

**STRATEGY:** *If you believe that your company is exceeding predetermined salary ranges by offering higher salaries to males who are performing essentially the same job, speak to an employment lawyer. This is a violation of EPA even if the reason is to attract minority applicants. And being denied equal pay because you are married, have children, or are a victim of gender-based stereotypes violates the law.*

---

### Comparable Worth

Pending cases may soon be decided to resolve the issue of comparable worth. Comparable worth is the concept of paying women equally for "comparable jobs." In the public sector some states and localities have compared jobs and found that some fit the definition when the value of the work and the amount of effort and independent judgment involved are equal. As a result, some women's wages have been raised. Comparable-worth cases are not presently recognized under the EPA, although a few female claimants are suing private employers in this area under federal and state sex discrimination laws.

## Tips and Wages

Millions of people in this country work in retail sales or as wait staff or beauticians. These services are typically paid on an hourly-plus-tips basis. Rules governing hourly jobs, such as the minimum wage that can be paid, overtime, and restrictions on child labor, are primarily based on the Fair Labor Standards Act (FLSA), also known as the federal Wage and Hour Law. Some states have passed more stringent laws. For example, every state has wage and hour laws that regulate when and how employees are paid. Certain states require that employees receive a meal period a few hours after beginning work; other states require breakfast periods as well. Rules concerning the amount of paid time employers are required to extend for coffee and lunch breaks vary from state to state, and employers must typically pay accrued wages no less than twice per month.

Like the EPA, the FLSA requires that male and female workers receive equal pay for work that requires equal skill, effort, and responsibility. It also defines when employers may give compensatory time (time given off from work instead of cash payments). For part-time workers, employers may not be required to provide any benefits other than those covered under state and federal law, including Social Security, unemployment insurance, and workers' compensation insurance. Speak to a representative at your state's department of labor regional office to get the facts.

If you earn more than $30 a month in tips, your employer can pay you less than the minimum wage (up to 50 percent less in certain instances) provided the total amount of wages and tips reaches the federally guaranteed minimum wage. However, employers are generally forbidden from taking tips away from you. Rules governing the sharing of tips, withholding requirements, and deductions from your salary or tips due to cash shortages, breakage, uniforms, or use of tools and equipment are governed by state law. Check with a local department of labor office to determine how much minimum pay you must receive if you get additional tips in your job.

## Overtime

If you are an hourly ("nonexempt") worker, the FLSA requires that you be paid at one and a half times your regular hourly rate if you work more than forty hours in a five-day workweek. Several classifications of salaried employees are exempt from the minimum wage and overtime requirements of the FLSA: outside salespersons, independent contractors, employees of certain retail establishments, amusement and recreation park employees, and others who meet various statutory tests, such as persons who hold bonda fide executive, administrative, or professional jobs. The rules governing whether you are considered an exempt executive, administrative, or professional worker are complex. For example, if you do not customarily direct the work of at least two other employees, have no discretionary powers at work, and merely are supposed to follow established procedures, you may be an hourly worker but misclassified as an exempt employee. Speak to a lawyer for more details.

In addition to claims of employee entitlement and problems regarding the computation of overtime, other disputes that sometimes arise are whether an employee can waive the right to overtime pay, what rights employers have in requiring people to work overtime, whether employers can equalize overtime on a day-to-day basis, and problems with unauthorized overtime.

In one case an employer docked a worker $3,300 for taking time off. She sued and won. The court ruled that when this occurred, the worker became reclassified as an hourly worker, and once any professional worker is classified as hourly, the company is liable for all overtime incurred during the past two years for the employee and similarly situated employees. The company was ordered to pay $750,000 in damages to the woman and twenty-three others.

---

**STRATEGY:** *If you are a salaried exempt professional, question all company policies that impose partial or full-day unpaid leaves. If you are an hourly employee, recognize that most compensatory plans (also called comp plans) allowing workers time off without pay in the work period following the week they worked excessive hours, or allowing them to work more than forty hours* *one week to make up for working fewer than forty hours in a previous week, may be illegal. Each workweek must be considered separately in determining overtime hours, regardless of the length of the pay period, except for certain occupations (e.g., police officers and firefighters); employers giving time off must compute the value of such benefits at one and a half times the regular rate of pay.*

Employers who fail to pay required overtime are liable for any unpaid overtime compensation and an equal amount as liquidated damages, plus attorney fees and costs. For willful violations, damages sometimes include earned overtime up to three years back, plus punitive damages.

Since the purpose of the FLSA is to ensure that employees are paid their full wages, employers may not make any deals to settle wage-hour claims for less than the full amount (even when a release is signed by the employee to defeat the rights of the worker). Although usually courts are pleased when prospective litigants compromise their differences, no such compromise is accepted under FLSA.

If you are an hourly worker, you may be entitled to overtime pay under the following conditions:

- If you arrive to work earlier than your starting time and do light work at the request of the employer
- If you typically work through lunch breaks at the employer's request
- If you take work home with the knowledge and permission of the employer
- If at home you are required to be "on call" and ready to report to work within an hour
- If you work several hours of overtime on a Friday and the employer states that you can leave work several hours early the following week

- If the job requires you to stay overnight for out-of-state assignments or travel extensively while on company business (but not for normal commuting travel to and from your home)

---

**STRATEGY:** *Speak to a lawyer if you are required to do extensive traveling on company business and are not paid for your time. The author recently represented a television reporter-producer who was encouraged to spend hundreds of hours each month traveling around the world to obtain provocative news stories. The author obtained a large five-figure settlement representing overtime pay even though the reporter was paid a salary and was considered exempt by her employer.*

---

Confer with counsel if you are unsure whether or not you are truly considered an exempt worker. Be sure that the company fairly rotates overtime between men and women. Discrimination often ensues when supervisors fail to equalize overtime (e.g., they offer substantially more overtime to males than females or minority workers).

The Wage and Hour Law is complex, and matters are often subject to detailed investigations. However, employers are generally required to give nonexempt workers as much advance notice as possible when they are expected to stay late. They should also rotate overtime, maintain a roster recording each worker's overtime, and establish rules as to how the roster system will work. Federal law requires employers who offer overtime to post signs outlining the federal minimum wage and overtime regulations conspicuously in places where workers enter and exit.

Additional rules concerning overtime:

- Generally, employers cannot force workers to waive their entitlement to overtime.

- If the company has no knowledge that an employee is working overtime and has established a rule or policy, conspicuously posted, that prohibits overtime work, an employee may not be entitled to overtime pay after making a claim.
- The FLSA does not protect employees who deliberately over-report their overtime hours. The employer may terminate an employee who falsifies overtime hours and may not be subject to claims of retaliation or unfair treatment.
- Generally, employees cannot refuse to work overtime unless they have a valid reason (e.g., taking care of a sick child). If the refusal to work overtime is not for good cause and the employer suffers undue hardship, this may be grounds for a valid termination and denial of unemployment benefits, even for union workers protected by collective bargaining agreements. However, if you believe you were fired unjustifiably, speak to a lawyer immediately.
- If you are requested to participate in a company-sponsored program after hours, such as a mercy session (e.g., a company-sponsored blood drive), and are an hourly worker, you may be entitled to overtime compensation.

Question all attempts by your employer to dock you for time taken to attend jury duty, to vote, and to handle medical emergencies. Most states do not allow employers to do this. If you are in doubt about a company's action in this area, call your local U.S. Labor Department Wage and Hour Division office for further details.

## Health Benefits

Only a few states require employers to provide workers with health care insurance. However, when health insurance coverage is voluntarily provided, employers may not discriminate; they must offer the same coverage to all employees regardless of gender, age, or disability. For example, if health insurance benefits are provided to the spouses of male workers, the same coverage must be provided to the spouses of female workers, and the extent of the coverage provided for dependents must be equal.

The law demands equality in health coverage for pregnant workers. Most state laws say that disabilities caused or contributed to by pregnancy, miscarriage, abortion, or childbirth and subsequent recovery are temporary disabilities and should be treated as such under any health or temporary disability insurance or sick leave plan available in connection with employment. This position is affirmed by federal law under the Pregnancy Discrimination Act of 1978 (PDA). Although companies are not required to provide any health care benefits, when they do, pregnancy must be treated the same way as any other medical condition; voluntary health care benefits must include coverage for pregnancy and pregnancy-related conditions and for those who are statistically more likely to incur high medical costs. (The PDA does not require employers to pay health insurance benefits for abortion except where the life of the mother would be endangered if the fetus were carried to term or where medical complications have arisen from an abortion.)

An employer cannot base employment decisions on the fact that a worker is pregnant, since employers must treat pregnancy the same as they would treat any other employee medical condition. If company health care is provided, maternity care must be included and coverage must be the same for spouses of males and females. Limitations on maternity coverage for preexisting conditions must be similar to limits on other conditions. If extended benefits (such as paid sick leave and benefits) are given for other disabilities, so, too, must extended benefits be given for pregnancies occurring during a covered period of the plan.

Once health insurance is provided, the employer is bound under federal law, including the Consolidated Omnibus Budget Reconciliation Act (COBRA) and the Employee Retirement Income Security Act (ERISA), to follow through on its promises unless the company reserved the right, in company handbooks and memos distributed to its workforce, to alter or amend promises of benefits at any time, with or without notice.

Many insurance policies have preexisting-condition clauses that disallow certain kinds of coverage for medical conditions that existed prior to the employee accepting employment. This is legal, as are benefits that are capped (i.e., no more than $X of reimbursement for a particular condition per year) and the requirement that you pay for all or part of the monthly premium.

The complexity of the employee benefits law is well established. New cases are constantly being decided and statutory developments implemented that have an impact on particular plans and practices. It is critical for you to constantly update and evaluate the effect of these legal developments on your own health and benefit plans. One area in particular—retirement health care benefits and successor benefits (when a person leaves a company to work in a new job)—has raised numerous problems. An employer's obligation to provide post-termination or retiree health benefits largely turns on whether those benefits are actually vested at the time of leaving. Claims for employee benefits are typically covered under federal ERISA law; speak to a qualified benefits or labor attorney for more details.

Many companies are cutting back on the amount of health coverage provided, and some companies are currently offering several plans at great expense. Often, after it is too late, employees learn that their health coverage is inadequate.

Always understand the minimum coverage you are receiving and what you must pay on your own for additional basic protection. Answers to the following questions can help you in this area.

QUESTIONS TO ASK REGARDING EMPLOYER-PROVIDED
HEALTH BENEFITS

- How much is your monthly premium? Is this taken directly out of your paycheck? Are you allowed to pay more on your own to get better coverage or shift your money to a more cost-effective plan?
- Does the company have a summary plan of benefits? If so, read the summary to get a better idea of the basic benefits offered. (It may still be necessary to read the entire plan to get more specific information and check the fine print.)
- What are the plan's exclusions and limitations? What mental and physical conditions does the plan not cover?
- Does the plan cover preexisting conditions?
- How much is your annual deductible (the amount you must pay before your insurance kicks in)?
- What is the process for filing claims? Do you have to pay and submit proof of payment before reimbursement, or can you submit claims directly from your physician? How long must you wait before reimbursement?
- Can you appeal a negative decision not to be reimbursed? If so, what is the process for filing an appeal?
- Is your family also covered?
- Does the plan pay for second opinions and preventive tests such as mammograms and Pap smears?
- If you are close to retirement age, what impact will Medicaid and Medicare coverage have on your benefits?
- If you are close to retirement, what guarantees regarding continued retiree health benefits will you receive?
- Does medical, dental, and hospitalization coverage stop the day you are fired or resign, or is there a grace period (e.g., through the end of the month)?
- Can you extend coverage beyond the grace period?
- Can you assume any group health policy (sometimes referred to as a conversion policy)?

**STRATEGY:** _The federal Health Insurance Portability and Account-ability Act of 1996 (HIPAA) was enacted effective June 1, 1997. This law benefits workers in several ways. It provides greater portability to employees with respect to their medical in-surance when they change employment. It also places limita-tions on when an employer may impose preexisting-condition clauses for new employees under an employer-sponsored med-ical plan. This reduces the chances of being excluded from a health plan or coverage due to a preexisting medical condition or illness upon being hired or while working. The law also lim-its the employer group medical plan from discriminating against individual employees based on health status. For example, un-derwriting by excluding injuries from medical plan coverage re-sulting from high-risk activities such as motorcycling, skiing, or bungee jumping may no longer be permitted._

Experts suggest this law reduces the circumstances where em-ployees are forced to unwillingly remain at a current job due to the fear that valuable medical coverage will be lost as a result of a job change.

Under the HIPAA, a group health plan generally may not apply a preexisting-condition exclusion to an employee or dependent unless the exclusion relates to a condition for which medical ad-vice, care, or treatment was recommended or received within the six-month period before the employee's hire date. Additionally, the maximum period that a preexisting-condition exclusion may be enforced is limited to twelve months for someone who enrolled when first eligible and eighteen months for a late enrollee.

Talk to an employment attorney whenever you believe you are unfairly denied or being excluded from your employer's medical coverage or when your COBRA coverage ceases. The HIPAA may augment COBRA coverage under certain circumstances. Be aware that as a result of the HIPAA, the chances of your medical coverage being denied has decreased, especially if you had similar coverage under a prior employer's plan.

## AIDS AND MEDICAL COVERAGE

The EEOC has ruled that companies may not exclude AIDS coverage from their medical plans altogether because such an exclusion violates the ADA. Some smaller companies that established self-insured plans were excluding coverage for preexisting conditions for a period of time (typically up to a year) after a person became employed. As a result, companies must proceed with caution and seek competent legal advice before implementing any self-insured plan that seeks to preclude coverage for HIV and AIDS sufferers. Additionally, any plan previously established that excludes persons with AIDS may now have to be modified.

## COBRA HEALTH BENEFITS

Federal COBRA law requires most private employers to continue to make existing group health insurance available to workers who are discharged or resign from employment. All employees who are discharged as a result of voluntary or involuntary termination, such as for poor performance, negligence, or inefficiency (with the exception of those who are fired for gross misconduct), may elect to continue plan benefits currently in effect at their own cost, provided the employee or beneficiary makes an initial payment within thirty days of notification and is not covered under Medicare or any other group health plan. The law also applies to qualified beneficiaries who were covered by the employer's group health plan the day before the discharge. Thus, for example, if the employee chooses not to continue such coverage, her spouse and dependent children may elect continued coverage at their own expense.

The extended coverage period is eighteen months upon termination of the covered employee; upon the death, divorce, or legal separation of the covered employee, the benefit coverage period is thirty-six months to spouses and dependents.

The law requires that employers or plan administrators separately notify all employees and covered spouses and dependents of their rights to continued coverage. After receiving such notification, the individual has sixty days to elect to continue coverage. Additionally, employees and dependents whose insurance is protected under COBRA must be provided with any conversion privilege otherwise available in the plan (if such coverage exists) within a six-month period preceding the date on which coverage would terminate at the end of the continuation period.

Some employers run afoul of the law in failing to follow rules regarding notification requirements, conversion privileges, excluded individuals, and time restrictions. In the event the employer fails to offer such coverage, the law imposes penalties ranging from $100 to $200 per day for each day the employee is not covered and other damages.

---

**STRATEGY:** *Know your COBRA rights before accepting any job and in the event you resign or are fired. This is especially true if you or a spouse or dependent is sick and needs the insurance benefits to pay necessary medical bills. You are entitled to such protection even if you have worked for the employer for a short period of time. Most short-term employees can generally enjoy COBRA protection for periods exceeding the length of their employment. The only requirement is that you must have been included in the employer's group plan at the time of the firing and that the employer was large enough (i.e., employed twenty or more workers, including part-timers, independent contractors, and agents, during the preceding year) under federal law to qualify.*

---

You cannot obtain benefits if you are fired for gross misconduct. This term is relatively ambiguous; the burden of proof is on the employer to prove that the discharge was for a compelling reason (such as starting a fight or stealing).

If an employer reduces your working hours to a point that makes you ineligible for group health coverage, or fails to notify you of the existence of such benefits, contact the personnel office immediately to protect your rights.

Other points to remember:

- A company's hands may not be tied in the event that a group health plan is modified or eliminated; an employer may be permitted to change or eliminate a current plan provided all qualifying beneficiaries and covered employees are allowed to participate similarly under new plans, if any.
- Coverage for adopted children, children born out of wedlock, and other dependents has been expanded under the Omnibus Budget Reconciliation Act of 1993 and recent court decisions.
- Speak to a lawyer if you or a dependent is excluded from COBRA protection because of the existence of a secondary health plan or other factors, such as because of an alleged discharge for gross misconduct.
- Never waive your COBRA rights when accepting severance payments or signing a release after a discharge.
- Be sure the company notifies you in a timely fashion so you can make the election properly before the short period of employer-provided coverage expires.

## ERISA Benefits

Employer-sponsored health, pension, and profit-sharing plans are governed by the federal Employee Retirement Income Security Act of 1974 (ERISA). ERISA sets minimum standards for benefit plans, the vesting of benefits, and communication to plan participants and their beneficiaries. This includes all plans, funds, or programs that provide medical, surgical, or hospital care benefits; retirement income or the deferral of income after retirement or termination (such as severance); or deferred compensation plans such as stock bonus and money purchase pension plans. The act covers six basic areas:

- Communications: what must be disclosed to employees, how it must be disclosed, and what reports must be filed with the federal government
- Eligibility: which employees may participate in a benefit plan
- Vesting: rules regarding when and to what extent benefits must be paid
- Funding: what employers must pay into a plan to meet its normal costs and to amortize past service liabilities
- Fiduciary responsibilities: how the investment of funds must be handled and the responsibilities of the plan administrators to oversee the plan and plan benefits
- Plan termination insurance: the availability of insurance to protect the payment of vested benefits

The law does not require employers to establish pension or profit-sharing plans. Once they do, however, virtually all private employers are regulated by ERISA in one form or another.

The first step to understanding and enforcing your ERISA rights is to ask for details regarding the nature of your benefits when you are hired. You are entitled to an accurate, written description of all benefits under federal law. Be aware of all plans, funds, and programs that will be established on your behalf. These may include the following:

**Defined contribution plans.** These include profit-sharing plans, thrift plans, money purchase pension plans, and cash or deferred profit-sharing plans. All these plans are characterized by the fact that each participant has an individual bookkeeping account under the plan which records the participant's total interest in the plan assets. Monies are contributed or credited in accordance with the rules of the plan contained in the plan document.

**Defined benefit plans.** These are characterized as pension plans that base the benefits payable to participants on a formula contained in the plan. Such plans are not funded individually as are defined contribution plans. Rather, they are typically funded on a group basis.

**Employee welfare benefit plans.** These are often funded through insurance and typically provide participants with medical, health, accident, disability, death, unemployment, or vacation benefits.

**ERISA plans.** These may not be as definite as the plans above. Rather, if the employer communicates that certain benefits are available, who the intended beneficiaries are, and how the plan is funded, the employer may be liable to pay such benefits even in the absence of a formal, written plan.

An investigation by the U.S. Department of Labor uncovered hundreds of companies misusing and diverting 401(k) employee pension programs. In 401(k) plans, workers save and invest their own money for retirement through automatic savings programs set up by their employers. When the plans are operated correctly, workers determine how much they contribute, the employer withholds the stipulated amount from employee paychecks, and the company forwards the money to a plan administrator, who invests worker contributions in a manner selected by the worker. The Department of Labor discovered that many small and midsize companies violated plan rules and federal law by delaying payment to plan administrators, diverted funds to pay other corporate expenses, or stole the money outright and never reported the contributions. In a recent 401(k) amnesty plan, the Department of

Labor reported that 170 companies admitted they failed to deposit $4.8 million in the retirement accounts of 16,800 workers. The money came from technology firms, law firms, doctors' offices, credit unions, and manufacturers in thirty-eight states, and payments ranged from $43 to $200,000. Some companies admitted using the money to cover business expenses. Note: Money withheld from workers' paychecks must be deposited to 401(k) accounts within fifteen business days after the end of the month the money is withheld. For more information, call (202) 219-9247 to get a copy of the free publication "Protect Your Pension" published by the Labor Department.

The best way to avoid such problems is to monitor and regularly scrutinize reports given to you by the employer concerning your current benefits. If your returns show constant losses, plan officials may not be investing your money properly. Speak to management about how you want your money invested. If your statements are coming late or at odd intervals, check with your benefits department to find out why. Demand such reports if they are not periodically forthcoming. If your retired friends say they can't get the pension plan to pay them what's due, start checking further. Always request such reports when you believe the company is having financial difficulties, such as when paychecks are not being distributed on time. Most important, keep track of how much you're contributing to the pension and then match your records to the reports you receive from the plan. These statements should indicate the amount you and your employer have contributed, plus the rate of return you've earned on your investments. If the numbers don't match, it is possible (especially with small companies) that the employer is illegally holding or diverting your contributions.

To safeguard benefits, ERISA mandates that assets in a beneficiary's pension be virtually "untouchable." This is accomplished by requiring that plan administrators file numerous reports with the U.S. Department of Labor, the Internal Revenue Service, and the Pension Benefit Guaranty Corporation (a federal agency located in Washington, D.C.), including plan descriptions, summary plan descriptions, material changes in the plan, description of modifications of the terms of the plan, an annual report (Form 550), an annual registration statement listing employees separated from services during the plan year, and numerous other reports for defined benefit plans covered by the termination insurance provisions with the Pension Benefit Guaranty Corporation.

Demand a copy of the employer's pension and/or profit-sharing plans from the plan administrator if the employer refuses to furnish you with accurate details. (You may have to pay for the cost of photocopying said plans when requesting them.) ERISA provides that plan participants are entitled to examine without charge all plan documents filed with the U.S. Department of Labor, including detailed annual reports and plan descriptions. If you request materials and do not receive them within thirty days, you may file suit in federal court. In such a case, the court may require the plan administrator to provide the materials and pay up to $100 a day until you receive them, unless the materials are not sent for reasons beyond the control of the administrator.

---

**STRATEGY:** *If you are fired just before the vesting of a pension (e.g., two months before the vesting date), argue that the timing of the firing is suspect and that public policy requires the employer to grant your pension. If the employer refuses, consult an experienced employment lawyer immediately.*

---

Contact the plan administrator immediately to protect your rights if your claim is denied or if you suspect there are problems with your plan. Under federal law, every employee, participant, or beneficiary covered under a benefit plan covered by ERISA has the right to receive written notification stating specific reasons for the denial of a claim. You have the right to a full and fair review by the plan administrator if you are denied benefits.

If you suspect the company has not acted properly with respect to your benefits, inquire about your account with the plan administrator. Determine whether the amount of each payment corresponds with the amount that was deducted from your paycheck and reflects any promised matching contributions. If you are not satisfied with the answers, contact your nearest Department of Labor office to discuss the matter with a representative. Request an investigation on behalf of you and your coworkers where warranted.

If you have a claim for benefits that is denied or ignored in whole or in part after making a request to a plan administrator, speak to a lawyer and consider filing a lawsuit in either state or federal court. If it should happen that plan fiduciaries misuse a plan's money, or if you are retaliated against for asserting your rights (such as being demoted, reassigned, or fired), seek assistance from the U.S. Department of Labor, or file suit in federal court. The court will decide who should pay court costs and legal fees. If you are successful, the court may order the employer or person you have sued to pay these costs and fees.

If your company goes out of business, files for bankruptcy, or has no assets, some states require the owners (i.e., stockholders) and officers to be personally liable to repay pension and other retirement benefits. Thus, all may not be lost if you discover that your benefits were diverted and the company goes out of business. Speak to a lawyer about this point.

The Pension Benefit Guaranty Corporation has created an office to help workers trace their pensions. By law, a pension plan that terminates is required to make only one attempt to get in touch with workers. The Pension Benefit Guaranty Corporation can assist you by making repeated attempts to find the plans of employers that have gone out of business. Contact this agency in Washington, D.C., and supply it with copies of any plan summaries and plan identification numbers, which are often printed on such papers. Permanently save all plan documents and summaries, because you never know when the information will come in handy to document and enforce a claim.

Speak to a benefits lawyer if your company orally modifies any plan benefits, if a summary description does not accurately depict essential elements of the plan, or if a division of the company you are working for is sold and the new company offers far less severance and other benefits than previously promised. When companies merge and workers are laid off or denied promised benefits they previously enjoyed, issues of severance and other post-termination and on-the-job benefits should be scrutinized by a competent lawyer to determine whether ERISA violations have occurred.

## Meals, Transportation, and Related Benefits

Generally, reimbursement for meals, transportation, and related expenses is includable in an employee's gross income. When such benefits are taxable, the benefits generally must be reported by the employer and are subject to federal income tax, Social Security, and federal unemployment withholding. Nontaxable benefits need not be reported by an employer to the IRS. However, a benefit is excludable from the employee's gross income if the value of the benefit is so small as to make accounting for it administratively impractical (e.g., a company-provided auto for six hours per month). If the company has a computerized accounting system, the burden is on the employer to demonstrate why it is unreasonable to track the benefits provided.

Employer-provided meals, meal money, and local transportation fare provided to employees are excluded if offered on an occasional basis (e.g., one, two, or three times per month) as a result of overtime and to enable the employee to work overtime. So, too, are special "provided meals" paid by the employee with a company charge account or employer-given cash at the time of the meal for the convenience of the employer. (This rule does not apply to actual meal money or cash reimbursements paid to employees.)

## Tuition Assistance

Tuition assistance is an effective way of bolstering employee performance and morale while benefiting the company with better skilled workers. When considering a tuition reimbursement program for your company, be aware of:

- Company objectives in offering the program
- Employee eligibility, such as who is qualified for reimbursement
- Limits to the kinds of reimbursable items
- Using company time to attend courses
- Proper reporting, including procedures for turning in receipts and the kinds of receipts required for reimbursement
- Situations when reimbursement is forfeited (e.g., not receiving a C grade or better, being fired for cause, or receiving an unsatisfactory job performance evaluation before the course is completed)

---

**STRATEGY:** *Be aware that employers are sometimes legally obligated to pay employees for attending company classes, especially when the employees' participation is mandatory and attendance is a condition of keeping the job or gaining a promotion.*

---

## Working Hours

Some states require coffee breaks, others do not. In addition, certain states require that employees receive a meal period a few hours after beginning work; other states require breakfast periods as well. Thus, check with the department of labor in your state for further details.

Must an employee be paid for on-call meal periods? In one case an arbitrator ruled that since the workers were in a state of constant readiness and could not leave the hospital, they were still on duty, even when taking meals, and such status was primarily for the benefit of the hospital.

Requests to eat in company facilities as a part of the job may constitute compensable work time. However, although a company may be liable to pay its workers when they are compelled to lunch at their workplace, there is little doubt that a company has the right to determine the timing of all breaks and how many workers must be present at a particular location at all times, if such a rule is established for a legitimate business reason.

## Time Card Procedures

Federal law requires that all companies keep an accurate record of an employee's work. Most companies consider it a serious work infraction, leading to dismissal, for a worker to punch in the time of another or falsify time card records. Never consider doing this for any reason.

# CHAPTER 4

# Recognizing Employee On-the-Job Rights and Conduct

Employees possess many on-the-job rights, including rights of privacy. These privacy rights are sometimes violated by executives, security personnel, private investigators, and fellow workers. The law allows employees to pursue a variety of legal causes of action when their rights have been violated, such as actions for invasion of privacy, intentional infliction of emotional distress, libel, slander, and wrongful discharge. Areas such as personal appearance rules, romantic relationships with coworkers, drug and AIDS testing, legal off-premises behavior, and many other subjects are generally protected by the U.S. Constitution. This chapter will discuss a variety of areas impacting workers and suggest strategies to overcome such problems.

## Privacy Rights of Employees

### LIE-DETECTOR TESTS

The federal Polygraph Protection Act of 1988 bans lie-detector tests (including polygraphs, deceptographs, voice-stress analyzers, psychological-stress evaluators, and similar devices) in *most* situations. For example, employers cannot regularly test employees as a matter of policy or in cases of continuing investigations where no suspects have been found, or use the test as a "fishing expedition" to intimidate or harass individuals or to determine whether an employee has used drugs or alcohol.

The law restricts most companies, regardless of size, in the areas of applicant screening, random testing of employees, and lie-detector use during investigations of suspected wrongdoing. (Federal, state, and local governments are exempt from the law; also exempt are certain federal contractors engaged in intelligence and security work, employers authorized by law to manufacture, distribute, or dispense controlled substances, and employers providing security services in some circumstances.)

Additionally, the law restricts employers from taking action against employees who refuse to submit to such tests. For example, if an employee refuses to take the test, he or she cannot be fired as a result. Although tests can be used in connection with the investigation of workplace thefts, embezzlement, sabotage, check kiting, and money laundering, employers must follow detailed safeguards to avoid the imposition of fines and penalties. Moreover, there must be a reasonable suspicion that the tested employee was involved in the activity being investigated, and the employer must provide the subject with a statement detailing the incident in question and the basis of the suspicion of wrongdoing. Fines and penalties include back pay, job reinstatement and related damages, attorney fees and costs to successful litigants, and civil penalties up to $10,000 and injunctive relief for actions brought by the U.S. Secretary of Labor within three years from the wrongful act.

Here is a thumbnail sketch of the relevant portions of the law.

**Effect on state laws.** In those states that currently have stronger laws prohibiting lie-detector tests (defined as any mechanical or electrical device used to render a diagnostic opinion regarding honesty), the federal law is of no consequence and state law governs.

**Prohibited uses.** Generally, employers are prohibited from directly or indirectly requiring, requesting, suggesting, or causing an applicant or employee to take any lie-detector test. Tests can be administered in connection with an investigation, but only *after* reasonable suspicion has been established and many procedural safeguards have been carefully followed. The procedural safeguards are as follows:

1. The individual must be given the opportunity to consult with and obtain legal counsel before each phase of the test.
2. The individual must be provided with at least forty-eight hours' notice of the time and place of the test.
3. The individual must receive notification of the evidentiary basis for the test (i.e., the specified incident being investigated and the basis for testing).
4. The individual must be advised of the nature and characteristics of the test and instruments involved (e.g., two-way mirrors or recording devices).
5. The individual must be provided an opportunity to review all questions to be asked at the examination.
6. The individual must be given a copy of the law that advises rights and remedies for employees and that gives him or her the right to stop the test at any time.

Additionally, all employers are required to post notices on bulletin boards that advise workers of the existence of this federal law and their rights thereunder.

**Accepted uses.** Although the federal law restricts the circumstances under which the tests can be given, it does allow for lie-detector use to investigate serious workplace improprieties. However, employees who submit to such a test must be given the test results together with a copy of the questions asked. Additionally, employers are forbidden from administering more than five tests per day, and each test must not run beyond ninety minutes.

All persons administering such tests must be qualified by law (i.e., bonded with at least $50,000 of coverage or an equivalent amount of professional liability insurance) and are forbidden from asking questions regarding religious, racial, or political beliefs, matters relating to sexual behavior, affiliations with labor organizations, or any matter not presented in writing to the examinee prior to the actual test. Nor can they recommend action to employers regarding test results.

Since employers must have a reasonable basis for suspicion of wrongdoing to order the test, companies must be sure that such suspicions are *well founded* lest they face liability. Additionally, all results of the exam and actions taken as a result of the test must be carefully guarded against careless dissemination to nonessential third parties. It is also interesting to note that the federal law forbids companies from allowing nonsuspects to voluntarily take the test to "clear their own name."

Finally, refusal to submit to such a test and the results of the test alone may not serve as basis for adverse employment action. Employers must possess other evidence, including admissions by the examinee or evidence indicating that the employee was involved in the activity being investigated, to justify a firing or denial of promotion.

If you believe you are being asked to submit to such a test in violation of federal or state law (or a collective bargaining agreement if you are a union member), were fired as a result of taking such a test, or that proper procedural safeguards were not followed, speak with a representative of your local department of labor, Civil Liberties Union, attorney general's office, or a private labor lawyer immediately to protect your rights. All private employers must be mindful of the law to avoid problems, and workers now have many rights in this area.

Lie-detector, voice-stress analyzer, psychological-stress evaluator, and other tests cannot be given as part of a "fishing expedition" to uncover facts. Employers may use the test only as part of an ongoing investigation, must be able to demonstrate the suspected employee's involvement in the matter under investigation, and must be careful to follow all pretest, test, and post-test procedures; the failure to follow any of the above can lead to serious repercussions.

## ACCESS TO PERSONNEL RECORDS

Each state has its own laws regarding an employee's or ex-employee's right to inspect his or her personnel file. In some states employees or their representatives have the right to review their personnel records pertaining to employment decisions. However, they generally cannot inspect confidential items such as letters of reference, information about other employees, records of investigation, or information about misconduct or crimes that have not been used adversely against them.

Some states have passed laws allowing employees access to their personnel records to correct incomplete or inaccurate information at a reasonable time and place. In such states you are usually not allowed to copy any of the documents in the file except for those you previously signed (such as an employment application or performance review). Such states usually allow you to make notes, however. In other states you generally do not have the right to review your records, so check the law in your state. (The Federal Privacy Act deals mainly with access to employee records. This law forbids federal government employers from disclosing any information contained in employee files without the written consent of the employee in question. Discuss the ramifications of this federal law with your lawyer.)

Even in states where access to records is not permitted, employers are prohibited from distributing confidential information, such as medical records, to nonessential third parties and prospective employers, and you are generally permitted to inspect all your files containing confidential medical and credit information. Some union employees covered under collective bargaining agreements have the right to examine their own records and to be informed of what information is used in making decisions relevant to their employment.

If you need legal help in your efforts to inspect the personnel file your employer (or past employer) has on you, and you don't have a personal attorney upon whom you can call, your local or state bar association will most likely have a referral service. Ask for an attorney experienced in employment law. Statutes of this sort are constantly changing; only those who specialize in employment law in your state may be up to date on the finer points that may affect you.

---

**STRATEGY:** *Since it is often difficult to review the contents of your personnel file, make and save copies of all documents the minute you receive them so you don't have to retrieve them later. In some arbitrations and lawsuits, employers are prohibited from introducing "memos in the file" that were never read or signed by you. Advise your lawyer about this.*

---

Some states grant workers the automatic right to include a rebuttal statement in their personnel file if incorrect information is discovered. Other states allow employees to do this when the employer will not debate such comments. A few states (notably Connecticut) have laws that require employers to send copies of rebuttal statements to prospective employers or other parties when information pertaining to a worker or her employment history is conveyed. Since each state treats the subject differently, review your state's law.

Some states require employers to seek workers' approval before employee records can be collected, distributed, or destroyed, and it may be illegal to distribute personal information without your consent. Thus, the circulation of confidential memoranda within a company has given rise to lawsuits, particularly where the employer did not take adequate precautions to determine whether derogatory information was accurate.

Some states (e.g., Illinois and Michigan) prohibit employers from gathering and maintaining information regarding an employee's off-premises political, religious, and other nonbusiness activities without the individual's written consent. In these states employees and former employees can inspect their personnel file for the purpose of discovering if any such information exists. If their file contains such information, the employer may be liable for damages, court costs, attorney fees, and fines.

With respect to medical records and investigations, the law generally recognizes that a duty of confidentiality can arise to protect this information and avoid dissemination to nonessential third parties. Under emerging state laws and case decisions, employers who request medical information may be liable for the tort of intrusion and for the tort of public disclosure of private data. Several states have recognized a claim for negligent maintenance of personnel files when files containing inaccurate medical information are made available to third parties. For example, Connecticut has enacted a statute requiring employers to maintain medical records separately from personnel files and permitting employees to review all medical and insurance information in their individual files.

---

**STRATEGY:** *Always try to review the contents of your personnel file, especially when you believe that the employer is treating you unfairly (for example, denying you a promotion or raise). If damaging or false information is discovered, try to photocopy such information if possible. Don't forget to inquire whether a rebuttal can be included in your file. Finally, if the employer refuses your request, investigate whether the law in your particular state permits you to review the contents of your file.*

---

## ACCESS TO CREDIT REPORTS AND MEDICAL RECORDS

The federal Fair Credit Reporting Act places certain restrictions on the use of credit reports and investigative consumer reports by employers. Under this law, employers are forbidden to use credit reports (defined as summaries of a person's credit history) for hiring or employment decisions. The same is true for investigative consumer reports (defined as descriptions of a person's creditworthiness and general reputation in her community based on interviews with coworkers, friends, and neighbors).

As a result of this law, employers cannot obtain any report without your permission. If your consent is obtained and a report is made, you have the right to receive a copy, including the name and address of the credit agency supplying it, together with a written description of your rights under the act.

When any adverse action is taken, such as your not receiving a promotion, you are entitled to receive notice of such adverse action, the name, address, and telephone number of the consumer reporting agency that provided the report to the employer (which includes an 800 number if one is available), *and* a written statement by the employer indicating that such information was not used in any way in the adverse action. Information also given with this is a statement that you can obtain a free copy of the report within sixty days of the notice and your right to dispute the accuracy or completeness of the report with the consumer reporting agency. The law also requires that the employer notify the credit reporting agency before receiving the report that it received your permission, provided you with the required notice, will not use the information to violate federal or state discrimination laws, and will not use the information to make any adverse action.

---

**STRATEGY:** *As a result of the law's requirements, speak to a knowledgeable employment lawyer immediately if you believe your rights have been violated in this area.*

---

Many states prohibit the unauthorized disclosure of an employee's medical records as well as the unauthorized acquisition of medical information. In Colorado, for example, the unauthorized acquisition of medical records or information is punishable as felony theft.

Some states require that an applicant or employee not be charged the cost of an employer-requested physical or that they be given a copy of the results. In other states (California, for example) the physician must obtain the job applicant's or employee's written consent before disclosing examination results to the employer. It is probably permissible for an employer to require you to take a physical as the last part of the screening process to get a job, provided all applicants are requested to participate in this process. However, be aware that some company doctors are not trained properly and ask discriminatory questions during the examination, or request answers to discriminatory questions contained on poorly drafted medical history forms; being denied employment on the basis of answers to such questions is illegal.

Thus, recognize that you may have rights in the event that confidential credit or medical information is conveyed to outsiders by your employer without your consent or knowledge or is used to your detriment. In fact, only relevant, accurate information should be maintained by the employer, and reasonable procedures should be adopted to assure the accuracy, timeliness, and completeness of such information. With respect to medical data, all information regarding an employee's health, diagnosis, and treatment of illnesses or other personal information revealed during medical consultations must be maintained in the strictest confidence to avoid violations of state privacy laws.

---

**STRATEGY:** *Employers should give applicants and employees the opportunity to review their records and correct mistakes before inaccurate information is disseminated. In many well-run companies, requests for information from law enforcement agencies,* *government agencies, unemployment insurance offices, credit agencies, security investigators, and search firms must typically be accompanied by subpoenas or official documents. This ensures the reliability of the identity of the source requesting such information. Additionally, unless prevented by injunction, it is a good idea for employers to advise employees of the source of the subpoena, the date when the information will be given, and an explanation of the person's rights.*

---

If you have any questions regarding your rights in this area, consult an experienced attorney or review applicable state law.

### EMPLOYEE SEARCHES

The law regarding employee searches involves a careful balancing of the employer's right to manage his or her business and the privacy rights of employees. For example, the Fourth Amendment to the United States Constitution provides protection for all persons against unreasonable search and seizure of their persons, homes, and personal property, and this doctrine applies when the employer is the government. However, most private employers are exempt from this doctrine (unless the private employer does extensive business with or is heavily regulated by the government) and are generally permitted to use a variety of techniques when suspecting a worker of misconduct. These include searching the employee's office or locker without his knowledge or consent and requesting the employee to open his briefcase or package upon leaving a company facility.

Although each case is decided on its own merits, the law generally states that office searches *are* permissible if an employer has a reasonable basis for suspecting the employee of wrongdoing and the search is confined to nonpersonal areas of his or her office. The reason is that the office and documents relevant to company business are the property of the employer and can be searched anytime.

However, clearly visible personal items cannot be searched, and employers cannot conduct a search if there is no reasonable ground for suspicion. Legitimate searches of an employee's briefcase, locker, or packages also depends upon whether the employee had a reasonable expectation of privacy.

The absence or presence of any regulation or policy placing employees on notice that routine searches would be conducted is the primary factor in determining whether or not searches of employees or their work areas or property are legal. For example, when signs are posted throughout a company reminding workers that personal property is subject to search, when memos are distributed stating that surveillance measures will be taken on a regular basis, and when handbooks are disseminated stating that personal property is subject to search in company lockers, case decisions indicate such measures reduce claims of illegal privacy invasions, particularly when such policies explain the necessity for conducting searches, set forth procedures minimizing personal intrusion, and advise employees that their refusal to cooperate may lead to discipline or discharge.

With such policies in place, one court found that packages may be searched. Another court decided that searching vehicles on company property was legal. One court even found a search valid on the basis that an employee had voluntarily accepted and continued employment notwithstanding the fact that the job subjected him to searches on a routine basis. This, the court concluded, demonstrated his willingness and implied consent to be searched (thereby waiving the claim that his privacy rights had been violated).

However, when the employer does not have such policies in place, the lack of published worker rules and regulations may actually encourage an expectation of privacy claim. For example, in one case the employer searched an employee's purse, which was contained in a company locker. The court ruled that this violated the employee's reasonable expectation of privacy because she was permitted to use a private lock on her locker and there was no regulation authorizing searches without employee consent.

You should also recognize that the expectation of privacy is greatest when a pat-down or other personal search of an employee is conducted. Knowledgeable employers are reluctant to conduct personal searches, especially if they are random or done without specific, probable cause with respect to the individual involved.

In one case an employer's security guards detained and searched an autoworker leaving a plant because he was suspected of stealing auto parts. According to testimony at the trial, the guards yelled at the employee in addition to shoving him. Although serious inventory shortages had been reported in the area where the employee was seen wandering shortly before leaving the plant, he was awarded $27,000 in damages after proving he had been singled out and treated unfairly by being subjected to the search and no stolen parts were found on his person during the search.

If you believe you are the victim of an employer's illegal search, ask yourself the following questions:

- Have similar searches been conducted on you or your property before? If so, did you acquiesce in the search?
- Have similar searches been conducted on other employees?
- Were you given a warning that the employer intended to conduct a search?
- Was the object of the search company property?
- Did the search have an offensive impact? Were you grabbed, jostled, struck, or held? Were you coerced, threatened physically, or mentally abused in order to make you cooperate?
- Were you held against your will? Were you so intimidated by the experience that you were afraid to leave?
- Were you chosen at random for a pat-down search with no actual suspicion of wrongdoing?
- Did the employer search your belongings in an area that was truly private?

- Were you stigmatized (e.g., fired) by a search when in fact you did nothing wrong?
- Did the employer search you in front of nonessential third parties, and was your business reputation harmed by such action?

If you answered yes to the last six questions, speak to an employment lawyer immediately to discuss your rights. You may have a strong case, especially if you were fired, placed on probation, suspended, or given an official reprimand after the search and you did nothing wrong. The tort actions most frequently alleged as a result of an improper employer search are assault, battery, defamation (in particular, slander), false imprisonment, invasion of privacy, and abusive discharge. For example, if you are detained against your will during the search, you may be able to allege a valid cause of action for false imprisonment.

This happened to a checkout clerk who was accused of failing to ring up merchandise purchases. The employee was searched and interrogated by security personnel and told to accompany them to another location for additional questioning. At the trial the company proved that the woman failed to ring up purchases. However, a jury awarded the employee $25,700 on the grounds of false imprisonment, because the woman was never told she could leave the room where she was being questioned and was forced to remain there for several hours.

Cases such as this illustrate that you may have rights that are violated during or after a search. For example, you may be able to sue the employer for slander and invasion of privacy if a search is conducted in front of nonessential third parties in a way that is suggestive that you are a thief.

## EMPLOYEE INTERROGATIONS

Employers can question workers in an effort to discover illegal acts. However, employees have rights during these interviews. Depending on the particular state where the act occurs, these may include:

- The right to receive an explanation regarding the purpose of the interrogation (e.g., are you a suspect?)
- The right to insist on the presence of a union representative at the interview if the worker is a union member and has reason to suspect it may result in disciplinary action
- The right to limit questions to relevant matters
- The right to refuse to sign any written statements
- The right to remain silent
- The right to speak to a lawyer before speaking
- The right to leave the room at any time

All of the above points must be carefully reviewed if you are wrongly accused or treated improperly in an interrogation. If the employer conducts the interrogation incorrectly, grave legal consequences can ensue. The following true case demonstrates this.

Three company representatives kept a supervisor in a manager's office for several hours until he finally signed a resignation notice and "admitted" his guilt concerning certain money given to him for driving duties. The man sued the company for false imprisonment and won. The court also found that the facts supported the tort of intentional infliction of emotional distress.

All employees should recognize that an employer may be violating your rights during an interrogation in the event you are restrained or confined by force or threat of force, thereby denying your freedom of movement (i.e., false imprisonment). It is no defense if you are detained during working hours; confinement cannot be done for the purpose of extracting a confession.

Do not hesitate to assert your rights if you believe you are being treated unfairly; if you are falsely accused of misconduct in front of others or are intimidated into answering questions at an interrogation, you may have a good case for defamation or false imprisonment.

## WIRETAPPING AND EAVESDROPPING

Although technological developments have enhanced surveillance capabilities and employers are increasingly using electronic monitoring devices to keep tabs on employee conduct during the workday (primarily designed to combat employee theft), confidential information about an employee is also sometimes acquired.

Wiretapping and eavesdropping policies are generally regulated and to some degree prohibited by federal and state law. Title III of the Omnibus Crime Control and Safe Streets Act of 1968 prohibits the deliberate interception of oral communications, including telephone conversations. Thus, conversations between employees uttered with the expectation that such communications are private (for example, in a ladies' bathroom) are confidential, and employers are forbidden from eavesdropping under this statute. Employers who fail to comply with this federal law are liable for actual and punitive damages and criminal liability for willful violations.

State law varies with respect to wiretapping, eavesdropping, and surveillance practices. In some states it is legal for individuals and companies to record telephone or in-person conversations with another person without first obtaining the other person's consent (you only need the approval of one of the two parties to tape). In such states the recording may subsequently be used as evidence in a civil or criminal trial under proper circumstances (e.g., that the tape was not tampered with or altered and that the voices on the tape can be identified clearly).

However, other states are not as liberal and forbid the interception of oral or wire communications unless both (or all) parties are advised and give their consent. Such states prohibit employers from operating any electronic surveillance device, including sound recording and closed-circuit television cameras, in employee lounges, rest rooms, and locker rooms (surveillance is permitted in actual work areas) and make it virtually impossible for employers to lawfully engage in surreptitious eavesdropping.

One company placed wiretaps on business telephones in certain stores. The court ruled that this was a violation under federal law and a violation of the employees' privacy rights under Georgia law. In another case a company monitored the calls of one of its sales representatives. A supervisor overheard the sales representative say she was going to accept another employer's offer. The supervisor told the employee what he had learned and tried to dissuade her from leaving. The employee left anyway and sued the company for invasion of privacy. The court ruled that the employer had violated the law by listening to her personal calls, and awarded her damages.

In another case a company president installed wiretapping machines on four business telephone lines. When a vice-president learned about this, he spoke with the company's lawyer and had the machines removed. He was later fired, and he sued the former employer; the court ruled he had a recognizable claim under Title II of the Omnibus Crime and Control Act.

Thus, in order to know your rights in this area, it is essential to know the laws of your particular state (since such laws vary widely).

Employers frequently maintain microphones between counter areas and the boss's office or instruct the office operator to listen in and monitor suspicious or personal telephone calls by employees. This is illegal in many situations. However, if the conversation is in a public area, if one of the parties consents to a taping, or if the employer had a genuine suspicion of wrongdoing and only monitored business calls and not personal calls, the eavesdropping or taping may be legal.

In most states it is illegal for employers to set up cameras in a nonwork area, take photographs, or use video cameras to monitor workers, especially in places where female employees have expectations of privacy (i.e., in rest rooms, locker rooms, bathrooms, and lounges). It is also illegal for employers or their workers to observe you disrobe or change clothes without your knowledge. (Workers generally do not have rights of privacy to stay in rest rooms for extended periods of time, particularly after being warned of such excessive respites and when the rest room visits are not medically related.) Also prohibited, by the National Labor Relations Act, is employer surveillance of employee union activity, discussions about unions, or union meetings. Speak to a lawyer immediately if you think your privacy rights have been violated.

Be aware that in certain instances "extension phone" monitoring (in which microphones are placed near a customer service desk to measure a worker's productivity and communication with the public or detect nonbusiness telephone use) has been upheld as legal. One employer did this and was sued by an employee claiming illegal interception of her conversations. The court ruled in favor of the employer, finding that the monitoring was done "for a legitimate business purpose" with the knowledge of the affected employee. This was proved, since written notification of the monitoring program was given to employees beforehand (who were monitored for training purposes).

In another case the legality of extension phone monitoring was also upheld when a supervisor used an extension phone to listen in on an employee suspected of disclosing confidential information to a competitor. The court found the supervisor's conduct (which was spurred by a customer's tip) to be legal.

Thus, it is best to research appropriate state law or speak to an experienced labor lawyer if you believe your rights in this area have been violated. This is because if an electronic surveillance law in your state imposes greater restrictions than federal law, an employer must comply with the requirements of *both* laws.

You should also know that photographing employees without their knowledge or consent for surveillance purposes may violate federal or state laws regarding invasions of a worker's privacy rights, depending on the facts. If the pictures are released to nonessential third parties and are strongly suggestive of guilt, and such release results in defaming your reputation, you may have a valid cause of action for defamation.

If you discover that your employer has wiretapped your business or home telephone with electronic devices and is eavesdropping on your business or private conversations, speak to a lawyer to determine whether your state permits the employer to listen in on an extension telephone used in the ordinary course of business. This is sometimes allowed (depending on state law) provided you were notified in advance that your business calls would be monitored. However, once you talk about private matters, it is generally illegal for the employer to continue to listen to calls. (You may be legally fired, though, for discussing personal matters while on company time.)

---

**STRATEGY:** *According to a recent report, more than one-third of the company members of the American Management Association said that they tape phone conversations, videotape employees, review voice mail, or check computer files and E-mail. A recent survey of Fortune 500 companies showed that nearly half collect data on their workers without informing them. But remember that in most states you have the right to be told that your phone conversations, interrogations, or interviews may be taped. Even if an employer is allowed under state law to set up a monitoring system, that doesn't give the employer the right to administer it improperly. As a general rule, private conversations should not be taped. And employers should decide, in advance, who will be allowed to review their surveillance tapes, because the dissemination of confidential information to nonessential third parties can be costly. For example, in one case an em-*

*ployer was ordered to pay $40,000 in damages. The company
taped employees' phone conversations in an effort to catch an
in-house thief. But the firm taped a conversation between a
worker and the worker's lover, then played the tape for the
worker's spouse!*

## E-MAIL MESSAGES

Does an employer have the right to monitor E-mail messages or
intercept your mail? This often depends on the facts of each case
and the law in your state. Few states have legislation to protect
workers from employers reading their E-mail, and more than one-
third of all companies responding to the recent American Management Association survey acknowledged searching E-mail for
business necessity or security.

In one recent case a white employee used the password of a
black employee to send an E-mail containing racist jokes to other
white employees at the company. A black employee received the
E-mail by mistake and notified other black employees at the company of its contents. A race and national origin discrimination action was filed by the black workers, but the court dismissed the
lawsuit, ruling that one single racist E-mail was not sufficient to
create a hostile work environment.

While you may consider your electronic-mail communications
to be confidential, think again, especially when the company has
announced a policy that electronic mail be used solely for business
purposes and that the company has the right at any time to review,
audit, and disclose all materials sent over or stored in its E-mail
system.

**STRATEGY:** *While employers may have the right to review E-mail
with such a policy in place, they generally cannot open your personal mail, especially mail marked "Personal and Confidential."*

*Speak to a knowledgeable employment attorney immediately if you feel your privacy rights are being violated.*

## EMPLOYEE TESTING

All forms of employee testing raise significant issues of potential violations of an employee's privacy rights. This includes honesty, psychological, and personality tests, genetic screening, substance abuse tests, and polygraph examinations (previously discussed in this chapter). This section will examine some of the issues involved.

### AIDS and Genetic Testing

Individuals with AIDS, as well as those with HIV, are covered by the Americans with Disabilities Act (ADA). Since AIDS is a protected disability under the law, employers cannot discriminate against an applicant or employee with the disease, and afflicted workers must receive reasonable accommodation as a result of their condition. This may include liberal use of leave time and restructuring of responsibilities on a voluntary basis. (Forcing an employee with AIDS to change her work habits may be considered an ADA violation.)

However, in order to be regarded as an impairment, the employee's HIV status must be known by the company. For example, one plaintiff was unable to prove that he had been discharged solely because of a perceived disability where the company did not know he was HIV-positive.

At present the law is not well settled in this area. While there are no federal laws prohibiting mandatory AIDS tests for workers, some states have laws related to the issue. As an example, AIDS testing of employees is required in various localities for food handlers, processors, and waiters, and virtually all states, government agencies, and the military mandate AIDS testing in blood donations. However, since AIDS is a protected illness under the ADA, prehiring and on-the-job AIDS tests are probably illegal in many circumstances and employers can be liable for refusing afflicted workers access to their jobs.

One employee with AIDS in California sued an employer when he was told he could not report back to work after a two-week hospital absence. Although he subsequently died, the California Fair Employment and Housing Commission found the company liable and ordered it to pay back wages totaling $4,359 to the man's estate. In another case in New York, a mail room clerk was fired after returning from a four-week absence when his employer confronted him about his health problems. The man contacted the AIDS discrimination unit of the state human rights division and settled the case for $8,000 and full health benefits for a five-year period.

HIV screening should not be required as part of preemployment or routine workplace medical examinations. Companies must also establish education and training programs to reduce potential workplace problems, especially in places such as hospitals where there is a higher risk of HIV exposure.

All companies should develop and follow comprehensive AIDS policies so that people with AIDS or HIV infection receive the same rights and opportunities as workers with other serious illnesses. Such policies must comply with all relevant state and federal laws and regulations and be based on the scientific fact that HIV cannot be transmitted through ordinary workplace contact. All policies should be communicated by supervisors and upper management, but all medical information concerning employees should be screened to maximize confidentiality.

The enactment of the ADA has significantly protected AIDS sufferers' privacy rights, since many preemployment and on-the-job medical investigation practices and procedures that were once considered legal are now prohibited. For example, intrusions into a person's medical background and history are now substantially reduced. Application forms can no longer solicit answers to questions about whether the applicant is an individual with a disability, has a medical condition, or has ever been hospitalized or treated for a mental or emotional problem. Questions such as how many days was the applicant absent from other jobs and whether the applicant is currently taking medication are illegal, and employers are required to establish policies for staff and health providers regarding the disclosure and use of employee medical information.

Employers should review company handbooks and draft statements protecting against the unnecessary dissemination of medical information, and institute policies requiring supervisors and health providers to consult with company lawyers before disclosing any medical information. Related problems that have emerged must be carefully addressed: for example, how can your company be sure that the results of any job-related medical tests will remain confidential so as to avoid charges of slander or libel and other invasions of privacy?

Even the issue of genetic testing is unsettled. Many major corporations are currently testing the relationship of inherited genetic traits to occupational disease to determine if there are certain predisposing risks to employees and job applicants. More and more companies are considering using such tests, and the extent to which the ADA will curtail their use is now being studied by labor lawyers throughout the country.

Thus, since the law in this area is unsettled, it is important to consult an experienced attorney to determine your rights, obligations, and options.

## Drug and Alcohol Testing

The fight against drug and alcohol abuse in the workplace often results in drug tests of employees. There has been a sharp rise in employer interest in drug and alcohol testing, fueled in part by high-profile drug deaths and publicity surrounding the marketing of drug tests. More employers are resorting to such tests, especially preemployment testing, to identify drug users and reduce the incidence of on-the-job accidents and absences.

Critics argue that indiscriminate testing violates employees' rights of privacy, due process, and freedom from unreasonable search and seizure, and that test results are often incorrect, unreliable, or disseminated to nonessential third parties. Proponents of testing cite its success (e.g., the military's program has dramatically lowered drug use in the armed forces) and the growing confidence in the reliability of current testing methods.

Generally, since private employers are *not* held to the same constitutional standards as local, state, and federal government employers, private employers *may* implement and conduct drug and alcohol tests provided certain procedural safeguards are followed to minimize potential offensiveness. This typically includes adopting a comprehensive testing policy and putting it in writing, periodically reminding employees of the stated drug or alcohol testing policy, reducing the incidence of errors, treating test results carefully (i.e., confidentially) to avoid improper dissemination, and following local, state, and federal laws and decisions in this area.

Despite the general legitimacy of such tests, some state and local governments have passed laws prohibiting the testing of employees for drugs or alcohol.

State law varies dramatically. Some states permit employee testing with required procedural safeguards to ensure that the testing is done in a reasonable and reliable manner with concern for an employee's rights of privacy. Other states only permit individual tests where a particular employee is suspected of being under the influence of drugs or alcohol and his impaired state adversely affects job performance.

Case decisions in other states prohibit employee testing in positions that are not safety- or security-sensitive as a matter of public policy, particularly programs involving a large number of employees where there is no suspicion of individual wrongdoing. In New York the state division of human rights prohibits drug or alcohol testing of applicants before and after an offer of employment has been made unless the testing is based on a "bona fide occupational qualification."

Since the law differs so dramatically from state to state, is constantly changing, and may be even more stringent than the requirements of the Americans with Disabilities Act, it is critical that you obtain advice from counsel.

Under federal law, companies represented by unions cannot unilaterally implement a testing program without bargaining with the union over changes and conditions of employment. To do so would violate the National Labor Relations Act. However, the Supreme Court has upheld an employer's right to test employees for drugs and alcohol, rejecting a union's argument that testing is reasonable under the Fourth Amendment only when based upon individualized suspicion that an employee is impaired by drugs or alcohol on the job. In one case affecting railway employees, the Court ruled that the government's policy of testing all employees was important in assuring the safety of the railways and therefore outweighed the privacy rights of nonsuspected workers en masse.

**The Drug Free Workplace Act.** The federal Drug Free Workplace Act of 1988 has had a major impact on federal contractors and grantees with federal contracts, requiring them to conduct antidrug awareness programs and require workers to report any drug-related convictions as a condition of receiving federal funds. The law requires company-contractors, ranging from weapons manufacturers to publishing companies, and employee-grantees, ranging from state governments to drug abuse treatment facilities, to publish strict statements prohibiting drugs and educating employees on substance abuse. Employers must also report to the procuring agency any workers convicted of workplace-related drug activities and certify that they will not condone unlawful drug activity during the performance of the contract.

Under the Drug Free Workplace Act, to receive a federal contract for the procurement of any property or service in excess of $25,000 or for any employer or individual receiving any grants, regardless of the dollar amount, from the federal government, an employer must certify that it will provide a drug-free workplace. This includes publishing and distributing a statement advising employees that the unlawful manufacture, distribution, dispensation, possession, or use of any controlled substance (including prescription drugs) is prohibited. The employer must institute a "drug-free awareness program" to inform employees about the dangers of drug abuse in the workplace, the employer's drug-free workplace policy, any drug counseling, rehabilitation, and employee assistance programs that are available, and the penalties (e.g., discharge) that may be imposed upon employees for violations of the antidrug policy.

Each employee working on the contract or grant must be given a copy of this statement. The statement must indicate that the employee will abide by the terms of the statement and that he/she will notify the employer if convicted of a criminal drug statute within five days of conviction (employees must be hired pursuant to written contracts informing them of these requirements). The employer must then notify the contracting agency of such occurrence within ten days of receiving this notice. Contractors and grantees must make a "good faith" effort to continue to maintain a drug-free workplace through implementation of the above.

Finally, each contract awarded by a federal agency is subject to the suspension of payments or termination of the contract if the agency determines that the contractor made a false certification, failed to notify the agency within ten days of an employee's drug conviction, or failed to notify employees of the dangers of drug use.

Although the federal law creates a heightened drug awareness policy, it does not mandate drug testing for company applicants or employees. Nor does the act explicitly sanction such testing as a way for a federal contractor to satisfy the requirements of the act. However, the existence of this law means that companies working for the federal government must conform to its more stringent guidelines rather than follow conflicting state laws.

There is great incentive for companies dealing with the government to comply with the requirements of this law. But the decision to test is still basically an individual one, particularly for private employers that do not deal with the government.

**The Americans with Disabilities Act.** Perhaps the most significant change affecting drug and alcohol testing involves the ADA. In reality, the ADA provides greater protections for individuals with disabilities than do many state laws.

The ADA specifically excludes from protection any employee or applicant who is currently engaged in the use of drugs. Although drug-testing processes are not specifically mentioned, the interpretive guidance to Section 1630.3 (a) through (c) states that "employers may discharge or deny employment to persons who illegally use drugs, on the basis of such use, without fear of being held liable for discrimination." Another section allows employers to prohibit alcohol as well as illegal drug use at the workplace, and states that they may require that employees not be under the influence of alcohol or illegal drugs in the workplace, and may hold an employee who uses illegal drugs or is an alcoholic to the same qualification standards for employment or job performance as other employees.

Thus, postemployment drug tests are permitted, and employees who are currently illegal drug users are not protected from adverse action. However, if an individual has successfully completed a supervised drug rehabilitation program or has otherwise been rehabilitated successfully and no longer uses drugs, or is presently participating in a supervised drug rehabilitation program and no longer uses drugs, that person cannot be penalized.

Administration of drug tests is not considered to be a medical examination, so prehiring drug tests by employers do not violate the ADA's prohibition on medical examinations prior to an employment offer. In light of this, many companies are considering administering drug tests earlier in the applicant-screening process to eliminate drug users and save the company the expense of a posthiring medical examination. Additionally, since the act neither prohibits nor encourages drug testing, employers probably have the right to conduct ongoing drug-testing programs with all employees.

---

**STRATEGY:** *If you work for a private employer and are not a member of a union, what concerns should you have when advised that the employer intends to test you for drugs and alcohol? First, if the employer has decided to test, you may be entitled to advance notification in work rules, policy manuals, and employment contracts to reduce perceived privacy rights in this area. For example, the manual should outline the steps management would take when it suspected that an employee was impaired on the job, such as immediate testing, with a description of how the test will be administered and the consequences flowing from a positive result, such as immediate discharge with no severance or other benefits. If no such notice was received before the test was administered, you could have a valid claim that your privacy rights were violated, especially when there was no rational reason for asking you to submit to the test (e.g., you were randomly selected) and you were requested to take the test without warning.*

*Second, even if your privacy rights are not violated, all tests must be administered in a consistent, evenhanded manner. For example, if you are black or a woman, and employees belonging to your classification of race or gender are being tested and fired as a result of such tests in far greater numbers than other classifications, a charge of race or sex discrimination might be valid under certain circumstances.*

*Third, test results must be treated in the same manner as other confidential personnel information. Unwarranted disclosure of this information (even within your company) when made with reckless disregard for the truthfulness of the disclosure, or excessive publication, can allow you to sue for damages. One employee in Texas was awarded $200,000 for defamation after*

*his employer internally and externally published written state-*
*ments regarding drug-screening results allegedly showing a*
*trace of methadone.*

*Additionally, a firing based on a positive test finding that*
*later proves inaccurate could lead to a multitude of legal causes*
*of action, including wrongful discharge, slander, and invasion of*
*privacy. Thus, if the employer fails to hire a reputable testing*
*company or the test's results are inaccurate, you can challenge*
*the test on this basis; be aware that six-figure verdicts are some-*
*times awarded for violations in this area.*

The Centers for Disease Control report that the most common test, the EMIT urine test, is plagued by a high degree of false positive results due to human error and inexperienced testing personnel. Other problems with this test are that it does not prove intoxication (i.e., the inability of the employee to perform his or her job duties) at the time the test is taken (which should always be the governing factor in any discharge decision) and may also indicate positive results for employees who have only used legal over-the-counter drug medications.

Thus, recognize that there may be ways to challenge the test results in the event you are fired or treated unfairly. You should speak to an experienced labor lawyer immediately if you believe that:

- The test was not administered fairly; i.e., no advance warnings were given or there was inconsistent enforcement
- The penalty for violations was too severe (e.g., an employee was fired for possessing a small amount of marijuana in his locker but proved he did not smoke the drug on company property)
- The reliability of test procedures and/or results is suspect
- The employer cannot prove the identity of the illegal drug allegedly found in the test

- The specimen was not properly identified as belonging to the accused worker
- The test was given randomly with no expectation that an employee had an impairment caused by persistent on-the-job drug or alcohol use (i.e., no observation of disorientation was present)
- No confirmatory tests were made following positive preliminary screening
- The company engaged in discriminatory practices relating to its testing procedures

Federal workers, employees engaged in security-conscious industries (e.g., those who are required to carry firearms), and employees who handle money or engage in transporting members of the public (bus drivers, train engineers, etc.) have fewer legal rights to oppose drug and alcohol tests, because of the nature of their jobs. For example, random drug testing was upheld for horse jockeys. The court ruled that horse racing was one of a special class of industries accustomed to heavy state regulation and that the need for safety and honesty to promote the integrity of the industry outweighed the jockey's significantly diminished expectations of privacy.

However, as stated above, even when testing is legal, employers must follow proper procedures to be sure that results are accurate and are not disseminated carelessly. Additionally, such tests are being challenged all the time, and the law is constantly changing in this area. For example, one New York court held that probationary schoolteachers could not be compelled to submit to urinalysis on the whim of the board of education without a reasonable suspicion that the teachers being tested had ever been drug users. In the absence of such suspicion, the court determined that the ordering of a urine test was "an act of pure bureaucratic caprice."

The same concerns that apply to drug tests are also applicable to alcohol tests. For example, instead of drawing blood, companies should use accurate breath-testing devices whenever possible to minimize offensiveness. Test procedures should ensure reliable test results. Results should be handled on a strict need-to-know basis inside and outside the company. Employees should be given an opportunity to explain any result, and the test results should be reconfirmed if possible.

Finally, companies that administer preemployment drug tests to applicants who test positive for drug use must be careful not to automatically disqualify them should the applicant apply for another chance of employment within a fixed period of time (such as six months thereafter). The reason is that such an individual may be deemed a "qualified individual with a disability" who may be able to prove successful completion of, or who is in the midst of successfully participating in, a rehabilitation program and is protectable under Section 104 of the ADA. Companies must avoid inflexible drug policies with a fixed waiting period for future employment and evaluate each case on its own merits and be careful of how they test. One worker filed a lawsuit in Louisiana after he was discharged for testing positive for marijuana. The main thrust of his lawsuit was that he had suffered great emotional distress when a company representative was required to stand by and watch as he urinated to provide a sample. He also alleged invasion of privacy under Louisiana law, wrongful discharge, intentional infliction of emotional distress, and defamation. The company argued that having a supervisor stand by was the only way to ensure that the test was not faked. However, the worker testified that he was taunted and insulted by the supervisor while taking the test. The jury agreed and awarded him $125,000, which was upheld on appeal, based on the theory of negligent infliction of emotional distress.

**Alcohol use and the ADA.** The act makes a distinction between drug users and alcoholics. Individuals disabled by alcoholism are entitled to ADA protection. This includes applicants who would automatically not be considered for a job in the past as a result of testing positive for alcohol. Now all employers with fifteen or more employees must determine if that individual is capable of performing essential functions of the position offered with reasonable accommodation. Some experts have suggested that, in light of the inherent problems associated with preemployment alcohol tests, employers should now consider eliminating such tests altogether.

Until enactment of the ADA the main federal law protecting handicapped individuals against discrimination was the Vocational Rehabilitation Act of 1973, which applied to government contractors and employers who received federal assistance. Today's numerous state and federal antidiscrimination laws, including the ADA, mean that all companies must follow strict procedures to ensure that their treatment of alcoholic employees conforms to the law, since these workers are entitled to reasonable accommodation and protection from discrimination on the basis of their physical handicap of alcoholism. Employers may still prohibit the use of alcohol on the job and require that employees not be under the influence of alcohol when they report to work. Additionally, workers who behave or perform poorly or unsatisfactorily due to alcohol use may, like other workers, be fired or reprimanded. The ADA does not protect workers who drink on the job, or current abusers who cannot perform their jobs properly or who present a direct threat to the property or safety of others.

Reasonable accommodation of an alcoholic often consists of offering the employee rehabilitative assistance and allowing the opportunity to take sick leave for treatment before initiating disciplinary action. To be safe, even if the employee refuses treatment, documentation must show that repeated unsatisfactory performance took place before a termination decision is made.

In one case a company was found liable for not offering leave without pay for a second treatment in a rehabilitation program. The judge commented that one chance is not enough, since relapse is predictable in the treatment of alcoholics. In another case the

judge outlined a series of steps an employer must take to avoid violating the law. His guidelines are instructive:

- Offer counseling.
- If the employee refuses, offer a firm choice between treatment
  and discipline. If the employee chooses treatment, the employer cannot take any detrimental action during a bona fide
  rehabilitation program.
- In case of relapse, automatic termination is not appropriate,
  but some discipline short of discharge may be imposed.
- Before termination, determine if retention of the worker would
  impose an undue hardship on the company. If removal is the
  only feasible option, the company must still evaluate whether
  the alcoholic condition caused poor performance; if so, the
  company should counsel and offer leave with pay first.

Typically, arbitrators consider the following factors when deciding any drug- or alcohol-related matter:

1. Whether possession or sale is involved;
2. The type of drug used;
3. If the alcohol- or drug-related conduct or sale occurred on
   company premises;
4. The history of drug or alcohol use;
5. The impact on the reputation of the employer; and
6. The effect on the orderly operation of the employer's business.

After considering test objectives (to screen applicants using
drugs, to test employees suspected of using drugs/alcohol, etc.)
smart companies adopt a plan and record it in work rules, policy
manuals, employment contracts, and/or collective bargaining
agreements to reduce perceived privacy rights of employees and
document company policy. For example, the manual might outline
the steps management will take if they suspect that an employee is

impaired on the job, including immediate testing, how the test will be administered, and the consequences flowing from a positive result. Before adopting a formal plan, employers should:

- Consider education and rehabilitation alternatives as well as all legal obligations
- Determine the scope of the testing program's coverage, which employees or applicants will be tested, under what conditions, and the selection of testing facilities
- Inform workers that employees are not permitted to come to work under the influence of alcohol or drugs, even when consumed off the company's premises
- Develop rules to cover off-premises conduct but be aware that invasion of privacy claims rise when off-premises conduct is monitored
- Inform employees that testing for substance abuse may be required to avoid OSHA penalties for employer negligence

---

**STRATEGY:** *If you do have a drinking problem, consult an employment lawyer immediately if you are told to either enter an alcoholic treatment program or be fired. One employee rejected such an ultimatum and was discharged. A federal court ruled that she was fired not because of her violation of company policy (as the company suggested), but ultimately as a result of her disability. She was awarded significant damages as a result.*

---

The line between reasonable and unreasonable requests to undergo drug and alcohol testing will continue to be more clearly drawn as court decisions and state legislatures articulate specific policies on this issue. There is no doubt that more drug policy and testing cases will reach the courts because of the strong desire in government and political circles to eliminate drug and alcohol abuse in the workplace. However, the information in this section should help you recognize that you may have rights before, during, and after any test is administered to you.

## SMOKING IN THE WORKPLACE

More workers than ever before are demanding the right to work in a smoke-free environment. This right is being upheld with increasing regularity through federal legislation, state laws, city ordinances, and case decisions.

Various federal agencies, including the Merit Board and the Equal Employment Opportunity Commission, have ruled that employers must take reasonable steps to keep smoke away from workers who are sensitive to it, and the Occupational Safety and Health Administration has issued similar requirements to enhance safety in the workplace. All of these developments have caused most employers to reevaluate their smoking policies and implement either formal or voluntary rules, depending upon applicable state and local laws.

Critics contend that such policies violate an individual's right to privacy. However, because of increased public sentiment and awareness in favor of such policies, and since in virtually all states an employer has a common-law duty to provide a reasonably safe workplace for its employees, the enforceability of on-the-job bans is increasingly being upheld throughout the country.

As a result, most employees have successfully eliminated smoking in the office where they work. Others are suing for and receiving unemployment compensation after resigning from their jobs. Still others are seeking disability pay. In one case a woman was awarded $20,000 in disability pay because she developed asthmatic bronchitis after being transferred to an office with several smokers. The court also ruled that unless her employer (a government agency) transferred her to a job in a smoke-free office within sixty days, she would be eligible for disability retirement benefits of $500 per month.

Some employers have even enacted policies denying jobs to applicants who smoke! And companies have become more tolerant and responsive to complaints by nonsmokers and are now more willing to accommodate their needs. It should be noted that such accommodations make sense because employers are fearful of formal litigation, OSHA investigations, union intervention, or EEOC involvement (which is being brought with increasing regularity in this area).

Most employers have put flexible smoking guidelines into place. Such policies have included permitting employees to vote on whether smoking will be permitted in conference rooms and common areas (such as cafeterias and lounges), provided this is permitted by state law. Some companies have even instituted inflexible no-smoking policies for all staff, visitors, and customers in response to recent legal and health trends.

Some manufacturers, prompted by the discovery that materials used in their plants can be hazardous to smokers, are announcing that workers will be discharged unless they stop smoking in warehouses and factories. Such policies are enacted with the approval of OSHA, since management has the right to designate rules pertaining to work assignments to ensure an employee's health and safety.

For example, it was reported that one major U.S. corporation introduced an absolute ban on smoking after the company discovered that mineral fibers used in nine of its acoustical-products plants could have adverse health effects on both smokers and nonsmokers. To date, such a policy has gone unchallenged from workers at its plants.

If you desire to work in a smoke-free environment, the following strategies may help you protect your rights and increase the chances of a successful lawsuit.

---

**STRATEGY 1:** *Gather the facts. Document the environmental condition of your work location to support your request. For example,* *it is important to determine the number of smokers, type of ventilation, physical arrangement of desks, how often people around you smoke, etc.*

---

**STRATEGY 2:** *Acquire medical proof. Visit a doctor if you suffer an illness from working in a smoke-filled environment. Note the prescriptions and the amount of time lost from work. It is also a good idea to visit your employer's medical department (if one exists) to document your condition.*

---

**STRATEGY 3:** *Speak to management. Present management with a letter from your personal doctor stating your need to work in a smoke-free area. If possible, request a transfer collectively with other workers.*

---

**STRATEGY 4:** *Consult a lawyer to determine your rights. The lawyer can assert several options on your behalf. For example, she can assist you in presenting demands directly to the employer or union representative, file an action in court, contact OSHA, or sue the employer under the Equal Employment Opportunity Act. Legal fees are sometimes awarded to successful litigants under these acts. (Although such action may be illegal, be aware that your employer may fire or penalize you for enforcing your rights. This possibility should be considered before you decide to hire a lawyer.)*

---

**STRATEGY 5:** *Confirm all grievances in writing. After the initial discussion, it is a good idea to document your request by presenting management with a letter similar to the following.*

---

## Sample Letter Requesting a Smoke-Free Environment

Your Name
Address
Telephone Number
Date

Name of Supervisor
Title
Name of Company
Address

Dear (Name of Supervisor):

   This will confirm the conversations we have had regarding the need to provide me (us) with a work environment free of tobacco smoke. Enclosed is information to support the request to eliminate smoking in work areas.

   Also enclosed is a petition signed by employees in our work location. As my (our) ability to work is constantly undermined by the unhealthy, toxic pollutants to which I (we) am (are) chronically exposed, I (we) will appreciate your giving this request priority and your prompt attention.

   Thank you for your cooperation in this matter.

Very truly yours,
Your Name

P.S. If a prompt response is not received, please be advised that I (we) may be forced to contact an OSHA representative for assistance. Hopefully, this will not be necessary.

*Sent certified mail, return receipt requested.*
cc: your personal physician, union delegate, other management personnel, etc.

(Send a similar version to management whenever you are exposed to any potentially unhealthful working condition.)

Wait a few days after sending such a letter. Then, if a satisfactory response is not made, you may wish to send an additional letter similar to the following.

### Sample Follow-up Letter Requesting a Smoke-Free Environment

Your Name
Address
Telephone Number
Date

Name and Title
Department
Company Name
Address

Dear (Name):

As of this date, I (we) have received no reply to my (our) request of (date). [If temporary or interim measures were tried but were unsuccessful, identify them here.]

To protect my (our) health while in your employ, it is vital that the company provide me (us) with a smoke-free work area so as to comply with the laws of this state (specify applicable statute). I (we) have asked organizations that are expert in the area of occupational health to provide you with additional information on my (our) behalf.

I (we) will appreciate your immediate response to this urgent matter.

Sincerely,
Your Name

Send copies to middle management, the president of the company, the medical director of the company, the union representative, and your personal physician.

---

**STRATEGY 6:** *Contact an appropriate agency for further information. Your regional department of labor, department of health, or OSHA office will provide you with more information. In addition, you may wish to contact an organization called GASP, which stands for the New Jersey Group Against Smoking Pollution. GASP has been an advocate of the rights of nonsmokers and maintains a list of nationwide pertinent cases, regulations, and lawyers who are knowledgeable in this area.*

---

**STRATEGY 7:** *Speak to a doctor about workers' compensation. If you incur medical expenses due to a smoke-related on-the-job illness, discuss filing a workers' compensation claim with your doctor.*

---

## CONSTITUTIONAL PROTECTIONS

Employers risk potential lawsuits based upon invasion of privacy, intentional infliction of emotional distress, and wrongful discharge, among other causes of action, for violations stemming from unlawful interference into an employee's personal relationships and other off-duty conduct. This section will examine areas such as employers' attempts to regulate free speech, personal appearance, relationships with coworkers, and related subjects typically protected by the U.S. Constitution.

### Free Speech

Beginning in the late 1960s, the United States Supreme Court ruled that government employees could not be fired in retaliation for the workers' exercise of free speech. In one leading case a teacher was fired for sending a letter to a local newspaper criticizing the school board. While acknowledging the government's need to conduct business efficiently, the court balanced the perceived harm to both parties and concluded that the basic right of free speech was more important (especially if government business was not disrupted). This and other cases came to allow public sector employees to speak out freely upon matters of public concern without fear of retaliatory dismissal. Later cases made a distinction in situations where government employees spoke out about matters such as office morale, transfer policies within a particular department, and creation of grievance committees, and the Court ruled that the U.S. Constitution does not protect employees from dismissal on the basis of insubordination in these areas.

---

**STRATEGY:** *Some companies overcome problems by proving that the reason for a discharge was a result of legitimate business criteria such as poor performance and not bias. They are advised by counsel to avoid enunciating that the reason for discharge or discipline was annoyance with a worker's protest or comments on matters of public concern when they can demonstrate other "traditional" reasons for the action taken. Be aware of this and act accordingly.*

---

The notion of free speech, privacy, freedom from discharge as a result of whistle-blowing, and related constitutional rights has now been expanded to private employees, particularly in states that have enacted broad civil rights laws. Are there limits on freedom of expression? Can companies restrict employees' political affiliations? When does something stop being a political issue and become a rights issue? In many states a private employer cannot discipline, fail to promote, or fire an employee because the company does not agree with the employee's comments on matters of public concern. Generally, even though the employer has the right to discharge employees at will without cause or notice, the enactment of special civil rights laws in these and other states protects workers who speak out freely when this activity does not substantially or materially interfere with the employee's bona fide job performance or the parties' working relationship. In states having such laws, companies are liable for damages caused by discipline or discharge, including costs of bringing the lawsuit.

On the other hand, decisions made by the courts and the NLRB have made it plain that there is no legal protection for activities that are (1) unrelated to working conditions, (2) flagrantly disloyal, (3) damaging to the employer's property or reputation, or (4) materially disruptive.

## Voting Rights

A majority of states have laws that prohibit employers from influencing how their employees vote. In some states private employers may not influence the political activities, affiliations, or beliefs of their employees and employers are prohibited from discharging employees because of their political beliefs. State statutes differ markedly, so research your state's law.

## Rights of Due Process

Generally, private employers do not have to give a hearing to employees accused of wrongdoing. However, if such a promise or right is contained in the company's policy handbook, written rules, or procedures, or has been extended to others in the past, a company may have a legal obligation to allow an employee to grieve company action at an internal hearing.

---

**STRATEGY:** *The best way employers can overcome liability is to avoid making promises or giving such rights to employees in the first place. If promises have been given, they must be followed accurately and uniformly to avoid charges of breach of contract or discrimination. For example, if a male employee was allowed* *to appeal a firing decision before a committee, the same option must be offered to a fired female worker.*

### Asserting Union Rights

The National Labor Relations Act prohibits the firing of an employee because of his or her involvement in any union activity, because the employee bargained collectively, or because the employee filed charges or testified pursuant to the act.

Contact your union, regional office of the National Labor Relations Board, state department of labor, or a lawyer if you believe your rights have been violated.

### Off-Duty Conduct

Attempts to regulate personal relationships and off-duty conduct of employees may subject employers to legal exposure. Disciplinary action in response to off-duty behavior that has no direct relationship to the workplace should not be tolerated.

To be successful in this area, employers must:

1. Demonstrate a legitimate business need;
2. Communicate reasonable policies in company handbooks, memos, or other written documents; and
3. Warn employees as to what constitutes objectionable conduct and the penalties for committing violations of stated company policy. Certainly, at a minimum, the regulations or policies enunciated must comply with your state's civil rights laws, must be consistent with other company policies, and cannot violate discrimination statutes in the process.

For off-the-job illegal conduct, a company typically has the right to fire a worker if the illegal conduct harms the employer's reputation or has a negative impact on job performance. A more prudent course of action, however, may be to suspend the worker without pay pending a conviction on the criminal charges, just to be safe.

Some employers fire any worker they suspect of criminal activity. But terminating a worker for erroneous off-the-job reasons or unfounded rumors of moonlighting could be grounds for a wrongful dismissal suit.

### Legal Activities Off-Premises

In some states a private employer cannot discipline, fail to promote, or fire an employee because the company does not agree with the employee's comments on matters of public concern. A majority of states have laws that prohibit employers from influencing how their employees vote. Attempts to regulate off-duty legal conduct is also sanctioned.

Most states have laws making it illegal for companies to fire workers who participate in legally permissible political activities, recreational activities, or the legal use of consumable products before or after working hours. Political activities include running for public office, campaigning for a candidate, and participating in fund-raising activities for a candidate or political party. Those activities may be protected if they are legal and occur on the employee's own time, off company premises, and without the use of employer property or equipment.

Recreational activities are defined as any lawful leisure-time activities for which the employee receives no compensation. The definition of consumable products even protects the rights of people who smoke cigarettes or drink alcohol before and after working hours and off the company's premises.

The right not to be demoted, retaliated against, or fired for engaging in these legally permitted activities generally depends on state law. To date, many states have passed laws making it illegal to be fired from a job because you are a smoker and smoke off-premises; the trend is for more states to follow. For example, in New York, employers cannot discriminate in hiring, promotion, and other terms of employment due to off-duty activities in four specific categories: political activities, use of a consumable product, recreational activities, and union membership or exercise of any rights granted under federal or state law (such as voting). However, a female employee was recently fired by a New York company for dating a coworker after hours. She sued the employer and argued that her discharge violated this law. The judge, however, ruled that having a sexual relationship was not included in the definition of a "recreational activity" as defined by the statute (skydiving, scuba diving, bungee jumping, and overeating were included) and ruled against her.

In the vast majority of states with such laws, it is illegal to refuse to hire smokers. It may also be illegal to discriminate against smokers by charging higher insurance premiums unless the company can demonstrate a valid business reason, such as higher costs. However, employees who smoke off-duty must still comply with existing laws and ordinances prohibiting smoking on-premises, such as only in designated areas. And just because it may be legal to drink alcohol off-premises late into the night does not give you the right to stagger into work drunk the next morning.

Employers who violate state law in this area are generally subject to a lawsuit by their state's attorney general seeking to restrain or enjoin the continuance of the alleged unlawful conduct. Hefty penalties are provided in some of these laws. Additionally, individuals may commence their own lawsuits and recover monetary damages and other forms of relief, including attorney fees, under the laws of many states.

Contact a representative at the American Civil Liberties Union in New York City for advice and guidance if you are being pressured to stop asserting legal political activities, affiliations, or political action. This includes banding together with other workers to protest poor working conditions. In one California case a group of individuals organized to promote equal rights of homosexuals at a large company via a class-action lawsuit. The court ruled that such activity was protected by state law.

Since some states do not have specific laws protecting employees who engage in political activity and other activities, and the laws vary, always consult with counsel and review applicable state law before engaging in questionable activities or taking action to protect such activities.

Regarding off-duty surveillance, a few states prohibit employers from gathering and maintaining information regarding an employee's political, religious, and other nonbusiness activities. In these states employees and former employees can inspect their personnel file for the purpose of discovering whether any such information exists. If their file contains such prohibited information, the employer may be liable for damages, court costs, attorney fees, and fines.

### Personal Appearance Rules

Some companies prescribe standards in dress and personal appearance. Although such codes have been attacked at times, they are legal provided the policies do not unfairly impact a group of workers, such as females. If a different rule is imposed for female employees than for male employees, such as requiring women waitresses to wear skimpy clothes while male counterparts wear whatever they wish, the policy may be discriminatory and a violation of Title VII for an adverse (disparate) impact based on gender. A grooming code that severely impacts women (e.g., requiring all female employees to have short haircuts), thus having an adverse impact under Title VII, may also violate the law unless the employer can demonstrate a legitimate business necessity (such as safety considerations) to enforce the rule.

When employers prove that a dress code is reasonable and job-related, it will probably be enforceable, and employers may terminate workers who refuse to follow reasonable rules. In many situations arbitrators and judges will uphold a company's personal appearance policy when it is justifiable. Good-grooming regulations are often imposed in an attempt to reflect a company's image in a highly competitive business environment. Reasonable requirements in furtherance of that policy may be legal if challenged, particularly if the company disseminated written rules advising workers of the consequences flowing from violations of such policies.

However, the law varies by state and depends on each set of facts. In one case, for example, a worker dyed her hair purple. She was given one week to change her hair color. When she rejected the boss's order, she was fired. The company was so incensed that it opposed her claim for unemployment compensation. It stated at a hearing that her job involved dealing with customers, many of whom were revolted by her unconventional hair coloring, and keeping her aboard would have resulted in loss of business. The company also believed it was misconduct and insubordination for the worker to refuse a reasonable request to change her eccentric hairstyle.

The worker defended her position by stating that the company had no right to dictate her personal appearance and that there was no evidence that customers complained about her purple hair. She stated that since several customers had complimented her new appearance, she was unjustifiably terminated in a manner that should not have precluded her from receiving unemployment benefits.

The court found there was no evidence that the color of the worker's hair significantly affected the employer's business or caused customer complaints. Although it stated that the company had the right to fire her as an at-will employee, it was unlawful to deny her unemployment benefits for her actions. It wrote: "We do not question the employer's right to establish a grooming code for its employees, to revise its rules in response to unanticipated situations, and to make its hiring and firing decisions in conformity with this policy. However, it is possible for an employee to have been properly discharged without having acted in a manner as would justify denial of unemployment benefits."

---

**STRATEGY:** *While rules requiring employees to wear uniforms may be legal, such rules can violate your rights if the cost of purchasing mandatory uniforms is deducted from your pay. This may be a violation of the Fair Labor Standards Act if your wages then drop below the minimum wage. It may also be a violation* *of federal and state discrimination laws if female employees are required to purchase uniforms while males are not.*

---

### Office Romances

Does management have the right to actively enforce a nonfraternization rule aimed at curbing interoffice romances? This varies depending on the facts. One supervisor who was fired commenced a lawsuit against a former employer. The supervisor had allegedly given his live-in lover a promotion that placed her above several employees with more seniority, even though the company had an unwritten, traditional rule forbidding social relationships between management and lower-echelon employees. When questioned by the home office, the supervisor admitted that he and the coworker were lovers; citing the nonfraternization rule, the company abruptly terminated him.

The supervisor took the company to court and argued that his employment contract brought with it the company's implied covenant of good faith and fair dealing, which the company violated when he was fired. He also stated that the nonfraternization rule was unfair, unreasonable, and selectively enforced.

The company responded that its nonfraternization rule became reasonable and necessary after the company discovered that attachments between supervisory employees and their subordinates led to accusations of favoritism, which had a negative impact on morale. The company also argued that since the employee had no written contract guaranteeing job security, he could be fired at any time for any or no reason.

The court found that the company was legitimately concerned with appearances of favoritism and employee dissension caused by romantic relationships. Given his actions, the terminated supervisor did not make a strong case that the company failed to act in good faith toward him.

Other courts have similarly upheld the dismissal of employees romantically involved with coworkers. A Wisconsin court ruled that there were no constitutional or statutory rights barring such a dismissal. In another case, termination because of marriage to the employee of a competitor was found not to violate public policy, and the worker's lawsuit for unfair discharge was rejected. Other employees have been fired for violating company fraternization rules by having extramarital affairs or taking a girlfriend to an out-of-state convention. However, since the law is unsettled in this area and each case is decided on its own set of facts and circumstances, never assume that a company's actions are legal in this area. Consult an employment lawyer for advice.

---

**STRATEGY:** *Although it may be legal to forbid employees from fraternization, all employees must be treated similarly to avoid violations. For example, if an employer reprimands a male employee for dating a coworker but fires a female employee for a similar infraction, the employer may be committing illegal sex discrimination.*

---

For off-the-job illegal conduct, a company typically has the right to fire a worker if the illegal conduct harms the employer's reputation or has a negative impact on job performance. The law is not so clear regarding attempts to regulate legal off-the-job behavior. Some cases have given employers the right to bar employees from cohabiting with persons who work for a competitor. In one such case a court upheld a company's written policy that stated: "The Company will not continue the employment of any person who lives in the immediate household of a person employed by a competitor." But in another case in a different state, an employer's rule prohibiting workers from dating employees of a competitor was found to be illegal.

### No Solicitation or Distribution Rules

Many companies prohibit employees from soliciting or distributing literature or other items. Typically, such policies are legal provided the company enunciates the policy in writing and applies it consistently. One company handbook states its policy as follows:

> To prevent disruptions of Company business and harassment of Company personnel, Employees may not:
> - Engage in soliciting donations or contributions;
> - Sell chances, raffle tickets, services, or merchandise;
> - Distribute merchandise or literature of any kind on company property during working hours. This includes soliciting or distributing literature to non-employees or visitors at any time.
>
> Under no circumstances may non-employees be allowed to distribute literature or solicit employees on company premises. Breaking any of these rules is considered serious misconduct and may be grounds for immediate discharge.

A few companies allow employees to solicit or distribute literature during "nonworking" hours—those periods, such as mealtimes, when they are not engaged in performing their work tasks and are away from designated working areas.

## Rest Room Visits

Workers generally do not have rights to privacy to stay in rest rooms for extended periods of time, particularly after being warned of such excessive respites and when the rest room visits are not medically related. However, if a medical condition justifies numerous trips to the bathroom (not for smoking or chatting), it may be wise for employers to avoid disciplining or terminating a worker without further investigation and careful planning in light of the increased protections and reasonable accommodation requirements afforded to covered employees under the ADA.

## Informants

Are company policies designed to encourage workers to inform on drug or alcohol abusers legal?

In one case, the NLRB ruled that the "informer" rule was valid. After noting that both management and the union agreed on the need to combat drug abuse, the referee decided that the basic premise of a drug-free atmosphere was vital and involved no violations of privacy.

---

**STRATEGY:** *Generally, an employee is under no ordinary obligation to divulge information on a coworker.*

---

## Right to Work in a Safe Workplace

HEALTH AND SAFETY IN THE WORKPLACE

Numerous changes benefiting workers have occurred in the area of health and safety. Federal and state laws have recently been passed that give employees the right to refuse dangerous work and receive accurate reports concerning toxic substances in their working environment. Increased activity by representatives of the federal Occupational Safety and Health Administration (OSHA) has also played a large role in protecting employees from unsafe working conditions.

**What is OSHA?** The 1970 Occupational Safety and Health Act requires employers to provide a safe and healthful workplace. This federal law applies to every private employer who is involved in interstate commerce, regardless of size. Additionally, some states have passed occupational safety and health plans approved by OSHA. Some of these laws are even stricter in their compliance and enforcement standards than the federal law. For example, in one case the Illinois Supreme Court ruled that the federal Occupational Safety and Health Act does not prohibit state officials from enforcing criminal penalties against employers who violate OSHA regulations.

In that case an Illinois company coated wires with toxic compounds. This practice continued despite knowledge by the company's supervisors that such manufacturing processes were producing harmful effects on workers. The company and several of its officers were indicted on criminal charges of aggravated battery and reckless conduct under state law. When the company appealed, the supreme court ruled that the state of Illinois was allowed to proceed with its own prosecution, notwithstanding the existence of the federal OSHA law, since "prosecutions of employers who violate state criminal law by failing to maintain safe working conditions for their employees will surely further OSHA's stated goal of assuring so far as possible every working man and woman in the nation safe and healthful working conditions."

The Occupational Safety and Health Administration (OSHA) is the federal agency created to enforce the law in this area. The law protects employees who band together to protest wages, hours, or working conditions. Under this law, workers are allowed to refuse to perform in a dangerous environment (e.g., in the presence of toxic substances, fumes, or radioactive materials) and to strike to protest unsafe conditions. Employees may also initiate an OSHA inspection of alleged dangerous working conditions by filing a safety complaint and cannot be retaliated against by taking such action when justified.

OSHA inspectors visit work sites to be sure that employers adhere to the rules. Penalties are sometimes imposed, including fines of up to $100,000 for each violation and/or imprisonment for up to three years for employers and key personnel who willfully or repeatedly violate OSHA laws or fail to correct hazards within fixed time limits.

The law includes an extremely broad general duty clause requiring all employers to furnish a workplace that is free from recognized hazards. This means that employers are required to comply with safety rules and are subject to inspections without notice (with an employee representative present) and that no employee who makes a complaint can be subject to retaliation, loss of work or benefits, or demotion.

**What protections are available to workers under OSHA?** Under this law, workers are allowed:

- To refuse to perform work in a dangerous environment (e.g., in the presence of toxic substances, fumes, or radioactive materials)
- To strike to protest unsafe conditions
- To initiate an OSHA inspection of dangerous working conditions by filing a safety complaint
- To participate in OSHA inspections, prehearing conferences, and review inspection hearings
- To assist the OSHA compliance officer in determining that violations have occurred
- To petition that employers provide adequate emergency exits, environmental control devices (e.g., ventilation, noise-elimination devices, radiation-detection tags, signs, and protective equipment), and the ready availability of medical personnel
- To request time off with pay to seek medical treatment during working hours
- To request eating facilities in areas that have not been exposed to toxic substances
- To request investigations when they are punished for asserting their rights

One of the most important aspects of the federal OSHA law is that it provides workers with protection against retaliation after asserting their rights. Employers cannot fire, demote, or transfer workers who assert their health and safety rights to any federal, state, or local agency empowered to investigate or regulate such conditions. Contact your union, regional office of the National

Labor Relations Board, OSHA representative, lawyer, or state department of labor if you believe your rights have been violated.

In one case seven machine-shop workers walked off their jobs, claiming it was too cold to work. The company fired them, stating they violated company rules by stopping work without notifying the supervisor. The workers filed a complaint alleging this was an unfair labor practice. The U.S. Supreme Court ruled that the employees had a constitutional right to strike over health and safety conditions, and that the firing violated the law. The workers were awarded back pay and job reinstatement as a result.

---

**STRATEGY:** *It is not necessarily a good idea to suddenly walk off your job when you believe you are working in a dangerous or unhealthful environment unless it is likely that the work is placing you in imminent danger of serious injury. You should first attempt to discuss such conditions with your supervisor, union delegate, or OSHA representative. This will make your demands seem more reasonable and minimize potential conflict.*

---

However, if you feel you have been punished for complaining about your safety and health rights, speak with a representative of your nearest OSHA office *immediately* (i.e., within thirty days of the time you discover the retaliation). Request an attorney or OSHA or union representative to file the complaint for you if you are too sick, since the complaint must be filed in a timely fashion to avoid dismissal under the statute of limitations.

Finally, be sure to fully discuss the facts with an OSHA representative *before* taking any action. After OSHA conducts the investigation, it may demand that your employer restore your job, earnings, benefits, and seniority if you have been illegally punished. OSHA is also empowered to institute a lawsuit in federal court to protect your rights, so be sure that you speak to a representative from your nearest OSHA office as soon as possible. You may also wish to retain an experienced labor lawyer. All of these options should be taken immediately to protect your rights in this area.

### RIGHT TO APPLY FOR AND RECEIVE WORKER'S COMPENSATION

Each state has enacted its own peculiar rules with respect to workers' compensation, which provides aid for employees who suffer job-related injuries. Under state compensation laws, the amount of money paid in benefits is linked to the workers' rate of pay prior to the injury and the kind and extent of injuries suffered. Workers' compensation is a substitute for other remedies you may have against the employer, such as bringing a private lawsuit for negligence. In many cases the issue becomes one of determining whether the injuries suffered were job-related and whether you are legally considered an independent contractor (not subject to workers' compensation laws) or an employee. The reason is that people typically prefer to sue the employer privately and obtain greater damages than are awarded under workers' compensation statutes.

---

**STRATEGY:** *Since the outcome of each workers' compensation case varies depending on the particular facts and unique state law, always seek the advice of a lawyer specializing in workers' compensation law. Issues such as how long you may delay before filing a claim, whether coverage is available for stress-related injuries, and what kinds of injuries are covered, together with strategies to help maximize the benefits received, can become complicated and typically require a lawyer's assistance and advice.*

---

Always notify your employer when you are injured while working. This is your right and you cannot be retaliated against in any way for taking such action. Fill out all necessary forms. If no forms are available, contact your nearest workers' compensation office for details. Speak to a lawyer immediately if a claim is contested. Visit several doctors to obtain accurate evaluations of your condition. Be sure you understand your rights if you are a part-time worker or are injured during work-related travel. The following list summarizes the kinds of injuries that are typically compensable:

- Preexisting conditions that the workplace accelerates or aggravates, such as a bad back, even if pain from the injury is delayed until a later time
- Injuries caused during breaks, lunch hours, and work-sponsored recreational activities, such as a company-paid party, and on-the-job injuries caused by company facilities, such as a shower located on the premises
- Diseases such as lung cancer if contracted by asbestos exposure at work as a result of the usual conditions to which the worker was exposed by her employment
- Injuries resulting from mental and physical strain brought on by increased work duties or the stress caused by a requirement that the employee make decisions on other employee dismissals. In some states this includes employees who develop a disabling psychosis because they cannot keep up with the demands of the job and a supervisor's constant harassment

An employer may not inquire whether you have ever filed for workers' compensation when you apply for a job. You also have the right to select your own physician for treatment, provided that physician is authorized by the state's workers' compensation board.

### RIGHT TO BE WARNED BEFORE A MASSIVE LAYOFF

Employees are entitled to be warned of large layoffs under the federal Worker Adjustment and Retraining Notification Act (WARN). Employers with more than one hundred workers are required to give employees and their communities at least sixty days' notice or comparable financial benefits (sixty days' notice pay) of plant closings and large layoffs that affect fifty or more workers at a job site. Speak to an experienced employment lawyer or contact your nearest regional office of the U.S. Department of Labor for more information. Companies must be careful when contemplating a substantial reduction of their workforce, and a representative from the Department of Labor can advise you if your rights are being violated.

A WARN claim applies not only to union employees working at plants. It can be asserted when a private employer (such as IBM or AT&T) lays off hundreds of workers at one time or when a company discharges large numbers of secretaries or dismantles an accounting, business, or financial department due to a reorganization.

For example, a federal judge in New York found that a major law firm violated the federal plant closure law when the 125-partner firm failed to give its 250 former staff attorneys and clerical help the required sixty days' notice. To avoid damages, it was reported that the law firm offered former employees one week's salary in return for their promise to opt out of the case, and about 150 accepted the offer. The others remained in the case and will receive significantly more compensation: one day's back pay for each day of violation up to sixty days; the value of medical expenses and other benefits paid directly to the affected employee; and the value of actual payments made to third parties on behalf of the affected employee.

The following thumbnail sketch will highlight important aspects of the act; suggestions will then be offered on the law's possible effects on workers and employers throughout the United States.

**What the law says.** Section 3(a) of the Worker Adjustment and Retraining Notification Act prohibits employers from ordering a plant closing or mass layoff until sixty days *after* the employer has given written notice of this to:

1. Affected employees or their representatives;
2. The state dislocated-worker unit; and
3. The chief elected official of the unit of local government where the closing or layoff is to occur.

Employers are defined as business enterprises that employ more than one hundred full-time workers (part-timers are characterized as those working fewer than twenty hours per week or less than six months in the preceding year) or who employ more than one hundred employees who in the aggregate work at least four thousand hours per week excluding overtime.

The act calls for covered employers to give notice of a plant closing or mass layoff. A *plant closing* is defined as the "permanent or temporary shutdown of a single site of employment, or one or more facilities or operating units within a single site of employment, if the shutdown results in an employment loss at the single site of employment during any 30 day period for 50 or more employees excluding part-time employees." *Employment loss* is defined under the law as "a termination other than for cause, voluntary departure or retirement, or a layoff for more than 6 months or a reduction in hours of work of more than 50 percent during each month of any 6 month period."

In contrast to a plant closing, a *mass layoff* is a reduction in force resulting in employment loss during any thirty-day period of fifty full-time employees who constitute at least 33 percent of the full-time employees at a single site of employment, or five hundred employees.

**Whom the law affects.** The law does not affect governmental or nonprofit organizations, and many layoffs of small companies may not be affected by the act's requirements due to the number of persons affected. Additionally, if the plant closing or mass layoff was caused by a natural disaster (flood, earthquake, severe drought, etc.), or was due to the closing of a temporary facility or completion of a project whose employees were hired with the understanding that their work was of limited duration, the law will not adversely affect the employer. The same is true for problems caused by strikes, lockouts, or permanent replacement of strikers.

There are other exceptions as well. The sixty-day rule does not have to be strictly followed if the employer, reasonably and in good faith, was forced to shut down the plant in a shorter time to obtain needed capital or business, or if the closing or mass layoff was caused by business circumstances not reasonably foreseeable at the time the required notice was to be given.

Finally, the law does not protect workers who lose their jobs less than sixty days after the effective date of a sale. This is because the act was intended to protect workers only from closings or layoffs prior to a sale. The law merely obligates the seller to give notice until the sale is completed; it is unclear to what extent, if any, the buyer would be liable thereafter.

**What are the penalties for noncompliance?** Any employer who orders a plant closing or mass layoff without furnishing appropriate notice may be liable in a civil action to each affected employee for:

1. One day's back pay for each day of violation up to sixty days. This amount is calculated at the higher of the employee's average regular rate or final regular rate of pay less any wages paid during the layoff period and any voluntary or unconditional payments (e.g., severance) paid to the affected worker that were not legally required
2. The value of medical expenses and other benefits paid directly to the affected employee
3. The value of actual payments made to third parties on behalf of the affected employee

Employers are also subject to fines not to exceed $500 per day to the appropriate unit of local government where the closing or layoff occurs unless the employer continues to pay benefits to affected employees as described above within three weeks of the shutdown or layoff. However, this fine may be reduced by showing that a "complained of wrongful act or omission" was in good faith and that the employer had reasonable grounds for believing that the act or omission was not a violation of law.

Critics contend that the law is weak because federal courts do not have the authority to *enjoin* (force an employer to reopen or rehire) plant closings and layoffs. The act only awards the above-cited economic sanctions plus reasonable attorney fees and costs to the prevailing party. Thus, some legislators interested in protecting the rights of employees are arguing that the act has no teeth and, at best, merely gives workers notice of the firing and possibly some severance pay if a job is eliminated prior to the sixty-day notice period.

Employers covered by the law must carefully orchestrate all moves *before* closing marginally profitable plants. Obviously, affected workers and the community must be notified properly, and additional benefits will have to be given to comply with the act's provisions.

---

**STRATEGY:** *Now that you have a better understanding of the law, if you believe you are being victimized by a substantial reduction in force and the employer is not applying the law properly, speak to an experienced labor attorney immediately or contact your nearest regional office of the U.S. Department of Labor for more information. Companies must be careful when contemplating substantial reductions of their workforce, and a representative from the Department of Labor can advise you quickly if your rights are being violated.*

---

Consider filing a lawsuit alleging WARN violations if you are terminated due to a large reorganization or downsizing (e.g., your whole department is suddenly axed) and are not given reasonable warning or a decent severance package. Thus, if you are fired suddenly and are part of a massive layoff, consult a lawyer immediately to discuss your rights and options under WARN.

Note that there are some exceptions to the law that do not help you. For example, the layoffs of workers employed by the same company but located at different sites cannot be combined to meet the threshold minimum. However, you may be entitled to recover damages under the law if you are a traveling salesperson working for the company like others all over the country and the entire field sales staff is fired en masse.

## Other Rights and Obligations of Employees

### CONFIDENTIAL INFORMATION AND TRADE SECRETS

Employees often resign from a job or are lured away to a rival company to compete directly against their former employers. Sometimes they take valuable customer lists, trade secrets, and confidential information (such as prices and requirements of key customers) with them. When the former company discovers this, a lawsuit may be filed to stop the employee from using such information. In other instances, a former employer may attempt to stop the individual from using information that was learned and acquired while working. Can this be done? The following information can decrease the chances that such problems will occur and give you a better understanding of the legalities in this area.

**Understand what constitutes a trade secret.** A trade secret may consist of any formula, pattern, device, or compilation of information used in business that gives a company an opportunity to obtain an advantage over competitors that do not know or use it. Although an exact definition is not possible, trade secrets are usually involved when:

- An employer takes precautions to guard the secrecy of the information
- The employer has expended significant money and effort in developing the information
- It is difficult to acquire the information outside of the company (i.e., it isn't generally known to outsiders)
- Employees are warned that trade secrets are involved and that they are obligated to act in a confidential manner

The most frequently disputed issue concerning trade secrets involves customer lists. A "secret" list is not a list of companies or individuals that can be compiled from a telephone directory or other source that anyone can examine. A list becomes confidential when the names of customers can be learned only by someone through his employment—for example, a salesperson secretly copies a list of customers that the company spent considerable time, effort, and money compiling and kept under lock and key.

When employees have become friendly with customers in the course of their previous employment, they are allowed to call on them for new employers. However, the law generally states that they are prohibited from using their knowledge of customer buying habits, requirements, or other special information when soliciting their former employer's accounts. If a salesperson knows that a particular customer will be in short supply of a product, for instance, he should not solicit that account, because he may expose himself to a lawsuit. This is because the law imposes a fiduciary duty of good faith and loyalty on all employees, sales and nonsales alike.

An employee cannot make deals with customers in which he or she promises to perform favors in return for secret kickbacks involving money or other benefits such as vacations. If you engage in such conduct without the company's knowledge and consent, the employer can terminate your employment and sue you for damages.

**Has a climate of confidentiality been created?** When an employer has made a special effort to remind employees of their obligation to protect the company's trade secrets, employees are sometimes held to a higher standard. For example, if posters are displayed in prominent areas reminding workers of their obligation to protect company secrets and this is published on a continuing basis in company journals, work rules, policy manuals, and memos, this reduces a person's argument that he or she didn't know it was wrong to convey confidential information to a competitor.

**Be aware that the transfer of confidential information may constitute a crime.** Some states have passed laws making theft of trade secrets a criminal offense. Legislation was enacted in New Jersey, for example, making it a high misdemeanor to steal company property, including written material. Other states, including Arkansas, California, Colorado, Maine, Michigan, Minnesota, Nebraska, New Hampshire, New Mexico, Ohio, Oklahoma, Pennsylvania, Tennessee, Texas, and Wisconsin, have similar laws. The state of New York has gone even further in addressing this problem by declaring it a felony for anyone to steal property consisting of scientific material.

In the federal system, crimes involving misappropriation of intellectual property have been prosecuted under the National Stolen Property Act and mail and wire fraud statutes. A criminal RICO action may also be asserted. Pursuant to the National Stolen Property Act, if valuable written material is stolen and transported to another state, the Federal Bureau of Investigation and the Justice Department can assist employers in apprehending workers because it is a federal crime to sell or receive stolen property worth more than $5,000 that has been transported across state lines.

Passage of the Economic Espionage Act, which makes trade secret theft a federal crime, specially addresses theft perpetrated via the Internet. Under Section 1832 of the act, it is a federal criminal act for any person to convert a trade secret to his or her own benefit or the benefit of others intending or knowing that the offense will injure any owner of the trade secret. The conversion of a trade secret is defined broadly to cover every conceivable act of misappropriation, and you can also be prosecuted for receiving or possessing trade secret information when you know it was given to you without the owner's authorization.

Penalties for violating this statute are steep. A person who commits an offense can be imprisoned up to ten years and fined up to $500,000. A corporation can be fined up to $5 million. The significance of this law is that those engaged in trade secret misappropriation can no longer be assured that liability will be limited to civil remedies and damages.

Since computers, E-mail, and other new technologies make it easier for employees at all levels to misappropriate valuable information and transfer it to others without removing bulky boxes, avoid the temptation to do so in light of this serious federal law.

## EMPLOYEE INVENTIONS AND SUGGESTIONS

Workers frequently create valuable suggestions, comments, ideas, designs, manufacturing processes, and inventions. These suggestions often lead to money-saving and money-making devices. If the invention is created while on the job or is used by an employer, is the company obligated to pay the employee for the use of such an idea? Who owns the device or invention created?

This section will clarify ambiguous law and give you a better understanding of how to avoid problems and protect yourself in this area. To be able to implement many of the strategies contained herein, it is important to first understand the following basic concepts.

**Work for hire.** A work for hire is defined as a work prepared by an employee within the scope of his or her employment or work specifically ordered or commissioned by the employer which the employee creates in reliance upon an express agreement. Thus, for example, when an employee is specifically engaged to do something (such as solve a problem, develop a new product, process, or machine), he or she is provided with the means and opportunity to resolve the problem or achieve the result and is paid for that work, then the employer is generally entitled to the fruits of the employee's labors. If a worker creates an invention while on the job, therefore, the invention may be owned by the employer under this legal principle.

**The shop right concept.** If an employee is not hired to invent or solve a particular problem, does the employee have the right to claim any rights to his or her discoveries? Maybe, depending upon the particular facts involved.

For example, under the shop right concept, when an employee makes an invention or discovery that is outside the scope of his employment but utilizes the employer's resources (equipment, labor, materials, or facilities) in making the invention, that invention may be owned by the employee subject to a "shop right" on the part of the employer. This shop right in certain instances may give the employer a nonexclusive, irrevocable license to use the invention indefinitely, without having to pay a royalty.

**Valuable ideas as opposed to patentable inventions.** Using a hypothetical case, Gwen develops a manufacturing process during nonworking hours which she thinks will save the company money. She tells her boss and the idea is incorporated into the company's production process. Gwen is not compensated for the idea. She resigns and sues to recover a percentage of the money saved by the idea's use.

Gwen's case is not as strong as it appears. The reason is that ideas, plans, methods, and procedures for business operations cannot normally be copyrighted. This is also true with respect to certain ideas as intellectual property. The law generally states that ideas belong to no one and are there for the taking.

Additionally, an idea is presumed to be a work made for hire and the property of the employer if an employee offers it voluntarily without contracting to receive additional compensation. Gwen would have a stronger case if she could prove that the idea was her own original, unique creation not requested or developed while working on company time or on the employer's premises, *and* that it was furnished because of a specific promise or understanding that she would be promoted or compensated once it was implemented by the employer.

Many workers are unknowingly exploited because they give away their ideas without understanding their rights. Review the following strategies if you wish to avoid being exploited in this area.

---

**STRATEGY 1:** *Articulate your idea, method, or process in writing. This is essential because it is difficult to prove you are the creator of a valuable idea unless it is set down on paper.*

---

**STRATEGY 2:** *Be sure the writing is detailed and specific. This can increase your chances of proving the idea is a protectable property interest. For example, if you write a proposal for a unique and original television show, be sure to fully describe the characters, budget, and script dialogue rather than briefly discussing the concept of the show.*

---

**STRATEGY 3:** *Avoid volunteering ideas. In one famous case a homemaker mailed an unsolicited cheesecake recipe to a baking company. The recipe was used and became a popular moneymaker. Although the woman sued the company for damages, she lost. The court ruled that no recovery was obtainable because the homemaker voluntarily gave her idea to the company.*

*The lesson to be learned from this case is clear. Since employers generally have no obligation to compensate employees for ideas, inventions, or suggestions that are conveyed voluntarily, think twice before doing this, particularly if company policy states that there is no obligation to pay anything if the idea is used, or that any payments made will be purely discretionary (i.e., not linked to any predetermined formula such as a percentage of specific company savings, revenue, or profits generated from the idea).*

---

**STRATEGY 4:** *Avoid signing any agreement or contract with work-for-hire provisions. Some companies request job applicants and employees to sign agreements stating that all inventions authored or conceived by the employee belong to the employer. Avoid this whenever possible.*

---

**STRATEGY 5:** *Negotiate a predetermined method of compensation and articulate your understanding in writing. For example, the agreement should mention the type of idea being conveyed and the manner of compensation for its use, and should stipulate that the employer will maintain the confidentiality of the idea and will not disclose, assign, or transfer the idea or its value to anyone else without your consent. The sample agreement below illustrates these points in greater detail.*

---

Note: If compensation is difficult to ascertain at the time the acknowledgment is negotiated, the agreement can state that the employee will be compensated in a manner mutually agreed upon by the parties and that the idea will remain the property of the employee or individual until such formula is determined.

## Acknowledgment of Receipt of Idea

Received on this day from (name of employee or individual) an idea concerning (specify) which was presented in the form of (specify) and which is hereby acknowledged.

The employer confirms that it has not used or implemented this idea in the past, that it is sufficiently original and has been conveyed with the expectation of receiving payment thereof, and, if used or implemented in any manner, shall cause (name of employee or individual) to be compensated according to the following: (specify).

The employer agrees to maintain the confidentiality of the material submitted herein by (name of employee or individual) and agrees not to disclose it, or the ideas upon which it is based, to any person, firm, or entity without (name of employee or individual)'s consent.

Accepted and consented to: Name of Employer
By: Name of Officer and Title        Date:
By: Name of Employee or Individual     Date:

---

**STRATEGY 6:** *Get a receipt. If you are unable to receive a signed acknowledgment similar to the above, you must be able to prove delivery of a valuable idea to another in order to protect your rights. For example, it is often wise to send a certified letter indicating that your idea was submitted in confidence with the expectation of being paid for its use. The letter on page 196 illustrates this concept.*

---

Note: Although such a letter cannot guarantee protection of your idea, it can increase the chances that you will not be exploited in this area. Try to send the materials by certified mail, return receipt requested, to prove delivery, and follow up the letter with a telephone call or another letter in the near future if you do not receive an immediate response. Finally, insist on having all materials returned, plus copies, if you receive an unfavorable reply; you don't want the materials floating around so other people can look at them and steal your idea.

Your Name
Address
Telephone Number
Date

Name of Officer
Title
Name of Employer
Address

Re: The submission of my original idea regarding (specify) consisting of (specify)

Dear (Name of Officer),

Per our earlier telephone conversation on (date), I have enclosed, per your request, my original idea regarding (specify) consisting of (specify).

You indicated an interest in this concept and advised me that the materials would be reviewed in confidence with no disclosure to any other person, firm, or entity without my prior written consent.

Finally, it was agreed that these materials are submitted with the expectation of furnishing appropriate acknowledgment of my authorship and payment to me in the event they are used after my written consent has been given.

Thank you for your interest in the matter and I look forward to hearing from you after you have completed your review.

   Very truly yours,
   Your Name

*Sent certified mail, return receipt requested.*

**STRATEGY 7:** *Avoid signing releases. Many employers and individuals request that creators sign releases before they will agree to review their ideas. Such releases typically state that the individuals assume no liability regarding the receipt or use of such material. Avoid signing any such document because they defeat the purpose of the strategies discussed in this section.*

**STRATEGY 8:** *Keep copies of all materials and letters that you send to others. Some people mail an unopened copy of the package back to themselves for this purpose. In the event of a dispute, the postmark date on the front of the envelope may establish that you were the sender of the package.*

**STRATEGY 9:** *Consult a lawyer. If your idea is sufficiently unique or potentially valuable, you may wish to consult an experienced copyright or patent lawyer whom you can trust.*

## CHAPTER 5

# All About Discrimination

Although employment discrimination is illegal, it is widely practiced throughout the United States. In fact, many hundreds of thousands of claims are filed each year with the various federal, state, and local agencies empowered to investigate, enforce, and protect the civil rights of workers.

Federal and state laws prohibit employers from discriminating against employees or potential employees on the basis of:

- Age
- Gender or marital status
- Race, color, or creed
- Religion or national origin
- Disability or physical handicap

This applies throughout all stages of employment: recruiting, interviewing, and hiring; promotion, training, transfer, and assignment; and discipline, layoffs, and discharge procedures. An illegal act can be committed by any member of an employer's staff, from the president down to the supervisor and receptionist! Typical remedies for illegal conduct are significant awards by judges, juries, or arbitrators.

When a recently fired employee consults with me in my office, one of the first points I consider is whether the individual has a valid claim of unfair termination based upon age, sex, or race discrimination. For example, assuming equal work, did the company pay the same salary and benefits to women as to men? Was a black employee fired justifiably because of excessive absences and lateness? Was an elderly sales employee the first to be fired because of a slipping sales quota?

As you will learn in this chapter, recognizing and fighting back against job discrimination is not always easy. The subtleties of this become apparent with the examples used above. Suppose a company fired a sixty-year-old salesperson because he wasn't meeting quota. That sounds like a legitimate reason, right? Maybe, but what if the company's sales were down in many of its territories? Were younger salespeople fired as well, or were they merely given a warning and placed on probation?

Using our other examples, were white workers with the same record of absences and lateness merely warned and not fired? Was the female employee fired for complaining that she did not receive the same benefits as her male counterparts? If so, discrimination has occurred which must be redressed.

The information in this chapter will help you recognize when you have been victimized by discrimination. You will learn what practices are illegal and how to file a timely complaint, prove your charges, and collect damages for your claim. If you are being forced to work in a hostile and offensive environment and are the victim of sexual harassment, you will learn how to send letters to document the exploitation. Recent Supreme Court cases dealing with major discrimination subjects will also be discussed and analyzed to make this chapter as timely as possible.

## Federal and State Discrimination Laws

The most comprehensive and significant federal legislation dealing with employment discrimination is Title VII of the Civil Rights Act of 1964, as amended by the Equal Employment Opportunity Act of 1972. This law applies to companies employing fifteen or more persons and affects private employers, employment agencies, and labor organizations.

In addition to federal laws regulating the employment process, most states have also enacted antidiscrimination statutes relating to employment. These state statutes and the agencies that enforce them are highly significant. For example, many small employers not covered by Title VII *do* fall within the jurisdiction of state law, and some local laws are even more strict and inclusive.

Some of these even prohibit discrimination based on marital status, physical handicap, or sexual orientation. If you are forty to seventy years of age, black, a woman, pregnant, disabled, or otherwise identifiable as a minority, the EEOC under the federally enacted Civil Rights Act of 1964 will provide protection against unfair dismissal. But many states and municipalities have enacted their own laws that offer even greater protection; for example, age discrimination protection may apply to the young as well as those who are middle-aged and older, and homosexuals may be protected under local sex discrimination laws. If you want to learn whether you have this extra protection, contact an appropriate state or city agency or employment agency for further details, or speak to a knowledgeable labor attorney.

A question frequently asked by employers is: Which law takes precedence? The answer, essentially, is *the law that is the strictest*. Thus, to ensure proper protection of your rights, try to be familiar with federal *and* state laws as well as those laws governing employment in your local business community or municipality. If there is a difference in coverage on the same subject, seek to enforce the law that is the most favorable to your situation.

We will now discuss the elements of sex, race, and age discrimination and related subjects in greater detail.

## Sex Discrimination

Sex discrimination law encompasses many facets. The law mandates equal pay for equal work. It requires equal treatment, policies, standards, and practices for males and females in all phases of the employment relationship, including hiring, placement, job promotion, working conditions, wages and benefits, layoffs, and discharges. It is generally discriminatory in all states and under federal law to:

- Refuse to hire women with preschool-age children while hiring men with such children
- Require females to resign from jobs upon marriage when there is no similar requirement for males
- Include spouses of male employees in benefit plans while denying the same benefits to spouses of female employees
- Restrict certain jobs to men without offering women a reasonable opportunity to demonstrate their ability to perform the same job adequately
- Refuse to hire, train, assign, or promote pregnant or married women, or women of childbearing age on the basis of gender
- Deny unemployment or seniority benefits to pregnant women, or deny granting a leave of absence for pregnancy if similar leaves of absence are granted for illness
- Institute compulsory retirement plans with lower retirement ages for women than men

Numerous cases of women winning large verdicts for sex discrimination have been reported recently. For example, Chevron reportedly agreed to pay more than $8 million to settle a class action filed by 777 female employees who claimed they were discriminated against in terms of pay, promotions, and assignments. A New Jersey judge upheld a $7.1 million sex discrimination jury verdict against a company after the plaintiff successfully alleged that senior managers removed her accounts she had helped build and gave them to male brokers. After twelve years with the company, the woman was accused of poor productivity and fired. The verdict included a $5 million punitive damages award.

Publix reportedly agreed to pay $81.5 million to settle a class-action lawsuit by 150,000 women who accused the big grocery chain of relegating them to dead-end, low-paying jobs. The settlement applies to all women who worked at any of the 535 Publix stores in Florida, Georgia, South Carolina, and Alabama since 1981. The suit was brought in 1995 by eight women who accused Publix of passing them over for raises and repeatedly denying them management jobs. They and four others who quickly joined the case said they watched as men with less experience and less seniority got promotions. Some said their requests were met with unwanted sexual advances from managers. The EEOC later joined the suit, and it was expanded to a class action covering past and current employees.

Although the Publix settlement is the largest involving supermarket chains, Lucky Stores reportedly paid $107 million to 14,000 women to settle similar allegations. Albertson's reportedly paid a $29.4 million settlement to women and Hispanic workers, and Safeway Stores reportedly settled for $7.5 million in a 1994 sex discrimination suit covering 20,000 employees in California.

In a suit against State Farm in 1992, $250 million was reportedly paid to women who said they were denied or deterred from positions as insurance agents. And Home Depot faces a similar challenge from more than 20,000 current and former female employees who filed a class-action lawsuit claiming the company's personnel structure is set up to limit their access to sales jobs and supervisor and manager positions. The lawsuit claims women are placed in positions with fewer opportunities, while men are given jobs with greater advancement potential. The suit also alleges a pattern of sexual harassment and unequal pay. The case is currently proceeding to a jury trial.

## THE LAW

The Civil Rights Act of 1991 implemented a series of sweeping changes in federal antidiscrimination laws. The legislation expanded procedural options and remedies available to women and overruled a series of important U.S. Supreme Court decisions that limited employees' legal recourse. In doing so, Congress amended six different statutes that together prohibit discrimination based on race, color, religion, gender, national origin, disability, and age. Those statutes are Title VII of the Civil Rights Act of 1964, the Americans with Disabilities Act of 1990, the Vocational Rehabilitation Act of 1973, the Age Discrimination in Employment Act of 1967, the Civil Rights Act of 1866, and the Civil Rights Attorney's Fees Awards Act of 1976. Virtually all employers are covered by these laws.

The 1991 act prohibits discrimination in all aspects of the employment process, including compensation, assignment, classification of employees, demotions, transfers, promotions, wages and working conditions, recruitment, testing, use of company facilities, training programs, fringe benefits, retirement plans, disability leave, hiring, and discharges.

Retaliation and on-the-job harassment are also prohibited. This means that if you file a charge of discrimination in good faith, you cannot be fired, demoted, or reassigned while the case is pending. However, if you knew the claim had no merit and filed it in bad faith, you could be fired legally.

Prior to the Civil Rights Act of 1991, claimants typically could only receive their jobs back, together with retroactive job pay and restoration of seniority benefits. Now, in cases where intentional race, gender (including pregnancy), national origin, skin color, religion, or handicap discrimination can be proved, the act also authorizes jury trials, reasonable witness and attorney fees to be paid to the individual harmed, punitive damages, and compensatory damages up to $300,000 depending on the size of the employer. Compensatory damages are defined as money paid to compensate individuals for future pecuniary losses, emotional pain and suffering, inconvenience and mental anguish, loss of enjoyment, and physical pain and suffering. Compensatory damages are typically available only for intentional discrimination and unlawful harassment, and do not apply where a job practice is not intended to be discriminatory but nonetheless has an unlawful disparate impact on women or persons within another protected class, such as workers over forty.

Sex discrimination, also called gender discrimination, is legislated by Title VII of the Civil Rights Act of 1964 as well as the revised Civil Rights Act of 1991. Gender discrimination covers a variety of subjects and is protected by many laws, including the Equal Pay Act of 1963, which makes it illegal to discriminate against women concerning salary or wages, and the Pregnancy Discrimination Act of 1978, which prohibits discrimination on the basis of pregnancy, childbirth, and related medical conditions and health benefits. For more information on these subjects, please consult a later section in this chapter.

You may be the victim of sex discrimination when:

- You are receiving disparate treatment (i.e., being treated differently from other employees);
- You are being denied employment opportunities primarily because you are a woman; or
- The effect of a company policy or rule has a disproportionally negative effect on women in your company, causing an adverse impact.

It is also illegal for companies to use advertising that denies women a chance to apply for a job or screening procedures that eliminate female applicants because the requirements are too demanding (e.g., requiring a college degree for secretarial work). No longer can women not be considered for physical jobs, nor is it lawful for employers to refuse jobs to women because they think that their turnover rate is higher, they take more sick leave, or they may become pregnant. As mentioned in Chapter 1, any questions to women regarding their families or childbearing plans are illegal. In certain cases the law is also making it easier for women to claim that the reason they were passed over for a promotion, such as not being made a partner in an accounting firm, was their gender and not their work performance (which is sometimes offered by employers as a pretext). Speak to a lawyer for more details.

## SEXUAL HARASSMENT

Another prohibited form of sex discrimination is sexual harassment. In 1986 the Supreme Court ruled that sexual harassment was actionable under Title VII of the Civil Rights Act of 1964. Many thousands of cases are filed yearly with the EEOC and state agencies. In fact, studies indicate that the vast majority of workingwomen (more than 85 percent) believe they have been sexually harassed on the job at one time or another.

The newspapers are full of large verdicts that women are receiving in this area. In one case a former airline employee was awarded $7.1 million in punitive and compensatory damages for a sex-discrimination-harassment charge. In another recent case the EEOC obtained a $1.85 million settlement in a sexual harassment case on behalf of a group of ten women who had worked for a company as secretaries or executive assistants. The women complained that the company's chairman sought sexual favors in exchange for job benefits and had engaged in a pattern and practice of harassment against them by forcing them to discuss sex acts, touching them in their private parts, and other harmful acts. The money is to be divided among the women based primarily on their seniority. Additionally, as part of the settlement, the employer must provide individualized counseling and training for all its employees nationwide, hire an outside consultant and several new employees to respond to sexual harassment complaints, and institute a toll-free number for reporting sexual harassment.

Sexual harassment cases are on the rise in a variety of non-traditional areas. For example, sexual harassment was found in one case when female employees were required to wear revealing uniforms and suffer derogatory comments from passersby. In another case a jury awarded $196,500 in damages to a man who claimed his supervisor demoted him because he refused her sexual advances. According to court testimony, the employee and his supervisor met one night in a hotel room, but the man refused to continue the relationship. The man proved he was demoted and passed over for a promotion as a result. In another case the termination of a male employee for rejecting the advances of his homosexual male supervisor proved costly to a company.

The Supreme Court recently ruled that same-sex sexual harassment is actionable. This cleared the way for *anyone* who is sexually harassed by supervisors or employees of the same sex to proceed with sexual harassment cases in federal and state courts.

Imaginative lawyers representing claimants in sexual harassment suits are also asserting other nontraditional causes of action in federal and state courts. These include wrongful discharge, fraud, intentional infliction of emotional distress for outrageous conduct, invasion of privacy, and assault and civil battery. Additionally, the Supreme Court in *Harris v. Forklift Systems, Inc.,* in 1993 made it easier for plaintiffs asserting such actions by ruling that they were not required to prove that any abusive conduct actually caused an injury or affected the person's psychological well-being. Lawyers representing claimants now only have to show that a "reasonable person" would have found the conduct to be offensive.

### Definition of Sexual Harassment

Unwelcome sexual advances, requests for sexual favors, and verbal or physical conduct of a sexual nature all constitute sexual harassment when:

- The person must submit to such activity in order to be hired;
- The person's consent or refusal is used in making an employment decision (e.g., to offer a raise or promotion); or
- Such conduct unreasonably interferes with the person's work performance or creates an intimidating, hostile, or offensive working environment (e.g., humiliating comments are repeatedly addressed to the complainant).

Defining what constitutes sexual harassment depends on the facts of each particular case. In *quid pro quo* cases (instances when employees of either gender are propositioned for sexual favors in order to receive a job, raise, or promotion), the issue may be clear-cut. If a person is passed over for a promotion or denied benefits in favor of an individual who submitted to sexual advances, the passed-over person is considered to be a victim of sexual harassment under federal and state guidelines.

Additionally, if a worker initially participates in social or sexual contact, but then rejects continued advances, that constitutes sexual harassment in most instances. The fact that the person does not regularly communicate her negative reaction may not exculpate the company from liability.

In hostile, intimidating, and unprofessional work environment cases, the issues are not always clear-cut. Typically, to establish a *prima facie* case, the employee must prove that:

1. She was subjected to unwelcome sexual conduct;
2. The unwelcome sexual conduct was based on her gender;
3. The unwelcome sexual conduct was sufficiently pervasive or severe to alter the terms and conditions of her employment and create an abusive or hostile working environment; *and*
4. The employer knew or should have known of the harassment and failed to take prompt and reasonable remedial action

Courts have ruled the following to constitute sexual harassment with respect to hostile, intimidating work environment cases:

- Extremely vulgar and sexually related epithets, jokes, or crusty language, provided the language is not isolated and is continuously stated to the complainant
- Sexually suggestive comments about an employee's attire or body
- Sexually degrading words describing an employee
- Repeated touching of the employee's body, provided the touching is unsolicited and unwelcome
- Showing lewd photographs or objects of a sexual nature to employees at the workplace
- Offensive or repeated requests for dates, even if the calls are made to the complainant after work
- Continued advances of a sexual nature that the employee rejects, even after the parties break off a consensual sexual relationship
- Requiring females to wear revealing uniforms and suffer derogatory comments from nonemployees

How the company investigates and acts on complaints may be a major factor in determining whether it will end up in court and incur substantial damages. In 1998 the Supreme Court clarified the law on sexual harassment in the workplace, making some lawsuits against employers easier to win while also possibly limiting the legal exposure of companies that have effective antiharassment policies in place (provided the effect of any harassment was not recognizable or severe). In a series of cases decided together, the Court first ruled that employers are *strictly liable* for the acts of their supervisors and managers when the harassment results in tangible harmful action, such as discharge, demotion, transfer, or other retaliation of the complainant. This is so regardless of whether the employer knew or should have known that harassment was taking place. Thus, when you can prove that serious harassment from a supervisor took place and resulted in damages (such as a lost job opportunity), the employer will probably lose the case.

However, when there has been no detrimental action taken (for example, an employee, although propositioned repeatedly by a supervisor, refuses his advances and gets promoted anyway), an employee is allowed to proceed with a lawsuit and recover modest damages, but the employer may defend itself by proving it has taken reasonable care to prevent and promptly correct any sexually harassing behavior (such as by adopting an effective policy with a complaint procedure) *and* proving that the employee failed to unreasonably take advantage of such corrective mechanisms by remaining silent instead of coming forward to complain.

As a result of these cases, courts will now carefully look to see if a comprehensive policy against sexual harassment was in place at the time the incidents occurred and whether the employer acted properly and promptly when notified of the complaint. When policies are vague or the complaint is not immediately and adequately investigated, or if the complainant is punished in any way for coming forward, the company may be found liable if the facts are true. Experts suggest that the practical effect of these rulings will be for employers to take a more active role in eliminating workplace harassment, such as by training workers in identifying and preventing lewd behavior.

Many employers have begun disseminating periodic reminders in policy manuals, journals, and letters distributed to employees that the company does not tolerate sexual harassment of any kind on the job, that anyone who experiences or observes such treatment should report this to management or their immediate supervisor (but not to the one doing the harassing) immediately, and that all communications will he held in strict confidence with no direct or indirect reprisals to the informant or complainant. In addition, companies are taking steps to instruct supervisors about sexual harassment and other forms of discrimination, what the adverse effects on the company could be, and ways to handle problems if they arise.

## How to Prove Sexual Harassment

Courts consider the nature and frequency of the acts, the conditions under which the conduct occurred, whether the company was promptly notified by the complainant, and what steps, if any, the company took after being notified. To prove a case of sex harassment, it is crucial to take prompt steps to document your claim. For example, if you are being teased on the job, it is wise to complain to a supervisor or manager *in writing* immediately after the incident occurred. Judges, arbitrators, and EEOC hearing officers are more willing to award damages for sex harassment when a formal complaint was made requesting that the offensive conduct stop and *the request was ignored.*

---

**STRATEGY:** *By sending a letter you notify the company of the allegations. When an employer does not properly investigate a claim, it can further compound the problem and be legally exposed. Most important, you have proof that a formal complaint was made. If the company then takes any negative action against you in retaliation, you may be able to prove the retaliation occurred after—and because—the letter was sent.*

*Send a copy of this letter to the president or other high officer of the company. Always keep a copy for your files. Save the receipt to prove delivery. If you feel you are the victim of harassment, discuss the incident with the other employees you trust to discover if they have suffered similar abuse. By doing so, you may strengthen a claim and be less at risk for making a complaint, since there is always safety in numbers. For example, it was recently reported that a sexual harassment and discrimination lawsuit against a well-known investment firm was amended to include twenty more women in a total of eleven states. The newest plaintiffs joined the action (which was started by one woman only) and alleged being subjected to lewd language, unwelcome touching, and being denied opportunities and privileges afforded men. The suit seeks class-action status on behalf of all women employed by the firm, in part for the company's alleged explicit descriptions and sexual talk in the basement of one of its offices.*

---

If possible, collect and save evidence (e.g., the pornographic pictures shown to you). Maintain a diary of all incidents of harassment recalling the location, events, time, persons involved, and name of any witnesses who may have observed the illegal conduct. Recall whether supervisors participated in creating or tolerating a sexually poisoned atmosphere.

Speak to an experienced employment lawyer immediately if:

- The matter is not resolved satisfactorily
- You are retaliated against for making a complaint, such as being demoted, reassigned, denied benefits or a promotion, receive an unfavorable job evaluation, or are fired
- You feel uncomfortable while being questioned about the events (i.e., the company is not conducting a fair and unbiased investigation and is accusing you of contributing to or causing the harassment by your dress, behavior, or language)
- The employer fails to take speedy action to investigate your complaints
- You wish to pursue money damages for stress, mental suffering, and physical injuries caused or induced by the harassment
- The company mistakenly determines that no harassment occurred, that the acts do not constitute harassment, that it had no knowledge of the incident and thus is not responsible, or fails to make a decision in an objective manner
- The employer disparages your character, job performance, or family life

- The employer refuses to allow you to grieve the incident through its complaint procedures

An experienced lawyer can tell you whether it makes sense to confront the harasser, use a company complaint procedure, immediately file a claim in court or with an appropriate federal agency (such as the EEOC) or a state agency, or, if more desirable and/or advantageous, to contact the employer and try to settle the matter out of court.

## Sample Letter Protesting Sexual Harassment

Your Name
Address
Telephone Number
Date

Name of Supervisor or Officer
Title
Name of Employer
Address

Dear (Name):

While working for the company, I have been the victim of a series of offensive acts that I believe constitute sexual harassment.

On (date), I (describe what occurred and with whom). I immediately (describe your reaction) and ordered that such conduct stop. However, on (date), another incident occurred when (describe what occurred and with whom).

I find such behavior intimidating and repugnant. In fact, (describe the physical and emotional impact on you), causing me to be less efficient on the job. Please treat this letter as a formal protest of such conduct. Unless such conduct ceases immediately, or in the event the company illegally retaliates against me for writing this letter, I will contact the Equal Employment Opportunity Commission to enforce my rights.

I do not wish to take such a drastic measure. All I want to do is perform my job in a professional environment.

Thank you for your cooperation in this matter.


Very truly yours,
Your Name


CONFIDENTIAL
*Sent certified mail, return receipt requested.*

---

**STRATEGY:** *Most states have laws that expressly prohibit sexual harassment; there are occasions when it might be advantageous to apply state law and file charges with a state agency instead of the EEOC. Talk to your lawyer about this. Consider filing a private tort lawsuit for assault and battery if you are touched, kissed, or rubbed without your consent. The advantage of being able to file a private lawsuit is that you may receive greater damages for your injuries and may be able to file a charge more than three hundred days after the acts occurred. Claimants who are not able to file a discrimination charge because the statute of limitations has expired may still be able to commence a private lawsuit in some cases. (By law, you are required to file a charge of discrimination with the EEOC within one hundred eighty days of the incident.)*

*In any event, do not be afraid to assert your rights when you are subjected to conduct you find uncomfortable. A course of strategy should be implemented immediately so you don't suffer more abuse and to protect your rights in this area. If you delay contacting an appropriate agency or lawyer, your inactivity may be viewed as a waiver of your rights or an acceptance of such illegal acts, which can jeopardize a claim.*

## RIGHTS OF MATERNITY, PREGNANCY LEAVE, CHILD CARE, AND DISABILITY

Childbirth leave and pregnancy-related disability are protected by numerous federal and state laws. In fact, the rights of pregnant workers have changed dramatically over the past few years.

Employers cannot treat pregnancy-related disability or maternity leave differently from the way they treat other forms of disability or leaves of absence. To do so violates both federal and state discrimination laws. The Pregnancy Discrimination Act of 1978, an amendment to Title VII of the federal Civil Rights Act of 1964, prohibits discrimination on the basis of pregnancy, childbirth, and related medical conditions. The law requires employers to review their health, disability, insurance, sick leave, benefit, job reinstatement, and seniority policies to ensure that they treat pregnancy-related disability and maternity leaves of absence the same as other temporary absences for physical disabilities.

The following general rules illustrate what employers may and may not do in this area:

- Employees who are on maternity leave (defined as the child-care period commencing after disability from the pregnancy and birth has ended) are entitled to accrue seniority, automatic pay increases, and vacation time on the same basis as other employees on medical leave.
- Employers may not require pregnant workers to exhaust vacation benefits unless all temporarily disabled workers are required to do the same.
- Employers may require a physical examination and doctor's certification of ability to return to work only if such is required of all temporarily disabled workers.
- Although employers may require workers to give notice of a pregnancy, such requirement must serve a legitimate business purpose and must not be used to restrict the employee's job opportunities.

- Employers are prohibited from discriminating in hiring, promotion, and firing decisions on the basis of pregnancy or because of an abortion.
- After a birth, an employer cannot prohibit a woman from returning to work sooner than company policy dictates.
- Employers are barred from forcing pregnant workers to take mandatory maternity leaves (i.e., forcing a woman to leave work against her wishes in anticipation of giving birth) as long as the employee is able to do her job.
- The decision as to whether payment for pregnancy disability leave will be given must be in accord with policies governing other forms of disability leave; if paid leave is provided for workers with other disabilities, the employer must provide pregnant workers with paid leave for their actual disability due to pregnancy and related childbirth.
- Time restrictions based on pregnancy-related leaves (e.g., that pregnancy leaves not exceed four months) must be reasonable and job-related; if not, they may be illegal. In addition, employers are generally required to provide disability benefits for as long as a pregnant woman is unable to work for medical reasons.
- It is illegal to place pregnant workers on involuntary sick leave if the company has no policy of placing workers with other forms of disabilities on involuntary leave; if a worker is physically able to work, the company cannot force her to leave merely because she is pregnant.
- An employer cannot refuse to hire a pregnant worker because it does not want to find a replacement when the employee takes a leave to give birth if her skills and qualifications meet or exceed those of other applicants.
- Women who take maternity leave must be reinstated under the same conditions as employees who return from leaves for other disabilities. For example, if an employer reinstates a worker who was absent from work due to a case of chronic

bronchitis, the employer must reinstate a worker after child-birth to avoid violating Title VII.

- If an employer accommodates partially disabled workers who cannot perform certain job assignments (such as lifting heavy objects because of a strained back), the employer is obligated to make similar arrangements for a pregnant worker.
- Employers cannot limit pregnancy disability benefits to married employees. Federal law states it is illegal to fire female workers who get married if the employer does not fire male workers who get married. Many state laws have gone even further to protect women; statutes have been enacted that prohibit employers from making any adverse decisions on the basis of a person's marital status even if the employer applies its policies equally to males and females.
- At the hiring interview, you cannot be asked questions about childbearing plans or pregnancy.
- Employers are not allowed to ask a pregnant employee to choose between a lower-level job and resignation.

The above rules may not apply, depending on the law and the particular facts and circumstances of your case. Always consult an experienced employment lawyer for advice and guidance.

Although pregnant workers were subject to poor treatment from employers in the past, the laws are now attempting to put pregnant women on an equal footing with other employees. The number of pregnancy discrimination claims filed with the EEOC increased by more than 33 percent between 1991 and 1995. While an estimated 84 percent of women expecting children work into the final month of pregnancy, and about one-third return to work within eight weeks and half within three months of giving birth, millions of women have lost their jobs after giving birth. Fortunately, with the passage of the Family and Medical Leave Act (discussed in the next section), pregnant women who work for employers with more than fifty full-time employees are guaranteed equivalent jobs when they return.

Speak to a competent employment lawyer if you feel you have been discriminated against on the basis of pregnancy. Women who are fired while pregnant should naturally suspect that pregnancy was the reason for the discharge. Consider filing a claim alleging pregnancy discrimination with the EEOC or appropriate state antidiscrimination agency. The filing is free, and you do not need a lawyer to assist you in the process. Information on how to file a discrimination charge is given later in this chapter.

Employers are often advised that even when a decision to fire has nothing to do with a woman's pregnancy, it may be wise to continue her employment until she voluntarily leaves to give birth, rather than fire her several months before the birth, to avoid the added costs and burdens of contesting a charge of pregnancy discrimination. Employers are also advised by their attorneys that if they must fire a pregnant worker, they should be sure that her file supports the decision (i.e., that unfavorable job performance appraisals and repeated written warnings are present in the file and the worker was repeatedly warned about her performance before the company was notified of her pregnancy).

*Strategies to Strengthen a Claim*

1. Tell your supervisor and other bosses immediately after you learn that you are pregnant. Once you become pregnant, you enter a protected class under the law, and the company may have to reevaluate any decision to fire you if that was being considered before your notification. Thus, in marginal performance cases, becoming pregnant could give you added job security. Some litigants lose their cases, however, because they cannot prove the company knew they were pregnant before taking adverse action. Do not be afraid to tell key people at the job site that you are pregnant, since this may work to your legal benefit.
2. Understand your options to take paid short-term and long-term disability leaves and unpaid leaves.

3. Be aware of how the company treated pregnant workers in the past for comparison purposes.

4. Remember that the payment of costs for pregnancy-related conditions may be limited to a specific dollar amount stipulated in an insurance policy, collective bargaining agreement, or other statement of employee benefits, provided limits are imposed for other health conditions.

5. Always read and understand your employer's health insurance policies and coverage before incurring medical treatment.

6. If you are offered a choice between enrolling in one of two health insurance plans, be sure to choose the one that covers pregnancy-related conditions so that you will be reimbursed on the same basis as for other medical conditions.

7. Employers are not generally responsible for providing health insurance covering abortions. However, they are required to offer sick leave and other fringe benefits as a result of an abortion. Additionally, while some health plans do not pay for abortions, they do cover complications resulting from the procedure, such as treatment due to excessive bleeding. Always read the fine print of your policy to determine your options.

Although the ADA does *not* consider pregnancy a covered disability (since it is classified as a temporary nonchronic impairment with no long-term impact), some state laws have ruled it as a per se disability requiring a company to make reasonable accommodation when requested by an employee. Under these state laws, the physical demands of pregnancy may require companies to allow pregnant workers to work at home or rearrange their work schedules. When a woman seeks reasonable accommodation during pregnancy, an employer should be responsive to the particular physical limitations that the employee brings forward on a case-by-case basis. Employers unwilling to comply with such a request are required to justify their decisions by demonstrating that compliance would create an undue hardship.

---

**STRATEGY:** *Check your state's law on this issue to understand the extent of protection available to you. If you find the law is favorable, consider requesting reasonable accommodation (such as reporting to work an hour later each day or being allowed to work from bed if you risk losing a baby without extensive bed rest). Speak to a lawyer for more details.*

---

Also speak to a lawyer whenever you believe that your pregnancy is being used as an excuse for downgrading your performance rating or removing you from the fast track for promotions. Employers must demonstrate legitimate business reasons for all decisions impacting you. This includes a scrutiny of your performance. When the company promotes a nonpregnant employee over you but cannot demonstrate the other person's superior qualifications, educational background, or accomplishments, speak to an experienced employment lawyer immediately. This is also true when you experience insensitive remarks, are not given the opportunity to make your own decisions regarding hazardous jobs, or believe that you have not been dealt with in a consistent, even-handed way compared to nonpregnant workers at the company.

*Pregnancy Leave and Reemployment*

Even before the enactment of the Family and Medical Leave Act (FMLA) in 1993, the rights of pregnant workers to have their jobs back within a certain period of time after giving birth and the ability to enforce the right to take paid maternity leave were being recognized in a number of states. Passage of the FMLA guarantees that pregnant workers who work for companies with fifty or more employees will get their jobs back after giving birth. The act affects private and nonprofit employers as well as federal, state, and local government employees, public agencies, and private elementary and secondary schools. It applies to companies that employ fifty or more employees within a seventy-five-mile radius for each working day for each of twenty or more calendar workweeks in the current or preceding calendar year. This is about half of the nation's workforce. Part-time employees and employees on leaves of absence are counted in this calculation provided they are on the employer's payroll for each day of the workweek. Conversely, employees who began employment after the beginning of a workweek, were terminated prior to the end of a workweek, or who worked part-time on weekends are not included in the equation.

Since companies with fewer than fifty employees are exempt, analyzing the number of employees who must be counted becomes an important consideration for organizations close to the "magic" fifty number. If a company hires temporary, contract employees or part-time workers who work twenty-five or fewer hours a week to get under the number, they will not be subject to the law's provisions.

An eligible employee, defined as someone who has been employed for at least twelve months and worked for the employer at least 1,250 hours during the twelve-month period immediately preceding the commencement of the leave, is allowed to take up to twelve weeks of unpaid leave in any twelve-month period for:

- The birth of a child (commencing from the date of the birth of the child)
- The adoption of a child (commencing from the date of the adoption)
- The care of a child, dependent son or daughter over the age of thirteen, spouse, or parent with a serious health condition
- Convalescence from a serious condition that makes it impossible for the employee to work

(Note: The twelve months of employment need not have been consecutive.)

Under the law, a "serious health condition" is defined as an illness, injury, impairment, or physical or mental condition requiring either inpatient care at a hospital, hospice, or residential medical care facility, or continuing treatment by a health care provider. Thus, an overnight stay in a hospital, any condition requiring absence from work of more than three consecutive calendar days, or a health condition that demands continued treatment by a health care provider may qualify. This includes voluntary or cosmetic treatments if inpatient hospital care is required, restorative dental surgery after an accident, and continued treatment for serious allergies, stress, or for substance abuse.

Thus, some employees who require continuing medical supervision (i.e., workers with early-stage cancer or who have major heart surgery) and must undergo frequent medical examinations or treatment but are nonetheless capable of working part-time still fit into the category of suffering from a "serious health condition" and qualify for leave time.

For those workers claiming serious health situations, the law permits an employer to obtain medical opinions and certifications regarding the need for a leave. The certification must state the date on which the serious health condition began, its probable duration, the appropriate medical facts within the knowledge of the health care provider regarding the condition, and an estimate of the amount of time the employee needs to care for a family member or herself. If an employer has doubts about the certification, it may require a second opinion from a different health care provider chosen by the employer. If the two opinions differ, a third opinion from a provider jointly designated or approved by the employer and the employee will be final and binding.

The law applies equally to female and male employees. Thus, a father, as well as a mother, can take family leave, at the same time or sequentially, depending on the family's preferences and economic considerations. (If both spouses work for the same company, the law limits the total amount of leave to twelve weeks for both in some situations, but not to care for themselves, their spouse, or a child.)

Although written notice is not generally required, workers who qualify for unpaid leave are required to give thirty days' advance notice unless this is not practicable or foreseeable, such as in a premature birth or sudden, unexpected illness. If thirty days' notice cannot be given, notice must be given as soon as practicable. You are required to make a reasonable effort to schedule the leave so as not to unduly disrupt the employer's operations.

It is not necessary to state that you require FMLA leave. Rather, it is sufficient only to indicate that time is needed and provide some details why. After your notice is received, the employer has an immediate obligation to provide you with a written statement concerning your rights, duties, and obligations within two business days. The written notice must provide you with answers to the following:

- Whether the leave will be counted against your annual FMLA entitlement
- Whether you are required to submit medical certification
- Your right to paid leave and if this will be substituted by the employer for FMLA purposes
- Any requirements for you to make premium payments to maintain health benefits
- Your liability for medical premiums paid by the employer during your absence if you do not return to work after the leave
- Your right to receive the same or an equivalent job upon your return
- Any requirement that you must present a certification stating your fitness before returning
- Whether you are considered a key employee under the FMLA and therefore not entitled to coverage

If such a timely notice is not received, the law presumes that you are qualified to take FMLA leave as soon as practicable. If you receive answers that you do not agree with, consult an employment lawyer immediately.

The key element of the law allows a person taking leave to be given her old job back or assigned an equivalent position, with equivalent benefits, pay, and other terms and conditions of employment, when she returns. The burden is on the employer to give the worker back her same or an equivalent job (not a comparable job) wherever possible.

An equivalent position is one that is virtually identical to the employee's former position in terms of pay, benefits, and working conditions, including privileges, perquisites, and status. It must involve the same or substantially similar duties and equivalent skill, effort, responsibility, and authority. The job must be in the same geographic proximity and offer the same opportunities for bonuses, profit sharing, salary increases, promotions, additional health insurance sick leave, and educational benefits.

No employer may deprive an employee of benefits accrued before the date on which the leave commenced. During the time the worker is on leave, an employer is not required to pay her but is required to maintain health insurance benefits, as well as life and disability insurance, pensions, educational benefits, and any annual sick leave that has accrued prior to the commencement of the family leave, at the level and under the conditions coverage would have been maintained if the employee had continued in employment. However, if the employer was legitimately about to lay off the worker just before being notified of the leave, the employee's right of reinstatement is no greater than what it was when the discharge occurred.

Nothing requires an employer to provide health benefits if it does not do so at the time the employee commences leave. However, if the employer was considering establishing a health plan during the employee's leave, the worker on leave is entitled to receive the same benefits other workers still on the job receive. However, an employer has the right to demand repayment for the group health care premiums paid by the employer during the leave if the employee fails to return after the period of leave to which she is entitled has expired and the reason was not caused by a recurrence or onset of a serious health condition or other circumstances beyond her control.

An employee may refuse to make the contributions during the leave period but still must be offered health insurance on the same terms and conditions when returning to work. If that occurs, the employer cannot require you to undergo a new health insurance qualifying period or a physical, or impose other restrictions that did not exist prior to your leave. Finally, if the health insurance plan benefits improved during your absence, you are entitled to those improved benefits upon your return.

There are numerous exceptions to be aware of. First, the FMLA prohibits a worker on leave from collecting unemployment or other government compensation. Part-time workers and those who have not worked for at least a year do not qualify for FMLA leave. In addition, an eligible employee may elect, or an employer is permitted, to substitute any accrued paid vacation leave, personal leave, or family leave of the employee under preestablished policies in handbooks or employee manuals for any part of the twelve-week period of family leave. As a result, companies are required to provide both paid and unpaid leave only up to a total of twelve weeks, and employers may count time off against paid vacation days or other accrued personal leave.

The leave request may not generally be intermittent or on a reduced schedule without the employer's permission or except when medically necessary; employers are permitted to require an employee taking intermittent leave as a result of planned medical treatments to prove the medical necessity of the leave and to transfer temporarily to an equivalent alternative position. Thus, for example, employers may have the right to demand that pregnant workers take the time off in a continuous period and then return. This provision gives employers greater staffing flexibility by enabling them to transfer employees who need intermittent leave or leave on a reduced schedule to positions that are more suitable for recurring periods of leave.

If you are a top executive (defined as being in the highest 10 percent of the company's payroll), the company may refuse your request to take leave when it would cause substantial economic harm. If you nonetheless take the leave, you are still eligible for continuation of medical benefits but the company is not obligated to take you back or guarantee that an appropriate job will be available upon your return. However, in such situations, no recovery of premiums may be made by the employer if the employee has chosen to take or continue leave after being denied her request for leave because she is ill or needs to continue the care of a relative or child. (If the employee refuses to come back because she took a better-paying job, the company can lawfully demand repayment.)

While you are on leave, economic benefits such as employer-contributed pension and profit-sharing payments and vacation pay do not continue to accrue unless you are receiving full pay with benefits. When in doubt, ask your employer about your entitlement to such continued benefits before you go out on FMLA leave.

The Secretary of Labor has the authority to investigate alleged violations of the FMLA. This includes requesting employers to submit their books and records for inspection. Violations are punishable by injunctive and monetary relief. For employers who violate the law, monetary damages include an amount equal to the wages, salary, employment benefits, or other compensation denied or lost to an employee. In cases where no compensation or wages are lost, the law imposes other forms of damages, such as the actual amount of out-of-pocket money paid to someone else to provide care. In the event a willful violation is proved, employers are liable for additional damages equal to the amount of the award. The law also imposes reasonable compensation for attorney fees, expert witness fees, and other costs and disbursements. Employers are forbidden from discriminating against workers who attempt to utilize the act or who protest alleged violations. Similarly, it is unlawful to retaliate against any worker by discharge or reduced benefits because the employee has filed a charge or instituted a proceeding concerning the law or is about to give (or has given) testimony regarding the FMLA.

## Hazardous Jobs

The Supreme Court has ruled that employers cannot ban women from certain hazardous jobs, even if the motive is preventing birth defects in fetuses those female workers may be carrying. In an important ruling, the Supreme Court decided that a manufacturer acted illegally by prohibiting women capable of bearing children from holding jobs involving exposure to lead during the manufacture of batteries. The Court determined that such a policy forces some women to choose between having a child and keeping a job, and this violated federal laws against sex discrimination.

*Conclusion:* Speak to a lawyer immediately or contact your nearest Equal Employment Opportunity Commission district office or state commission on human rights office if you believe you were fired, demoted, or denied benefits on the basis of pregnancy. An experienced labor lawyer or agency representative can help you weigh your options to achieve the quickest and most satisfactory results.

Do not be pressured or intimidated into accepting a decision that appears to be unfair. To avoid misunderstandings, request a full explanation of your benefits and options with a duly authorized representative of the company. Go in with a ballpark proposal and be prepared to *negotiate* certain benefits, because many items are negotiable (no matter what you are told). Then if you are unsatisfied, weigh all your options carefully and be apprised of the law in this area to protect your rights. Remember, all actions taken by the employer must be justified under the law. The burden of proving that decisions are appropriate and necessary falls on the employer, since any practice that excludes employment or denies benefits on the basis of pregnancy is closely scrutinized. In addition, if there is an investigation into such charges, a company faces the risk of having the Equal Employment Opportunity Commission and other agency investigators evaluate treatment accorded other employees returning after nonmaternity leaves of absence.

Thus, never be afraid to assert your rights. You may discover that the employer will have no choice but to respond favorably to your demands to avoid potential problems and investigations.

## RETIREMENT PLANS AND FRINGE BENEFITS

Besides unequal pay for equal work, retirement, pension plans, and fringe benefits are often found to be unequally applied; any program that favors one gender over another violates federal and state discrimination laws.

Be aware that the following practices have been declared illegal in the application of fringe benefits pertaining to vacations, insurance coverage, pensions, profit-sharing plans, bonuses, holidays, and disability leaves:

- Providing benefits to employees and their spouses and families on the basis of a particular status (e.g., "head of household" or "principal wage earner")
- Making certain benefits available to wives of male employees but denying them to husbands of female employees
- Basing provisions of a pension plan on norms applied differently according to gender
- Denying a job or benefit to pregnant employees or applicants

These are just some of the ways employees commit violations pertaining to benefits. If you have doubts about any current practices, seek competent legal advice at once.

## PREEMPLOYMENT SCREENING

Although common illegal practices in this area were discussed in Chapter 1, it is worthwhile to mention this again. Unfortunately, many employers ask illegal questions of females at job interviews, particularly with respect to their marital status. Federal Equal Employment Opportunity Commission guidelines and state regulations declare that the only lawful question that may be asked of a female applicant is "What is your marital status?"

Familiarize yourself with the kinds of questions that are illegal at job interviews. Then if you refuse to answer such questions and are denied a job as a result, you may wish to consider filing charges with the EEOC or appropriate state rights organization alleging sex discrimination on the basis of such illegal inquiries.

## Age Discrimination

Federal and state discrimination laws are designed to promote employment of older persons based on their abilities, irrespective of age. The most important federal law, the Age Discrimination in Employment Act (ADEA), protects workers over forty from being arbitrarily fired, refused a job, forced to retire, or treated unfairly with respect to pay, promotions, benefits, health care coverage, retirement plans, and other employment opportunities because of age. The ADEA governs all private employers with fifteen or more workers. It also protects employees of labor organizations, unions, and local, state, and federal governments. Many states have enacted even tougher laws protecting workers by reducing the number of employees an employer must have to be subject to the law or reducing the cutoff age for inclusion into a protected class (age thirty in a few states).

The following thumbnail sketch outlines what employers can generally do under the ADEA and state discrimination laws pertaining to age:

• Fire older workers for documented, inadequate job performance or good cause (e.g., excessive tardiness or absences)

- Entice older workers into early retirement by offering additional benefits, such as bigger pensions, extended health insurance, or substantial severance packages, that are *voluntarily* accepted
- Force employees to retire if the worker is sixty-five or older, has worked as an executive for the past two years, and is entitled to a pension exceeding $44,000, or if the job calls for physical fitness (e.g., airline pilots or police officers) and age is recognized as a bona fide occupational qualification (BFOQ) factor in fitness and job performance
- Lay off older workers when younger employees are similarly treated
- Refuse to hire older applicants when successful job performance absolutely requires that a younger person be hired for the job (e.g., in the case of flight controllers)
- Make adverse decisions provided the acts are taken as a result of a demonstrated good-faith business decision that does not have a discriminatory impact on all older workers at the company

Some employers may legally discriminate against older workers when they hire independent contractors (which the law doesn't generally protect) or employ fewer than fifteen workers and there is no state antidiscrimination law to protect the rights of older workers. Always check the law of your state to see what protection is available if you work for a small employer or are an independent contractor. Additionally, since some state agencies process discrimination cases more quickly than the EEOC and provide greater damages and remedies under applicable state law, consider pursuing your rights with a state agency or in state court after discussing your options with a labor lawyer.

The following actions are generally prohibited by federal and state law:

- Denying an older applicant a job on the basis of age
- Imposing compulsory retirement before age seventy
- Forcing older employees into retirement by threatening them with termination or loss of benefits, unless the company has instituted a valid seniority system or retirement plan
- Firing older workers because of age
- Denying promotions, transfers, or assignments because of age
- Penalizing older employees with reduced privileges, employment opportunities, or compensation because of age

Significant damages are recoverable when workers receive unfair treatment because of age. These may include job reinstatement in the event of a firing, wage adjustments, back pay and double back pay, future pay, promotions, recovery of legal fees, witness fees, and filing costs, compensatory damages up to $300,000 depending on the size of the employer, and punitive damages. Recourse can also include the institution of an affirmative action program on behalf of fellow employees, counseling, and enhanced outplacement assistance.

Whenever an older employee (over forty) is fired and that individual is claiming discrimination, the issue is basically whether the company's decision was made because of age or was the result of a reasonable, nondiscriminatory rational business reason. Typically, the older worker must use circumstantial evidence to prove an employer's motive was improper. This is sometimes done by demonstrating she was between forty and seventy years of age, was doing satisfactory work, and was fired, and the position was then filled by a substantially younger employee under forty. If a younger male employee replaces her, the female employee may also have a claim for sex discrimination. However, when employers support firing decisions with documentation of poor work performance or other factors, an older female worker's chances of proving age discrimination diminish.

**STRATEGY:** *It is easier to prove age discrimination when age-related statements are made to or about the claimant ("You are too old"; "Why don't you retire?") or by using statistics (e.g., that the company fired ten older workers in the past six months and replaced them all with employees under forty).*

However, when staff did not make liability-sensitive statements, remarks, or threats with respect to age and the employee is unable to demonstrate statistical proof that the company had a practice of firing older workers and replacing them with younger ones, the chances of success with a claim are reduced. A Supreme Court ruling that an employer's decision to lay off mostly older workers close to receiving vested retirement benefits did not, in and of itself, constitute age discrimination (even though the older workers were more severely affected by the discharge than younger workers) has not helped the cause of older workers asserting age claims. In that case the Court found that since the employer proffered a rational business justification for firing a large number of older workers (i.e., to save the company money, since older workers with the most seniority had the highest salaries), no illegality occurred. (The Supreme Court did say that the individuals might consider filing ERISA claims to protect forfeited retirement and severance benefits as a result of the company's actions.)

The following is a discussion of areas where age discrimination often occurs.

**Preemployment screening.** Employers sometimes set requirements that are too high or commit violations through illegal ads. Many make statements or ask questions during the hiring interview that are illegal. For example, discrimination against older applicants occurs when they are told by an interviewer that:

- They are "overqualified"
- They lack formal education credits even though they are

highly qualified by previous work experience and a college degree is not necessary for successful job performance
- They must take a preemployment physical that is unnecessary, not job-related, or not requested of all other applicants
- They are required to answer questions such as "How old are you?", "What is the date of your birth?", or "Why did you decide to seek employment at your age?"

With respect to preemployment questions concerning age, be aware that under federal and state guidelines, employers can only ask the applicant if he or she is between eighteen and sixty-five, and if not, to state his or her age. Any other type of question concerning age is illegal. If you refuse to answer such a question and believe you were denied a job as a result, consider contacting the EEOC, a local human rights commission office, or your state attorney general's office to pursue your rights.

**Physicals.** Companies sometimes require potential employees to take preemployment physicals. This is not legal as a result of the passage of the Americans with Disabilities Act. Physicals can be given only if they are directly related to successful job performance (e.g., a firefighter's job) and are required by all employees after a job has been offered, not before. Thus, employers are allowed to offer a job that is conditioned on passing a physical exam.

**Advertising.** Pay special attention to language in advertisements used to attract job candidates. As stated in Chapter 1, the ADEA prohibits companies from publishing advertisements indicating any preference, limitation, specification, or discrimination based on age. Thus, targeted advertisements containing language such as "Industrial management trainee, recent college degree," "Sales trainee, any recent degree," "Prefer recent college grad," or "Corporate attorney, 2–4 years out of law school" are illegal. However, help-wanted notices or advertisements that include a term or phrase such as "college graduate" or other education criterion, or specify a minimum age less than forty, such as "not under twenty-one," are not prohibited by federal statute.

**Job requirements.** When preparing criteria for a particular job, companies sometimes set a higher requirement than is necessary, to attract higher-caliber applicants. This may discriminate between classes of applicants. If you are an older applicant and believe a potential employer has established unwarranted requirements (such as a college degree) that are not job-related, be aware that you may have a valid case of age discrimination.

Simply showing that a younger individual was hired over a qualified older applicant does not prove age discrimination if the employer can show its decision was based on an honest evaluation of the candidate's qualifications (e.g., the rejected applicant would be bored or likely to leave upon finding a better job, or both). Furthermore, an employer is under no obligation to provide a laid-off employee with a job for which that person is overqualified. And when eliminating a position, an employer does not assume an obligation to retain or create a position for the displaced employee simply because the employee is within a protected class, such as being a female or over forty.

**Progressive discipline and warnings.** The practice of progressive discipline, in which notice is given to the employee of a company's dissatisfaction with his work performance, is used to reduce the risk of wrongful termination lawsuits. By documenting the incidence of employee disciplinary measures through precise records of conferences, warnings, probationary notices, remedial efforts, and other steps, employers sometimes demonstrate that an eventual termination was not due to a discriminatory motive but stemmed from a good-faith business decision.

Many companies, however, apply their system of discipline and warnings in a haphazard fashion and fail to use the same punishment for similar infractions. This often invites a discrimination lawsuit if there are several employees with a chronic problem (such as absenteeism) and the older worker (or the female) is the first to be fired for that reason while workers under forty (or males) are only given a warning.

---

**STRATEGY:** *If you are an older worker who believes that an employer is treating you more harshly than younger workers for identical infractions, or you are receiving dissimilar, unfair on-the-job treatment with respect to benefits, promotions, or other matters, speak to an employment lawyer for advice.*

---

**Seniority rights and vacation time.** Nothing in the federal laws barring age discrimination prohibits employers from altering the terms of a benefit seniority system provided the new system is not a subterfuge for engaging in arbitrary age discrimination. For example, when companies change vacation pay policies by putting a cap on the amount of annual paid vacation a person can take, regardless of seniority (thus penalizing older workers who have more seniority), or reduce medical insurance and retiree benefit plans, such acts are legal where justified by significant cost considerations. However, the burden falls on the employer to justify that its actions are lawful.

**Retirement plans and forced retirement.** This is an area where older executives are often exploited. It occurs when companies exert pressure on older workers to opt for early retirement or face firing, demotion, a cut in pay, or poor recommendations. Companies contemplating a large layoff or seeking to reduce payroll through early retirement incentives must do so carefully to avoid charges of age discrimination. Under the ADEA and in most states, it is illegal to impose compulsory retirement before age seventy unless the employee is a "bona fide executive" receiving an annual company-paid retirement benefit of at least $44,000 per year after reaching sixty-five, or is in a "high policy-making position" during a two-year period prior to reaching age sixty-five.

Some states have passed similar laws to protect older employees from being victimized by forced retirement and mandatory retirement plans. For example, New York has a law that prohibits most public employees from being forced to retire, no matter how old they get (except for firefighters, police officers and other law enforcement positions). Private sector employees (with limited exceptions for some executives and tenured college faculty members) are also protected.

If the employer can show that a retirement plan is "bona fide" (e.g., plan benefits are based on an employee's length of service), that the employee's decision to accept early retirement is voluntary, and that the reasons for the plan are nondiscriminatory (i.e., not based on age), a plan may not violate the ADEA. If an employee can no longer perform her job duties, the employer may be allowed to discharge her or, alternatively, force her to retire (depending on the circumstances).

Ask yourself the following questions if you believe you were fired because of age:

- Did you request a transfer to another position before you were fired? Was it refused? If so, were similar requests granted to younger workers?
- How were you terminated? Were you given false reasons for the termination? Did you consent to the action or did you protest (such as by sending a certified letter to the company refuting the discharge)?
- Were you replaced by a younger worker under forty (or between forty and fifty if you are between sixty and sixty-five)? Were younger workers merely laid off and not fired (i.e., rehired several months later)?

Positive answers to these questions may prove you were fired as a result of age discrimination. Your case will be strengthened when fellow employees are also victimized. In one case, for example, 143 persons were forced to retire prematurely from an insurance company at the age of sixty-two. The large number of older employees all the same age made it difficult for the company to claim it was a valid reduction in force (called RIF), and the workers collectively received more than $6 million in back wages.

Before implementing a RIF, companies must take steps to ensure they have acted properly. For example, if they have a practice of permitting "bumping" or transfers before a discharge, not extending such opportunities to older workers during a RIF may give rise to a claim of disparate treatment. Selection of individuals for layoff based on their current cost of retention may also be unlawful where wage and benefit rates are found to be a function of length of service and, as such, an arguable product of age.

**Waivers.** To avoid charges that a person was not given sufficient time to reflect and weigh the options of an early retirement offer and thus was constructively discharged, employers are now required to prepare written releases that give retirees and older workers time to consider the offer, seek advice from a lawyer, and even repudiate the decision within seven days after signing the document. Historically, Congress did not recognize the ability of employers to enforce the waiver of age discrimination claims. As a result, some lucky workers who signed releases prior to 1990 were able to cash their settlement checks and still sue an employer thereafter.

The enactment of the federal Older Workers Benefit Protection Act (OWBPA) has eliminated confusion, provided its provisions are properly followed. The act makes clear that in relation to a firing or resignation of a worker over forty, a company can protect itself from potential violations of ADEA claims by utilizing waivers, provided:

1. The waiver is part of an agreement that specifically states the worker is waiving his ADEA rights and is not merely a general release;
2. The agreement containing the waiver does not disclaim any rights or claims arising after the date of its execution;

3. The worker receives value (such as an extra month of severance) in exchange for signing the agreement;

4. The worker is advised in writing of the right to consult an attorney of his choosing before signing the agreement;

5. The worker is advised in writing of his right to consider the agreement for a period of twenty-one days before it is effective; and

6. The worker is given at least seven days following the execution of the agreement to revoke it.

When employers request the signing of releases or waivers in connection with mass termination programs and large-scale voluntary retirement programs, the act is even more strict. All individuals in the program must be given at least forty-five days to consider the agreement, and each employee must also be provided with numerous facts, such as the class, unit, or group of individuals covered by the program, any eligibility factors for the program, time limits applicable to the program, the job titles and ages of all individuals selected for the program, and the ages of all individuals not eligible for the program.

## Discharge

The law states that it is illegal to fire anyone on the basis of age. Thus, as we have seen, whenever an older employee is fired, the issue is basically whether the employer's decision was made because of age or was the result of a reasonable, nondiscriminatory business factor. Usually, the older worker must use circumstantial evidence to prove that the employer's motive was improper. This is sometimes done by demonstrating that he or she was between forty and seventy years of age, was doing satisfactory work, and was fired, and the position was then filled by a substantially younger employee. It can also be proved by direct evidence, such as statements made to the claimant, and with statistics.

## Handicap Discrimination

The federal Americans with Disabilities Act (ADA) was enacted in 1990 to widen the scope of protection available to disabled workers. Employers with fifteen or more workers must avoid disability discrimination in all phases of the job. Employers are required to eliminate any inquiries on medical examinations and forms designed to identify an applicant's disabilities. Persons with disabilities cannot be disqualified from applying for a job because of the inability to perform nonessential or marginal functions of the job. Employers must scrutinize all job requirements so they do not inadvertently screen out qualified disabled applicants. Under the ADA, it is unlawful to refuse to hire people with disabilities who have equal skills after the employer provides reasonable accommodation, such as purchasing a telephone headset for a person with a hearing impairment.

The following list will familiarize you with typical obligations employers must generally follow during the hiring process:

- Employers cannot ask disability-related questions in interviews (such as "Do you presently have a disability?" or "Do you have any impairments that prevent you from performing the job you've applied for?").
- Employers cannot inquire about the kind of accommodation a person needs in order to perform the job properly if hired.
- A medical exam can be requested only after hiring, provided it is an essential condition for employment for all entering employees in that position.
- All contracts with employment agencies, unions, and insurance plans cannot be discriminatory.
- Employers cannot deny employment opportunities to an applicant or employee because of the need to make reasonable accommodation for a disability.
- Employers must avoid employment tests or selection criteria that have a disparate impact on individuals with disabilities

unless the tests or criteria are shown to be job-related and supported by business necessity.

- Employers may deny jobs to handicapped workers if they can demonstrate the position poses a danger to the individual's health and welfare or that hiring would significantly interfere with productivity or create dangers to others.

The main object of the ADA is to protect any person with a physical or mental impairment that substantially limits one or more life activities. This covers a broad range of disabilities, including deafness, AIDS, cancer, and learning disabilities. It does not generally include job-related stress, compulsive gambling, or pregnancy. (State law may be more inclusive as to what constitutes a covered disability, such as for infertility and obesity in some cases, so speak to a lawyer for more details.)

Recently, the EEOC expanded the category of mental disabilities by issuing enforcement guidelines on the application of the ADA to persons with psychiatric disabilities. The guidelines include major depression, bipolar disorder, anxiety and personality disorders, and schizophrenia as illnesses perceived to be protected disabilities when they chronically and severely impact normal activities related to learning, thinking, concentrating, sleeping, interacting with others, and caring for oneself for several months (without regard to the effects of medication). The guidelines suggest that, wherever possible, employers grant liberal time off and the adjustment of supervisory methods, use of a job coach, and reassignment of the mentally disabled employee to a different position unless and until undue hardship to the employer results.

Critics contend that these new guidelines unfairly impact employers. However, the guidelines are not binding on the courts, whose interpretations of employers' obligations to psychiatrically disabled employees under the ADA are not as restrictive.

In addition to job applications and screening procedures, every aspect of the employment relationship is protected, from employee compensation, terms, and privileges to job classifications, fringe benefits, promotions, training opportunities, and discharge.

Although the ADA does not require an employer to give preferential consideration to persons with disabilities, a person with a disability cannot be excluded from consideration for a raise, promotion, or on-the-job opportunity because of an inability to perform a marginal function. For example, an employer may not classify disabled applicants or employees in a way that limits their opportunities or status because of their disability. Different pay scales may not be adopted for workers with developmental disabilities if the job duties of such individuals are the same as for other workers. It is also impermissible to exclude or deny equal jobs or benefits to an individual because of that person's relationship or association with a disabled person. Thus, an employer should not fire an individual because that person does volunteer work with AIDS victims.

The law does not cover workers who cannot work because of total disability; the law only protects workers with disabilities who are capable of *continuing* working if the employer provides reasonable accommodation. On-the-job accommodations that must be provided to handicapped employees include:

- Restructuring or modifying work schedules
- Offering part-time work
- Permitting the employee to work at home
- Reassigning an individual to a vacant position
- Providing readers or interpreters for blind or deaf persons
- Acquiring or altering equipment or devices
- Making existing facilities readily accessible to the disabled
- Adjusting marginal job requirements
- Allowing flexibility in arrival and departure times for people who require special vehicles for transportation or who are confined to wheelchairs

Employers are required to make such accommodations only if the disability is known, if the accommodation requested is reasonable, and if the employee is truly partially disabled. An employer is relieved of responsibility to accommodate a disabled employee when to do so would impose an undue hardship. Factors considered in determining whether undue hardship exists are the nature and the costs of the accommodation to the employer, the overall financial resources of the employer (i.e., number of employees, overall size of the business, etc.), and other related factors. Courts will look at the type of the operation, overall budget, profitability of the employer, and the financial impact of the suggested accommodation in determining whether undue hardship exists. The facts concerning what constitutes undue hardship vary from case to case; however, if the employer can afford to accommodate, it must generally do so.

The ADA also specifies that reasonable accommodation includes job restructuring, part-time or modified work schedules, and reassignment to vacant positions. Under ADA, an employer may not reduce the number of hours an employee with a disability works because of transportation difficulties, and an employee must be given consideration for a flexible schedule as long as that employee maintains the same number of working hours as are required of other workers in that position. In situations where, because of a disability, an employee is no longer able to perform the essential functions of his/her current job, a transfer to another vacant job for which the person is qualified is considered a reasonable accommodation; if such a position is available within the company, an employer must make every effort to transfer the employee to it.

Undue hardship has many interpretations under the ADA. Larger, more profitable companies may have greater difficulty maintaining that the cost of an accommodation constitutes undue hardship than will smaller, less profitable businesses. Experts suggest that less than half of the persons with disabilities currently employed need job accommodations requiring expenditures by the employer and that less than 15 percent need job accommodations that cost more than $500.

As a result of the ADA and various state laws, employers now have enhanced obligations to current employees who develop disabilities while working. Wrongful discharge of such persons could result in severe penalties, particularly for workers who contract the AIDS virus, develop alcohol problems affecting their attendance or performance, or even become obese. (Although the ADA defines drug addiction as a disability, which means that you cannot be refused a job or be fired because of past drug addictions, there is no protection for current drug users. You can be legally terminated for using drugs on the job or working in an impaired state because of current drug use.)

Although employers are generally permitted to terminate workers who become completely disabled, every opportunity must be extended to give handicapped workers the opportunity to work at less demanding jobs or offer other accommodations. Employers must also provide you with existing short- or long-term disability benefits and other existing medical coverage (as well as an enhanced severance package if you can negotiate it) before you leave. Thus, always try to obtain the best post-termination benefits if you are fired and possess a disability. Contact a lawyer immediately to discuss your rights and options.

With respect to promotions and training, employers cannot use standards, criteria, or other administrative methods that discriminate on the basis of disability. Employers can, however, refuse to assign or reassign an individual with an infectious or communicable disease to a food-handling job. An employer may also state as a defense the fact that an employee poses a direct threat to the health or safety of other employees.

**Acquired disabilities while working.** Under the ADA, employers now have enhanced obligations to current employees who develop disabilities while on the job. Wrongful discharge of such persons could result in severe penalties, particularly for workers who contract the AIDS virus, become drug users off the premises, or develop alcohol problems affecting their attendance or performance.

**AIDS and AIDS-related diseases.** More than 1 million Americans—1 in 250—are now thought to be infected with HIV. Most people infected are young adults between the ages of twenty-five and forty-four, the age category that contains half the nation's workers. AIDS and AIDS-related diseases are protected "handicaps" within the meaning of the Rehabilitation Act and are considered covered disabilities under the ADA. As mentioned earlier, however, in order to be regarded as an impairment, the employee's HIV status must be known by the company.

## Racial Discrimination

Title VII of the Civil Rights Act and various other federal and state laws prohibit intentional discrimination based on ancestry or ethnicity. Some employers practice blatant forms of minority discrimination by paying lower salaries and other compensation to blacks and Hispanics. Others engage in quota systems by denying promotions and jobs to individuals on the basis of race or color. Federal laws prohibit employers of fifteen or more employees from discriminating on the basis of race or color. Virtually all states have even stronger antidiscrimination laws directed to fighting job-related race and minority discrimination. In some states, companies with fewer than eight employees can be found guilty of discrimination.

Both federal and state laws generally forbid private employers, labor unions, and state and local government agencies from:

- Denying an applicant a job on the basis of race or color
- Denying promotions, transfers, or assignments on the basis of race or color
- Penalizing workers with reduced privileges, reduced employment opportunities, and reduced compensation on the basis of race or color
- Firing a worker on the basis of race or color

Typically, the EEOC or related state agency will investigate charges of race discrimination or race-related retaliation. The EEOC has broad power to secure information and company records via subpoena, field investigations, audits, and interviewing witnesses, both employees and outsiders. Statistical data may be presented to demonstrate a pattern or practice of discriminatory conduct. As in other forms of discrimination, the contents of an individual's personnel file and the files of others in similar situations are often examined. Data on workplace composition may reveal a pattern or practice of exclusion or channeling. Regional or national data may shed light on whether a decision locally made was, in fact, racially discriminatory.

In cases where circumstantial evidence is presented to prove race discrimination, the burden is on the plaintiff to raise an inference of discrimination. This is often done through the use of statistics and payroll records.

**Common areas of exploitation.** Although it is legal for employers to pose questions at the hiring interview that test your motivation, maturity, willingness to accept instruction, interest in the job, and ability to communicate, inquiries made to further discriminatory practices are illegal. Common areas of exploitation encompass questions pertaining to color, national origin, citizenship, language, and relatives. For example, it is illegal to ask the following questions under federal Equal Employment Opportunity Commission guidelines and state regulations:

Color: What is your skin color?

National origin: What is your ancestry? What is your mother's native language? What is your spouse's nationality? What is your maiden name?

Citizenship: Of what country are you a citizen? Are your parents or spouse naturalized or native-born citizens? When did they acquire citizenship? Are you a native-born citizen?

Language: What is your native tongue? How did you acquire the ability to read, write, and speak a foreign language?

Relatives: Names, addresses, ages, and other pertinent information concerning your spouse, children, or relatives not employed by the company. What type of work does your mother or father do?

---

**STRATEGY:** *You have the right to refuse to answer any of the above questions at the hiring interview. If you choose not to answer them, you can politely inform the interviewer that you believe the questions are illegal and refuse to answer them on that basis. If you are then denied the job, you may have a strong case for damages after speaking with a representative from the EEOC, your state's human rights commission, or a knowledgeable lawyer provided you can prove the denial stemmed from a refusal to answer such questions.*

---

Another common area of race discrimination occurs when companies deliberately impose higher hiring standards than necessary, which tends to exclude minorities. All employment requirements must be directly related to the job; minorities cannot be excluded unnecessarily.

---

**STRATEGY:** *Proving you were individually excluded from a job based on your race or color may be difficult. It is often helpful to obtain statistical data to show that the employer's practices are illegal. For example, if ten positions for an engineering job were filled and none of the jobs was offered to a minority (or a woman), that may be sufficient to infer that the company violated the law. You would need assistance from a competent lawyer or discrimination specialist to prove this because the rules necessary to prove statistical disparities are complex.*

*You may have an easier time of demonstrating race dis-*

*crimination when you are directly treated unfairly on the job. For example, if you are repeatedly harassed and called names on the job, or are treated differently from nonminorities (e.g., you are absent several days from work and are suspended or placed on formal probation, while white workers with the same or a greater number of absences are only given an informal warning), it is best to gather this factual information for discussion with an executive or officer in your company's personnel department. In light of the Supreme Court decision* Wards Cover v. Antonio, *you may have an easier time proving race discrimination on an individual basis as opposed to relying on statistical disparities. This is because in certain cases employers now only have to offer a business justification for actions that are shown by statistics to have an unfair impact on minorities. The burden then shifts to the complainant to demonstrate that the alleged business justification is not legitimate.*

## AFFIRMATIVE ACTION PLANS

The Supreme Court recently cast doubt on the constitutionality of federal affirmative action programs that award benefits on the basis of race. The Court ruled that any such programs will be subject to the most searching judicial inquiry and will survive only if they are narrowly tailored to accomplish a compelling governmental interest. This ruling is a clear defeat for employers who take positive steps to recruit individuals on the basis of personal characteristics and classifications, including race, gender, religion, and veteran status, when the number of such individuals within the company is far below the number of such individuals within the community where the company is located. It is also a setback for employers who seek to ensure that such individuals, when employed, have an equal opportunity for benefits and promotions within the company.

The effect of the Supreme Court decision was immediate. The

Office of Federal Contract Compliance Programs (OFCCP), charged with overseeing and administering the largest affirmative action program in the United States (more than ninety thousand organizations have contracts with the federal government valued at $50,000 or more), announced that the requirement for "goals and timetables" in mandatory affirmative action plans for federal government contractors is not to be construed as a quota system to be achieved through race-based or gender-based preferences. The OFCCP is trying to clarify that its affirmative action program is different from preferences or set-asides and does not amount to reverse discrimination.

Employers are now eliminating any race- or gender-based preferences in their hiring policies; if a formal plan has already been established, companies are considering eliminating any references to formal goals and/or timetables (such as not requiring that any specific position be filled by a person of a particular race, gender, or ethnicity) and not establishing a minimum number of minority employees that must be employed by a certain date.

For companies acting as government contractors, all that is now required is that an employer be responsive to the needs of under-represented groups and make informal good-faith efforts to hire those best suited for the job. This is not even necessary for other private employers, since there is no affirmative duty for companies hiring minority employees to institute affirmative action policies.

Most companies with formal EEO policies contained in company handbooks and manuals are now modifying or deleting the language that guarantees the institution of any formal plan.

It is unclear just what kind of affirmative action programs are still permissible. Persons favoring affirmative action argue that the Supreme Court decision did not kill affirmative action, particularly in cases where no women or minority workers are included in a company's workforce. Even if this is not true, your company still cannot take illegal action toward minorities. But any employment program with numbers, goals, or timetables that can even remotely lead to quota preferences is now probably illegal. Speak to an employment lawyer to determine your rights and options.

## Religious Discrimination

The Civil Rights Act of 1964 prohibits religious discrimination and requires employers to reasonably accommodate the religious practices of employees and prospective employees. Various state laws also prohibit discrimination because of a person's observance of the Sabbath or holy days. In many states employers may not require attendance at work on such a day except in emergencies or in situations in which the employee's presence is indispensable. Absences for these observances must be made up at some mutually agreeable time or can be charged against accumulated leave time.

The following summarizes what companies are obligated to do to avoid lawsuits:

- Employers have an obligation to make reasonable accommodations to the religious needs of employees.
- Employers must give time off for the Sabbath or holy days except in an emergency.
- If employees don't come to work, employers may give them leave without pay, may require equivalent time to be made up, or may allow the employee to charge the time against any other leave with pay, except sick pay.

Employers may not be required to give time off to employees who work in key health and safety occupations or to those whose presence is critical to the company on any given day. Employers are not required to take steps inconsistent with a valid seniority system to accommodate an employee's religious practices. They are not required to incur overtime costs to replace an employee who will not work on Saturday or Sunday. Employers have no responsibility to appease fellow employees who complain they are suffering undue hardship when a coworker is allowed not to work on a Saturday or Sunday due to a religious belief while they are required to do so. Finally, employers are generally not required to choose the option the employee prefers, as long as the accommodation offered is reasonable. However, penalizing an employee for refusing to work on Christmas or Good Friday most likely constitutes religious discrimination, depending on the facts.

The definition of a "religious belief" is quite liberal under the law. If your belief is demonstrably sincere, the belief can be considered religious even if it is not an essential tenet of the religion of which you are a member. The applicant's or employee's knowledge that a position would involve a conflict does not relieve the employer of its duty to reasonably accommodate absent undue hardship.

In most cases the court weighs the facts to determine whether the employer offered a reasonable accommodation or that undue hardship existed; the plaintiff will attempt to show that the hardship was not severe or that the accommodation offered was not reasonable. What constitutes undue hardship varies on a case-by-case basis. Generally, undue hardship results when more than a *de minimis* cost (e.g., overtime premium pay or the breach of a collective bargaining agreement) is imposed on the employer.

---

**STRATEGY:** *The "undue hardship" defense is an exception that companies try to assert to successfully circumvent current law in this area. When you request time off for religious practices, document the date and nature of the request and the reasons given by the employer (or the alternatives considered by the company) in meeting or denying that request. If your request is denied, insist on an explanation. Speak to counsel to fully explore your options, such as filing a charge of religious discrimination with the EEOC or a state agency, or suing the employer in either state or* *federal court. You have certain rights if you are a true religious observer whose beliefs conflict with your work schedule.*

## Retaliation Discrimination

Employees who legitimately assert discrimination rights by filing charges in federal or state court, with the EEOC, or through state agencies, or who complain to the employer before taking action, are protected from adverse retaliation by an employer. If you reasonably believe that a Title VII violation was committed, an employer cannot take any action adverse to such rights, such as failing to promote, discharging, or unduly criticizing you as a direct result of that action.

Acts taken by an employer as a direct result of your filing charges or threatening to go to the EEOC or bringing a lawsuit are viewed by the courts as retaliatory. Many employers who are accused of discrimination have valid defenses and can overcome such charges. However, they foolishly take steps deemed to be in retaliation against an individual's freedom to pursue such claims and eventually suffer damages resulting from the retaliatory actions, not the alleged discrimination!

The following list identifies common areas where retaliation occurs:

- Transfer or reassignment that is undesired (even with no loss in pay or benefits)
- A transfer out of the country
- Threats, when repeatedly made and when disruptive to your job performance
- Harassment on the job
- Giving unfavorable references to a prospective employer, or otherwise interfering with your efforts to obtain a new job
- Attempting to persuade a current employer to discharge a former employee

- Firing you or forcing retirement by eliminating the position and offering only lesser alternative positions
- Denying or suspending severance payments
- Retroactively downgrading your performance appraisals and placing derogatory memos in your personnel file
- Refusing to promote or reassign you or adding preconditions for a requested reassignment
- Transferring you to a job with poorer working conditions
- Increasing your workload without good reason
- Adversely changing the company's vacation or benefits policy
- Delaying the distribution of tax and Social Security forms
- Interfering with an employment contract

---

**STRATEGY:** *Never falsely accuse an employer of a wrongful act in the attempt to obtain leverage, because you may not be legally protected if you then suffer harmful retaliation. However, you are protected against retaliation in a variety of nondiscriminatory areas such as complaining about overtime policies, safety (OSHA) violations, and filing a workers' compensation claim. Speak to a lawyer for advice and guidance if you believe you were treated unfairly as a result of complaining about an employer's illegal acts.*

---

## Strategies to Enforce Your Rights

Recognizing discrimination is only part of the battle; proper steps must also be taken to enforce your rights. As previously mentioned, the law entitles victims of discrimination to recover a variety of damages. This may include reinstatement or job hiring; receiving wage adjustments, back pay, and double back pay; receiving promotions and future pay; recovering legal fees, filing costs, and fees paid for expert witnesses; receiving punitive damages and compensatory damages up to $300,000 depending on the size of the employer; and other damages depending on the facts of your case. Even if you work in a right-to-work state and can be fired, it is illegal to be fired because you belong to a protected class, such as being a woman, over forty, a minority, handicapped, or a religious believer.

To start the ball rolling, it is necessary to file a formal charge. No one can stop you from filing a complaint; the law forbids employers from threatening reprisals or retaliation (such as loss of a promotion) when action is taken. The following must be included in the complaint:

1. Your name
2. The names, business addresses, and business telephone numbers of all persons who committed and/or participated in the discriminatory act(s)
3. Specific events, dates, and facts to support why the act(s) was discriminatory (e.g., statistics, whether other employees or individuals were discriminated against, and if so, the person(s) victimized, and by whom)

The complaint must be signed and sworn to by the complainant. However, it is not necessary for the complaint to be lengthy or elaborate. The main purpose is to make sufficient allegations to trigger an investigation. That is the advantage of filing charges with an appropriate agency; charges of discrimination are initiated and investigated at no cost to you. An investigator from the EEOC or state agency prepares and types the complaint. If your claim seems plausible, the EEOC or other agency will develop the claim on your behalf. A copy of the complaint, together with a request for a written response, is then sent to the employer. The employer must respond to the charges within several weeks. This is done either by a general denial of the claim or by the filing of specific facts and reasons to support the employer's position.

The following text illustrates the brevity of a valid complaint:

I am a female. On (date) I was notified by my supervisor (name) at (name of employer) that I was fired. I asked (name) to tell me why I was fired; he said it was because I called in sick six times in the past year. I know of several male employees who called in sick more than six times and who were not fired.

Based on these facts I believe I have been discriminated against on the basis of my gender.

After charges and countercharges have been examined by an investigator, the employer and the complainant may eventually be invited to attend a conference if the investigator believes the complainant's charges possibly have merit. Cases that are deemed to be too far-fetched or insufficient on their face are dismissed before the no-fault conference. If you receive a notice from the EEOC that your case has been dismissed (sometimes referred to as lacking probable cause), it must advise you of your rights. The letter will state that if you wish to proceed with your case, you must file a formal lawsuit in federal court within ninety days or forfeit your claim. This is called a right-to-sue letter.

The purpose of a no-fault conference is to discuss your case. At that time the investigator may make arrangements to visit the employer's premises, examine documents and other pertinent records, and interview key employees and witnesses. Because an employer may have an incentive to dispose of the matter early on to save excessive legal fees, lost manpower time, and potential damages, approximately 40 percent of all complaints are disposed at the settlement conference.

---

**STRATEGY:** *Although it is not necessary to retain a lawyer to represent you at or before the no-fault conference, the chances of settling your case are much higher with a lawyer present. An employer will bring its counsel, and you may be intimidated. Additionally, an experienced lawyer can evaluate your claim and advise how much it is realistically worth. Since many EEOC* *claims take years to be heard, a lawyer will advise you whether a settlement offer is valid and should be accepted, particularly after considering the lengthy delays that are frequently involved.*

*The conference is conducted by an investigator. Pressure may be placed on the employer to offer a monetary settlement or some other form of restitution (such as a promotion) to avoid the large legal expenses that would be incurred in the course of an ongoing investigation and eventual hearing. And some employers may be fearful that the investigator will examine its business records, including employment applications, interoffice memos, and pay records if a settlement is not reached.*

---

If your case cannot be settled at the conference, many options are available, including:

- Hiring a lawyer privately and suing the employer in a civil lawsuit, typically in federal court
- Representing yourself *pro se* (without a lawyer) and suing the employer in federal or state court
- Having the agency act on your behalf to protect your rights and proceeding to a fact-finding hearing and determination
- Having the EEOC or Department of Justice commence a lawsuit for you and/or others similarly situated in a class-action lawsuit
- Hiring a lawyer and commencing a private lawsuit in state court and, if applicable, alleging other causes of action as well as violations of discrimination laws

The advantage of suing an employer privately is that you may receive a quicker settlement. The EEOC and other agencies have many thousands of claims to process and follow; your case could take years before it is acted upon. Even if you receive a favorable decision (referred to as a finding of probable cause), the employer can appeal the agency's decision, adding years to the delay before an administrative trial is commenced. A lawyer working for you may be able to move the matter along more quickly. However, private lawsuits can be very expensive. That is why it is best to initially contact the nearest district office of the EEOC or state agency and speak with an intake person or investigator, or contact a lawyer and discuss your options before taking action.

State and local laws are often more favorable than federal law in terms of the standards of proof required, the amount of damages awarded, and other factors. It may be advantageous to file charges with these agencies instead, so do not automatically assume your case must be filed with the EEOC. Talk to an employment lawyer to discuss your options and maximize a claim.

When you retain a lawyer, he or she may first contact the employer by letter. The letter may specify the potential charges and invite the employer to discuss settlement before the matter proceeds to the next step. Cases are often settled this way before a formal discrimination charge is filed.

*Final tip:* No matter what course of action is considered, do not delay unnecessarily. In many situations you must file a formal complaint within 180 days of the time the alleged act(s) occurred to avoid the expiration of the statute of limitations. Some complainants take their time and unfortunately discover their cases are dismissed because they waited too long to file.

## Summary of Steps to Maximize a Discrimination Claim

1. If you believe you have been victimized by employment discrimination, consider filing a discrimination charge with the EEOC and/or your state agency. In some states, filing a charge with either the EEOC or state agency will be treated as filing with both. Speak to a labor lawyer for advice, because some state statutes provide greater protection and some state agencies have more powers than the EEOC.
2. EEOC offices are listed in the telephone directory under

United States Government or you can call (800) 669-4000. State agencies can be located by calling your state's department of labor or an EEOC office in your area.

3. Typically, you must give your name if you want an investigation to proceed, but you cannot be retaliated against for filing a charge.

4. Although some state agencies permit a longer period (e.g., up to three hundred days depending on state law), to be timely, you must file a charge with the EEOC within one hundred eighty days of the date the last incident occurred.

5. Although you may file a private lawsuit in federal court, once you file a charge with the EEOC you cannot litigate the matter privately until the EEOC dismisses your case (finds no probable cause), rules in your favor, or allows you to opt out. In either situation you then have ninety days to file a private lawsuit, to be timely, after receiving a final disposition notice (a right-to-sue letter) from the EEOC.

6. Obtaining a favorable decision does not automatically mean that you will receive big bucks. The employer may appeal a state agency or EEOC decision and force you to sue it in federal court.

7. Call the EEOC officer assigned to your case regularly to determine the status of the investigation and action taken in your case. Be assertive and follow the progress of your case. Whenever you receive a request for information, provide this immediately to the investigator.

8. If you are unhappy with the progress of the investigation or how the case is being handled, consult an attorney for guidance and advice. Consider joining a class-action lawsuit if one already exists against your employer or ex-employer. By doing so, however, you may have to withdraw from your own action.

9. Be patient. The EEOC often takes years to render its decision and the employer may delay the final outcome years more by refusing to settle and appealing the case further.

Some investigators leave the agency while working on a case and a new investigator has to be assigned, causing further delay. Thus, recognize that in most situations, even with a good case, you may not receive justice for many years.

# PART III

# How to Avoid Being Fired Unfairly and What to Do if You Are

Until recently, employees had few options when they received a "pink slip." This was because of a legal principle called the employment-at-will doctrine, which was generally applied throughout the United States. Under this rule of law, employers hired workers "at will" and were free to fire them at any time with or without cause and with or without notice. From the nineteenth to the mid-twentieth century, employers could discharge individuals with impunity for a good reason, a bad reason, or no reason at all with little fear of legal reprisal.

Some state legislatures began scrutinizing the fairness of this doctrine beginning in the 1960s. Courts began handing down rulings to safeguard the rights of nonunionized employees. Congress passed specific laws pertaining to occupational health and safety, civil rights, and freedom to complain about unsafe working conditions.

Now there has been a gradual erosion of the employment-at-will doctrine in many areas. Some states have enacted public policy exceptions that make it illegal to fire workers who take time off for jury duty or military service. Some courts have ruled that statements in company manuals, handbooks, and employment applications constitute implied contracts which employers are bound to follow. Other states now recognize the obligation of companies to deal in fairness and good faith with longtime workers. This means, for example, that they are prohibited from terminating workers in retaliation when they tattle on abuses of authority (i.e., whistle-blowing), or denying individuals an economic benefit (a pension that is vested or about to vest, commission, bonus, etc.) that has been earned or is about to become due.

A few states are even allowing wrongfully terminated workers to sue in tort (as opposed to asserting claims based on contract) and recover punitive damages and money for pain and suffering arising from the firing. Employees who have sued under tort theories for wrongful discharge have recovered large jury verdicts (sometimes in the six figures) as a result. Innovative lawyers are asserting federal racketeering (RICO) claims, seeking criminal sanctions and treble (triple) damages against companies. This is in addition to fraud and misrepresentation claims against individuals responsible for making wrongful termination decisions.

Given the changed legal climate, it is understandable that more people are seeking information about their rights and are fighting back after being fired. For example, they are requesting and *receiving* benefits that include severance pay greater than the company's last offer, accrued bonuses, continued medical, dental, and life insurance coverage, office space, telephones, secretarial help, résumé preparation, and outplacement guidance while looking for a new job.

This section of the book deals with important considerations to remember and follow when you are fired.

In Chapter 6 you will learn how to recognize when you are fired illegally. This is the first step in understanding when you have been exploited and collecting what you are due. It also stresses correct negotiating strategies to assist you in maximizing severance and other termination benefits. You will learn the right questions to ask and points to clarify at the termination session to increase what can be obtained. Actual letter agreements are included to illustrate how to confirm the deal in writing after it is accepted. Additionally, you will learn what to look out for when requested to sign a release or settlement agreement prepared by your employer.

Although it is unlikely that you will succeed in getting your job back after reading this chapter, you can discover how to enforce your rights without hiring a lawyer. You will also learn the steps to take when a satisfactory settlement is not achieved through informal means. If you are victimized but cannot obtain benefits with your ex-employer and cannot afford a lawyer, you will learn where to obtain assistance through various federal, state, and local agencies. In addition, you will discover ways to collect evidence and strengthen a claim before a lawyer is retained.

# CHAPTER 6

# Recognizing When You Have Been Fired Illegally

Not every firing is illegal. If you are fired in a state that still recognizes the employment-at-will doctrine, you may have little bargaining power in getting your job back. However, you are still entitled to monies earned and due *before* the firing, such as commissions, profit sharing, and perhaps bonuses, even in states that follow this doctrine.

And notwithstanding this law, you may still have a statutory right to fight the discharge. This is because all states have laws protecting workers who are fired due to discrimination, whistleblowing, and other acts; these laws operate independently of the employment-at-will principle.

The first step in determining when action should be taken is to know the particular laws in your state. This can be done by consulting an experienced employment attorney or investigating the law yourself in order to determine whether you have been fired illegally.

## Statutory Restrictions

A variety of federal and state statutes restrict an employer's freedom to discharge employees. These form the legal basis for many challenges to firings. The most comprehensive and significant federal legislation is Title VII of the Civil Rights Act of 1964, as amended by the Equal Employment Opportunity Act of 1972. Under this law, employers cannot fire workers based upon personal characteristics of gender, age, race, color, religion, national origin, and nondisqualifying physical handicaps or mental impairments unrelated to job qualifications. If you believe that your termination from a job was due to discrimination, see Chapter 5 for information on discrimination and the law. The law also protects workers who exercise their First Amendment and other rights from reprisals. If you have lost your job because you spoke up about health and safety conditions, or because you refused to take a lie-detector test, see relevant portions of Chapter 4. Other factors may enter into the legality of a firing, and a discussion of these follows.

## CREDIT PROBLEMS

The Consumer Credit Protection Act of 1973 forbids employers from firing workers whose earnings have been subjected to a wage garnishment arising from a single debt. However, employees may presumably be fired after other garnishments. Some states have enacted laws that give workers additional protection; check the applicable law in your state.

## SEVERANCE AND RETIREMENT BENEFITS

The Employee Retirement Income Security Act of 1974 (ERISA) prohibits the discharge of any employee who is prevented thereby from attaining immediate vested pension rights or who was exercising rights under ERISA and was fired as a result.

You are also entitled to certain rights as a participant in an employer's pension and/or profit-sharing plans. ERISA provides that plan participants are entitled to examine without charge all plan documents, including insurance contracts, annual reports, plan descriptions, and copies of documents filed by the plan with the U.S. Department of Labor. If you request materials from a plan (including summaries of each plan's annual financial report) and do not receive them within thirty days, you may file a suit in federal court. In such a case the court may require the plan administrator to provide the materials and pay you up to $100 a day until you receive them (unless the materials were not sent for reasons beyond the control of the administrator). See later in this chapter for more about your rights under ERISA.

### ASSERTING A SEXUAL HARASSMENT CLAIM OR CHARGE OF RETALIATION

Federal law prohibits employers from retaliation after an employee complains about sexual harassment, files formal charges with the EEOC or a state agency, or commences a lawsuit in court. Consult Chapter 5 for more information about this subject.

### FIRED AS PART OF A LARGE LAYOFF

If you are part of a massive layoff and not given at least sixty days' notice or sixty days' severance pay, this is a violation under the federal Worker Adjustment and Retraining Notification Act (WARN). This law prohibits employers from ordering a plant closing or massive layoffs until sixty days after the employer has given written notice of this to affected employees or their representatives, the state dislocated-worker unit, and the chief elected official of the unit of local government where the closing or layoff is to occur. If you are fired suddenly and are part of a massive layoff, consult a lawyer immediately to discuss your rights and options under WARN. Information about WARN is contained in Chapter 4.

**STRATEGY:** *This claim does not only apply to union employees working at plants. As noted earlier, it can be asserted when a private employer (such as IBM or AT&T) lays off hundreds of executives at one time or when a company discharges large numbers of secretaries or dismantles an accounting, business, or financial department due to a reorganization.*

## ASSERTING UNION RIGHTS

The National Labor Relations Act prohibits the firing of any employee because of his or her involvement in union activity, because of filing charges, or because of testifying pursuant to the act. Contact the closest regional office of the National Labor Relations Board if you believe you have been fired for one of those reasons.

The law also protects employees who band together to protest about wages, hours, or other working conditions. For example, if a group of nonunion employees complains about contaminated drinking water or about failure to receive minimum wages or overtime pay, their employer could be prohibited from firing them if their charges are proved.

## FIRED FOR SERVING IN THE MILITARY

Several federal laws, including the Veterans' Re-employment Rights Act and the Military Selective Service Act, protect the rights of veterans and military personnel. These laws provide that employees who are in military service be regarded as being on an unpaid leave of absence from their civilian employment. For example, if you are on extended reserve duty (up to four years) or are called up for short-term emergency duty merely to serve in a motor pool across town, you must be offered a job with the same pay, rank, and seniority upon your return. An employer is prohibited from forcing an employee to use vacation time for military training. Employers are obligated to assist employees who return from military service and cannot deny promotions, seniority, or other benefits because of military obligations. Thus, if an employee was promoted or promised a raise right before a call-up, he must receive a job in line with the promised promotion and raise upon return, together with reinstatement of all benefits and those benefits (e.g., additional pay) that would have been earned if he had continued to work.

Companies that receive job applications from military personnel and reservists relating to work after termination of active-duty status and don't hire them must fully document the reasons for denial. Any employer not following these rules is subject to investigation and action by the local U.S. Attorney's office or a private lawsuit filed by the claimant in the federal district court sitting in any county where the employer maintains a place of business. Charges can also be brought under the Veterans' Benefits Improvement and Health Care Authorization Act. These laws prohibit discrimination in all aspects of employment, including hiring, promotion, and discharge on the basis of military membership.

## ATTENDING JURY DUTY

The Jury System Improvements Act of 1978 forbids employers from firing employees who are impaneled to serve on federal grand juries or petit juries. Most states have enacted similar laws.

## REPORTING RAILROAD ACCIDENTS

Two federal laws govern here. The Federal Railroad Safety Act prohibits companies from firing workers who file complaints or testify about railroad accidents; the Federal Employer's Liability Act makes it a crime to fire an employee who furnishes facts regarding a railroad accident.

## Public Policy Exceptions

The information contained in the previous section gives you a better understanding about the numerous federal laws protecting workers from being fired unfairly. But many courts and state legislatures have carved out other exceptions to the employment-at-will doctrine based on public policy considerations.

For example, workers are protected from discharge who refuse to violate criminal laws by committing perjury on the employer's behalf, participating in illegal schemes (e.g., price-fixing and other antitrust violations), mislabeling packaged goods, giving false testimony before a legislative committee, altering pollution control reports, or engaging in practices abroad that violate foreign, federal, and state laws. Also protected are workers who perform a public obligation, exercise a public duty (e.g., attend jury duty, vote, supply information to the police about a fellow employee, file workers' compensation claims) or observe the general public policy of the state (e.g., refuse to perform unethical research). These public policy exceptions to the employment-at-will doctrine are widely recognized and are followed in many states.

Tattling on abuses of authority, or whistle-blowing, is now protected conduct in many states. Michigan has enacted a Whistle-blower's Protection Act, which typifies the laws in such states. This law protects employees from retaliation after they report suspected violations of laws or regulations, and provides specific remedies, including reinstatement with back pay, restoration of seniority and lost fringe benefits, litigation costs, attorney fees, and a $500 fine.

People who work for federal agencies are also protected from being fired for whistle-blowing. In one case a nurse was dismissed after reporting abuses of patients at a Veterans' Administration medical center. She sought reinstatement and damages before a federal review panel. The panel ordered that she be reinstated and awarded her $7,500 in back pay.

The following true cases illustrate examples of firings that were found to be illegal in this area:

- A quality control director was fired for his efforts to correct false and misleading food labeling by his employer.
- A bank discharged a consumer credit manager who notified his supervisors that the employer's loan practices violated state law.
- A financial vice-president was fired after reporting to the company's president his suspicions regarding the embezzlement of corporate funds.

However, be aware that not all whistle-blowing conduct is protected under this public policy exception. Some companies have successfully fired workers who questioned internal management systems, "blew the whistle" without properly investigating the facts, bypassed management, or tattled in bad faith.

---

**STRATEGY:** *All individuals wishing to protect their job should seek competent legal advice before engaging in whistle-blowing activity, since the law is often unclear and each case is decided upon its own particular merits.*

---

## Implied Contract Exceptions

In addition to federal and state statutory restrictions on an employer's freedom to discharge employees and the public policy exceptions outlined above, there are newer protections that may restrict the at-will authority of employers to terminate employment without having to state a reason for the termination. This protection is in the form of "implied contract" terms created by representations and promises published by employers in their employee handbooks.

During the first half of the twentieth century, a number of state courts ruled that company retirement, sick leave, and fringe benefit plans described in their employee manuals were enforceable promises of compensation. Today, rights to your employer's retirement and benefit plans are protected by federal law under ERISA (Employee Retirement Income Security Act), discussed earlier.

But ERISA did not affect the right of an employer to terminate your job "at will" without having to give the reason for firing you. Employers then began to use their employee handbooks to dress up their images as good places to work by promising job termination only for "good cause" or under specified procedures. A number of state courts began to view these promises as enforceable "implied contracts," even though they may not have been read by the employee until after accepting employment and they were not signed by either party, as is customarily required to enhance contract enforceability.

Many state courts have ruled that the promises in employee handbooks may be legally enforceable as implied contracts. In spite of this progress, many questions still exist. What if the employer promises, then makes a disclaimer, equivalent to taking back the promise? What if after you are hired your employer changes the employee handbook, taking back some of the promises contained in the version in effect when you were hired and upon which you relied? For how long are the promises effective? And there are more questions.

Basically, the first step to protecting your rights in this area is to investigate whether the company has enunciated its firing policies in writing. If such statements exist in work rules, policy manuals, periodic memos, or handbooks, these must be analyzed to determine if the words are sufficiently definite to constitute promises you can rely upon. Courts are sometimes ruling that statements in employee handbooks are not legal promises but merely sales puffery aimed at enhancing morale. And the existence of disclaimers may be legally sufficient to void the enforceability of such promises. So, too, may the same result occur if the company reserves the right to print revisions to the manual after you are working, revisions that eliminate promises contained in earlier editions of the manual you were given, and relied upon, when being hired.

Since each case must be analyzed on its particular facts, if you believe that you are being deprived of your rights as stated in your employer's employee manual, see an attorney experienced in employment rights. The lawyer may find that an implied contract exists.

The implied contract exception to the employment-at-will doctrine may extend to oral promises made at the hiring interview. For example, if you are told by the company president at the hiring interview, "Don't worry, we never fire anyone around here except for a good reason," a legitimate case might be made to fight the firing provided you could prove that the words were spoken and that it was reasonable to rely on them (i.e., that they were spoken seriously and not in jest).

However, be aware that not all oral promises are enforceable against an employer, particularly when you are promised "a job for life." Promises of lifetime employment are rarely upheld due to a legal principle referred to as the statute of frauds. Under this law, all contracts with a job length exceeding one year must be in writing to be enforceable. As a result, courts are generally reluctant to view oral contracts as creating permanent or lifetime employment. Usually, such contracts are viewed as being terminatable at will by either party. Thus, a "lifetime contract" may theoretically be terminated after one day!

Some states have laws that limit the duration of an employment contract to a specified number of years (e.g., seven). Thus, if you currently have a contract that you believe is for lifetime employment, it may not be enforceable. Consult an experienced labor attorney if you hope to obtain such a contract in the future.

**STRATEGY:** *To successfully assert this claim, it is essential to have previously received a copy of the company's manual and read it carefully. If you can prove that promises are clearly contained in a manual, and you relied on them to your detriment, you may be able to assert a valid lawsuit under the laws of some states. Remember, if a company fails to act in accord with published work rules or handbooks, it may be construed as violating an important contract obligation in some states.*

Types of promises to look for (which may give you additional rights during and after a firing) include:

- Allowing you to appeal or mediate the decision through an internal nonbinding grievance procedure
- Requiring the employer to give reasonable notice before any firing
- Stating you can be fired for cause only after internal steps toward rehabilitation have been taken and have failed
- Guaranteeing the right to be presented with specific, factual reasons for the discharge before the firing can be effective

### FIRED IN BREACH OF CONTRACT RIGHTS

If you are fired in a manner inconsistent with or different from rights in a written contract or collective bargaining agreement (if you belong to a union), you may be entitled to damages. If a contract exists, examine it upon termination. The failure to give timely notice as required by a contract, or failure to follow the requirements set forth in a contract, may expose a company to a breach of contract claim. In some instances, it can even cause the agreement to be extended for an additional period.

## Implied Covenants of Good Faith and Fair Dealing

Courts in some states have further eroded the at-will doctrine by imposing a duty of good faith and fair dealing on long-term employment relationships. For example, one man with forty years of service claimed he was fired so his company could avoid paying commissions otherwise due on a $5 million sale. A Massachusetts court found this to be true and awarded him substantial money even though he had been hired at will. Another employee was fired after working fourteen years without a written contract or job security. However, the court ruled that the company fired him merely to deprive him of the vesting of valuable pension benefits in his fifteenth year of service. The employee was awarded $75,000 in damages.

Typically, the duty of employers to act in good faith and fair dealing only applies to cases where an employee has been working for the company for many years or where a person is fired just before he or she is supposed to receive anticipated financial benefits (commissions, bonuses, accrued pension, profit sharing, etc.).

In one case, however, the Montana Supreme Court reasoned that the covenant of good faith and fair dealing is a duty imposed by law. The court upheld a $50,000 jury award of punitive damages (more than twenty-five times the compensatory damage award) because the employer had promised to write a favorable letter of recommendation in exchange for an employee's resignation. Despite this promise, the employer delivered a letter of recommendation merely stating the complainant's dates of employment. Additionally, the employer returned a copy of the original letter of resignation despite the employee's request for the original. These actions, the court found, justified the jury's finding of "fraud, oppression or malice."

But not all longtime workers are entitled to such protection. Remember that if an employer fires you for a lawful reason (i.e., for cause), the fact that you have been with the company for a substantial time or are eligible for a substantial benefit may *not* make the firing illegal under a covenant of good faith and fair dealing theory.

---

**STRATEGY:** *If you are fired at the end of the year and are denied a year-end bonus or other benefits about to vest in the following year, consult a lawyer immediately to enforce your rights. (The author believes that pension or stock option benefits about to vest within six months to a year of a firing can often be obtained via negotiations. For a bonus, a stronger claim can be made if you are fired within three months of the expected payment date. Sometimes a company will agree to keep you on unpaid leave status during the appropriate period as a way of qualifying. Speak to your lawyer about this negotiating strategy for more details.)*

---

If you cannot get your job back using a violation of good faith and fair dealing argument, you or a lawyer may be able to negotiate for you to obtain benefits you were expecting and would have received but for the firing. You should also consider asserting a claim for benefits based on ERISA rights. However, if an employer fires you for a lawful reason—that is, for cause—the fact that you are about to become eligible for a substantial benefit may not make the firing illegal.

### FIRING DUE TO A LEGITIMATE ILLNESS OR ABSENCE

You cannot be fired if you were injured on the job and file a workers' compensation claim, or are absent for a medical reason relating to pregnancy or for taking maternity leave of less than twelve weeks in any given one-year period (in violation of the federal FMLA if you work for an employer with more than fifty full-time employees). However, an employer may have the right to fire a worker who is excessively absent due to illness. In that case a viable option might be for you to file for and collect benefits under the company's short- or long-term disability plan.

The above legal theories are exceptions to the traditional employment-at-will rule and may be useful in recovering greater benefits or damages when you are fired. The law varies greatly from state to state, and each case warrants attention based upon its particular facts and circumstances. However, this information should help you determine if you have been fired illegally or unfairly. For example, you should now understand many of the instances when firings become *suspect*. These include:

- When you are about to receive a large commission or vested stock option rights
- If the company fails to act in a manner specified in its employment applications, promotional literature, policy statements, "welcome aboard" letters, handbooks, manuals, written contracts, correspondence or memos, benefit statements, or disciplinary rules
- If you are fired right after returning from an illness, pregnancy, or jury duty
- If you are fired after complaining about a safety violation or other wrongdoing
- If you are over forty, belong to a minority, are partially disabled, or are a female and believe you were fired primarily because of such personal characteristics
- If you are a longtime worker and believe the firing was unjustified
- If you received a verbal promise of job security or other rights that the company failed to fulfill

In many situations the company may still have a right to fire based on the traditional employment-at-will rule. But even in those states that adhere to the rule, you can obtain *additional* benefits by demonstrating your knowledge of the above exceptions and appealing to the company's sense of decency and fair play.

Since laws change rapidly, consult with an experienced labor attorney or research current case decisions and statutory developments in your state to be sure you know your rights in this area whenever you are fired or treated unfairly.

Many employers fire workers without warning—for obvious reasons. By firing workers suddenly, employers believe they will keep workers off balance, without sufficient time to anticipate the discharge and plan ahead.

No matter how you learn the news, it is important to remain calm so you can carefully consider your options. The fact that you are fired suddenly (as opposed to being given a warning) does *not* mean you should accept fewer benefits than you deserve. The following strategies will help you increase severance benefits and/or damages in the event you are fired.

The first question to ask yourself when you are fired is whether the employer had a valid legal basis for doing so. The preceding material mentioned various instances where employers are prohibited from discharging workers, even those employed at will. However, these are not the only prohibited kinds of actions. For example, do you have a written contract? If so, what does it say? Employers cannot fire you in a manner inconsistent with the terms of the written contract. Thus, if you are hired for a definite term (for example, one year), you cannot be fired prior to the expiration of the contract term except for cause.

### REVIEWING YOUR CONTRACT

Review what your contract says about termination. For example, many companies have written contracts with their executives. Some of these agreements run for a period of one year and state that if timely notice of termination is not given at least thirty days prior to the expiration of the one-year term, the contract will automatically be extended and renewed under the same terms and conditions for an additional year. If the company fires the executive two weeks before the end of the year, or forgets to send timely notice, the employee could have a legal basis to insist on working for an additional year. Or he or she would then have strong claim to negotiate for additional compensation rather than filing a lawsuit.

Were you hired for a definite term—for example, your contract states, "This agreement is effective for a period of one year commencing on February 1, 2001, and terminating on January 31, 2002"? If so, the employer can only terminate you prior to the effective termination date—January 31, 2002—*for cause.*

The following are examples of cause that justify contract terminations:

- Theft or dishonesty
- Falsifying records or information
- Punching another employee's time card
- Leaving the job or company premises without prior approval from a supervisor
- Insubordination or disrespect of company work rules and policies
- Willful refusal to follow the directions of a supervisor (unless doing so would endanger health or safety)
- Assault, unprovoked attack, or threats of bodily harm against others
- Use of drugs or possession of alcoholic beverages on company premises or during company-paid time while away from the premises
- Reporting to work under the influence of drugs or alcohol
- Disclosing confidential and proprietary information to unauthorized third parties
- Unauthorized possession of weapons and firearms on company property

- Intentionally making errors in work, negligently performing duties, or willfully hindering or limiting production
- Sleeping on the job
- Excessive lateness or irregular attendance at work
- Failing to report absences
- Sexually harassing or abusing others
- Making secret profits
- Misusing trade secrets, customer lists, and other confidential information

Does the contract restrict you from working for a competitor or establishing a competing business after termination? This is referred to as a restrictive covenant or covenant not to compete, which may or may not be enforceable depending on the particular facts and circumstances. (Restrictive covenants are discussed in detail in Chapter 7.) If so, be sure you receive a detailed opinion concerning your rights.

Thus, remember that your rights may be enhanced or diminished depending upon the type of contract in existence.

## Oral Promises of Job Security

As previously discussed, courts in some states are ruling that employees have the right to rely on oral representations made before hiring or during the working relationship. Interviewers, recruiters, and other intake personnel are often careless and make statements that can be construed as promises of job security. They sometimes use words such as "permanent employment," "job for life," or "just cause termination" and make broad statements concerning job longevity and assurances of continued employment (such as "Don't worry—no one around here ever gets fired except for a good reason") or specific promises regarding career opportunities.

When such statements are sufficient to be characterized as promises of job security, when you can prove the actual words were spoken, and when you can demonstrate that you relied on such statements to your detriment, you may be able to contest the firing if you work in a state that recognizes this exception to the employment-at-will doctrine. The following actual case is a good illustration.

An executive worked for a company for thirty-two years without a written contract. The man was suddenly fired. He sued his company and argued that he had done nothing wrong to justify the firing. At the trial the executive proved that:

- The company's president told him several times that he would continue to be employed if he did a good job.
- The company had a policy of not firing executives except for cause.
- The man was never criticized or warned that his job was in jeopardy.
- He had a commendable track record, his employment history was excellent, and he had received periodic merit bonuses, raises, and promotions.

The executive won the case because the facts created an implied promise that the company could not arbitrarily terminate him.

---

**STRATEGY:** *Try to remember and document what was said, when, where, who said it, and the names of any witness(es) who were present whenever such promises were made. This may help your case at a later date if you are fired in a manner inconsistent with such promises.*

---

A word of caution: Some employers design employment applications or contracts that specify that employment is at will, that no one has made additional promises regarding job security, and that you acknowledge not receiving such promises. You may have a difficult job arguing this point (regardless of verbal promises) when you sign such a document.

## Written Promises of Job Security in Company Manuals

If company manuals promise job security, has the employer followed stated policy? It is important to review all manuals, handbooks, memos, correspondence, benefit statements, "welcome aboard" letters, employment applications, policy statements, and disciplinary rules. Know what they say regarding firings. For example:

- Can you appeal the decision?
- Must the employer give you a warning before firing?
- Are there specific rules regarding severance?
- Can you be fired at will or only for cause?
- Is there a system of progressive discipline, or can you be fired immediately without notice?
- Are there internal grievance policies?
- Can you arbitrate the dispute rather than litigate?
- Do you have the right to receive a written reason for the firing?
- Do you have the right to review your personnel file after the firing?

You may be able to contest the firing and sue for damages if the employer has favorable policies in writing that aren't followed. Thus, review all company policies as soon as possible to determine if promises have been broken.

---

**STRATEGY:** *Sometimes it is difficult to review these materials after a discharge. You may not be on the premises and may be unable to obtain such documents because many employers insist that* *ex-employees return all company property upon being fired. If this is the case, ask friendly coworkers to lend you their materials for review. Photocopy relevant text as soon as possible. Better still, if you have suspicions you may be fired, plan ahead by gathering copies of these materials before you are asked to leave. Bring this information to your lawyer at the initial consultation. This will enable him or her to give you a more accurate opinion as to whether the employer has violated an implied contract term. For example, if the employer has a written policy allowing terminated employees to appeal the firing to a grievance committee, you may wish to do so. If the employer refuses to allow you to file such an appeal despite its stated policy, you might be able to contest the firing as a result.*

Whenever an individual is fired, I try to gain an advantage for my client by scrutinizing all company policies regarding firings to see if they were followed. If not, this is used as leverage in negotiating for additional severance and other benefits.

## Personnel Records

As previously discussed, some states permit workers to review and copy the contents of their personnel files. For example, California law provides that an employee is to be given access to personnel files used to determine his or her qualifications, promotions, pay raises, discipline, and discharge. Other states allow both employees and terminated employees to inspect personnel files maintained by employers. Some states also permit inspection by a representative designated by the employee.

Additionally, most states give employees the right to review information supplied to the employer by a credit reporting agency under the Fair Credit Reporting Act of 1971, as well as to review all medical and insurance information in the file. However, confidential items such as letters of reference, records of internal investigations regarding theft, misconduct, or crimes not pertaining to the employee, and confidential information about other employees are generally prohibited from being viewed.

Sometimes these files do not support firing decisions because they contain favorable performance appraisals, recommendations, and memos. If you can only be fired for cause and the employer gives you specific reasons why you were fired, your file may demonstrate that such reasons are factually incorrect and/or legally insufficient. If this occurs, you may have a strong case against the employer for breach of contract.

---

**STRATEGY:** *Try to make copies of all pertinent documents in your file while working for the employer (particularly favorable records). If you have received excellent performance reviews and appraisals and the file indicates you received large merit salary increases and other benefits, you may be able to contest the firing and be rehired. Or you may use this information to successfully negotiate more severance than the company is offering.*

---

In some states you can bring legal proceedings to expunge false information that is contained in your file and is known by the employer to be false. These states even allow you to collect attorney fees, fines, court costs, and damages in the event you discover false information or records of off-premises activities (political, associational, etc.) that do not interfere with your work duties.

## Refusals to Pay Expected Financial Benefits

Many companies fire workers to deprive them of the fruits of their labors. This includes a year-end bonus, commissions, wages, accrued vacation, or pension benefits that are about to vest. In some states, if an employer fires someone just before he or she is supposed to receive anticipated benefits, the firing may be illegal.

Even if the firing is legal, you may be entitled to collect this money in negotiations or during a lawsuit. For example, the department of labor in most states requires employers to pay accrued vacation and earned wages to terminated workers. Additionally, you may be able to receive a pension if you are about to qualify for a vested pension but are fired. This is because employers are forbidden in most states and under the federal Employment Retirement Income Security Act from firing longtime workers who are close to receiving such benefits. Consult an experienced labor lawyer immediately if you believe you have been victimized in this area.

Salespeople who earn commissions are now receiving additional statutory protections in this area. Many states now require that companies promptly pay commissions to their independent sales representatives (or agents) who are fired. When prompt payment is not made, companies may be liable for penalties up to *three times the commission amount* plus reasonable attorney fees and court costs if the case is eventually litigated. Some of the states that have enacted laws protecting sales representatives and their commissions are Alabama, Arizona, California, Florida, Georgia, Illinois, Indiana, Iowa, Kansas, Kentucky, Louisiana, Maryland, Massachusetts, Minnesota, Mississippi, Missouri, New Hampshire, New Jersey, New York, North Carolina, Ohio, Oklahoma, South Carolina, Tennessee, Texas, and Washington, and more states are bound to enact similar legislation.

Additionally, you may have a valid claim if you are fired right before the payment of a year-end bonus. Some employers require workers to be employed on the day bonus checks are issued as a condition of payment. However, workers are sometimes fired unfairly and are denied bonuses that have been earned. As noted, I once represented a man who had worked a full year and was expecting a bonus of $22,500 to be paid on February 15 of the following year. The company's policy required workers to be employed on the date of payment in order to receive the bonus. My client was fired on February 10 for alleged misconduct due to an unauthorized absence taken the day before. The employer refused to pay severance or the bonus.

I proved that my client had a justifiable excuse for missing work on the day in question. Further, I argued that the employer's policy of paying earned bonuses only if the worker was still employed the following year was unfair. Although I was unable to obtain his reemployment, I did manage to obtain severance pay equivalent to two weeks for every year of employment, as well as the expected bonus.

---

**STRATEGY:** *Always request a bonus if you are fired close to the end of the year and are entitled to a bonus by contract or job history (i.e., you consistently received bonuses in prior years). If the employer tells you that bonuses are only paid if you are still working on the day the check is issued and that you were fired before then, argue that you would have received the bonus but for the firing. And argue that you are entitled to a pro rata share of the bonus if you are fired close to but before the end of the year. For example, if you are fired on December 1, negotiate to receive eleven-twelfths of the bonus you were expecting.*

---

## Offers of Severance Pay

Although there is generally no legal obligation to pay severance monies, most employers in the United States *do* offer such payments when a firing is due to a group layoff, business conditions outside the employee's control (such as reorganization), or reasons other than employee misconduct. However, there may be a legal obligation to pay severance when:

- You have a written contract stating that severance will be paid
- Oral promises are given regarding severance pay
- The employer voluntarily promises to pay severance
- The employer has a policy of paying severance and this is documented in a company manual or employee handbook
- The employer has paid severance to other employees in similar firings and thereby has created a precedent

If you are fired and are not offered severance, it is advisable to request a meeting with a qualified representative of the employer to discuss clarification regarding severance and available wage equivalents.

Many employers are fearful of the increasing amount of employee-related litigation and are flexible in easing the departure of terminated individuals. Thus, you should begin the discussion by appealing to corporate decency and fair play. For example, it might be stated that severance pay is needed because you anticipate it will take longer to find a suitable job than the amount of severance currently offered. Always be polite and act professionally; being vindictive or making threats won't solve anything.

Most employers have different policies regarding severance depending on the industry and company. However, it is recommended that you attempt to receive *one month* of severance for every year worked as a starting point. If this can be achieved, you can leave the company knowing that you have received a fair severance offer.

Although severance pay is a common problem for individual employees whose employment has been terminated, the extensive merger and acquisition activity in recent years has caused the issue of severance pay to become one of large-scale financial and legal significance. If your company is sold and you continue to work for the new employer, you may be able to assert rights under the federal Employee Retirement Income Security Act and welfare benefit plans in the event the new employer denies severance to a group of workers at a later date.

Additionally, you may have grounds for a valid lawsuit in the event you have a vested pension but are fired just weeks short of becoming entitled to greater severance, larger monthly pension payments, and improved medical and insurance benefits. This happened to an executive who sued his former employer in federal court.

The case involved the termination of a former vice-president of a large manufacturing company after thirty-two years of service. At the time of the firing, the man earned $132,500. Although the executive was fully vested before he was terminated, he was approximately one month short of becoming entitled to substantially higher pension payments and additional severance. He sued his former employer under Section 510 of ERISA, which makes it illegal for employers to discharge anyone for the purpose of cutting off their employee benefits or stopping them from collecting vested pension rights.

After the employee persuaded the jury that the reasons advanced for his discharge were unworthy of credence and were motivated by a discriminatory purpose—to deny him additional benefits (which the employer could not rebut)—he won the case and recovered damages of $650,000, representing additional pension and severance payments.

Cases such as this demonstrate the responsibility of employers to comply with all pension laws and ERISA regarding severance when a business is sold or when company policy has created an expectation that the purchasing company will continue an established severance policy crediting employees with prior years of service from the selling company.

If you begin working for a new employer who ceases business operations (i.e., declares bankruptcy) within a relatively short period of time after the hiring, you may have a valid claim of severance from the selling company under certain conditions.

Courts are beginning to recognize the rights of employees to severance in many situations, particularly when there is a massive layoff or group sale of assets due to a merger or acquisition.

---

**STRATEGY:** *You should not automatically acquiesce to a denial of benefits if you are fired and not offered severance, whatever your particular situation. Most workers are now receiving severance when they are fired; others are negotiating and receiving greater severance than the company's first offer. Statistics from my own law practice support this. The vast majority of all clients who hire me to negotiate firings obtain more severance and other benefits than the amount first offered directly to them by the employer.*

---

## Reliance on Hiring Promises

What if you resign a current job because you are offered a position with a new employer, but the job offer is then withdrawn? What happens if you are fired immediately after starting the new job? Unfortunately, this happens to thousands of workers each year in the United States.

Fortunately, you may be protected by a legal principle called *promissory estoppel*. In a Minnesota case, for example, the court rejected the company's argument that employers should be permitted to change their minds regarding job offers when they hire at will.

I once represented a man who flew to Texas and was offered a prestigious sales position. He resigned from a lucrative job to begin working for the new employer. Two weeks later he was fired when the company stated he "didn't fit in." The man attempted to get his old job back but was unsuccessful. He hired me to collect damages resulting from this unfair treatment. The case was settled satisfactorily out of court after I instituted a lawsuit on his behalf.

**STRATEGY:** *Always obtain a written contract with a new employer before you resign from a current employer. The contract should guarantee employment for a minimum period of time (such as three months) to avoid exploitation.*

Recognize that you may have rights if you are offered a job and rely on this promise of employment to your detriment. Consult an experienced labor lawyer immediately if this happens to you.

## Issues for Older Workers

The Age Discrimination in Employment Act (ADEA) prohibits employers from firing workers between the ages of forty and seventy because of their age. Similar discrimination laws have also been enacted in most states.

If you are an older worker and are being pressured to retire voluntarily by accepting an early retirement option or face the risk of being fired, demoted, or given a cut in pay, you may have grounds for an age discrimination complaint with the Equal Employment Opportunity Commission (EEOC) or a state agency such as the division of human rights. See Chapter 5 for information on age discrimination and the law.

Early retirement programs in and of themselves are legal and do not violate federal age discrimination laws so long as participation is voluntary. However, if you are offered a financial package containing early retirement inducements, be sure that it really contains worthwhile incentives such as additional pension benefits (i.e., extra years of age and service for pension calculations), lump sum severance payments (e.g., an extra year's pay), cash inducements, and retirement health programs.

Avoid accepting early retirement packages that penalize you if you return to the workplace with a new job. Some companies, for example, permanently discontinue health coverage when the employee takes another job where coverage is provided. The problem here is that you could wind up working for the new employer for a short period of time (say, six months) and find yourself out of a job. Accepting this condition would cause you to forfeit valuable health benefits that are essential during your older years.

If the employer offers decreasing benefits with increasing age, this may penalize you unfairly. Before accepting an early retirement package, understand that you may have a difficult time finding a new job or starting your own business because of your age. You should also recognize that inflation may eat away at your pension if you don't have a secure financial nest egg. Finally, if you are an older worker being asked to sign a waiver or release in exchange for more severance or early retirement inducements, be aware that the federal Older Workers Benefit Protection Act may give you added protection and should be reviewed with your attorney.

## Determining if the Decision Was Fair

When a terminated worker consults with me regarding his or her discharge, I consider the following to determine whether the firing was justified and/or legal:

- Are there mitigating factors that excuse or explain the employee's poor performance or misconduct?
- Was the employee victimized by a supervisor's bias or subjective evaluations rather than objective criteria?
- How long has the employee worked for the company? What kind of overall record does the employee have?
- Is termination appropriate under all of the circumstances?
- Does the punishment fit the crime?
- Has the employer followed a consistent policy of terminating workers with similar infractions?

- Is the employer retaliating against the employee because of a refusal to commit illegal or unethical acts, obeying a subpoena, falsifying records, or serving on extended jury duty or in the military rather than a bona fide business reason, disciplinary problem, or poor performance?
- Has the employee been fired because she filed a sex harassment complaint, is pregnant, or refused to submit to sexual favors?
- Is the fired employee being deprived of severance or other financial benefits that are due? Is this contrary to the employee's contract, letter agreement, company handbook, or employee manual?
- Is the firing contrary to a written contract?

If any of these considerations apply to you, consult an experienced employment attorney immediately.

## Massive Layoffs and Plant Closings

You may be entitled to receive WARN benefits including salary and/or severance for an additional period up to sixty days if you weren't given ample notice before losing your job. The application of the Worker Adjustment and Retraining Notification Act is detailed in Chapter 4.

Speak to an experienced attorney immediately if you believe that the law is not being properly followed in your case. Additionally, you may be entitled to receive free training in your local community where the plant closing or discharge en masse occurs. Contact the nearest U.S. Department of Labor office for further details if you are victimized in this area.

## Negotiating Strategies to Recover Maximum Compensation and Other Benefits

The first rule of thumb to remember when you are fired is to try to stall for time. Certainly, you should request additional time to think things over when informed of the firing decision. Stalling for time can help you learn important facts. This includes many of the points discussed earlier in this chapter: requesting to see your personnel file to review and collect favorable documents; learning who made the decision to fire you to see if there is a possibility of appealing that decision or whether that person had proper authority to terminate you; reconstructing promises of job security that were made; reviewing employment manuals; etc. This information can help you in negotiations for additional severance and other benefits.

If possible, do not accept the employer's first offer regarding severance. Always request a negotiating session to obtain more benefits. The following negotiation points are the actual strategies I give my clients; they can help you obtain a better severance arrangement, whatever your situation.

### WAGES (ALSO REFERRED TO AS SALARY CONTINUATION)

1. Try to stay on the payroll as long as possible.

2. Negotiate for the employer to continue to provide medical, dental, and hospitalization coverage (paid for by the employer) while you are receiving severance wages.

3. Avoid arrangements where you are offered severance for a specified period (e.g., six months) that automatically cease when you obtain a new job. Rather, make the offer noncontingent on new employment or arrange that differential severance will be paid in a *lump sum* if you obtain a new job prior to the expiration of the severance period. (For example, arrange that three months' worth of severance will be paid in a lump sum if a new job is ob-

tained three months before the six months of salary continuation expires.)

4. If severance pay is to be paid in a lump sum, consider asking for it immediately, not in installments over time.

5. Recognize that if you receive salary continuation rather than a lump sum payment, you may be ineligible in some states for unemployment benefits until the salary continuation payments cease; thus, consider the benefits of a lump sum payment rather than extended salary continuation where warranted.

6. Avoid accepting the employer's first offer; *negotiate, negotiate, negotiate.*

7. Attempt to receive at least *four weeks'* severance for every year of employment.

## OTHER COMPENSATION

1. If you have relocated recently at the request of the employer, try to obtain additional relocation allowances.

2. Discuss accrued vacation pay, overtime, and unused sick pay. Be sure you are paid for these items.

3. If you were fired without notice, ask for two additional weeks of salary in lieu of the employer's lack of notice.

4. If commissions are due or about to become due, insist that you be paid immediately; do not waive these expected benefits.

## BONUS

1. Understand how your bonus is computed.

2. If you were entitled to receive a bonus at the end of the year, ask for it now.

3. Argue that the firing deprived you of the right to receive the bonus if the employer refuses to pay; or

4. Insist that your bonus be prorated according to the amount of time you worked during the year if this argument is rejected.

## PENSION AND PROFIT-SHARING BENEFITS

1. Ask for details regarding the nature of your benefits. Under federal law, you are entitled to an accurate, written description of all benefits.

2. Be aware of all plans, funds, and programs that may have been established on your behalf. These may include the following:

**Defined contribution plans.** These include profit-sharing plans, thrift plans, money purchase pension plans, and cash or deferred profit-sharing plans. All of these plans are characterized by the fact that each participant has an individual bookkeeping account under the plan which records the participant's total interest in the plan assets. Monies are contributed or credited in accordance with the rules of the plan contained in the plan document.

**Defined benefit plans.** These are characterized as pension plans that base the benefits payable to participants upon a formula contained in the plan. Such plans are not funded individually as in defined contribution plans. Rather, they are typically funded on a group basis.

**Employee welfare benefit plans.** These are often funded through insurance and typically provide participants with medical, health, accident, disability, death, unemployment, or vacation benefits.

**ERISA (Employee Retirement Income Security Act) plans.** These may not be as definite as the above. Rather, if the employer communicates that certain benefits are available, whom the intended beneficiaries are, and how the plan is funded, the employer may be liable to pay such benefits even in the absence of a formal, written plan.

3. If you are fired just before the vesting of a pension (e.g., two months before the vesting date), argue that the timing of the firing

is suspect and that public policy requires the employer to grant your pension. If the employer refuses, consult an experienced lawyer immediately.

4. Demand a copy of the employer's pension and/or profit-sharing plans from the plan administrator if the employer refuses to furnish you with accurate details. (You may have to pay for the cost of photocopying.) As a participant in the company's pension and/or profit-sharing plans, you are entitled to certain rights and protections under the Employee Retirement Income Security Act of 1974 (ERISA). ERISA provides that all plan participants are entitled to examine without charge all plan documents, such as insurance contracts and copies of all documents filed by the plan with the U.S. Department of Labor, including detailed annual reports and plan descriptions.

Under ERISA, if you request materials from a plan (including summaries of each plan's annual financial report) and do not receive them within thirty days, you may file suit in federal or state court. Contact the plan administrator for the company immediately in writing if your claim is denied or if you do not receive an adequate response shortly after a firing. If no adequate response is received, seek assistance from the U.S. Department of Labor or a competent employment lawyer to protect your rights. If you file suit, the court may require the plan administrator to provide the materials and pay up to $100 a day until you receive them, unless the materials were not sent for reasons beyond the control of the administrator.

5. Contact the plan administrator immediately to protect your rights if your claim is denied or if you have not received a proper accounting or payment of your retirement benefits from your employer. Under federal law, every employee, participant, or beneficiary covered under a benefit plan covered by ERISA has the right to receive written notification stating specific reasons for the denial of a claim. The letter on page 296 illustrates this. Additionally, you have the right to a full and fair review by the plan administrator if you are denied benefits.

If you have a claim for benefits that is denied or ignored in whole or in part after making such a request, you may file suit in a state or federal court. If it should happen that plan fiduciaries misuse a plan's money, or if you are discriminated against for asserting your rights, you may seek assistance from the U.S. Department of Labor, or you may file suit in a federal court. The court will decide who should pay court costs and legal fees. If you are successful, the court may order the person you have sued to pay these costs and fees. If you lose (i.e., if it finds your claim to be frivolous), the court may order you to pay these costs and fees.

## OTHER BENEFITS

1. Request continued use of an office, secretary, telephone, or mail facilities to assist you in your job search, if appropriate.

2. Consider requesting a loan to tide you over while looking for a new job, if appropriate.

3. Consider requesting continued use of your company car or ask to buy the car or take over the lease at a reduced rate, if appropriate.

4. Request that the employer pay for outplacement guidance, career counseling, and résumé preparation services including typing and incidental expenses, if appropriate.

## MEDICAL, DENTAL, AND HOSPITALIZATION COVERAGE

1. Does coverage stop the day you are fired, or is there a grace period? Ask for a copy of the applicable policy.

2. Can you extend coverage beyond the grace period?

3. Be sure to have your benefits explained to you if you do not understand them.

4. Can you assume the policy at a reduced personal cost? This is sometimes referred to as a *conversion policy.*

5. If you are married and your spouse is working, you may be covered under your spouse's policy. If so, do you want to continue paying for your own policy?

6. Be sure the employer has notified you regarding your rights under COBRA (the Consolidated Omnibus Budget Reconciliation Act of 1985).

## Sample Demand Letter for ERISA Retirement Benefits

Your Name
Address
Telephone Number
Date

Name of Officer or Employer
Title
Name of Employer
Address

Re: My ERISA Retirement Benefits

Dear (Name of Officer):

As you know, I was terminated (or resigned) on (specify date). However, I have not received a written description of all my retirement benefits under federal ERISA law. (Or, if applicable, state: I have not received the correct computation of all benefits due me. Or: I believe I was fired shortly before the vesting of a pension, in violation of my ERISA rights.)

Your company has a legal obligation to provide me with accurate information concerning all applicable profit-sharing, pension, employee welfare, benefit, and other plans. Therefore I would like you to send me (specify what you want, such as to receive a copy of the employer's formal pension and/or profit-sharing plans, recomputation of your benefits, or offer of a pension).

It is imperative that I receive a response to my request

immediately in writing to avoid having me take prompt legal action to enforce my rights.

Hopefully, this will not be necessary and I thank you for your prompt attention in this matter.

Very truly yours,
Your Name

*Sent certified mail, return receipt requested.*

**The COBRA law and post-termination health benefits.** The most important provisions of the Consolidated Omnibus Budget Reconciliation Act of 1985 (COBRA) require many private employers (who employ more than twenty workers on a typical business day) to continue to make group health insurance available to workers who are discharged from employment. Most people benefit, since the cost of maintaining such insurance is cheaper; the individual pays for coverage at the employer's group rate rather than the cost of an individual policy.

All employees who are discharged as a result of a voluntary or involuntary termination (with the exception of those who are fired for gross misconduct) may elect to continue plan benefits currently in effect *at their own cost* provided the employee or beneficiary makes an initial payment within thirty days of notification and is not covered under Medicare or any other group health plan. The law also applies to qualified beneficiaries who were covered by the employer's group health plan the day before the discharge. Thus, for example, if the employee chooses not to continue such coverage, his or her spouse and dependent children may elect continued coverage at their own expense.

The extended coverage period is eighteen months upon the termination of the covered employee; upon the death, divorce, or legal separation of the covered employee, the benefit coverage period is thirty-six months to spouses and dependents.

The law requires that employers or plan administrators separately notify all employees and covered spouses and dependents of their rights to continued coverage. After receiving such notification, the individual then has sixty days to elect to continue coverage. Additionally, employees and dependents whose insurance is protected under COBRA must also be provided with any conversion privilege otherwise available in the plan (if such coverage exists) within a six-month period preceding the date that coverage would terminate at the end of the continuation period.

In the event the employer fails to offer such coverage, the law imposes penalties ranging from $100 to $200 per day for each day the employee is not covered.

---

**STRATEGY:** *Be sure you know your rights under COBRA in the event you are fired. This is especially true if you or a spouse or dependent is sick and needs the insurance benefits to pay necessary medical bills. You are entitled to such protection even if you have worked for the employer for only a short period of time. See Chapter 3 for more about this law.*

---

Remember, however, that you cannot obtain benefits if you are fired for gross misconduct. This term is relatively ambiguous; the burden of proof is on the employer to prove that the discharge was for a compelling reason (fighting on the job, stealing, working while intoxicated, etc.). Also be aware that some employers reduce a person's working hours to a point that makes them ineligible for group health coverage. However, COBRA may still be available to workers in these situations.

If an employer refuses to negotiate continued health benefits as part of a severance package or fails to notify you of the existence of such benefits, write a letter or contact the personnel office immediately to protect your rights. If the letter is not answered or if the employer refuses to offer continued COBRA benefits after a discharge for any reason, consult an experienced employment lawyer immediately.

COBRA requires that most employers offer continuation of coverage for an additional eighteen months to former employees who were discharged as a result of a voluntary or involuntary termination (with the exception of gross misconduct); all terminated employees have the option to continue medical plan benefits at their cost. You must be notified within sixty days of your right to continue such coverage. Send a letter whenever you do not receive such a notification shortly after a firing. A well-drafted letter can spur the company into action and protect your rights.

### LIFE INSURANCE

1. Can you convert the policy to your benefit at your own cost? Don't forget to inquire about this.

2. Is there any equity in the employer's life insurance plan that accrues to you upon termination? Inquire about this and ask for a copy of all policies presently in effect.

### YOUR COVER STORY

1. Clarify how the news of your departure will be announced. Discuss and agree with management on the story to be told to outsiders.

2. Consider whether you want it to be known that you resigned for personal reasons or that you were terminated due to a "business reorganization." These are neutral explanations that are preferable to firings for misconduct or poor performance.

3. *Recognize that if you resign, you may be forfeiting unemployment benefits.* Thus, avoid resigning wherever possible. Although you may prefer that outsiders be told you resigned for personal reasons, confirm with the employer that you will be able to apply for unemployment benefits. That way your local department of labor will be advised that there was a termination (as opposed to a resignation, since this is what really happened) and you can still tell outsiders you resigned.

4. Request that a copy of a favorable letter of recommendation be given to you *before* you leave the company. The letter should state the dates of your employment, the positions held, and that you performed all of your job duties in a diligent and satisfactory fashion. If possible, the letter should be signed by a qualified officer or supervisor who worked with you and knows you well. Do not rely on promises that the employer will furnish prospective employers with a favorable recommendation, since many fail to do this after employees leave the company. Thus, *always* attempt to have such a letter *in hand* before you leave.

The letter below is an example of the kind of recommendation you may find acceptable. It is best not to include the specific reason for the parting in such a letter. This will enable you to offer whatever reasons you feel appropriate under the circumstances.

5. Request that key members of the company be notified of your departure in writing. If possible, approve the contents of such a memo before distribution. Written memos can dispel false rumors about your termination. A positive memo, such as the one on page 301, may assist you in obtaining a new job. Remember, news of a firing usually spreads rapidly; you don't want to be the subject of false rumors or innuendo.

## Sample Letter of Recommendation

Date

To whom it may concern:

I am pleased to submit this letter of recommendation on behalf of (name of employee).

(Name of employee) worked for the company from (date) through (date). During this period (name of employee) was promoted from (specify title) to (specify title).

During the past (specify) years, I have had the opportunity to work closely with (name of employee). At all times I found him/her to be diligent and dependable, and (name of employee) rendered competent and satisfactory services on the company's behalf.

I heartily recommend (name of employee) as a candidate for employment of his/her choosing.

Very truly yours,
Name of Officer

## Sample Termination Memo

MEMORANDUM

To: Employees of (Name of Company or pertinent division)
From: (Name of Officer or Supervisor)
Subject: Resignation of (Name of Employee)

I wish to inform you that (name of employee) has decided to pursue other interests and has elected to resign effective (specify when) from the company.

(Name of employee) has contributed greatly to the growth of the (specify) division and he/she will indeed be missed.

We all wish (name of employee) the best of continued good health and success.

## GOLDEN PARACHUTES

1. Determine if you are entitled to receive additional benefits under a severance contract or golden parachute. Generally, golden parachutes are arrangements between an executive and a corporation that are contingent upon a change in control of the corporation. Typically, additional cash and other economic benefits are paid to the terminated individual following the discharge (provided the employee is not fired for cause). Although most compa-

nies cover only a limited group of key employees, some companies have determined that it is appropriate to cover a much larger group.

2. Speak to an experienced employment attorney immediately to protect your rights if the employer refuses to provide all the benefits specified in your contract.

## Protecting the Severance Arrangement

After you have negotiated your severance package and are satisfied that you have adequately covered all of your options and benefits, you must decide whether to accept the company's final offer or retain a lawyer in the attempt to obtain additional compensation.

Before retaining a lawyer, be sure that you feel comfortable with him or her and that the lawyer will be able to render competent services on your behalf. This can be accomplished by following many of the strategies contained in Chapter 10.

---

**STRATEGY:** *When you are owed wages, accrued overtime pay, vacation pay, an earned bonus, commissions, stock options, or other compensation, or believe the employer violated the law, the lawyer may first advise you to send letters of protest on your own in the attempt to obtain an amicable settlement. The letters serve several functions: in addition to helping you settle the matter privately (and saving money allocated for legal fees), they can help your lawyer if the company refuses to respond or responds inaccurately or negatively. A letter can help you document your claim and often places the employer or its actions in a poor light.*

---

Whomever you retain, it is important that the lawyer get started on your matter immediately. Time is crucial in all termination cases; action must be taken immediately to demonstrate the seriousness of your resolve. In fact, the longer a lawyer waits before contacting the employer, the weaker a case can become. That is why the author prefers to contact the employer within a week or two after the individual has been fired.

When my office is retained to represent a terminated individual, a letter is sent to the employer by messenger or certified mail, return receipt requested, usually the day I am hired. This ensures that the employer is notified quickly that I have been hired to discuss and negotiate the circumstances surrounding the person's termination, the inadequacy of the severance offer, the amount of money in commissions or other benefits still due, and other considerations. The initial demand letter is kept brief because I do not want to "tip my hand" and state my case to someone I have never spoken with. Of course, it is always desired that the employer contact me as soon as possible. *This helps my negotiating position.*

A variety of techniques are used during negotiations; I typically stress that the employer should offer more to settle the matter amicably and avoid time-consuming and expensive legal action. I write a simple demand letter when I represent a terminated employee seeking severance.

An officer of the employer or a company attorney usually contacts me after receiving such a letter. Negotiations then ensue to determine if the matter can be settled out of court. Usually it is. I believe this is due to several factors. First, most employers want to avoid the poor publicity that can arise from a protracted court battle. Second, when companies are contacted by attorneys representing terminated employees, they must weigh whether it is wise to offer additional compensation to settle out of court versus spending thousands of dollars in legal expenses and lost work hours resulting from defending the charges in formal litigation. Finally, if the firing is illegal, company exposure can amount to hundreds of thousands of dollars in actual damages (which doesn't include interest, attorney fees, and costs that are sometimes awarded).

A pragmatic approach is often taken and most matters are settled. The employee receives additional severance and other benefits and the employer avoids a lawsuit. Remember that the mark of a good settlement is that no side is truly happy with the result. The employer believes too much money was paid to settle; conversely, the employee sometimes feels that he or she received too little. However, given the confines of the legal system (the long delays before the case is actually tried, the tremendous expenses involved, etc.), many terminated employees often achieve a fair out-of-court settlement for their troubles.

If you decide that contacting a lawyer is not necessary when you obtained a fair and equitable settlement on your own, request that the employer confirm the deal in writing. Such a letter will clarify the points agreed upon and document the severance arrangement that has been made. If the employer fails to abide by an important term (such as a promise of salary continuation for six months), the letter can increase your chances of success if you decide to sue for breach of contract.

The following letter was given to a former client of mine who recently negotiated to receive an additional one year's severance arrangement and other benefits with my assistance. Note the protections insisted on by the employer in the latter part of the agreement.

## Employer Confirmation of Severance Agreement

Date

Name of Employee
Address

Dear (Name of Employee),

This will confirm our agreement regarding your employment status with (name of employer).

We agreed as follows:

1. Your services as Vice President of (specify division) will terminate by mutual agreement effective (date).

2. Although your services as Vice President will not be required beyond (specify date), you agree to be available to (name of employer) through (specify termination date) to render advice, answer any questions, and provide information regarding company business.

3. Through (specify termination date) except as provided in paragraph 4 below, you will continue to receive your regular biweekly salary of (specify) and you may continue to participate in those company benefit plans in which you are currently enrolled. In addition to your final paycheck, you will receive from the company on or about (specify termination date) or given as provided for in paragraph 4 hereunder, the sum of (specify) less applicable deductions for local, state, and federal taxes, as a bonus for the present year.

4. If you obtain other regular, full-time employment prior to (specify termination date), then, upon commencement of such employment (date of new employment), your regular biweekly salary payments and your participation in company benefit plans, as described in paragraph 3 above, shall cease; however, medical and dental coverage previously provided you shall be continued for an additional period of three months at a cost to be borne by (name of employer). In such event, you will receive in a lump sum, less applicable deductions for taxes, the remaining amount you would have received on a biweekly basis from the date of new employment through (specify termination date) plus the (specify sum) bonus, less taxes, payment referred to in paragraph 3 within two weeks of your date of new employment. You agree to notify the company

immediately of the date on which such regular full-time employment will commence.

5. You acknowledge that the sums referred to in paragraphs 3 and 4 above include any and all monies due you from the company, contractual or otherwise, to which you may be entitled, except for any vested benefit you may have in the (name of employer) Savings and Investment Plan and the Pension Plan.

6. (Name of employer) will provide you with available office space, telephone service, and clerical help on an as-needed basis at (address) until you obtain other regular full-time employment or (date), whichever occurs first.

7. You agree to cooperate fully with (name of employer) in their defense of other participation in any administrative, judicial, or collective bargaining proceeding arising from any charge, complaint, grievance, or action which has been or may be filed.

8. You, on behalf of yourself and your heirs, representatives, and assigns, hereby release (name of employer), its parents, their subsidiaries and divisions, and all of their respective current and former directors, officers, shareholders, successors, agents, representatives, and employees from any and all claims you ever had, now have, or may in the future assert regarding any matter that predates this agreement, including, without limitation, all claims regarding your employment at or termination of employment from (name of employer), any contract, express or implied, any tort, or any breach of a fair employment practice law, including Title VII, the Age Discrimination in Employment Act, and any other local, state, or federal equal opportunity law.

9. You acknowledge that you have had the opportunity to review this agreement with counsel of your own choosing, that you are fully

aware of the agreement's contents and of its legal effects, and that you are voluntarily entering into this agreement.

10. You agree that any confidential information you acquired while an employee of the company shall not be disclosed to any other person or used in a manner detrimental to the company's interests.

11. Neither you nor anyone acting on your behalf shall publicize, disseminate, or otherwise make known the terms of this agreement to any other person, except to those rendering financial or legal advice, or unless required to do so by court order or other compulsory process of law.

12. The provisions of this agreement are severable and if any provision is held to be invalid or unenforceable it shall not affect the validity or enforceability of any other provision.

13. This agreement sets forth the entire agreement between you and the company and supersedes any and all prior oral or written agreements or understandings between you and the company concerning this subject matter. This agreement may not be altered, amended, or modified except by a further writing signed by you and (name of employer).

14. In the event (name of employer) becomes insolvent, bankrupt, is sold, or is unable in any way to pay the amounts due you under the terms of this agreement, then such obligations shall be undertaken and assumed by (specify parent company) and all such sums shall be guaranteed by (name of parent company).

15. In the event that any monies due under this agreement are not paid for any reason, then the release referred to in paragraph 8 shall be null and void and of no effect.

If the foregoing correctly and fully recites the substance of our agreement, please so signify by signing in the space below.

Dated:

Very truly yours,
Name of Employer
By: Name of Officer, Title

Accepted and agreed:
Name of Employee

In the event the employer refuses to provide such a letter, it is advisable to send a letter to the company by certified mail, return receipt requested, confirming the arrangement that has been made. The letter should state that if any terms are ambiguous or incorrect, a written reply will be sent to you immediately. If no response is received, you will be able to rely on the terms of the letter in most situations. The following is a good example.

## Employee Confirmation of Severance Agreement

Your Name
Address
Telephone Number
Date

Name of Corporate Officer
Title
Name of Employer
Address

Re: Our severance agreement

Dear (Name of Corporate Officer),

This will confirm our discussion and agreement regarding my termination:

1. I will be kept on the payroll through (specify date) and will receive (specify) weeks' vacation pay, which shall be included with my last check on that date.

2. (Name of company) shall pay me a bonus of (specify) within (specify) days from the date of this letter.

3. (Name of company) will purchase both my nonvested and vested company stock, totaling (specify) shares at the buy-in price of (specify) per share, or at the market rate if it is higher at the time of repurchase, on or before (specify date).

4. (Name of company) will continue to maintain in effect all medical, dental, hospitalization, and life insurance policies presently in effect through (specify date). After that date, I have been advised that I may convert said policies at my sole cost and expense and that coverage for these policies will not lapse.

5. I will be permitted to use the company's premises at (specify location) from the hours of 9:00 A.M. until 5:00 P.M. This shall include the use of a secretary, telephone, stationery, and other amenities at the company's sole cost and expense to assist me in obtaining another position.

6. I will be permitted to continue using the automobile previously supplied to me through (specify date) under the same terms and conditions presently in effect. On that date, I will return all sets of keys in my possession together with all other papers and documents belonging to the company.

7. (Name of company) will reimburse me for all reasonable and necessary expenses related to the completion of company business after I submit appropriate vouchers and records within (specify) days of presentment thereto.

8. (Name of company) agrees to provide me with a favorable letter of recommendation and reference(s), and will announce to the trade that I am resigning for "personal reasons." I am enclosing a letter for that purpose which will be reviewed and signed by (specify person) and returned to me immediately.

9. Although unanticipated, (name of company) will not contest my filing for unemployment insurance benefits after (specify date), and will assist me in promptly executing all documents necessary for that purpose.

10. If a position is procured by me prior to (specify date), a lump sum payment for my remaining severance will be paid within (specify) days after my notification of same. Additionally, the stock referred to in paragraph 3 above will be purchased as of the date of my employment with another company if prior to (specify date) and will be paid to me within (specify) days of my notification.

If any of the terms of this letter are ambiguous or incorrect, please advise me immediately in writing specifying the items that are incorrect. Otherwise, this letter shall set forth our entire understanding in this matter, which cannot be changed orally.

(Name of corporate officer), I want to personally thank you for your assistance and cooperation in this matter and wish you all the best in the future.

Very truly yours,
Your Name

*Sent certified mail, return receipt requested.*

Be sure to draft the agreement accurately, since all ambiguities are usually construed against the person who writes such a letter. In addition, be prepared to send follow-up letters. Using the preceding case as an example, it would be wise to notify the company in writing if you obtained another job prior to the severance cutoff date. This is confirmed as shown in the following sample.

## Sample Letter Requesting Unpaid Severance

Your Name
Address
Telephone Number
Date

Name of Corporate Officer
Title
Name of Company
Address

Re: Subsequent development to our agreement dated (specify)

Dear (Name of Corporate Officer),

I hope all is well with you and yours.

As a follow-up to our letter of agreement dated (specify), I am informing you that I have accepted employment with another company effective (specify date).

Therefore, I expect to receive a lump sum payment representing all unpaid severance through (specify date) plus (specify) weeks of vacation pay on or before (specify date).

Furthermore, I believe I am entitled to compensation for my stock totaling (specify amount) within (specify number of days).

As of this date, I am returning all keys to the office by messenger together with keys to the company car. I have also included the last voucher for company-related expenses.

Thank you for your prompt cooperation in these matters.

Very truly yours,
Your Name

Enc.


# RELEASES

Always be cautious if the employer asks you to sign a release. Generally, releases extinguish potential claims. Employees sometimes voluntarily sign such documents when they are fired, without fully understanding the ramifications of such an act. Later they regret taking such action after consulting a lawyer and learning they forfeited valuable rights without receiving much in return.

Since you may be out of luck if you sign such a document, consider the following strategies *whenever* you are asked to sign a release.

---

**STRATEGY 1:** *Never sign a release unless you are satisfied with the company's offer. You should never relinquish a potentially valuable right without obtaining something of value in return.*

---

**STRATEGY 2:** *Read the release carefully before signing it. Most releases are complicated documents. Many have settlement* *agreements, releases, waivers, and nondisclosure provisions all contained in one document.*

*What does the release say? Are you prohibited from telling others about the terms of your settlement? This is referred to as a "gag order" provision. Many employers insert gag order clauses in the release which require all settlement monies to be forfeited and returned in the event you reveal the terms of the settlement to others. Obviously, you should question this provision and avoid signing it if possible.*

*Does the release prohibit you from working for a competitor or starting a competing business? Without such a clause you are free to work for the employer of your choosing. This is a valuable right which should never be given up easily.*

---

**STRATEGY 3:** *Negotiate additional clauses for your protection. First, make sure the release will be null and void if any monies due under the agreement are not paid. Second, a guarantee might be included that obligates the parent company to pay all remaining sums due under the agreement in the event a subsidiary corporation becomes bankrupt, insolvent, or fails for any reason to pay the amount due. These are examples of the kinds of points to consider and implement in your agreement.*

---

**STRATEGY 4:** *Obtain mutual releases where appropriate. Try to get the employer to give you a release whenever you are giving one to the employer. This is because you want to be sure that the employer can never sue you at a later time for something you did.*

---

**STRATEGY 5:** *Speak to a lawyer immediately whenever the employer requests that a release be signed. Not understanding the consequences of their actions, people often waive valuable rights by signing such agreements. For example, you may be waiving valuable claims based on discrimination, breach of contract, un-*

*fair discharge, additional commissions or other monies owed. Never sign a release until you are knowledgeable of all potential rights that you are giving up.*

---

A competent lawyer can also take other practical steps for your protection. For example, he or she can insist that the release be held in escrow until all sums due under the agreement have been paid. This means that the employer could not rely on the signed release until it had fully performed all of the obligations required by the release. This is important and should never be overlooked.

If you believe the release was signed under conditions of fraud, duress, or mistake, it can be rescinded provided you act promptly. Thus, it is essential to consult a lawyer immediately.

Finally, as previously stated, the federal Older Workers Benefit Protection Act codifies existing law by providing that an older worker may not waive rights or claims of discrimination under the Age Discrimination in Employment Act unless the waiver is clear, voluntarily signed, part of an agreement where additional severance pay, early retirement benefits, or other monies are given, and the individual is given at least twenty-one days to consider the agreement containing such a waiver and seven days to change his or her mind after he or she signs it. Speak to a lawyer to advise you of your rights if you are asked to sign a complicated waiver that you believe does not comply with the requirements of this law.

# CHAPTER 7

# Related Post-Termination Issues

## Resigning Properly

Most people do not know how to resign properly. The slightest mistake can expose you to a lawsuit or cause the forfeiture of valuable benefits. Some people resign without receiving a firm job offer from a new employer. Later, after learning the new job did not materialize, they are unable to be rehired by their former employers and spend months out of work unnecessarily.

It doesn't have to happen this way. Problems such as these can be avoided by thinking ahead. A proper resignation occurs when you are able to step into a new job with increased benefits without missing a day's pay, have no legal exposure, and collect what you are owed from the former employer.

The following rules should be considered whenever you are thinking about resigning from a present job.

**1. Sign a written contract with a new employer before resigning.** This is essential. A written contract with a definite term of employment (e.g., six months or one year) may protect you from situations in which the new employer changes his or her mind and decides not to hire you, or fires you after a short period of time. Since this often has devastating consequences, you should *never* leave a job without first obtaining a signed, written contract or letter agreement from a new employer. If the new employer is hesitant about putting the deal in writing, think twice before making the move to "greener pastures."

**2. Review your current contract or letter of agreement.** What does it say regarding termination? For example, if the contract states that written notice is required to be sent by registered mail thirty days prior to the effective termination date, be sure to comply with those terms. Otherwise, your failure to do so could cause the employer to sue you for breach of contract.

Does your contract or letter of agreement contain provisions restricting you from working for a competitor, disseminating confidential or proprietary information learned on the job, or calling on accounts previously served by you during your current employment? Such clauses are called restrictive covenants or covenants not to compete, and may or may not be enforceable depending upon the particular circumstances and facts.

**3. Is it necessary to give notice?** In most jobs, notice is not required. However, if you are entitled to a large bonus or commission in the near future, avoid resigning before you have received such a benefit.

**4. Should you resign by letter?** Most people think it is proper to resign by letter, but it is not always in your best interest to do so. A letter can clarify resignation benefits, request prompt payment of monies previously due, or put you on record that the resignation will not be effective until some later date. If this is important, then a letter should be sent. However, you should keep the letter brief and avoid giving specific reasons for the resignation, because this can preclude you from offering other reasons in the event of a lawsuit.

**5. Should you resign if given the choice?** Many people mistakenly believe that it is better to resign than be fired. *This is not always true.* By resigning, you may waive valuable benefits, including severance pay and bonuses. This is because many employers have written policies stating that no severance or other post-termination benefits will be paid to workers who resign. Additionally, in many states you are not entitled to unemployment insurance benefits after voluntarily resigning from a job. If you are a commission salesperson, it is more difficult to argue that you are entitled to commissions due on orders shipped after a resignation (as opposed to after a firing).

Thus, always think twice about resigning if the employer gives you the option of resignation or discharge. In fact, I usually prefer my clients to be fired rather than resign whenever possible, since in this way potential damage claims and severance benefits may remain intact.

If you are worried about what outsiders may think, you can always negotiate that the employer will tell outsiders you "resigned for personal reasons" even if you were fired. The golden rule is to never quit. In conclusion, always speak to an experienced labor lawyer *before* resigning from any significant job, since by resigning you may be forfeiting valuable rights unnecessarily.

**6. Keep your lips sealed.** Never tell friends or business associates of your decision to resign before telling your current employer. The expression "loose lips sink ships" is certainly true in this area.

**7. Avoid bad-mouthing.** It is not a good idea to tell others about the circumstances surrounding the resignation, particularly if you are leaving on less-than-pleasant terms. Many employers have sued former employees for defamation, product disparagement, and unfair competition upon discovering that slanderous comments were made. Additionally, when the statement disparages the quality of a company's product and at the same time implies that an officer or principal of the employer is dishonest, fraudulent, or incompetent (thus affecting the individual's personal reputation), a private lawsuit for personal defamation may also be brought. Some companies withhold severance pay and other benefits as a way of getting even. Thus, avoid discussing your employer in a negative way with anyone.

**8. Return property belonging to the employer.** Disputes sometimes occur when property belonging to the employer is not returned. You must return such property (automobile keys, confidential customer lists, samples, etc.) immediately upon resignation to avoid claims of conversion, fraud, and breach of contract. And if you are returning items by mail, get a receipt to prove delivery.

Remember, in most states an employer cannot withhold earned salary or accrued vacation benefits for any reason. Thus, assert your rights and demand your money.

## Restrictive Covenants and Related Problems

As explained in detail in Chapter 2, restrictive covenants are agreements that prohibit a person from directly competing with, or working for the competitor of, one's employer. Historically, promises by employees not to compete with employers after termination of a job were enforceable provided a bona fide business interest existed that required protection, there was no undue hardship on the employee, and the restriction was not unreasonable in terms of time and/or geographic scope, did not violate public policy, and was not considered a restraint of trade. Utilized by companies to protect hard-won business and retain prized employees, such agreements were generally protected by the courts.

However, many courts are now viewing such covenants as unfair because they limit a person's ability to earn a living. As a result, executive mobility is becoming harder to contain. When judges decide that such contracts go too far in restraining employees, they either modify the terms (making them less restrictive) or declare such covenants to be totally unenforceable and of no legal effect.

There are no set rules regarding the enforcement of restrictive covenants. *Each case must be analyzed on its own particular merits.* Some kinds of noncompete pacts stand a better chance of being upheld than others. These include situations where the seller of a business agrees not to start a competing business that could injure the buyer's interests, where trade secrets are involved, or where the employer paid additional consideration (e.g., a bonus of $10,000 was given to the employee as inducement to sign a contract containing a restrictive covenant).

## Defamatory Job References

Defamation can occur in the workplace whenever an employer communicates information about an employee. For example, defamatory statements are often made to outsiders and prospective employers regarding an employee's job performance or problems on the job. Third parties are sometimes shown an employee's personnel file or performance evaluations. Such records often contain derogatory comments which are later proved to be untrue. In other situations inaccurate memoranda are circulated within a company. This causes serious consequences when the employer does not take adequate precautions to determine whether derogatory information in the memoranda is accurate.

Failure to recommend a former employee for a new position can give rise to a potential cause of action for libel or slander even when the employee has sustained no actual economic harm. This is because all states generally recognize a valid defamation lawsuit when false written or spoken words are communicated to a third party which disparage a person in his trade, office, or profession and when the employer (or former employer) negligently failed to check the accuracy of such statements.

Two forms of wrongs fall under the larger heading of defamation. *Slander* arises when an unfair and untrue oral statement is communicated to a third party and damages the individual's reputation. The spoken words must pertain to a person's poor moral character, unreliability, dishonesty, financial instability (e.g., a false statement that the person is filing for bankruptcy or is always being sued), or failure to live up to contractual obligations or business responsibilities. *Libel* arises when an unfair and untrue statement is made about a person in writing. The statement becomes actionable when it is read by a third party and damages the person's business or personal reputation. Such comments are frequently made in a letter or memo.

Mere statements that an employee was discharged from employment, or truthful statements pertaining to that employee's work habits, are not defamatory. Truth is a total defense against claims of libel or slander. Charging a worker with bad manners, being careless or a troublemaker, not having sufficient skills, or not adequately performing a job will not qualify as defamation.

However, statements that the individual was discharged for cause or unsatisfactory performance, incompetence, or insubordination coupled with the employer's refusal to give a recommendation may be potentially damaging, and thus actionable as defamation.

In some states the law protects employees fired on false charges of bad conduct who themselves reveal the charges (as opposed to a false communication or reference made by the employer).

As previously indicated, defamation does not only arise from dissemination of damaging information to prospective employers. It can also occur on-site. Harshly criticizing an employee can make an employer vulnerable in a defamation lawsuit. For example, if you are accused in front of others of stealing company property and slanderous remarks are made (such as "You are a crook"), your employer may be guilty of defamation if the remarks are proved false.

Defamation may also arise through acts impugning a person's reputation from the firing itself. In one case a man was discharged after he failed a lie-detector test. The employee proved the company defamed him by firing him under circumstances strongly implying he was guilty of theft. After demonstrating that the test results were improperly evaluated by an unqualified and unlicensed polygraph examiner and that he was not guilty of the theft, the man was awarded $150,000.

To avoid exposure in this area, many employers are now advising staff to merely confirm an individual's former employment, the dates of employment, and last position held. They are being advised that it is wise never to offer an opinion about an employee's work performance unless it is conclusively positive.

Most states have ruled that employers have a qualified privilege when discussing an ex-employee's job performance with a prospective employer. This means that the employer may be excused for disseminating information about an individual that later turns out to be false if the person responsible for disseminating such information did so in the course of his or her normal duties (such as a personnel supervisor who writes performance appraisals about individuals).

However, a qualified privilege can be lost or abused and an employer can be liable if an executive or personnel supervisor knowingly makes false defamatory comments about a former employee due to reckless disregard for the truth, ill will, or spite.

The first thing to remember in any defamation lawsuit is that you must prove that false statements were made. This is often hard to do. For example, if you are told by an employee recruiter that he or she heard slanderous comments from your former employer, the recruiter would have to testify in court in order for you to prevail, and many people are reluctant to do this.

In addition, truth is an absolute defense in any defamation lawsuit. This means that if your employer disseminates harmful information that is true, or you are fired for a legitimate reason that is properly documented and can be proved by the company, you may lose your case.

Finally, many cases are lost when employers assert a qualified privilege defense.

However, even if a lawyer determines that commencing a lawsuit in this area is not in your best interest, you can compel an employer to stop disclosing harmful information to others. That is why it is critical to consult an experienced labor lawyer immediately to analyze and protect your rights.

Damages do not have to be proved in all instances. The law treats certain statements as defamatory per se, which means that the person or business does not have to prove actual damages to win a verdict; money can be recovered simply because the statement is untrue. Examples of per se statements are:

- Accusing a person of serious misconduct in her business, trade, or profession (e.g., that a doctor or group medical practice she is affiliated with has trouble paying its bills, is discontinuing its operations and filing for bankruptcy, is fi-

nancially unstable, incompetent, of poor moral character, unreliable, or dishonest)
- Imputing to a person the commission of a criminal offense
- Charging a person with dishonesty (e.g., "She is a crook and steals money from the company")
- Accusing a person of serious sexual misconduct (e.g., "She is a whore")
- Stating that a person has a loathsome or deadly disease (such as AIDS)

In a few states "service letter" statutes have been passed giving fired workers legal protection. Under the laws in these states, employers are required to give a terminated worker a true written statement regarding the cause of his or her dismissal. Once such an explanation is received, the employer cannot furnish prospective employers with reasons that deviate from those given in the service letter.

In those states an employer can be sued for damages for refusing to tell you why you were fired, for providing you with false reasons, or for changing its story and offering additional reasons to outsiders or during legal proceedings (i.e., at a trial or arbitration).

Thus, it is a good idea to discover the reasons why you were fired, particularly in those states that have passed service letter statutes. This can be done by sending the employer a letter similar to the following.

## Sample Letter Protesting Inaccurate Job References

Your Name
Address
Telephone Number
Date

Name of Officer of Employer
Title
Name of Employer
Address

Dear (Name of Officer),

On (date), I applied for a job with (name of potential employer). At the interview, I learned that you had submitted an inaccurate, unfavorable reference about me.

You supposedly said the reason I was fired was that I was excessively late on the job. We both know this is incorrect. I had the opportunity to review the entire contents of my personnel file after I was dismissed. Not one reference was made anywhere in the file to lateness.

Kindly cease and desist from making any such unfavorable remarks about my job performance, particularly to potential employers. If I learn that you disregard this request, be assured that my lawyer will take immediate legal action to protect my rights.

Thank you for your prompt cooperation in this matter.

Very truly yours,
Your Name

cc: potential employer
*Sent certified mail, return receipt requested.*

## Sample Letter Demanding Written Explanation
## for Discharge

Your Name
Address
Telephone Number
Date

Name of Officer of Employer
Title
Name of Employer
Address

Re: My termination

Dear (Name of Officer),

On (date) I was fired suddenly by your company without notice, warning, or cause. All that I was told by (name of person) was that my services were no longer required and that my termination was effective immediately.

To date, I have not received any explanation documenting the reason(s) for my discharge. In accordance with the laws of this state I hereby demand such information immediately.

Thank you for your prompt cooperation in this matter.

Very truly yours,
Your Name

*Sent certified mail, return receipt requested.*

## How to Increase Your Chances of Success at Unemployment Hearings

Many people who are fired forfeit valuable unemployment insurance benefits. This is because they do not know how to act or represent themselves properly at unemployment hearings. Many are told by unemployment personnel that a lawyer or other representative is not required and that preparation for the hearing is unnecessary. They then attend the hearing and are surprised to learn that the employer is represented by experienced counsel who has brought witnesses to testify against their version of the facts. Additionally, some are unprepared for the grueling, humiliating cross-examination lasting several hours that they may be subjected to. Other people lose at the hearing because they do not know the purpose of their testimony or what they must prove to receive benefits.

This section will offer strategies to increase your chances of obtaining benefits at unemployment hearings when your case is contested by a former employer.

### KNOW THE LAW

Each state imposes different requirements for collecting unemployment benefits, such as the maximum amount of money that may be collected weekly, the normal waiting period required before payments begin, the length of such benefits, and the maximum period you can wait before filing and collecting. States also differ on standards of proof required to receive such benefits. You must know such essential details before filing. This can be done by contacting your nearest unemployment office.

The following questions are some of the points to consider asking:

- How quickly can I file?
- When will I begin receiving payments?

- How long will the payments last?
- What must I do (i.e., must I actively look for employment in order to qualify and continue receiving benefits)?
- How long did I have to work for my former employer in order to qualify?
- What must I prove in order to collect if my ex-employer contests my claim?
- When will the hearing be held?
- Will I have an opportunity to review the employer's defense and other documentation submitted in opposition before the hearing?
- How can I learn whether witnesses will appear on the company's behalf to testify against me?
- How can I obtain competent legal counsel to represent me?
- How much will this cost?
- Is a record made of the hearing? If so, in what form?
- Is the hearing examiner's decision final and binding, or can the decision be appealed?
- Can I recover benefits if I was forced to resign?
- Is the burden on the employer to demonstrate that I was fired for a good reason (such as misconduct), or is the burden on me to prove that I did not act improperly?
- Can I subpoena witnesses if they refuse to appear voluntarily on my behalf? Will the hearing examiner assist me in this regard?
- Are formal rules of evidence followed at the hearing?

As you can see, collecting benefits may not be a simple matter, especially if your claim is contested by an ex-employer.

When a terminated worker comes into my office, one of the first points I consider is whether the employee was discharged for a valid reason. In most states you *can* collect unemployment benefits if you were fired due to a business reorganization, massive layoff, job elimination, or other reasons that were not your fault. In many situations you can even collect if you were fired for being unsuited or unskilled for the job or for overall poor work performance.

However, you generally *cannot* collect if you resign voluntarily (unless you were forced to resign for a good reason) or if you were fired for *misconduct*.

The following are common examples of acts that often justify the denial of unemployment benefits based on misconduct:

- Insubordination or fighting on the job
- Habitual lateness or excessive absence
- Intoxication or drug abuse on the job
- Disobedience of company work rules or policies
- Gross negligence or neglect of duty
- Dishonesty or unfaithfulness

Although these examples appear to be relatively straightforward, employers often have difficulty proving that such acts reached the level of misconduct. This is because hearing examiners typically seek to determine whether a legitimate company rule was violated and whether or not that rule was justified.

When representing terminated individuals, I am mindful of the standards that hearing examiners, judges, and arbitrators use in making decisions at unemployment hearings and arbitrations. Many of these guidelines are relevant to successfully asserting one's claim for unemployment benefits and are repeated here for your benefit.

- Did the employer have a clear rule against the kind of behavior that resulted in the firing?
- Is the rule reasonably related to the orderly, efficient, and safe operation of the employer's business?
- Did the employer provide all employees with a reasonable opportunity to learn the company's rules?
- Did the employer provide all employees with reasonable notice regarding the consequences of violating such rules?

- Has the employer administered and enforced the rules consistently and without discrimination among all employees?
- Did the employer take steps to fairly investigate the circumstances involved in the alleged offense?
- Did the employer obtain substantial evidence of the alleged act through this investigation?
- Did such acts meet the standard of law required to prove misconduct?
- Are there mitigating factors that reasonably explain the employee's conduct?
- Was the firing fair under all of the circumstances?
- Were the employer's witnesses credible in proving the action taken?

These considerations demonstrate the degree of sophistication that is often required to prevail at unemployment hearings. That is why you should carefully consider whether you require representation by experienced counsel at the hearing. If you are anticipating receiving the maximum benefits allowed (in some states this may exceed $325 per week) and expect to be unable to find gainful employment for a long period of time (e.g., six months), it may be advantageous to hire counsel.

The following information will help you prepare and increase your chances of success if you decide that representation is not necessary.

### PREPARING FOR THE HEARING

Once you file for unemployment insurance and learn that the employer is contesting your claim, it is your responsibility to follow the progress of the case carefully. Plan on attending the hearing on the date in question. If you cannot be present, speak to a clerk responsible for scheduling, explain your reasons, and ask for another convenient date. This should preferably be done in person. Indicate future dates when you know you can appear. Call that individual the day before the old hearing date to confirm that your request has been granted.

An unemployment hearing is not different from a trial. Witnesses must testify under oath. Documents, including personnel information, warnings, performance appraisals, and so on, are submitted as exhibits. The atmosphere is rarely friendly. Thus, you must prepare in advance what you will say, how you will handle tough questions from the employer, and what you will try to prove to win the case.

When preparing for the hearing, be certain that all your friendly witnesses (if any) will attend and testify on your behalf. If necessary, ask a representative from the unemployment office to issue a subpoena compelling the attendance of key disinterested witnesses (such as coworkers) who refuse to voluntarily attend and testify. Unfortunately, people who tell you they will appear do not always do so, and it may be necessary to subpoena them. If the unemployment representative has no authority to do this, wait until the first day of the hearing. Explain to the judge or hearing examiner the necessity of compelling the appearance and testimony of key witnesses. The judge may grant your request depending on the relevance and reasonableness of it.

Organize your case before the day of the hearing to maximize your chances of success. Collect all evidence so it can be produced easily at the hearing. Practice what you will say at the hearing. This will relax you and help you to organize the important facts. You can even prepare an outline of key points to be discussed and questions to ask each witness and employee of the ex-employer.

## THE HEARING

Arrive early on the hearing day and advise a scheduling clerk of your appearance. Bring your evidence and come properly attired (preferably in business clothes).

**STRATEGY:** *In some states you can review the entire contents of your unemployment file before the hearing; don't forget to ask for this if appropriate.*

When your case is called, all relevant witnesses will be sworn in. Stay calm. The judge or hearing examiner will conduct the hearing and ask you questions. Speak directly and with authority. Show the judge your evidence. Talk directly to the judge and respond to his or her questions. Show respect. Always refer to him or her as "Your Honor" or "Judge" and never argue with the judge. If you are asked a question while speaking, stop immediately and answer it. Make your answer direct and to the point.

Avoid being emotional. Avoid arguing with your opponent at the hearing and avoid interrupting his or her presentation.

After your opponent finishes testifying, you will have the opportunity to cross-examine such testimony and refute what was said. In addition, do not be afraid if the employer is represented by an attorney. If you feel intimidated, tell the judge that you are not represented by counsel and are not familiar with unemployment hearing procedures. Ask the judge to intercede on your behalf when you feel your opponent's attorney is treating you unfairly. Most judges are sympathetic, since unemployment hearings are specifically designed for you to present your case without an attorney.

**Obtaining a decision.** Decisions are not usually obtained immediately after the hearing. You will probably be notified by mail (sometimes two to six weeks later). Be sure to continue filing for benefits while waiting for the decision. Many people forget to do this and lose valuable benefits in the process.

You should begin collecting weekly or biweekly benefits immediately after receiving a favorable decision. Additionally, you should receive a lump sum check representing benefits previously due.

**Should you appeal?** If you are notified that you lost the decision, read the notice carefully. Most judges and hearing examiners give specific, lengthy reasons for their rulings. If you feel that the ruling was incorrect or you disagree with the judge's opinion, you may wish to file an appeal and have the case reheard. However, it is best to speak with an experienced attorney to get his or her opinion before doing so. You may discover that your chances of success with the appeal are not as good as you think. Appeals are not granted automatically as a matter of right in many states. If the judges on the appeals board believe that the hearing judge's decision was correct factually or as a matter of law, the decision will go undisturbed.

Recognize that the odds of winning the appeal are not in your favor. Often, the amount of time needed to review the transcript or tape of the proceeding(s), prepare an appeal brief, and reargue the case makes it too expensive and time-consuming. Thus, depending on the particular facts of your case, appealing the hearing may not be worth it. However, if new material facts come to light or relevant witnesses are willing to come forward and testify at the appeal hearing, this could make the difference. That is why you should always consult with an experienced labor lawyer before making such a decision.

# CHAPTER 8

# Employment Litigation and Alternatives

After you have left your job, willingly or otherwise, how do you collect what your employer owes you if it has not been paid to you freely and promptly? Much depends on why you left the job, and under what conditions. If you left voluntarily with prior notice and under favorable circumstances from a reputable employer, you should have no problem. But what if you were fired? What if you were fired on charges of misconduct or poor performance? What are your defenses?

If you have a discrimination claim under Title VII of the Civil Rights Act of 1964, you have recourse in federal or state court with the Equal Employment Opportunity Commission or a state human rights agency.

State statutes vary widely, but in general they tell when back wages must be paid following job termination. Many states provide for penalties and payment of attorney fees if you are not paid in a timely fashion. The definition of back wages normally includes everything of dollar value owed to you, including bonuses, deferred compensation, accrued vacation, sick leave, and pension rights. Note that most courts will consider only wages due to you up to the time of the court award, not projected or future losses.

In any event, when seeking back wages, you can enforce your rights either by suing directly or through the assistance of your state labor department. (Note, however, that you are not protected by the federal Fair Labor Standards Act or state wages statutes if you are a nonemployee independent contractor.) You should always consider and follow through on your options as quickly as possible when seeking back wages and other benefits.

Tens of thousands of employment-related lawsuits are filed in state and federal courts annually. Common lawsuits are for discrimination complaints and breach of contract actions to collect wages, commissions, and benefits. This chapter will provide you with an explanation of the various legal forums you may be exposed to when asserting your rights. Strategies will be provided to help win a case in court, after an appeal, through arbitration, and through small-claims court, and how to settle a matter out of court through mediation.

## Litigation

The party commencing a lawsuit (called the plaintiff) must have proper subject matter and personal jurisdiction to avoid having the case initially dismissed. Having subject matter jurisdiction means filing the action in an appropriate court. For example, an ERISA benefits claim must be filed in a federal district court; a case involving significant wages cannot be filed in small-claims court. Before starting a lawsuit, speak to a lawyer to be sure you are filing your case in the proper court.

It is also necessary to demonstrate personal (*in personam*) jurisdiction. Typically, if the person or business being sued (called the defendant) lives or works in the state where the action is filed, or has close ties with that state (e.g., ships goods into or travels to that state to conduct business), then personal jurisdiction may be determined to exist by a judge. It will also be necessary to select the correct venue (the proper county) where the lawsuit should be filed. For example, in a wrongful discharge lawsuit, the proper venue is the county where the plaintiff or defendant resides. Since venue laws vary from state to state, ask your lawyer where the suit should be brought, to avoid having the case dismissed.

**STRATEGY:** *Where applicable, ask your lawyer about the advantages and disadvantages of commencing the lawsuit in either state or federal court. Some experts believe that federal court judges are generally more highly regarded for their legal skills than state judges and that litigants are often able to obtain a trial quicker in federal court. However, if a dispute is with an employer located within your state, you may not be able to file a lawsuit in federal court unless you are asserting a discrimination charge or other matter dealing with federal laws (such as a wage and hour or overtime violation). Conversely, if you are being sued, it may be advantageous to keep the case in a state court to "slow down" its progress.*

Before starting any action, it is important to thoroughly analyze whether your case has merit. Does the defendant have a strong defense? Will you be able to prove your case? Will the defendant be interested in settling the matter before protracted and expensive litigation occurs? Carefully examine the strengths and weaknesses of any case before starting. Analyze whether the defendant has sufficient assets (such as money in the bank and property). After going through lengthy litigation and expense if the matter is not settled out of court, you don't want to win the case but be unable to collect the award.

There are investigative companies who, for a fee, can advise you about the defendant's asset picture. Your lawyer can tell you where such companies are located. You may also find them listed in the telephone yellow pages. Always discuss these concerns with your lawyer before the decision to litigate is made.

## COURTS

A court is a place where trials are held and/or the law is applied. Depending upon one's choice and other factors, a trial may be conducted and decided by a judge only or by a judge and jury. In some appellate courts and the United States Supreme Court, only judges are present to hear arguments and make decisions.

A court can only preside over matters to which it has jurisdiction. Courts of original jurisdiction are the first courts to preside over a matter. A court of appellate jurisdiction is a higher court that reviews cases removed by appeal from a lower court.

Each state has its own court system, which operates separately from the federal court system. There are basically two levels of state courts: trial courts and appellate courts. General trial courts are typically divided into two separate, distinct courts, one to hear criminal matters and one to adjudicate civil matters. Civil trial courts may be further divided depending upon the amount of money or the subject matter at issue. In New York, for example, original jurisdiction small-claims courts adjudicate civil matters up to $3,000; the civil court adjudicates matters up to $25,000; and the supreme court presides over civil matters involving more than $25,000 or other issues.

The federal court system is divided into twelve districts or circuits and has jurisdiction over the following:

- When a federal law is at issue, such as bankruptcy, copyright and patents, maritime, and postal matters
- When one state is suing another state
- When a person or entity (i.e., a corporation) is suing a person or entity residing in another state and the amount in controversy exceeds $50,000

Within the federal system are separate limited jurisdiction courts that hear matters exclusively pertaining to bankruptcy (U.S. Bankruptcy Court), tax issues (U.S. Tax Court), suits against the federal government (U.S. Court of Claims), and disputes concerning tariffs and customs (U.S. Court of International Trade).

The United States Supreme Court is the country's highest court. It considers cases from the highest courts of each state, decisions of the U.S. Court of Appeals (the highest federal appeals court), and cases where the constitutionality of federal laws comes into play.

The vast majority of lawsuits, including unemployment and workers' compensation hearings, originate in state courts. If you are thinking of filing a lawsuit, speak to an employment lawyer or visit the clerk of any local court to determine where the correct place is to start. Each state has its own unique filing, procedural, and jurisdictional requirements, which must be correctly followed so the case will not be dismissed. It is essential to get proper advice from a lawyer before starting any legal process.

## Starting an Action

A civil lawsuit must be commenced (i.e., filed) within a certain period of time after the dispute arose to avoid dismissal on the basis of being untimely (called the statute of limitations). Each state and federal court has its own rules concerning the maximum amount of time you can wait before a lawsuit must be filed; it is crucial to know how much time you have before contemplating litigation. If you wish to join others in one suit (called a class action), it is necessary to contact the law firm representing the class within the required period of time to be able to join and be included in the lawsuit.

A lawsuit is started by preparing and filing a summons and complaint with the court. A summons is a single piece of paper typically accompanied by the complaint that, when served on the defendant (e.g., an employer), notifies the defendant of a lawsuit. A complaint is a legal document that starts the lawsuit. It alleges pertinent facts and legal causes of action that the plaintiff will rely on in the attempt to collect damages. For a lawsuit to proceed, it is necessary that the summons and complaint be served on the defendant either in person (typically with the help of a process server or sheriff) or by certified mail, return receipt requested, in states that permit mail service. If the defendant is not notified of the existence of the lawsuit or if the complaint is not drafted accurately and fails to state a legally recognized cause of action, the case may be dismissed. If a lawsuit is dismissed without prejudice, it may be started over; lawsuits dismissed with prejudice are considered final, and may never be brought again.

Once the summons and complaint are served on the defendant, it must be filed with the proper court together with the payment of the initial filing fee (which can be as much as $250 in some states). Filing these documents is rather easy. At the courthouse, a clerk accepts the fee and documents, stamps the papers to indicate the date and time received, and issues a receipt. The documents then become part of a file, which is stored at the court. The file is given to the presiding judge of the case when appropriate (such as during oral arguments before trial and at the trial). A judge is assigned to preside over every filed case. The judge will rule on various pretrial motions, move the case along to the trial, conduct the trial, and render a judgment based on the evidence when a jury is not involved.

After the complaint is served, the defendant has a period of time (usually no more than thirty days) to submit an answer. An answer is the defendant's reply to the plaintiff's charges in a civil lawsuit. Properly drafted answers typically deny most of the plaintiff's charges, list a number of legal reasons (called affirmative defenses) why the case should not proceed, and may or may not contain counterclaims. A counterclaim is a claim asserted by the defendant in a lawsuit. Sometimes the plaintiff loses the case and the defendant wins the case through its counterclaim.

Each case is decided by its unique facts. The fact that you are the plaintiff means only that you filed the lawsuit first; it does not guarantee success of the matter in any way. However, if the defendant fails to respond to the lawsuit by filing an answer, it may lose the case by default. (If you are sued, *always* consult an attorney after receiving a complaint to ensure that a timely answer will be filed.)

## DAMAGES

Damages are compensation or relief awarded to the prevailing party in a lawsuit. Damages can be in the form of money or a directive by the court for the losing party to perform or refrain from performing a certain action. The following briefly describes various forms of damages:

*Compensatory damages.* This is a sum of money awarded to a party that represents the actual harm suffered or loss incurred. Since damages cannot be presumed, one must prove what the actual out-of-pocket losses are. For example, projections of future lost profits will not be awarded unless they are definite and certain.

*Incidental damages.* Incidental damages are traditionally direct out-of-pocket expenses for filing a lawsuit and related court costs (such as process server fees). These direct costs of litigation are sometimes awarded to the prevailing party in a litigation as part of the party's loss.

*Liquidated damages.* This is an amount of money agreed on in advance by parties to a written contract to be paid in the event of a breach or dispute. If it is not possible to compute the amount of the loss, a judge may uphold the amount specified. However, in many circumstances, when the amount specified has no actual basis in fact, a judge may disregard it, viewing the amount merely as a penalty.

*Nominal damages.* This is a small amount of money (e.g., $1.00) awarded by the court. Sometimes a party may win the lawsuit but not have proved suffering or any actual damages.

*Punitive damages.* Also called exemplary damages, punitive damages represent money awarded as punishment for a party's wrongful acts beyond any actual losses. When punitive damages are awarded, a judge is often sending a signal to the community that similar outrageous, malicious, or oppressive conduct will not be tolerated. Under the laws of many states, punitive damages can be awarded only in certain types of lawsuits, such as personal injury and product liability actions, and not lawsuits to enforce employment contracts or business agreements.

*Specific performance.* This is a directive by the court for the party being sued (i.e., the defendant) to perform a certain action such as sell a business or not work for a competitor pursuant to a clause in an employment contract. Specific performance is typically not awarded if monetary damages can make the party seeking the relief whole.

*Injunction.* This is a court order restraining one party from performing or refusing to perform an action or contract.

*Mitigation of damages.* This is a legal principle that requires a party seeking damages to make reasonable efforts to reduce damages as much as possible; for example, to secure comparable employment or file for unemployment benefits if a job cannot be obtained in the short term.

Sometimes an employer is interested not only in obtaining damages but in seeking to stop you from establishing a competing business or working for a competitor. An action can be commenced called a preliminary injunction. The employer (as the moving party) will request a hearing immediately after the lawsuit is filed. A request for an immediate hearing is called an *order to show cause.* If a judge rules in favor of the motion, the injunction will be granted. If a judge decides in favor of the defendant, the injunction will be denied, but, depending on the circumstances, the case may be allowed to proceed like any other lawsuit to ascertain damages.

After the answer is received from the defendant, the discovery phase of the case begins. Several pretrial devices, including interrogatories, depositions, and motions, are used by lawyers to elicit information from the opposing side, gather evidence, and prepare for the trial. The discovery phase can last several years in a complicated case and can be very expensive in terms of attorney fees and the costs of taking depositions, procuring documents, and paying for postage and related expenses.

Interrogatories are written questions sent to an opponent to be answered under oath. One problem with interrogatories is that the opposing party's attorney may draft the responses to prevent, insofar as possible, damaging statements from being conveyed.

Depositions often lasting several days are taken by both sides in complicated labor cases. A deposition is a pretrial proceeding in which one party is questioned under oath by the opposing party's lawyer. A stenographer is present to record all statements and preserve the testimony. Depositions are used to collect information and facts about the case, narrow the issues to be proved at trial, and discredit (impeach) the testimony of the witness.

It is essential that your lawyer properly prepare and advise you before your deposition is taken. Many cases have been lost due to unprepared responses elicited from a witness at a deposition. If your testimony is materially different (inconsistent) at the trial from statements you gave at the deposition, your credibility may be seriously undermined; giving a totally different statement about something at the trial could dramatically reduce the chances of success. Incorrect answers at the deposition might also give the opposing attorney grounds to file a motion to dismiss the case in its entirety or throw out various causes of action. A motion to dismiss asserts that even if the plaintiff's allegations are true and there is no genuine issue as to important facts, no legal basis exists for finding the defendant liable.

Sometimes attorneys file motions to get a ruling on admissibility of evidence or ask the court to assist in obtaining documents and records that have not been turned over by the other side (although promised).

Once the discovery phase of the case is completed, a judge will order a pretrial conference. Both attorneys are asked to appear to discuss the case and the possibility of settlement. Some judges make active attempts to settle cases at these conferences. If the conference is successful and the case is settled, the parties will prepare a written stipulation that describes the terms of the settlement. Typically, the judge will review and approve all settlements before they are implemented.

---

**STRATEGY:** *Think carefully before accepting any settlement. Most civil actions take up to five years to be tried. By accepting a fair settlement early on, you have use of the money, which can be invested to earn more money. You may eliminate large legal fees, court costs, and the possibility of eventually losing the case after a trial. However, if you have a good case, it may pay to wait before discussing and accepting a settlement. Most trial attorneys believe that large settlements are obtained for their clients by waiting until the case reaches the courthouse steps.*

---

The decision on whether to accept a settlement should always be made jointly with your attorney, who knows the merits, pitfalls, and true value of the case better than you. However, do not allow a lawyer to pressure you into accepting a smaller settlement than you deserve. Some attorneys seek smaller immediate settlements out of laziness because the settlement represents money in the bank to them.

Instruct your attorney to provide you with a detailed explanation of the pros and cons of settling your case. Inform him that you prefer to control your affairs, including the decision of settling a claim. Do not let your attorney push you around. Your attorney cannot settle the case without your approval. If he does, he can be sued for malpractice. If you are not satisfied with your lawyer's advice or conduct, consult another attorney for a second opinion before settling the matter. Do this before taking action, because once you sign the settlement papers, you probably cannot change your mind and continue with the case, since release language contained in such documents generally prohibits you from doing so.

If a matter cannot be settled, the judge will discuss with both attorneys how the case will proceed. The identity and order of witnesses and exhibits to be submitted at the trial will be agreed to before the trial begins. In many types of labor cases, either party can request that a jury decide the case rather than a judge. A jury trial usually involves twelve people, although some states allow as few as six. Some states permit a civil jury's decision to be less than unanimous.

The first step of the trial begins with jury selection if a jury has been requested by either side. Prospective jurors are questioned (referred to as the *voir dire*) to see if they are qualified to sit on the panel. Lawyers seek answers to certain questions in the attempt to learn if a person has an open mind and is not biased. After attorneys for both sides dismiss certain people and retain others, the jury is picked and the trial begins. The plaintiff's lawyer will begin the trial with an opening statement. This is a speech designed to tell the judge or jury about the nature of the case, what the plaintiff intends to prove from the facts, and what kind of damages are sought.

After the defendant's attorney gives his opening statement, the trial begins. Witnesses are called by the plaintiff, and witnesses give their direct testimony under oath. The opposing attorney has the right to question (cross-examine) each witness in turn. All other evidence, such as documents and exhibits, is submitted, and other witnesses are questioned.

## EVIDENCE

Evidence is information in the form of oral testimony, exhibits, physical items, or affidavits used to prove a party's claim. Exhibits are tangible evidence presented for the purpose of supporting factual allegations or arguments. Testimony of expert witnesses may also be introduced as evidence.

In a civil case the plaintiff has the burden of proving its case by a legal standard called preponderance of the evidence ("more likely than not") through witnesses, charts, documents, photographs, and other forms of physical evidence. In a criminal case the prosecution must prove a person's guilt beyond a reasonable doubt. This is a more difficult standard to achieve.

During the trial one side will try to get evidence admitted into the court record for consideration by a judge or jury when deciding the case. The other party, through his or her lawyer, will seek to exclude such evidence through objections—for example, by stating that the evidence is irrelevant or legally inadmissible. A judge will either deny the objection and allow the evidence to be admitted or sustain the objection and exclude the evidence. The introduction of evidence in any case depends upon an attorney's arguments and the judge's interpretation of that state or federal court's rules. Certain types of evidence, such as hearsay evidence (a witness's testimony about what someone else said outside of the courtroom), must be excluded (and may be excluded in advance of a trial).

Each party has the opportunity to discover what evidence the other intends to introduce at the trial to prove its version of the facts. This is done through depositions where a witness's testimony is taken under oath and during discovery procedures whereby records and other physical information is turned over to the other side for evaluation. In most states it is against the law to destroy evidence.

---

**STRATEGY:** *Because the success or failure of a case often depends on the type of evidence introduced and admitted (or excluded) from the record at a trial, it is important to hire an employment lawyer who is very knowledgeable about the rules of evidence. For maximum success, always hire an employment lawyer who possesses competent trial skills.*

---

After the plaintiff's case is completed, the defendant presents its side of the case. When both sides are finished, each attorney gives a summation. This is a review of the facts, testimony, and other evidence. If no jury is involved, the judge will render a decision. Typically, both parties have to wait a period of time (up to thirty days) before receiving the judge's written decision.

If a jury is involved, a judge will instruct its members as to what *law* is applicable to the facts and statements they have heard. The jury will then leave the courtroom and return with its determination. In rare cases a judge may disregard the jury's findings and grant a motion for judgment notwithstanding the verdict (called a JNOV) when he or she believes there was insufficient evidence to support a jury's conclusion.

After the judgment is made, either party can appeal the decision by filing a written document called a brief. Information about appeals is discussed in the next section. It is also important to take proper steps to collect the judgment if the losing party doesn't pay. This may involve placing a lien on real estate property owned by the losing party or attaching such property to prevent the transfer, assignment, or sale without your consent. Speak to your attorney for more information about how this can be accomplished.

---

**STRATEGY:** *Litigation is complicated, time-consuming, and subject to many hazards. Unless absolutely necessary, or unless the case involves a small amount of money that can be handled by yourself in small-claims court, do not attempt to file papers and represent yourself (pro se) in a lawsuit without an attorney.*

---

The following is a summary of key strategies to follow in any lawsuit, whether you are the plaintiff or the defendant:

1. Hire a lawyer skilled in conducting trials. Many attorneys do not litigate cases, which is a specialty.
2. Play an active role in all phases of the case. Request that

your attorney routinely send you copies of all incoming and outgoing correspondence on a regular basis. This will help you monitor and question the progress of your case.

3. Never ignore a summons and complaint if you are served. Ignoring a summons and complaint can result in the imposition of a default judgment with huge damages, penalties, and interest assessed against you without your filing a defense. Speak to a lawyer immediately to protect your rights.

4. Never ignore a subpoena if you are summoned to court to appear as a witness. A subpoena is an order requiring your presence to testify. If for some reason you cannot be present on the date specified, speak to the clerk of the court for advice and guidance. Ignoring a subpoena can result in a fine, imprisonment, or both.

5. Be prepared at all times. Competent attorneys work with their clients in anticipation of the upcoming deposition and trial. There should be no surprises in what you will testify to and what the opposing lawyer will ask you. Your lawyer should advise you how to react if you do not understand a question or do not wish to answer.

6. Consider alternative methods to settle your dispute. This includes arbitration and mediation (which are discussed later in this chapter). Ask your lawyer to actively seek and encourage a settlement where warranted.

7. Determine if the opposing party has sufficient assets to pay a successful verdict before starting an action.

8. Before you get in too deep, assess the chances of winning or losing and how much a lawsuit will cost to commence or defend.

## APPEALS

The vast majority of employment-related lawsuits never go to trial; they are either discontinued or settled. However, every case that is tried has a loser, and the losing party must decide whether or not to appeal the unfavorable decision.

An appeal is a request that a higher court review the decision of a lower court. In those states that have an intermediate appellate court, the losing party challenging a trial court decision first brings the appeal to the intermediate court. In the federal court system the losing party brings the appeal to the court of appeals in the appropriate circuit. For serious criminal cases (i.e., felonies), the right to an appeal is mandatory. In civil cases an appeals court may have the discretion not to consider the appeal in certain circumstances. After the appeal is decided by an intermediate appellate court, the case can be further reviewed by the highest state appeals court (although some state cases are reviewed by the U.S. Supreme Court). In the federal system, after the appeal is decided by the U.S. Court of Appeals, the Supreme Court of the United States has the power and discretion to review and rule on the history of the case and the most recent appeal.

Appeals judges read the transcript of the trial together with legal documents called briefs to determine if the trial judge or jury erred in the decision. Typically, the intermediate appellate court will concern itself with issues of law as opposed to facts. It is rare that the appellate court will overturn a jury's factual decision. Rather, a verdict can be reversed if the wrong law was applied, incorrect jury instructions were given by the judge, or significant legal mistakes occurred, such as important evidence being mistakenly excluded by a judge from the trial.

Less than 20 percent of all criminal cases and 30 percent of all civil cases are reversed on appeal. Most decisions do not get reversed, but if a person or business has spent several years and thousands of dollars pursuing or defending a valid claim, the additional money spent on an appeal can be worth it, particularly if the delay caused by the appeals process works to an appellant's advantage.

Speak to a lawyer immediately if you receive an unfavorable trial verdict. There is a limited period of time (often thirty days) in which to file a notice that you intend to appeal. This must be done without delay to preserve your rights. To evaluate the chances of a successful appeal, it is necessary to carefully reconstruct (in an objective fashion) the reason the case was lost. Consider whether to hire a specialist in appeals matters. Although your current attorney is familiar with the case, there are distinct advantages to hiring an attorney who makes a living writing briefs and arguing oral appeals (it is an art). Be certain you know how much the appeal will cost. Always sign a retainer agreement that clearly spells out attorney fees, costs, and disbursements.

Remember that no matter which lawyer handles the appeal, it is generally costly and time-consuming and frequently does not produce anticipated results. However, if you win a big case and the employer appeals, there is little you may be able to do but contest the appeal.

## Mediation

Mediation is an alternative to resolving employment disputes via formal litigation or arbitration. A neutral intermediary (the mediator) defines the conflicting interests of the parties, explains the legal implications, and attempts to help the parties reach and prepare a fair settlement. When settlements are achieved, they are typically reached more quickly and cheaply than litigation because opposing parties have not hired opposing counsel to fight it out in court. More and more employment-related cases are now being resolved this way. For example:

- When an employer alleges it was justified in firing an executive for cause prior to the expiration of the stated term in an employment agreement
- When an employer is confronted with a breach of contract or wrongful discharge case

- When a worker threatens to file a lawsuit alleging sexual harassment
- When there is a significant dispute over the terms of an important clause in an employment contract

The parties may prefer to work out their problems in the privacy of a business suite instead of a crowded public courtroom and negotiate the terms of a settlement based on their best mutual interests. If a mediator (usually a trained lawyer, businessperson, or retired judge) is hired to assist in the process, he or she will not make decisions for the parties but will help them reach an agreement within the realistic limits of their budget.

Resolving a dispute by mediation requires that both parties agree to mediate the dispute. It also requires a good-faith effort by the parties to resolve the dispute, not to determine who is right and who is wrong. Nonbinding mediation may not work when one party strongly believes he or she is entitled to punitive or extra damages that can be awarded only by a judge via litigation.

## HOW MEDIATION WORKS

Various community associations, private enterprises, and the American Arbitration Association (AAA) offer mediation services. The AAA is most often selected to assist parties in the mediation process. It is a public service nonprofit organization that offers dispute settlement services to business executives, employers, trade associations, unions, and all levels of government. Services are available through AAA's national office in New York City and through twenty-five regional offices in major cities throughout the United States (see the appendix).

A list of various mediation and dispute resolution organizations is included at the end of this chapter.

Once both parties agree to try to solve their differences through mediation, a joint request for mediation is usually made through an AAA regional office. The request identifies the parties involved in the dispute, gives their current addresses and phone numbers, and briefly describes the controversy and the issues involved. The employee and the company should include whatever information is helpful to appoint a mediator.

The AAA assigns a mediator from its master list. The parties are then given information about the mediator. Typically, the mediator has no past or present relationship with the parties. A mediator is free to refuse the appointment or resign at any time. Likewise, the parties are free to stop the mediation or ask for the services of a different mediator. If a mediator is unwilling or unable to serve, or if one of the parties requests that the mediator resign from the case, the parties may ask the AAA to recommend another mediator. The mediator is compensated on either an hourly or a daily basis. Both parties are informed of potential mediator fees and are sometimes requested to sign a document evidencing approval of the compensation arrangement and an agreement to share fees.

Before choosing a mediator, inquire if the mediator's approach is suited to your needs. Ask the following questions at the initial interview:

- How does the mediator operate?
- How much experience and training does the mediator have?
- What is the mediator's background?
- How many sessions are required?
- How much will mediation cost?

After the initial interview takes place and the mediator is found to be acceptable, he or she will arrange the time and place for each conference with the parties. At the first conference the parties will be asked to produce information required for the mediator to understand the issues. The mediator may require either party to supplement such information. The mediator will explain what the parties should expect. Good mediators explain that the process is entirely voluntary, that they are not judges and have no power to dictate solutions, and that the parties are free to terminate the mediation process at any time.

A mediator does not have authority to impose a settlement but will attempt to help the parties reach a satisfactory resolution of their dispute. Although usually trained in law, the mediator is not supposed to give legal advice. While parties do not have to be represented by counsel at the mediation sessions, most claimants and employers retain attorneys in employment and business disputes.

Conferences are private. The mediator will meet with both parties, and then sometimes with each privately. Other persons, including witnesses, may attend only with the permission of the parties and at the invitation of the mediator.

The mediator is hired as a consultant, jointly retained, to help the parties work their way through their problems to resolution. At some point the mediator may make a recommendation or proposal. Both parties can agree or disagree or come to a compromise of their own. The mediator will draft a report confirming the agreement. The report is then submitted to the parties for submission to their attorneys for incorporation into a formal document, such as a settlement agreement.

If the parties fail to agree, or do not agree with the mediator's recommendation, they can break off the mediation, consult another mediator, give up, settle their dispute without a mediator, or go to court. The following is a typical mediation scenario from start to finish:

1. The mediator and parties meet at the initial conference. The mediator's role is explained and the responsibilities and rights of the parties are set forth.
2. The mediator designs a schedule for the sessions.
3. The parties sign a formal retainer agreement with the mediator.
4. A method is adopted for obtaining whatever information is required to understand the parties' problems.

5. The mediator identifies the various areas of agreement, defines the issues to be resolved, and assists the parties in their negotiations.
6. A final settlement may be proposed.
7. The mediator arranges for the terms of the settlement to be transmitted to the attorneys of the parties for filing in court, if necessary.

Some mediators do not possess sufficient skills or training to be effective. Others have been criticized for not ending the process when the interests of each party are not receiving balanced treatment. If the mediator is a lawyer, he or she often has to make an adjustment in attitude. Unlike the lawyer, who tells the client what to do, a mediator must allow the parties enough freedom to structure their own unique solutions to problems. Mediation by attorneys has raised the concern of whether one lawyer can adequately advise two parties with opposing interests and whether a mediator can invoke the attorney-client privilege in any future litigation. For example, if lawyers are present with the parties at mediation sessions and incriminating or damaging statements are made by a client, a lawyer may seek to prevent a judge or jury from hearing such statements in court when the mediation fails. A judge may not allow such oral testimony to be admitted in court depending on a number of facts, such as whether the parties formally agreed beforehand that such statements were confidential and could not be introduced in subsequent court hearings.

---

**STRATEGY:** *To avoid problems, interview the mediator carefully; be sure to hire the mediator only on the basis of a written retainer agreement. If you believe the process is not working or do not feel comfortable with the person hired, terminate the relationship immediately and discuss further options with your attorney or other professional adviser.*

---

Understand that mediation will not work unless both parties are willing to cooperate and recognize the savings and other benefits to be achieved versus litigation, such as:

- Eliminating the anxiety of preparing a case before going to court
- Avoiding potential poor publicity
- Maintaining privacy
- Obtaining a quicker result
- Eliminating uncertainty as to outcome when the case is tried in court
- Maintaining a desire to continue good business relationships

If either party has a great need to even the score, mediation will probably fail. Speak to your professional adviser to determine if mediation is a proper means of resolving any employment dispute before resorting to litigation or arbitration. Once involved in mediation with a company representative, inquire if that person has sufficient authority to resolve and settle the matter on the company's behalf once a resolution is imminent. Finally, since your lawyer may be able to meet and question important witnesses, the benefits of learning more about your adversary's case may make the exercise worthwhile even if a settlement is not forthcoming. (In some employment lawsuits, nonbinding court-ordered mediation is required before a trial begins. Speak to your lawyer for more details.)

## Arbitration

Arbitration is a formal mechanism for resolving disputes that differs from litigation. Hearings are conducted by arbitrators rather than by judges and are not limited by strict rules of evidence. Arbitrators can consider all relevant testimony when making an award, including some forms of evidence (e.g., hearsay, questionable copies of documents) that would be excluded in a regular court. Arbitrators have the authority to hear witnesses out of order. Their decision is usually final and unappealable. (Limited circumstances for appeals are mentioned later in this section.)

To obtain an arbitration, the law requires both parties to agree to the arbitration process beforehand in writing to prevent claims of unfairness by the losing side. Typically in an employment contract, lease, loan agreement, or other document, the relevant clause may state some version of the following: "Any controversy or claim arising out of or relating to this agreement or the breach thereof shall be settled by binding arbitration in accordance with the rules of the American Arbitration Association, and judgment upon the award rendered by the arbitrator(s) may be entered in any court having jurisdiction thereof."

## ADVANTAGES OF ARBITRATION

*Expense.* Substantial savings can be achieved through arbitration. Attorney fees are reduced because the average hearing is shorter than the average trial (typically less than a day versus several days). Time-consuming and expensive pretrial procedures, including depositions, interrogatories, and motions, are usually eliminated. Out-of-pocket expenses are reduced because stenographic fees, transcripts, and other items are not required.

*Time.* Arbitration hearings and final awards are obtained quickly; cases are usually decided in a matter of months, compared to several years in formal litigation.

*Privacy.* The arbitration hearing is held in a private conference room, rather than a courtroom. Unlike a trial, the hearing cannot be attended by the general public.

*Expertise of arbitrators.* Arbitrators usually have special training in the area of the case. In a breach of an entertainment contract dispute, for example, arbitrators serving on the panel are typically respected lawyers or other professionals with significant experience in the entertainment industry. Their knowledge of trade customs helps them identify and understand a problem more quickly than a judge or jury.

*Increased odds of obtaining an award.* Some lawyers believe that arbitrators are more likely than judges to split close cases down the middle. The theory is that arbitrators bend over backward to satisfy both parties to some degree, since their rulings are final and binding. This tendency to compromise, if true, benefits claimants with weaker cases.

## DISADVANTAGES OF ARBITRATION

*Finality.* Arbitrators, unlike judges, need not give formal reasons for their decisions. They are not required to maintain a formal record of the proceedings. The arbitrator's decision is binding. This means that an appeal cannot be taken if you lose the case or disagree with the size of the award except in a few extraordinary circumstances where arbitrator misconduct, dishonesty, or bias can be proved.

*Arbitrator selection.* The parties sometimes agree that each will select its own arbitrator. In such cases it may be assumed that the chosen arbitrators are more sympathetic to one side than the other. However, arbitrators are usually selected from a list of neutral names supplied by the AAA. This method generally eliminates bias.

*Loss of sympathetic juries.* Some knowledgeable lawyers believe that juries tend to empathize more with certain kinds of people such as salespeople, fired employees, destitute wives, and older individuals. Arbitrators are usually successful lawyers and businesspeople whose philosophical orientation may lean more toward companies than toward individuals.

*Loss of discovery devices.* Some claimants must rely upon an adversary's documents and records to prove their case. For example, sales agents, authors, patent holders, and others often depend upon their company's (or licensee's) sales figures and accurate record keeping to determine how much commission and royalties they are owed. The same is true for minority shareholders who seek a proper assessment of a company's profit picture.

These people may find a disadvantage in the arbitration process. Trial lawyers have ample opportunity to view the private books and records of an adversary long before the day of the trial. This is accomplished by pretrial discovery devices, which include interrogatories, depositions, and notices to produce documents for inspection and copying. However, these devices are not readily available to litigants in arbitration. In many instances records are not available for inspection until the day of the arbitration hearing. This makes it difficult to detect whether they are accurate and complete. And it is often up to the arbitrator's discretion whether to grant an adjournment for the purposes of reviewing such records. Such requests may be refused.

Sexual harassment and sex discrimination issues are currently being resolved in arbitration as well as by litigation. Often an employee prefers that her matter *not* be resolved through arbitration because in many states punitive and other special damages are not granted in an arbitrator's award. However, if you signed an employment agreement containing an arbitration clause, you may be forced to arbitrate your case (including claims made by a fired employee for age discrimination under the Age Discrimination in Employment Act), especially if you work in the securities industry.

---

**STRATEGY:** *Courts favor resolving cases through arbitration when agreed beforehand by the parties. Thus, it is essential to understand the ramifications of signing any employment agreement or contract containing an arbitration clause.*

---

## SUMMARY OF STEPS LEADING TO THE HEARING

Commencing the hearing is a relatively simple matter once arbitration has been selected as the method of resolving a dispute. A party or her lawyer sends a notice called a Demand for Arbitration to the adversary. See page 357 for an example of this notice. Copies of the demand are sent to the American Arbitration Association, along with the appropriate administrative fee. The AAA is most often selected to arbitrate disputes. As previously noted, it is a public service nonprofit organization that offers dispute settlement services through the national office in New York City and dozens of regional offices in major cities throughout the United States (included in the appendix).

The notice briefly describes the controversy. It specifies the kind of relief sought, including the amount of monetary damages requested. A response to the charges is then sent by the opposing party, usually within seven days. This may also assert a counterclaim for damages. Either party can add or change claims in writing until the arbitrator is appointed. Once this occurs, changes and additional claims can only be made with the arbitrator's consent.

After the AAA receives the Demand for Arbitration and reply, an AAA administrator usually supplies the parties with a list of potential arbitrators. The list contains the arbitrator's name, current occupation, place of employment, and appropriate background information. The parties mutually agree to nominees from this list. Potential arbitrators are obligated to notify the AAA immediately of any facts likely to affect their impartiality (e.g., prior dealings with one of the litigants), and disqualify themselves where appropriate. (If the parties do not agree beforehand to the number of arbitrators, the dispute is decided by one arbitrator, unless the AAA determines that three arbitrators are appropriate.)

Once the arbitrator is selected, the AAA administrator schedules a convenient hearing date and location. There is no direct communication between the parties and the arbitrator until the hearing date; all requests and inquiries are received by the administrator and relayed to the arbitrator. This avoids the appearance of impropriety. The parties are free to request a prehearing conference to exchange documents and resolve certain issues. Typically, however, the parties, administrators, lawyers, and arbitrator meet face-to-face for the first time at the actual hearing.

## THE ARBITRATION HEARING

Most hearings are conducted in a conference room at an AAA regional office. A stenographer is present, if requested (the requesting party generally bears the cost). The arbitrator introduces the parties and typically asks each side to briefly summarize its version of the dispute and what each intends to prove at the hearing.

## Sample Demand for Arbitration

American Arbitration Association
Commercial Arbitration Rules
Demand for Arbitration

Date

Name of Employer
(Name of party upon whom the demand is made)
Address
Telephone

Named claimant, a party to an arbitration agreement contained in a written contract dated (specify) providing for arbitration, hereby demands arbitration thereunder.

(Attach arbitration clause or quote hereunder, such as)
"Any controversy or claim arising out of or relating to this contract, or any breach thereof, shall be settled in accordance with the Rules of the American Arbitration Association, and judgment upon the award may be entered in any court having jurisdiction thereof."

NATURE OF DISPUTE: Breach of contract action
CLAIM OR RELIEF SOUGHT: (amount, if any) $50,000 plus attorney fees as payment of salary through the termination date of employment agreement
TYPE OF BUSINESS:
Claimant: Executive          Respondent: Financial
HEARING LOCALE REQUESTED: New York, NY

You are hereby notified that copies of our arbitration agreement and of this demand are being filed with the American Arbitration Association at its New York Regional Office, with the request that it commence the administration of the arbitration. Under Section 7 of the Commercial Arbitration Rules, you may file an answering statement within seven days after notice from the Administrator.

Signed
(May be signed by attorney)

Name of Claimant
Address
Telephone

Name of Attorney
Address
Telephone

To institute proceedings, please send three copies of this demand with the administrative fee, as provided in Section 48 of the Rules, to the AAA. Send original demand to Respondent.

The complainant's case is presented first. Witnesses are called to give testimony (usually under oath). After witnesses finish speaking, they are usually cross-examined by the opposing party's lawyer. They may also be questioned by the arbitrator. The complainant introduces all its witnesses, documents, and affidavits until it has finished presenting its side of the case.

The opposing party then introduces its witnesses and documents to defend its case and/or prove damages. After the opposition has concluded its case, both sides are usually requested to make a brief summary of the facts (i.e., what they felt was proved at the hearing). Sometimes the arbitrator may request that legal briefs be submitted that summarize the respective positions of the parties before rendering a final decision.

## Sample Award of Arbitrator

In the Matter of Arbitration between
Sally Smith
and
Doe Corporation Inc. Case No.

I, the undersigned Arbitrator, having been designated in accordance with the arbitration agreement entered into by the above-named parties, and dated (specify), and having been duly sworn and having heard the proofs and allegations of the parties, AWARD as follows:
1. Within ten (10) days from the date of this AWARD, Doe Corporation Inc. ("Doe") shall pay to Sally Smith ("Smith") the sum of Twenty-Five Thousand Eighteen Dollars ($25,018.00), plus interest in the amount of Two Thousand Two Hundred Dollars ($2,200.00).
2. The counterclaim of Doe against Smith is hereby denied in its entirety.
3. The administrative fees of the American Arbitration Association totaling Eleven Hundred Dollars ($1,100.00) shall be borne equally

by the parties. Therefore, Doe shall pay Smith the sum of Five Hundred Fifty Dollars ($550.00) representing one-half (50%) of the filing fees previously advanced by Smith to the AAA.

4. Each Party shall pay one-half (50%) of the Arbitrator's fee in this arbitration.

5. This AWARD is in full settlement of all claims and counterclaims submitted in this arbitration.

Signature of Arbitrator
Dated:

## AWARD OF ARBITRATOR

Arbitrators are generally required to render written decisions within thirty days unless the parties agree to some other time period. The arbitrator can make any award that is equitable. She can order the losing party to pay additional costs, including AAA filing fees and arbitrator fees. Legal fees may be awarded if the arbitration clause so provides. See page 359 for a sample Award of Arbitrator.

Arbitrators volunteer their time for hearings lasting under two full days; they are paid a reasonable per diem rate (up to $1,000) for additional hearings. If the parties settle their dispute prior to a decision, they may request that the terms of the settlement be embodied in the consent award.

Arbitrators have no contact with the parties after the hearing is concluded. The parties are notified in writing by the AAA administrator and are sent a copy of the award. The decision in a typical employment case is brief—usually no formal reasons are given to explain why a particular award was rendered or the basis on which damages were calculated.

It is practically impossible to appeal a losing case. The arbitrator has no power once the case is decided. The matter can be reviewed only by a judge, and judges cannot overturn the award on the grounds of insufficient evidence. The only ways a case can be overturned on review are:

- For arbitrator dishonesty, partiality, or bias
- When no valid agreement was entered into that authorized the arbitration process
- When an issue that the arbitrator was not authorized to decide was ruled upon

Awards are modifiable only if there was a miscalculation of figures or a mistake in the description of the person, property, or thing referred to in the award.

### How to Increase the Chances of Success in Arbitration

Since the arbitrator's award is final and binding, it is essential to prepare and present a case properly the first time around, because you won't get a second chance. The following strategies may help increase the chances of success.

*Hire a lawyer.* People have the right to appear themselves (*pro se*), but it's best to have a lawyer represent you at the hearing, particularly if the dispute involves a large amount of money or complicated legal questions. The familiar expression "He who represents himself has a fool for a client" is certainly applicable in arbitrations. Seek the services of an experienced lawyer who is familiar with the intricacies of the arbitration process. Ask your prospective lawyer how many times he or she has represented clients in arbitration within the past several years. If the answer is "never" or "only a few times," look elsewhere for representation.

*Prepare for the hearing.* It is important that both you and your lawyer submit evidence to prove the case, so:

- Organize the facts. Gather and label all documents needed at the hearing so they can be produced in an orderly fashion.
- Prepare a checklist of documents and exhibits so nothing will be forgotten during the presentation.
- Make copies of all documents for the arbitrator and adversary.
- If some of the documents needed are in the possession of the other party, ask that they be brought to the hearing or subpoenaed.
- Interview witnesses.
- Be sure that friendly witnesses will attend and testify; if there is a possibility that additional witnesses may have to appear, alert them to be available on call without delay.
- Select witnesses who are believable, who understand the case and the importance of their testimony, and who will not say things at the hearing to surprise you.
- Coordinate the witnesses' testimony so your case will seem consistent and credible.
- Prepare witnesses for the rigors of cross-examination.
- If a translator is required, make arrangements in advance.
- Prepare a written summary of what you hope each witness will prove and refer to it at the hearing.
- Anticipate what the opponent will say to defeat your claim, and be prepared to refute such evidence.
- Practice your story to put you at ease and help organize the facts.
- Prepare a list of questions your lawyer should ask the opponent at the hearing.
- Dress appropriately by wearing conservative business clothes.
- Act professionally and show respect for the arbitrator.
- Listen to the arbitrator's questions and instructions; never argue with the arbitrator.
- If a question is posed while you are speaking, stop talking immediately.
- Answer all questions honestly and directly.

- Avoid arguing with your opponent at the hearing; interrupt his presentation only where absolutely necessary.

Finally, most losing parties voluntarily comply with the terms of an unfavorable award. However, if your opponent decides not to pay, you can enforce the judgment in a regular court. Speak to a lawyer for more details.

## Small-Claims Court

Before considering filing a lawsuit in small-claims court, attempt to resolve your dispute in a reasonable fashion. It is often best to write a demand letter to your employer or ex-employer and send it certified mail, return receipt requested. In addition to documenting your claim, the letter will advise the company that the matter must be corrected to your immediate satisfaction or you will take additional action. If there is no response to your letter, send a follow-up letter reporting that your initial letter has not been answered. The letter should also state what your next step will be if this letter is ignored.

If you cannot get satisfaction in an employment, financial, or business dispute by personal negotiations, you might consider suing in small-claims court. Small-claims courts, which help you collect wages, commissions, and money in an inexpensive manner without hiring a lawyer, hear over 1 million cases a year in the United States. They can be used in many situations. For example, you may wish to sue for money damages when your employer fails to pay you or someone damages your property and refuses to pay for repairs. Many small-claims courts have night sessions, and matters are resolved quickly, sometimes within a month from the time an action is filed. The maximum amount of money you can recover varies from state to state. It is usually up to $5,000.

The following guidelines describe the procedures of a typical small-claims court. However, the rules vary in each city and state.

Before you contemplate starting a lawsuit, call the clerk of that court and ask for a written explanation of the specific procedural rules to be followed.

*Who can be sued?* Small-claims court can be used to sue any person, business, partnership, corporation, or government body owing you money. If you sue in small-claims court and recover a judgment, you are precluded from suing again to recover any additional money owed to you. Thus, if your claim greatly exceeds the maximum amount of money that might be awarded in small-claims court, consider hiring a lawyer and instituting suit in a higher court.

*Do you have a valid claim?* In order to be successful, you must have a valid claim. This means that you must:

- Identify the person or business that damaged or caused you harm;
- Calculate the amount of damages you suffered;
- Show that there is some basis in law to have a court award you damages; and
- Be sure that you were not the main cause of your own harm, that you haven't waited too long to start the action (statute of limitations), and that you did not sign a written release.

*Where to sue.* Call your local bar association, city hall, or the county courthouse to discover where the nearest small-claims court is located. (In some states small-claims court is called justice court, district court, municipal court, or justice of the peace court.) In most states suit must be brought in the county in which the person or business you are suing lives or does business. Confirm this with the small-claims court clerk and ask what days and hours the court is in session. Also find out the maximum amount of money you can sue for, what documents are needed to file a complaint, the filing fee, and whether this can be paid by cash, check, or money order.

*What can you sue for?* You can sue only to collect money. Thus, before you begin to sue in small-claims court, estimate the amount of money you wish to collect. When calculating the amount of your claim, include all incurred expenses, including gasoline bills, tolls, telephone costs, losses due to time missed from work, sales tax, and interest, if applicable. Save all your receipts for this purpose.

---

**STRATEGY:** *In certain states an employer's willful failure to pay earned vacation money, wages, or other accrued compensation or promised benefits may cause it to be liable for extra statutory damages (such as an additional 25 percent) plus legal costs and expenses. Check your state's law to ascertain whether this applies in your case.*

---

*Starting the lawsuit.* You begin the lawsuit by paying a small fee (about $5) and either going to the court in person or mailing in a complaint that states the following information:

- Your name and address
- The complete name and address of the person, business, or company you are suing (the defendant)
- The amount of money you believe you are owed
- The facts of your case
- The reasons you (the plaintiff) are seeking redress

If you are filing a claim on behalf of an individually owned business, you must list the name of the owner in addition to the name of the business. If you are filing a claim on behalf of a partnership, you must list the name of the partnership as the plaintiff. (Some states do not allow a corporation to sue someone in small-claims court.)

Be sure to write the accurate and complete name and address of the defendant on the complaint. Write the corporation's formal name rather than its "doing business as" (d/b/a/) name. Thus, if you are suing a corporation, contact the county clerk's office in the county where the corporation does business to obtain its proper name and address. Better still, call the department of corporations in your state to obtain such information.

At this time you may also be required to prepare another form called a summons, which notifies your opponent of the lawsuit. Sometimes the clerk will do this. Ask the clerk whether the court will mail the summons by registered or first-class mail, personally serve the defendant on your behalf, or whether you must hire a professional process server. If a professional process server is required, ask what is necessary to prove that service was accomplished. You may have to pay the process server an additional fee (between $20 and $50). However, if you win your case, you can ask the judge to include the process server's fee in the award. When the clerk gives you a hearing date, be sure that it is convenient and you have no other commitments.

Some states require that you send a "thirty-day demand letter" before filing a small-claims action. The letter should briefly describe your money loss and what you want the employer to do to remedy the situation. Add that you are giving the employer thirty days to make a good-faith response. Otherwise, you will begin legal action. Send the letter certified mail, return receipt requested, and consider sending copies to your state attorney general's office and your attorney. If the letter is answered and the ex-employer refuses to pay, you may learn what position it intends to take at the trial. If your letter is ignored, that is evidence in court.

*The defendant's response.* When the person or company you are suing receives the summons, the defendant or his or her attorney can:

- Deny your claim by mailing a written denial to the court
- Deny your claim by personally appearing in court on the day of the hearing

- Sue you for money you supposedly owe (this is called a counterclaim)
- Contact you to settle the matter out of court

If an offer of payment is made, ask to be reimbursed for all filing and service costs. Notify the court that you are dismissing the action only after you receive payment. (If you are paid by check, wait until the check clears.) Do not postpone the case. Tell your opponent that unless you are paid before the day of the trial, you are prepared to go to court and either commence with the trial or stipulate the offer of settlement to the judge.

If a written denial is mailed to the court, ask the clerk to read it to you over the phone or go to the court and read it yourself. This is your right and may help you prepare for your opponent's defense. The following is an example of a simple denial in an answer: "I deny each and every allegation in the face of the complaint." Now you must prove your allegations in court to recover your claim

*Your duties as the moving party.* It is up to you to follow the progress of your case. Call the clerk and refer to the docket number to discover whether the defendant received the complaint and whether it was answered. If you discover that the defendant did not receive the complaint by the day of the trial, request that the clerk issue a new complaint to be served by a sheriff or process server. Go to court that day anyway, to be sure that the case is not dismissed because of your failure to appear.

If the complaint is personally served and your employer does not appear at the trial, he will be in default and you may be awarded a judgment automatically. In some states you still have to prove your case in order to be successful. Defendants sometimes file motions (legal affidavits) requesting the court to remove the default judgment on the grounds that there was a valid reason for not attending the hearing. If this motion is granted, your trial will be rescheduled.

If you are unable to come to court on the day of the trial, send a certified letter, return receipt requested, to the clerk, asking for a continuance. The letter should specify the reasons you will be unable to appear and include future dates when you will be able to come to court. Send a copy of this letter to your opponent. When you receive a new date, send your opponent a certified letter, return receipt requested, informing the employer of the revised date. Requests for continuances are sometimes not honored. Call the clerk on the day of the original trial date to be sure that your request has been granted. Be prepared to send a friend or relative to court to ask for a continuance on your behalf if a continuance has not been obtained by the day of the trial.

*Preparing for trial.* You have several weeks to prepare for trial. Use the time wisely. First, be sure that your friendly witnesses, if any, will attend the trial and testify on your behalf. Select witnesses who are believable and who will not say things that will surprise you. In some states you can present the judge with signed affidavits or statements of witnesses who are unable to appear at the trial. Some states also permit judges to hear testimony via conference telephones.

If necessary, the clerk can issue a subpoena to ensure the attendance of important witnesses who you believe may refuse to attend and testify. A subpoena is a document that orders a person to testify or produce books, papers, and other physical objects on a specified date. If the subpoena is issued and the person refuses to appear, a judge can direct a sheriff to bring the witness into court or even impose a jail sentence for a willful violation of the order.

When you come to court for the trial, check to see if the clerk has received any subpoenaed documents. If such records are crucial to your case and have not been received, you can ask for a continuance. If you have subpoenaed an individual and do not know what he or she looks like, ask the clerk to call out the name to determine if he or she is present so you can proceed with the trial.

To maximize your chances of success, organize your case before the trial. Gather and label all your evidence so that you can produce the documents easily. You may also wish to speak with a lawyer or call a lawyer's referral service for legal advice. Many communities have such advisory organizations, and they are willing to inform you, without charge, about relevant cases and statutes. This may help you know to what damages you are legally entitled. You may cite these laws, if applicable, at the hearing.

*The trial.* Arrive early, locate the correct courtroom, find the name of your case on the court calendar, and check in with the clerk. You should be properly attired, preferably in business clothes. Come prepared with all relevant documents. Examples are:

- Receipts and canceled checks
- Correspondence
- Contracts
- Letters of protest demanding unpaid wages
- Unpaid invoices
- Contemporaneous memos of promises and statements made to you
- Signed affidavits or statements from friends and witnesses unable to appear at the hearing
- An accountant's statement of lost wages
- Prior years' tax returns
- Diagrams or charts
- Copies of applicable statutes, cases, and regulations

When your case is called, you and your opponent will be sworn. The judge or court-appointed arbitrator will conduct the hearing and ask you questions. Be relaxed. Keep your presentation brief and to the point. Tell why you are suing the defendant and what monetary damages you are seeking. Show your evidence. Bring along a short written summary of the case. You can refer to it during the trial, and if the judge does not come to an immediate decision, he or she can use your outline for reference. Talk directly to the judge and respond to his or her questions. Show respect. Always refer to him or her as "Your Honor" or "Judge." Listen to the judge's instructions and never argue. If the judge asks you a question while you are speaking, stop immediately. Then answer the question honestly and to the point. Be diplomatic rather than emotional. Avoid arguing with your opponent in court and never interrupt his or her presentation.

After both sides finish speaking, you will have the opportunity to refute what your opponent has told the judge. Do not be intimidated if he or she is accompanied by a lawyer. Simply inform the judge that you are not represented by counsel and are not familiar with small-claims court procedures. Ask the judge to intercede on your behalf if you feel that your opponent's attorney is treating you unfairly. Most judges will be sympathetic, since small-claims courts are specially designed for you to present your case without an attorney.

*If you are a defendant.* Follow the same procedures as the plaintiff: prepare your testimony; contact your witnesses to be sure that they will appear at the trial and testify on your behalf; collect your exhibits and documents; arrive early on the day of the trial and check in with the clerk. If you have any doubts about your case, try to settle with the plaintiff before the judge hears the case. Request that the case be dismissed if your opponent fails to appear. Your opponent will speak first if he or she appears. Wait until he or she is finished speaking before telling your side of the story. Point out any inconsistencies or flaws in your opponent's story. Conclude your remarks by highlighting the important aspects of the case.

*Obtaining judgment.* Some small-claims court judges render oral decisions on the spot. Others issue a decision in writing several days after the hearing. This gives them time to weigh the testimony and exhibits. If your opponent failed to attend the hearing, judges usually render a judgment of default immediately after your presentation.

If you win the case, make sure you know how and when payment will be made. Check to see that all your disbursements, including court costs, filing fees, service of process, and applicable witness fees, are added to the amount of your judgment. Send a copy of the decision by certified mail, return receipt requested, to your opponent, together with a letter requesting payment. Some states require that payment be made to the court; others allow payment to be made directly to you.

Do not hesitate to act if you do not receive the money. First, contact the clerk and file a Petition for Notice to Show Cause. This will be sent to the defendant, ordering the employer to come into court and explain why it has not been paid. You should also file an Order of Execution with the sheriff's, constable's, or clerk's office in the county where the defendant is located or owns a business. This will enable you to discover where the defendant has assets. The sheriff or other enforcement agent has the power to go out and collect the judgment by seizing personal property, freezing the defendant's bank accounts, placing a lien on any real estate, or even garnisheeing an individual's salary where appropriate. The clerk of your small-claims court should tell you exactly what to do to collect your judgment.

*Final comments:* By bringing suit in small-claims court, you usually waive your right to a trial by jury. However, the defendant can surprise you. Some states allow defendants to move a small-claims court case to a higher court and/or obtain a trial by jury. If this occurs, you will need a lawyer to represent you, and his or her services could cost as much as your claim in the dispute.

Some states do not allow losing plaintiffs to appeal, but if you can and do appeal, be aware that an appeals court will overturn the decision of a small-claims court judge only if there is strong proof that the judge was biased or dishonest. This may be difficult to prove.

## Workers' Compensation

Each state has enacted its own particular laws with respect to workers' compensation benefits, which provide aid for employees who suffer job-related injuries.

In all states, employers with more than several workers are obligated to maintain workers' compensation insurance through a company or be self-insured for the benefit of their employees (not independent contractors). The advantage to employers is that they cannot be sued in court for injuries sustained by workers during the course of employment even if an accident was caused by an employer's fault (negligence). Lawyers representing injured workers typically prefer that their clients not receive workers' compensation benefits because the potential of being awarded money for damages in a personal injury lawsuit is vastly greater.

Not every on-the-job injury is covered under workers' compensation. State courts seem to be divided on whether an injured employee can recover for horseplay. Many states will not award benefits to a person who is injured while intoxicated or who deliberately inflicts injury on himself. Furthermore, an employee who is injured while traveling to or from work is not generally entitled to benefits unless the employer has agreed to provide the worker with the means of transportation, pay the employee's cost of commuting, or if travel is required while performing his/her duties. For example, if the employee regularly dictates office memos into a dictating machine within a vehicle, the car may be deemed part of his/her workplace.

If a worker leaves the employer's premises to do a personal errand, no compensation should be due. However, if injury is incurred when an employee is returning from company-sponsored education classes, goes to the rest room, visits the cafeteria, has a coffee break, or steps out of a nonsmoking office to smoke a cigarette, workers' comp boards and courts typically recognize that employers benefit from these "nonbusiness" employee conveniences and often award compensation.

Always alert your employer immediately if you are injured on the job. Under compensation laws in most states, each employer must promptly provide medical, surgical, optometric, or other treatment for injured employees, as well as provide hospital care, crutches, eyeglasses, and other appliances necessary to repair, relieve, or support a part of the body. Your company's medical team may eliminate unnecessary treatment, but an injured employee may select her own physician or authorized treatment, provided that physician is authorized by the state's workers' compensation board.

Employers may engage the services of a competent physician to review the medical care an injured worker is receiving. Such a person may be able to determine, for example, whether less expensive home care is more appropriate than hospital care. A medical consultant can also evaluate claims from the employee's doctor to see if they are self-serving.

---

**STRATEGY:** *Do not be afraid of reporting an accident or filing a claim in writing. Most states prohibit companies from firing, demoting, or otherwise punishing an employee for filing or pursuing a valid workers' compensation claim. Do this as quickly as possible so your case is not dismissed as being untimely. While you are receiving medical treatment, save all receipts of drug purchases, trips to the doctor (including tolls and cab fares), and all related purchases. You are generally entitled to full reimbursement for all direct out-of-pocket expenses, including payment for doctors, hospitals, rehabilitation, and related therapy costs. Dependents are entitled to receive death benefits in case of death, and you will be compensated for the loss of a limb or body part (such as an eye) based on a predetermined schedule. You are also entitled to compensation for loss of wages and income. The type of disability you suffered (i.e., temporary, permanent, partial, and/or total disability) will determine the amount of money you receive each week and how long you will receive such benefits. Each*

*state has maximum limits for weekly benefits that typically do
not exceed 75 percent of a worker's regular weekly salary.*

---

Do not hesitate to consult a lawyer specializing in workers'
compensation injuries or a personal injury lawyer where applicable, particularly if your employer refuses to provide benefits. A
lawyer can protect your rights in many ways. For example, if anyone other than your employer or coworker was even partly responsible for the accident, you may be free to file your own
liability insurance claim against that person or business. If for any
reason your accident is not covered by workers' compensation because you are an independent contractor or because the company
has no coverage, you may be able to file a lawsuit against your
employer in the same fashion that you could sue anyone who
causes you personal injury. In such a case, additional damages
such as attorney fees, money for mental pain and suffering, loss of
companionship to a spouse, and even punitive damages may be
awarded.

Under certain circumstances you may also be able to collect Social Security benefits, retirement benefits or unemployment compensation, and health insurance payments while you are collecting
disability benefits. A labor lawyer or one who specializes in workers' compensation law can advise you. A knowledgeable lawyer's
services may be required to argue your case at the hearing stage
before an administrative law judge, especially when the issues are
not clear-cut (such as when and where the accident occurred, to
determine initially if workers' compensation is applicable).
Lawyers handling workers' compensation matters are generally
quite knowledgeable about medical conditions and dealing with
doctors. Resolving an issue of whether an accident caused a partial or permanent disability can involve tens of thousands of dollars in future wages.

It may also be necessary to retain the services of a lawyer if you
want to pursue an unsuccessful verdict at the appeals stage. Thus,

consult a specialist for advice and guidance where applicable. (Typically, workers' compensation lawyers work on a contingency-fee basis.)

## Mediation and Dispute Resolution Organizations

American Arbitration Association (AAA)
140 West 51st Street
New York, NY 10020
(212) 484-4000

American Bar Association (ABA)
Section of Dispute Resolution
740 15th Street NW
Washington, DC 20009

National Institute for Dispute Resolution
1901 L Street NW, Suite 600
Washington, DC 20036
(202) 862-7200

Council of Better Business Bureaus
4200 Wilson Boulevard, Suite 800
Arlington, VA 22203
(703) 276-0100

The above organizations may be able to provide additional information about specific areas of dispute resolution. Many offer catalogs of publications, as well as brochures of general information.

## Important Federal and State Agencies to Contact

### For Civil Rights Violations

Commission on Civil Rights, Washington, DC

American Civil Liberties Union
132 West 43rd Street
New York, NY 10036
(212) 944-9800

National Association for the Advancement of Colored People,
Washington, DC

National Organization for Women, New York, NY

## For Discrimination Complaints

American Civil Liberties Union, New York, NY

Equal Employment Opportunity Commission
1801 L Street NW
Washington, DC 20506
(800) 669-EEOC; (800) 669-4000 for a list of regional offices
(202) 663-4264

U.S. Department of Labor
200 Constitutional Avenue NW
Washington, DC 20210
(202) 219-6666

## Concerning the Elderly

American Association of Retired Persons, Washington, DC

National Council on the Aging, Washington, DC

Social Security Administration, Washington, DC

Equal Employment Opportunity Commission, Washington, DC

American Association of Retired Persons
601 E Street NW
Washington, DC 20049
(800) 424-3410

## For Discrimination Concerning the Handicapped

Equal Employment Opportunity Commission, Washington, DC

U.S. Department of Transportation, Washington, DC

State Attorney General's Office

Pension and Welfare Benefits Administration, Washington, DC

President's Committee on Employment of People with Disabilities
1331 F Street NW
Washington, DC 20004-1107
(202) 376-6200

Social Security Administration, Washington, DC

## For Safety and Health Complaints

U.S. Department of Labor

Occupational Safety and Health Administration (OSHA)
Frances Perkins Building
200 Constitution Avenue NW
Washington, DC 20210
(202) 219-6091

## For Information on Labor Unions

AFL-CIO, Washington, DC
(202) 637-5000

National Labor Relations Board
1099 14th Street NW
Washington, DC 20005-3419
(202) 273-1991

## For Pension Information

Division of Public Disclosure
U.S. Department of Labor
Room N5507
Washington, DC 20210
(202) 219-8771

Pension Rights Center
918 16th Street NW, Suite 704
Washington, DC 20006
(202) 296-3778

Pension Benefit Guaranty Corporation
Case Operations and Compliance
1200 K Street NW
Washington, DC 20005
(202) 326-4000

Pension and Welfare Benefits Administration
1730 K Street NW, Suite 556
Washington, DC 20006
(202) 254-7013

# CHAPTER 9

# Legal Problems of Sales Representatives

Sales representatives (most often called sales reps, reps, agents, or brokers) are persons or organizations that contract to sell the products of manufacturers or other organizations (called principals). When the sales rep is an independent contractor instead of an employee, there are a number of unique legal problems that must be faced. Unlike most workers, sales reps risk income fluctuation because of factors often removed from their control. For example, after orders are procured, reps sometimes suffer losses of earnings when principals fail to ship merchandise, fail to provide a proper and accurate accounting of commissions owed, or terminate the relationship (in the absence of a written contract with a definite term) at their whim with little or no notice, without cause.

There are currently millions of salespeople in the United States who earn their livelihood in a variety of selling areas including furniture, apparel, gifts, mass marketing, industrial goods, and a multitude of others. However, reps are often exploited, most without knowing it. They sign contracts prepared by the legal staffs of their principals which are typically slanted for the benefit of the company. Others do nothing when their commissions are unjustifiably withheld.

Fortunately, the legal position of sales reps is growing stronger with each passing year. Fifteen years ago there were no federal or state laws to protect the plight of the independent salesperson. Now many states have passed legislation *ensuring* the prompt payment of commissions after the working relationship ends.

Some state laws even require written contracts that specify how commissions are earned, when they must be paid, and the penalties that ensue when these procedures are not followed.

No matter what industry they sell in, reps must be knowledgeable about the pitfalls of their business and know how to protect themselves before, during, and after their relationship with a principal terminates. This chapter summarizes many of the strategies I offer clients to help them protect their business. You will learn how to investigate a principal before accepting a line, and many of the important points to negotiate and confirm in writing before starting work. If you receive a contract from a company, you will learn what clauses favor the principal and how these clauses can be modified to better your interests. If you have an oral contract with a principal, you will learn how your status can be substantially improved and protected.

This chapter will explain why it is important to save all correspondence and sales records while working to receive an accurate accounting, and how to act properly, enforce your rights, and receive all commissions due after the relationship has ended. Also covered is a discussion of current state laws protecting sales reps and strategies to remember when using these laws to your advantage.

Additionally, you will understand when it is often advantageous to proceed with arbitration (as opposed to litigation) to collect what is owed, plus tips to help win your case regardless of the forum used to settle the dispute. In short, whether you are a novice salesperson or an experienced pro, you will become more informed and less vulnerable to being subjected to the injustices of your trade.

## Considerations Before Taking On a New Line

The first step in reducing the chances of being exploited is to take the time to investigate the principal and the line you are considering representing. For example, some reps are hired as a result of conversations with company officials. Agreements made via the telephone should be entered into with *great caution*. By meeting the principal, inspecting the manufacturing facilities, and talking in person with key personnel you will be working with (such as the sales manager), you can avoid future problems. Many times, after agreeing to a specified commission rate and other key terms and investing time and money selling goods for the company, reps are told that the person who offered the package did not have the authority to bind the company or is no longer working there. On other occasions, salespeople have been told over the telephone to "show us what you can do and write your own ticket" only to find stiff opposition from the company once their orders have been placed. These abuses need not occur and can be prevented by taking the following simple steps:

1. Always find out with whom you are talking, his or her position, and the extent of his or her authority to bind the company.
2. Do *not* rely on promises that terms will be worked out at a later date.
3. If you are unfamiliar with a principal or the track record of the manufacturer, ask for the names of a few customers who are currently being shipped products or receive services. Call them to obtain information about the company.
4. Learn who previously represented the company and why he or she is no longer in that position. Then talk to the former salesperson. You may learn that the person resigned because she wasn't being paid on time, or had her commissions unfairly reduced or her territory cut without her consent when the principal unilaterally designated certain accounts as house accounts.
5. Try to investigate the principal's financial history by asking such questions as:

- What is its financial status and credit rating?
- Does it ship damaged goods with a high rate of return?
- Does the firm have a high rate of sales turnover?

Once you are satisfied with the firm's reputation, financial picture, and track record, you must carefully negotiate your working arrangement. Too many reps begin working without clearly defining their contract, which often leads to future misunderstandings and problems. The following is a comprehensive checklist which describes numerous points to request, including fallback points, during the negotiating session.

## TERRITORY

- Specify the precise territory you will represent.
- Try to obtain a status as the exclusive rep in that territory (i.e., that the principal cannot appoint another rep to sell goods in your territory).
- Obtain the principal's consent to sell *all* of its products, including those introduced in the future, if possible.
- Specify that you will receive commissions for all sales made in your territory regardless of whether the order is procured by you or received directly by the company without your assistance.
- Specify that there will be no house accounts (i.e., noncommissionable accounts) in your territory.
- Define split commission policies in advance. For example, what commission will you receive on orders accepted by customers in your territory but shipped into another salesperson's territory?

## COMMISSIONS

- Be sure to specify when your commissions will be earned: Will they be earned when the order is accepted? When the order is accepted and shipped? When the order is accepted, shipped, and invoiced? Or when the order is accepted, shipped, invoiced, and paid for? Some principals will only pay commissions after the order is shipped and *paid for* by the customer. Avoid this arrangement if possible. Try to receive commissions after shipment rather than when the customer pays for the product. If you cannot obtain this, try to get a portion of the commission upon acceptance of the order (such as 50 percent within one week of acceptance) and the balance when shipment is made and payment is received.

- Consider negotiating guaranteed shipping arrangements where applicable. This can provide you with payment in lieu of shipment if the company fails to deliver its merchandise. Under this scenario, the company guarantees it will ship a specified percentage of all accepted orders. If the company fails to ship this percentage, you will be paid on the difference.

- Be sure you understand whether the commission is a gross or net amount. If a net amount, understand how and when deductions are computed. For example, principals often deduct unfair amounts as a result of returns, freight charges, billing and advertising discounts, collection charges, large orders, special customers, off-price goods, and reorders. Avoid such deductions if possible.

- What about taxes and tooling expenses? Are these excluded from your earnings?

- Discuss the amount of commissions to be paid if monies are received after a collection agency or law firm collects delinquent arrears.

- Ask to receive credit and payment for reorders (i.e., repeats of merchandise previously purchased by the customer).

- Discuss commission rates for large orders, special customers, off-price goods, and reorders.
- Establish an arithmetic formula for determining commission rates on off-price goods. *Never* leave this to the company's sole discretion. For example, on goods sold at 75 percent of the regular selling price, commissions normally due the rep at 8 percent should only be reduced to 6 percent.
- If no arithmetic formula is agreed upon, insist that the parties will discuss and agree on every off-price order but in no event will the rep receive less than a specified percent.
- Discuss and agree on split commission policies (sales in your territory that are shipped into another rep's territory, or vice versa).
- If additional services are contemplated for warehousing, detailed forecasting, collections, etc., be sure to request additional payment for such services which are separate and apart from commissions due.
- Define your status as an independent contractor and determine who pays for expenses and taxes, if applicable.
- Ask for a stipulation that commission rates cannot be changed suddenly without your written approval. Many employees and independent sales agents are exploited in this fashion. Also watch out for house accounts and related problems. House accounts are customers that are either nonsolicitable or noncommissionable; if the employer insists on this, be sure you understand in advance what customers and accounts will not earn commissions so you don't waste valuable time and effort on them.
- Be sure you negotiate to receive accurate commission reports *together* with copies of all accepted orders and invoices. Proper accounting is vital for all people earning commissions, and employers frequently exploit people in this area. Many people rely on the honesty and integrity of their companies as to the accuracy of the figures presented to them.

Although most employers are generally honest, mistakes frequently occur.

- By negotiating to receive complete documentation in addition to the commission statement, you will be in a better position to detect errors and mistakes. Additionally, the fact that you may get a computer printout commission statement does not mean that you are obtaining 100 percent accurate accounting. Duplicate invoices are often photocopied in error. In addition, some companies give each of their commission employees and agents a different computer number. If these numbers are fed into the computer incorrectly, other people may receive credit for your sales. Also be careful if your invoices are delayed and the company informs you that you will receive supplementary sheets at a later date. Many people forget to tally these sheets and lose valuable commissions.

- Specify what happens to commissions if you resign or are fired. This is a common problem that is typically not addressed when the job begins. Try to negotiate the right to receive commissions for orders that are accepted prior to the termination or resignation but are shipped *after* the termination date. Additionally, you may wish to receive commissions for reorders through the end of the selling season customary in your industry and/or for blanket orders or purchases that are to be filled for a period of time after the termination date. Remember, if you don't ask for these things, the employer will only pay you commissions up to the termination date.

- Finally, if you successfully negotiate items discussed above, insist on the right to receive copies of all orders and shipping information after the termination date while your commission arrangement is still in effect. Companies have a legal obligation to keep records of all accounts, particularly when their employees and sales agents are entitled to commissions. This duty is most apparent after the individual resigns or has been terminated, since it is virtually impossible to obtain information on sales figures after you no longer work for the company.

*Advance on commissions.* Ask if you are entitled to a *draw* or *advance* against commissions. (This arrangement is not typically made with sales employees but with independent sales representatives and agents.) Salespeople and employees are sometimes advanced money to be applied against and reimbursed by future commissions. When advances are made that do not exceed commission earnings, you are *not* generally personally liable to return the difference (no matter what the company tells you) unless you promised before to do so. The reason is that courts generally consider advances to be additional salary unless language in an employment agreement or conduct of the parties expressly indicates that such advances were intended to be a loan. Even if you leave the company before commission earnings exceed a draw, you will probably not be liable to return the excess.

---

**STRATEGY:** *At the hiring interview or after, never agree to be personally liable for repayment and never acknowledge to anyone that you intend to repay any excess advance. To protect your rights in this area, do not sign or endorse draw checks containing the word "loan" on the face of the check, and do not sign an employment contract stating that advances are not considered part payment of salary but rather a personal indebtedness to be repaid at some future date when commission earnings do not exceed the draw; never sign a promissory note or letter to this effect.*

---

Request that the employer cannot stop or reduce the draw at any time without prior notice when commission earnings do not exceed draw. Since you may be relying on a draw to pay your bills and expenses until commissions are received, you don't want to be left high and dry.

JOB SECURITY

- Specify the start date.
- Try to get as much job security as possible—for example, stipulate that you can continue to represent the principal on a yearly basis or as long as your sales volume exceeds a specified dollar amount.
- If you cannot get at least a one-year contract, negotiate to receive as much notice of termination as possible (e.g., that you can only be fired on six months' notice). Sometimes, reps negotiate additional notice periods as the amount of time representing the principal increases. For example, a thirty-day notice period becomes sixty days after the first year and ninety days after the second year, etc.
- During this notice period, specify that you can continue representing the line and will be paid for all orders obtained by you or procured in your territory, even if shipped after the termination date of the contract.
- Specify that any notices of termination must be sent certified mail, return receipt requested, so you will be sure to have received such notice. (If notice is sent by regular mail, the company may be in breach of contract.)

TERMINATION OF EMPLOYMENT

- Clarify when commissions stop but *avoid* arrangements where they cease immediately upon termination.
- Negotiate to receive commissions for a certain period of time after termination—through the end of the selling season or for a specified period of time thereafter (ninety days after termination is a good figure).
- In addition to commissions, be aware that reps in certain industries are negotiating additional *severance* after termination. This means that if you are fired without cause, you can

receive the average monthly commission during the last year multiplied by the number of years worked.

- A fallback provision using this concept can be to receive severance based on the increase of sales volume in your territory from your efforts. For example, if you took over a territory with a volume of $1 million annually and built that to $2 million annually, you would receive an additional three months' severance; volume exceeding $4 million annually would entitle you to six months' severance, etc.
- Specify when a final accounting will be made and commissions paid after termination.
- Discuss the handling of commissions on orders "pending" or "in the works" for sales expected but not yet consummated.

## PROPER ACCOUNTING

- Always request copies of all accepted orders and invoices within a certain period of time after shipment. Typically, you should negotiate to receive this information, together with an accurate commission statement and commission check, no later than the thirtieth day of the month following the month of shipment.
- Avoid arrangements where the company requires that you protest commission statements within a certain period of time after receipt (such as ten days), and if no notice regarding errors is received, they will be deemed correct.
- Demand the right for you, your accountant, or your attorney to inspect the company's books and records at least once annually upon reasonable written notice at your own cost. If errors are discovered exceeding 5 percent of what you were told was owed, make the company pay for the cost of the inspection.

## POINTS TO AVOID

- Never accept an arrangement where you are paid commissions on a quarterly, semiannual, or annual basis.
- Avoid agreeing that you will work exclusively and on a full-time basis for the company, unless this is financially in your best interests.
- Avoid arrangements where you must *personally* solicit the product and cannot hire a sales associate, partner, road salesperson, or employee to assist in your selling endeavors.
- Avoid mandatory attendance at national sales meetings at your own expense.
- Resist arrangements where you must call on all accounts in your territory a certain number of times annually, service these accounts, and maintain accurate selling records and lead sheets.
- Be aware of situations requiring you to actively assist in any collection efforts requested by the company. If there is such a requirement, ask what activities will be included. For example, are you merely required to call on the account periodically to ask for payment, or must you hire and pay for a collection agency on behalf of the principal?
- Never sign contracts containing restrictive covenants prohibiting you from working for a competitor, calling on certain customers, or revealing confidential information or trade secrets after termination, particularly before speaking to a lawyer knowledgeable in this area.
- Resist arrangements requiring you to maintain minimum general and automobile liability coverage in excess of a specified dollar amount per occurrence.
- Avoid signing contracts with clauses stating that any litigation must take place in the state where the principal is located or mainly does business.

Other Negotiating Points

- Ask the company to provide you with proof of product liability insurance naming your rep firm as a beneficiary on its policy and indemnifying you and holding you blameless in any liability or lawsuit (including the payment of legal fees incurred in defending yourself in a lawsuit) caused by injury to a customer by a product negligently designed or manufactured by the principal, or regarding patent, trademark, or copyright matters affecting the principal or its products.
- Be sure your contract states that there can be no modifications of any terms previously agreed upon unless reduced to writing and signed by both parties. This will eliminate the most flagrant abuses to reps—namely, sudden reduction of your commission rates and accounts in your territory without your approval.
- Be sure your contract states that it is binding on all successors and assigns. This way, if the company is sold, the new principal will be required to honor your contract and continue to engage you as the rep.

## Confirming the Agreement in Writing

Once you and the company have agreed to key terms, it is essential to confirm the deal in writing. Legal disputes usually arise in this area because principals hire reps on a handshake. A handshake, or oral agreement, indicates only that the parties came to some form of agreement; it does not say what the agreement was. Failure to spell out important terms often leads to misunderstandings and disputes. Even when key terms are discussed, the same spoken words that are agreed upon have different meanings from the salesperson's and company's perspective. Written words limit this sort of misunderstanding.

The following sample agreement was prepared by the National

Electrical Manufacturers Representatives' Association (NEMRA). It illustrates many of the points described in the previous section and is the kind of formal agreement that should always be signed by both parties to avoid future problems. (Bear in mind that this is a "sample" agreement and that it does not contain a number of favorable terms that salespeople must consider, such as an arbitration clause.)

## Sample Principal-Rep Agreement

THIS AGREEMENT made this _____ day of _____ by and between _____ a corporation incorporated under the laws of the State of _____ having its principal office at _____ hereinafter referred to as "Manufacturer,"
and
a corporation incorporated under the laws of the State of _____ having its principal office at _____ hereinafter referred to as "Representative," as follows:

Appointment and Acceptance
Manufacturer appoints Representative as its exclusive selling representative to sell products (enumerated in Provision No. 3 hereof) in this territory (defined in Provision No. 2 hereof); and Representative accepts the appointment and agrees to sell and promote the sale of the Manufacturer's products.

Territory
Representative's territory shall consist of the following:

Products
The products of the Manufacturer to be sold by the Representative are:

Amount of Compensation
Representative's compensation for services performed hereunder shall be ___% of the "net invoice price" of the Manufacturer's

product shipped into Representative's territory. However, when engineering, execution of the order, or shipment involves different territories, the Manufacturer will split the full commission among the Representatives whose territories are involved. The Manufacturer will make this determination and advise the interested Representatives at the time the order is submitted to the Manufacturer. The sum of the split commission shall add up to a full commission and no Representative whose territory is involved shall receive less than ___% of the full commission.

Computation and Payment of Commission

a) Commissions are due and payable on or before the ___ day of the month following the month in which the customer is invoiced; and if not paid when due, the amount not paid will accrue interest at ___% per annum from the date due until paid.

b) Manufacturer will send Representative copies of all invoices at the time Manufacturer invoices customer, and each invoice shall indicate the amount of commission due Representative.

c) At the time of payment of commissions to Representative, Manufacturer will send Representative a commission statement showing:

1. the computation of all commissions earned during the ninety (90) day period prior to its issuance (listing all invoices covered by the statement), and

2. commissions paid during that period (listing the invoices on which commissions are being paid), and

3. commissions due and owing Representative.

d) "Net invoice price" shall mean the total price at which an order is invoiced to the customer, including any increase or decrease in the total amount of the order (even though such increase or decrease takes place after the effective date of termination), but excluding shipping and mailing costs; taxes; insurance; and any allowances or discounts granted to the customer by the Manufacturer.

e) There shall be deducted from any sums due Representative:

1. an amount equal to commissions previously paid or credited on sales of Manufacturer's products which have since been returned by the customer or on allowances credited to the customer for any reason by the Manufacturer, and

2. an amount equivalent to commissions previously paid or credited on sales which Manufacturer shall not have been fully paid by the customer, whether by reason of the customer's bankruptcy, insolvency, or any other reason which renders the account uncollectible (if any sums are ever realized upon such uncollectible accounts, Manufacturer will pay Representative its percentage of commission applicable at the time of the original sale upon the net proceeds of such collection).

f) "Order" shall mean any commitment to purchase Manufacturer's products which calls for shipment into Representative's territory or which is subject to split commission in accordance with Provision No. 4 hereof.

Acceptance of Orders

All orders are subject to acceptance or rejection by an authorized officer of Manufacturer at its home office and to the approval of the Manufacturer's credit department. Manufacturer shall be responsible for all credit risks and collections.

If Manufacturer notifies customer of its acceptance or rejection of an order, a copy of any written notification shall be transmitted to the Representative. At least once every month, Manufacturer shall supply Representative with copies of all orders received directly by the Manufacturer, copies of all shipping notices, and copies of all correspondence and quotations made to the customers in the territory.

Terms of Sale

All sales shall be at prices and upon terms established by the Manufacturer and it shall have the right, in its discretion from time to time, to establish, change, alter, or amend prices and other terms and conditions of sale. Representative shall not accept orders in the

Manufacturer's name, or make price quotations or delivery promises without the Manufacturer's prior approval.

Representative's Relationship and Conduct of Business

a) Representative shall maintain a sales office in the territory and shall devote such time as may be reasonably necessary to sell and promote the sale of Manufacturer's products within the territory.

b) Representative will conduct all of its business in its own name and in such manner as it may see fit. Representative will pay all expenses whatever of its office and activities and be responsible for the acts and expenses of its employees.

c) Nothing in this agreement shall be construed to constitute Representative as the partner or employee or agent of the Manufacturer, nor shall either party have any authority to bind the other in any respect, it being intended that each shall remain an independent contractor responsible only for its own actions.

d) Representative shall not, without Manufacturer's prior written approval, enlarge or limit orders, make representations or guarantees concerning Manufacturer's product, or accept the return of or make any allowance for such products.

e) Representative shall furnish to Manufacturer's credit department any information which it may have from time to time relative to the credit standing of any of its customers.

f) Representative shall abide by Manufacturer's policies and communicate same to Manufacturer's customers.

g) Manufacturer shall be solely responsible for the design, development, supply, production, and performance of its products and the protection of its trade names. Manufacturer agrees to indemnify and hold Representative harmless from and against and to pay all losses, costs, damages, or expenses whatsoever, including reasonable attorney's fees, which Representative may sustain or incur on account of infringement or alleged infringement of patents, trademarks, or trade names, or breach of warranty or claims of breach of warranty in any way resulting from the sale of Manufacturer's products. Manufacturer will indemnify Representative from and hold it harmless from and against all liabilities, losses, damages, costs, or expenses, including reasonable attorney's fees, which it may at any time suffer, incur, or be required to pay by reason or injury or death to any person or damage to property or both caused or allegedly caused by any products sold by Manufacturer.

h) Manufacturer shall furnish Representative, at no expense to Representative, samples, catalogs, literature, and any other material necessary for the proper promotion and sale of its products in the territory. Any literature which is not used or samples or other equipment belonging to the Manufacturer shall be returned to the Manufacturer at its request.

i) Whenever Representative, at Manufacturer's request, takes possession of Manufacturer's products for the purpose of delivering such products to customers for any other purpose, the risk of loss or damage to or destruction of such products shall be borne by the Manufacturer, and Manufacturer shall indemnify and hold Representative harmless against any claims, debts, liabilities, or causes of action resulting from any such loss, damage, or destruction.

Terms of Agreement and Termination
This agreement shall be effective on the _____ day of _____, and shall continue for ____ years(s) until the _____ of _____. It shall be automatically renewed from year to year thereafter unless terminated by either party upon ____ days' notice to the other by registered mail or certified mail prior to the end of the initial term of this agreement, or any renewal term.

Rights Upon Termination
Upon termination of this agreement for any reason, Representative shall be entitled to:

(a) Commissions on all orders calling for shipment into Representative's territory which are dated or communicated to Manufacturer prior to the effective date of termination, regardless of when such orders are shipped; and

(b) Its share of split commissions on orders dated or

communicated to Manufacturer prior to the effective date of termination, regardless of when such orders are shipped.

(c) Commissions referred to in this Provision No. 10 shall be paid on or before the ___ day of the month in which the Manufacturer receives payment for the orders.

General

This agreement contains the entire understanding of the parties, shall supersede any other oral or written agreements, and shall be binding upon, or inure to the benefit of, the parties' successors and assigns. It may not be modified in any way without the written consent of both parties. Representative shall not have the right to assign this agreement in whole or in part without Manufacturer's written consent.

IN WITNESS WHEREOF, the parties have executed this agreement the day and year above written in multiple counterparts, each of which shall be considered an original.

Manufacturer:
By:
   Title:
Representative:
By:
   Title:

Although a written contract cannot guarantee that you will be satisfied with the company's performance, it can provide additional remedies in the event of a principal's nonperformance. That is why most reps in all industries within the past ten years are no longer accepting being hired on a handshake. They now recognize that they can be better protected by including favorable clauses in clearly drafted contracts. For example, by specifying *in writing* that commissions will continue to be paid on all orders accepted prior to termination but shipped thereafter, including reorders, many thousands of dollars in commissions can be obtained that typically would *not* be available in an oral agreement. And by specifying in the agreement that all changes must be *in writing* and approved by both parties, you can eliminate common areas of exploitation that would not be accomplished without a written agreement.

When written agreements are used, be sure that all changes, strike-outs, and erasures are initialed by both parties and that all blanks are filled in. If additions are necessary, include them in a space provided or attach them to the contract itself. Then note on the contract that addenda have been added and accepted by both parties. This prevents questions from arising if addenda are lost or separated, because it is difficult to prove there were any without mention in the body of the contract.

## Turning an Oral Contract into a Written Agreement

A formal agreement similar to the above is not always required to serve your purposes; in some cases an oral contract can be an acceptable substitute. Before I describe how this may be accomplished, a few words about oral contracts are appropriate. An oral contract is a verbal agreement between the salesperson and the company defining their working relationship. Such contracts may be binding when the duties, compensation, and terms of employment are agreed to by both parties.

Salespeople often have oral agreements because their companies refuse to give them written contracts. Many principals like to use oral contracts because there is no written evidence to indicate what terms were discussed and accepted by both parties when they entered into their working arrangement. If disputes arise, it is more difficult for the salesperson to prove that the principal failed to abide by the terms of the agreement. For example, if a 5 percent commission rate was accepted verbally, a dishonest principal could deny this by stating that a lower commission rate on certain items had been accepted. The salesperson would then have to prove that both parties had agreed upon a higher commission figure.

When a legal dispute arises concerning the terms of an oral contract, a court will resolve the problem by examining all the evidence that the salesperson and company offer and weighing the testimony to determine who is telling the truth. Thus, to avoid problems, all salespeople should try to obtain a written contract to clarify their rights. However, if your company refuses to sign a written agreement, there are ways to protect yourself if you have an oral contract. Your chief concern should be directed toward obtaining written evidence indicating the accepted terms (i.e., concerning such areas as your commission rate, assigned territory, job security, notice-of-termination requirements, and proper accounting).

If your company refuses to sign a written agreement, it is advisable to write a letter to the principal whenever you reach an oral agreement relating to your job.

Whatever the deal that is agreed upon, the letter should be drafted similar to the following.

## Sample Letter Agreement

Name of Rep Firm
Address
Date

Name of Company Officer
Title
Company Name
Address

Dear (Name of Company Officer),

It was a pleasure meeting with you yesterday. Per our discussion, this will confirm the terms of my engagement as a sales representative for your Company commencing (date) under the following terms and conditions:

I agree to represent the company in: (specify states or territory). This territory will be covered exclusively by me with no other sales reps covering this territory, and there will be no house accounts in this territory.

I will receive a commission of (specify) percent of the (specify) gross (net) invoice amount for all orders shipped in my exclusive territory regardless of how the order is obtained or received by you or your company.

There will be no deductions from my commission except for (specify). Commission checks together with accurate statements will be sent to me on or about the (specify) day of the month following the month of shipment and the Company agrees to send me copies of all invoices of shipments in my territory on a weekly basis.

[*Optional:* In addition, the Company will contribute a showroom participation fee of ($X) payable on the first day of each month of this Agreement, which is a separate charge and not to be deducted or collected against any commissions due me.]

I will be considered an independent contractor and will be responsible to pay all applicable Social Security, withholding, and other employment taxes.

To cancel our agreement, either party must send the other written notice no less than thirty (30) days prior to the effective termination date. Upon termination for any reason, I shall be paid commission on all shipments made for a period of six (6) months after the effective termination date for orders in house before the effective termination date.

If any of the terms of this letter are ambiguous or incorrect, please advise me immediately in writing; otherwise, this letter shall set forth and constitute our entire understanding of this matter which may not be modified or changed to any extent, except in writing, signed by both parties.

Very truly yours,
Name of Rep; Firm Name

*Sent certified mail, return receipt requested.*

Be as specific as possible when referring to subjects that you and the company have agreed upon. Write the letter with precision, since ambiguous terms are resolved against the letter writer. Be sure to keep a copy of the letter for your own records and save the certified mail receipt. If at a later date the terms of the oral agreement are changed (for instance, additional territory is assigned to you), write another letter specifying the new arrangement that has been reached. Keep a copy of this letter and all correspondence sent to and received from your company.

## Determining Your Status for Tax Purposes

Many salespeople lack knowledge as to what constitutes independent contractor versus employee status for tax purposes. The IRS generally opposes independent contractor status, since employers are not required to withhold income and employment taxes. Additionally, since independent contractors can manipulate their earnings and deductions (they are entitled to claim all of their business-related expenses on Schedule C, where expenses offset gross business income), many dollars of compensation income often go untaxed. This section will examine the legal distinction between being treated as an independent contractor and being treated as an employee for tax purposes, and will offer strategies to avoid problems in this area.

There is no precise legal definition that explains what an independent contractor is. In fact, each state has its own laws in determining whether a salesperson is an employee or an independent contractor. When the courts attempt to determine the difference, they analyze the facts of each particular case. The most significant factors that courts look at when making this distinction are:

1. The company's right of control over the salesperson;
2. Whether or not the company carries indemnity or liability insurance for the salesperson; and
3. Whether the parties have a written agreement that defines the status of the salesperson.

The company's right of control is best explained by the use of examples. Courts have found people to be employees if their employers:

- Had the right to supervise the details of their operations; that is, required salespeople to collect money owed from accounts on behalf of the company
- Provided the salesperson with a company car or reimbursement for some or all expenses
- Restricted the person's ability to work for other companies or jobs (i.e., person devoted full-time efforts to this job)
- Required the person to call on particular customers
- Provided the person with insurance and workers' compensation benefits
- Deducted income and FICA taxes

This list is not meant to be all-inclusive; these factors are listed to help you determine whether the law in your state treats people as employees or independent contractors.

Since the law is so unsettled and frequently varies from case to case and state to state, federal legislation was introduced in the Senate to standardize this problem. Unfortunately, the bill was not passed; however, the bill is instructive, because it outlined a set of rules to be applied. By following these rules, you may be able to minimize problems or document your position in the event of an audit. According to the bill, an independent contractor:

1. Controls his own work schedule and number of working hours;

2. Operates from his own place of business or pays rent if an office is provided;

3. Risks income fluctuation, since his earnings are a result of output and results (i.e., sales), rather than number of hours worked; and

4. Has a written contract with an employer before he begins working that states he is not considered an employee for purposes of the Federal Contributions Act or the Federal Unemployment Tax Act; and income is not withheld at the source; and the contract states that the salesperson must pay his own self-employment and federal income tax.

Following these rules can help apply the correct status determination if it is contested by the IRS. In addition, a properly drafted contract with all of your principals and sales associates can protect you in many other areas as well. Don't forget to implement this if possible.

## Steps to Take While Working

While representing a principal, there are a number of steps you can take to reduce the chances of being exploited. These include checking your commission statements carefully and notifying the company immediately when you detect errors, saving all correspondence, records, and documents to confirm all deals and actions, reviewing your contract periodically to be sure both parties are complying with all of its terms, and documenting all promises made to you. (Example: "You are the best salesperson around here so we would never fire you without notice except for a good reason.")

Proper accounting is vital for any salesperson who works on a commission basis. Most reps rely on the honesty and integrity of their principals as to the accuracy of the figures that are presented to them. In most instances companies do give a proper accounting. However, many principals use questionable methods of record keeping. I have represented many sales clients who have been denied hundreds of thousands of dollars by dishonest principals who failed to record sales properly and to render credit for all shipped orders, and only paid these commissions after being threatened with legal action.

These are just a few of the abuses either intentionally or unintentionally practiced upon salespeople. The fact that you may get a computer printout commission statement does not mean you are obtaining 100 percent accurate accounting. Duplicate invoices are often photocopied in error. In addition, some companies give each of their salespeople a different computer number. If these numbers are fed into the computer incorrectly, other salespeople will receive credit for your sales. You should also be particularly careful if your invoices are delayed and the company informs you that you will receive supplementary sheets at a later date. Reps often forget to tally these sheets and lose valuable commissions.

Additionally, in order to prove you have a justifiable reason to view your company's books and records during pretrial discovery, you may be asked to provide a court with information that reveals what you are looking for. Usually, these requests must be supported by written documentation so you will not be viewed as being disruptive and engaging in a "fishing expedition." For example, you may have to make specific references to accounts or be required to furnish the dates of the sale in addition to the products that were sold. Thus, save all of your records. Remember that companies have a legal obligation to keep records of all accounts, particularly if their salespeople receive commissions. This becomes important after the salesperson resigns or is fired, since it is often impossible for him or her to obtain information on sales figures for goods that were shipped and paid for after the salesperson left the company.

If the principal will not voluntarily turn over this information, it may be necessary to compel him to do so by means of discovery procedures. Discovery procedures play an important role in virtually every lawsuit, and both parties use them to obtain information before the case is brought to trial. It first must be established to the court's satisfaction that money may be due and owing before you are entitled to examine the records in the hope that something helpful will turn up. However, if you can show that the company's documents and records will help your case, extensive discovery is usually allowed by the court.

Thus, save your commission statements, copies of checks, letters, memos, and other documents received from the company while you are still working. All of this information may prove useful to your attorney later.

Reps are also wise to accumulate documents to confirm all deals, actions, and modifications of working arrangements. If the company decides to reduce your commission rate or draw, or change your territory, and your contract specifically forbids any changes unless in writing and agreed to by both parties, send a letter to document your protest. If you don't take steps to indicate your dissatisfaction, you may appear to have consented to such changes by conduct.

## Steps to Take if You Are Fired

Your principal may have the right to fire you, but you could be entitled to damages, depending on the circumstances. Implement the following strategies when you are fired or believe you are about to be fired:

1. Insist on receiving a final statement of commissions and other benefits to determine if you are owed any money.
2. Know the law regarding the prompt payment of commissions. Reps in thirty-four states are entitled to receive their final commissions shortly after being fired. These states

have sales rep protection laws which can be used to your advantage because they provide damages up to three times the commission amount owed plus reasonable attorney fees, costs, and disbursements when reps must resort to litigation in the event of a principal's noncompliance. Many of these state laws also require the parties to have written agreements specifying how commissions are earned and when they are due.

Spurred by Congress's failure to enact the Sales Representative Contractual Relations Bill of 1984 and quietly lobbied by sales groups with little opposition or knowledge from business interests, certain states are now recognizing inherent problems in the principal-agent relationship and are correcting them by legal means; expect more states to follow this trend and pass similar legislation in the coming years. All reps and rep firms must be aware of the laws in *each* state in which they sell to enhance their rights in this area.

Each state law differs regarding time requirements and penalties imposed. For example, in New York, commissions must be paid to a rep covering accounts in the state within five business days after termination of the working relationship or when commissions are earned. Ohio mandates payment within thirteen days of termination or after commissions become due, while the time limit for reps selling to accounts in Texas is thirty days after termination, but only if there is no written contract between the parties defining when commissions are earned and payable.

In the above states, the following penalties are imposed on companies not paying reps in timely fashion as specified: New York, twice the commission amount plus reasonable attorney fees, costs, and disbursements; Ohio, exemplary damages up to three times the commission amount plus attorney fees and costs; Texas, three times the damages sustained by the rep plus attorney fees and court costs.

While the time requirements and penalties may differ, all of the thirty-four state rep protection laws apply to principals (defined as a person or company who manufactures, produces, imports, or distributes a product for wholesale) typically located out of state who hire independent contractor sales reps to call on customers and solicit orders for commissions in another state. Multiple state laws may sometimes apply, giving reps the opportunity to *forum shop,* or use the state law that is most favorable under certain circumstances. That is why all reps should be knowledgeable about each state law in their selling territory for optimum advantage.

*Insist on written contracts for protection.* Some states, including Tennessee, Florida, Alabama, New York, Georgia, and Texas, require companies to issue written contracts spelling out important terms and to give reps a signed copy for their records after being hired. For many years I have advocated negotiating and obtaining written agreements to avoid many problems frequently encountered by reps (including sudden termination, erosion of accounts into house accounts, and reduction of commission rates without warning). Properly drafted, written contracts can eliminate many of these abuses and should be insisted upon whenever applicable. *If the principal refuses, remind him that this is the law.*

*Be aware of contract terms that avoid the effects of these laws.* Sophisticated principals are attempting to reduce the harsh effects of these laws by including a number of clauses in agreements with reps. Some include an arbitration clause requiring that all controversies be settled by arbitration in the city where the company's main office is located. This can have a chilling effect, since many out-of-state reps are reluctant to travel to a distant locale and incur expensive travel and related costs to obtain a hearing. Arbitration can work favorably for a principal, since the arbitrators selected are usually no-nonsense attorneys and businesspeople who are not as likely to be swayed by sympathy as juries are and are not required to make decisions strictly on relevant law. When principals are found liable, it is less likely that the arbitrators will tack on additional damages (i.e., triple commission payments).

Additionally, *never* agree to a clause similar to the following: "The parties agree that the law of X state [where the principal is located, but not your state] will apply and govern in any case, controversy, or proceeding." If legal action becomes necessary to protect your rights, you will be forced to seek an attorney licensed to practice in the other state, you could be bound by the law of that other state, and you will be forced to attend countless hours of proceedings in an out-of-state location. The cost to you in lost time and distraction may easily exceed the value of the award you are seeking from the principal.

Many reps, anxious to obtain a company's line, often fail to question or understand the effect of such language and waive valuable rights under the laws of *their* major sales territory or home state. Thus, avoid signing contracts containing such a clause.

---

**STRATEGY:** *Even if you do sign a contract waiving your favorable state's law, some rep acts make such clauses void and unenforceable.*

---

*Always send a detailed written demand for unpaid commissions.* This should be done by certified mail, return receipt requested, to document your claim and prove delivery. Such a demand will "start the clock" for the purposes of determining the number of days that commissions remain unpaid and put the principal on notice that additional damages and penalties may be owed for a continued breach. Remember, a written demand is essential in enforcing your rights.

Consider litigation to collect what is due. I used to advise sales rep clients that it was not worth pursuing a claim when less than $3,000 in commissions was owed, since legal fees, costs, and disbursements typically ran more than $2,000 when a case was brought to trial. Now, however, even small claims are worth pursuing in view of the extra legal fees, costs, and up to triple damages that are now being awarded. Since it is conceivable that a principal could be liable for $12,000 on an original $3,000 claim, do *not* be afraid to consider litigation where appropriate; you may be able to collect additional damages, costs, and fees in the process.

If you are owed a small amount of money (i.e., less than $3,000), consider instituting proceedings in small-claims court. Recognize, however, that since you may only be permitted to bring suit in the county where the principal resides or has its main office, the travel and incidental expenses involved may not make it worthwhile to pursue your rights.

*Seek legal advice before you take any action.* This is essential so you can receive an accurate opinion regarding your chances of success and an estimate of damages that are recoverable. The matter must also be analyzed to determine which state's law will apply. For example, if you sell to customers located in Texas, Arkansas, and Mississippi, can you apply Texas law (and triple damages) to your unpaid commissions from sales in Arkansas and Mississippi or only for sales in Texas? Since many of these acts are relatively new, and the law is unclear, sound legal advice can guide you accordingly. Your lawyer may also help you draft a demand letter or a letter stating your position, or a response to a letter received from a manufacturer, which could strengthen your position if litigation becomes necessary.

Obviously, *never* sign a release unless you know exactly what you are owed before settling a claim with a principal. And whenever you receive final commission checks, never cash them if they contain language such as "in full and final payment" without first speaking to a lawyer. In some states you can write a restrictive endorsement on the back of the check. Example: "Under Protest. Endorsement of this check does not constitute a waiver of any and all claims for commissions owed," and you will still be able to sue for the balance. In other states your cashing the check will *preclude* you from recovering anything further, despite any protest language. Thus, photocopy and save copies of all checks you receive and speak to a lawyer before endorsing and depositing such checks.

The lawyer you consult should be an experienced labor attorney with particular knowledge of problems typically encountered by salespeople and reps. At the initial interview, bring with you all pertinent written information including contracts, letters of intent, company memoranda, shipping lists, invoices, commission statements, etc. Tell the lawyer everything related to your problems, since all communications are privileged, and this will save time and make it easier for him or her to evaluate your case.

Once the lawyer receives all pertinent facts, he or she should then:

- Decide whether your case has a fair probability of success considering the law in the state in which the suit will be brought;
- Give you an accurate estimate as to how long the lawsuit will take; and
- Make a determination of the approximate legal fees and disbursements.

If the lawyer sees weaknesses in your case and believes that litigation will be unduly expensive, or if he or she desires to try to settle the matter without resorting to time-consuming litigation, he or she may send an initial demand letter similar to that on page 410. Many cases are settled by my office after the sending of such a letter.

In any event the chosen course of action should be instituted without delay so you will be able to receive remuneration as quickly as possible. This will also ensure that the requisite time period to start the action—the statute of limitations—will not have expired.

Strategies about how to hire a lawyer properly and work effectively with one are explained in more detail in the next chapter.

## Considering Arbitration Versus Litigation

Arbitration is an alternative to formal litigation whereby disputes are settled without resorting to the court system. Cases are resolved by arbitrators who are not bound to make their decisions using strict rules of legal procedure. Since arbitration differs markedly from civil litigation, both the salesperson and the company must mutually agree upon the arbitration process.

Arbitration is faster and cheaper than litigation in most cases. While it may take a civil case up to four years to be resolved, the same case in arbitration might take six months from the date of filing the complaint to the day of decision. Those salespeople seeking a quick resolution of their problem will find this characteristic of arbitration to be very appealing. There is far less preparation required for an arbitration case than for a full trial. The average arbitration lasts less than a day, in comparison to a trial, which may last several days. If you are paying attorney fees by the hour or by the hour plus a flat fee for trial work on a per diem basis (as opposed to contingency fees), the arbitration route affords you considerable savings. Some people favor arbitration because the arbitrators who are selected are fully familiar with the trade practices in your industry. This reduces court time because they are able to "trim the fat" and concentrate on the contractual provisions in dispute.

## Sample Demand Letter

Law Offices of Sack & Sack
135 East 57th Street, 12th Floor
New York, NY 10022
Telephone (212) 702-9000
Telecopier (212) 702-9702

Date

Name of Principal Officer
Title
Name of Principal Company
Address

Dear (Name of Principal Officer),

Please be advised that this office is General Counsel to the National Association of Sales Agents (NASA) and represents (name of rep, address).

Demand is hereby made for commissions totaling (specify), which have been earned by my client pursuant to the agreement between the parties and which remain unpaid despite due and diligent demand.

I also understand that you have failed to render a detailed, accurate accounting regarding additional orders and reorders procured by my client which have been shipped to his customers and orders which have been received directly by your firm and shipped to my client's accounts, resulting in additional commissions due.

In this regard, I suggest that you or your representative contact this office immediately in the attempt to resolve these issues in an amicable fashion to avoid expensive and protracted litigation which, under the laws of the state of (specify) may also include triple commission damages, reasonable costs, attorney fees, and interest on the above-stated amount if commissions are not paid within (specify) days of your receipt of this letter and a lawsuit is instituted.

Hopefully this can be avoided and I thank you for your prompt cooperation and attention.

Very truly yours,
Steven Mitchell Sack

SMS/nc
cc: client
*Sent certified mail, return receipt requested.*

However, there are several disadvantages to the arbitration process for salespeople. If you opt for arbitration, you may lose your most powerful weapon—that is, *the right to view your company's books and records.* In most states the pretrial discovery procedures available in a court case are either limited or eliminated by arbitration. For example, you may not be able to force the company to turn over its books until after the arbitrator(s) has been appointed. The arbitrator has the power to decide what company records and documents you can view. His or her decision is discretionary and can be denied. Moreover, if records are produced at the hearing (sometimes for the first time), you and your attorney may have little time to analyze them before proceeding. Thus, in cases where the salesperson must rely on the company to demonstrate what is owed, and when such records are not available to the salesperson going into the dispute, litigation may be a better forum than arbitration. Conversely, when you know exactly what is owed and don't need the company to produce its records, then arbitration may be more advantageous.

Also be aware that arbitrators are less sympathetic than juries (who are more likely to rule on the side of the independent rep rather than the large company). This could unfairly hurt your case, especially if you are fired suddenly without cause, right before procuring a large order to which a claim for commissions is being made.

For all of these reasons, deciding if arbitration should be used to resolve your dispute is not a simple matter. Always discuss the pros and cons applicable to your particular case with your lawyer before agreeing to it.

# CHAPTER 10

# Hiring a Lawyer to Protect Your Rights

Do you know how to get the most out of your lawyer and how to work effectively with one? This chapter will tell you how to avoid potential misunderstandings involving lawyer billing, what to include in retainer agreements, and how to recognize when your problem is not being handled competently or in a timely fashion. You will learn what to bring to the initial interview and what to say, how to negotiate a fair fee arrangement, and how to stay informed and keep your lawyer working on your case.

## When You Need a Lawyer

Labor laws and regulations are unduly complicated, and people often need attorneys to guide them properly. The time to determine whether you need an employment lawyer is before legal action is considered. Common situations that might call for legal help are:

- Deciding to resign from a lucrative job
- Considering filing a discrimination case with the EEOC or a state agency, or filing a private lawsuit in federal or state court
- Before commencing or threatening to file a lawsuit for breach of contract, commissions, wages, bonuses, benefits, or other monies due

- Negotiating severance and other benefits resulting from a firing
- Defending a charge of violating a restrictive covenant
- Reviewing a proposed independent contractor or employment agreement

The best time to determine whether a lawyer is needed is before legal action is contemplated or necessary, and the best way to decide if a lawyer is needed is to speak to one. Hopefully, you won't be charged for brief information given over the telephone.

## How to Find a Lawyer

Select a lawyer with care. The right choice can mean recovery of thousands of dollars or satisfactory resolution of a conflict or other problem and peace of mind. The wrong choice can cost money and aggravation.

Your first step is to speak to an experienced labor attorney to determine if your problem warrants assistance. If it does, then a consultation should be scheduled so your problem can be reviewed in greater detail.

The place to start is to call a lawyer you have dealt with in the past and ask for the name of an employment law specialist. You should also inquire if your matter warrants a consultation. If the lawyer you speak to is willing to conduct the consultation, ask if he or she has sufficient expertise to provide you with competent advice. This is important. Most lawyers who represent clients in other fields are not qualified to represent people in labor matters because the law has become quite specialized. Just as you would not consult a heart surgeon about a skin problem, you should not consult a lawyer who does not regularly handle labor matters (i.e., does not devote at least 50 percent of his or her working time to representing individuals with employment-related disputes). If the lawyer tells you that she does not commonly handle your type of problem, ask for the names of other lawyers she is willing to recommend. Clients often receive excellent assistance through lawyer referrals.

---

**STRATEGY:** *Recognize that many attorneys who competently represent clients in one area (e.g., criminal law) are not qualified to represent the same client in an employment matter because most lawyers become familiar with certain types of cases, which they handle promptly, efficiently, and profitably. When lawyers accept matters outside the realm of their daily practice, the chances of making mistakes or not handling matters promptly increase. Ask the attorney what proportion of his working time is spent dealing in the field of law related to your problem. Finally, be wary of recommendations from people whose advice may be self-motivated.*

---

If you don't deal regularly with a lawyer, you may have to ask friends and relatives for referrals. However, this may not be wise unless the person tells you about a lawyer who handled a *labor matter* (not a house closing or divorce) satisfactorily. You may also wish to call your local bar association and ask for the names of labor lawyers. Some associations maintain legal referral services and lists of labor lawyers who will not charge you more than $25 for a half-hour consultation. Bar association personnel who handle incoming telephone requests are generally unbiased when referring names of lawyers. However, inquire whether the names supplied are experienced practitioners or inexperienced neophytes; be sure to ask for the names of experienced lawyers only.

Be wary of attorney advertising. Some lawyers have misled the public with their advertising. One common method is to run an advertisement stating that a particular matter costs only $X. When a potential client meets the attorney, she learns that court costs and filing fees are that amount, but attorney fees are extra. Also beware of advertisements that proclaim the lawyer is a "specialist." Most state bar associations have not adopted specialist certification programs.

## The Initial Interview

After you find a lawyer who will discuss your case with you, set up an initial interview. At the initial consultation you should obtain a sound evaluation of your legal problem and decide if you should hire the lawyer. When scheduling the consultation, be sure to ask how much it will cost and what documents, including copies of your contract, letters, performance appraisals, and reviews, should be brought to the meeting.

All discussions with the lawyer at the consultation are privileged and confidential, so don't be afraid to discuss your matter in great detail. After the consultation is over, you should have received a detailed analysis of:

- What your rights are
- Whether your case has a fair probability of success if additional action is taken
- What action should be taken by you to maximize your claim (sending a letter of protest to document your position, collecting pertinent information, etc.)
- What action would be taken by him or her to protect your rights
- What your objectives should be in taking legal action
- Potential problems relating to federal and state statutes and case decisions in the state where a lawsuit would be brought
- Approximately how long the lawsuit will take
- The approximate legal fees and disbursements

If the lawyer sees weaknesses in your case and believes that litigation will be unduly expensive, or if he or she desires to try to settle the matter without resorting to time-consuming litigation, the lawyer may recommend sending a letter to the employer for negotiation purposes.

The vast majority of cases are settled out of court after such a letter is sent. Never underestimate the power of a lawyer's letter once it is received by an employer. In any event, the chosen course of action should be instituted without delay so you will be able to receive remuneration as quickly as possible. This will also ensure that your case falls within the requisite time period to start an action—i.e., that the statute of limitations will not have expired.

A competent lawyer should leave you with a good feeling after your consultation. During the initial meeting the lawyer should be attentive, not allow distractions or interruptions to disrupt the consultation, present an outward appearance of neatness and good grooming, not act in a boastful manner (beware of the lawyer who brags "I never lose a case"), and should discuss fee arrangements up front. Some lawyers have a tendency to wait until all work is done and submit large legal bills. The failure to discuss the fee arrangement at the initial interview may be a sign that the lawyer operates this way.

## The Fee Arrangement

Once you have decided to hire the lawyer, it is important to discuss the fee arrangement immediately so there will be no surprises. Questions to ask include the following:

- What is the lawyer's fee?
- If you are billed on an hourly basis, will the lawyer estimate the maximum amount of money you will be charged?
- How are time charges computed? Will you be charged for telephone calls with the lawyer? What kind of billing statement will you receive? Are costs and disbursements (telephone charges, travel, filing fees, photocopying expenses, etc.) included, or are they extra?

- Is it better to be charged on a contingency basis? If so, what percentage of any money received in a settlement or lawsuit will be payable to the attorney? Are you required to pay an initial retainer to be applied against the contingency fee? Is this recoverable against the lawyer's fee if money is recovered?

To avoid problems and reduce misunderstandings, *always* insist on receiving a written retainer agreement before hiring the lawyer. The following are actual examples of retainer agreements given to my clients in various labor-related matters. The first letter is sent whenever a client retains my office to engage in settlement negotiations after a firing; the second letter is sent when negotiations are unsuccessful and litigation is necessary.

## Sample Retainer Agreements

Law Office of Steven Mitchell Sack
135 East 57th Street, 12th Floor
New York, NY 10022
Telephone (212) 702-9000, ext. 34
Telecopier (212) 702-9702

Date

Name of Client
Address

Re: Name of Employer

Dear Jordan,
This letter will confirm the terms of my engagement as your attorney regarding the above.
I met with you, reviewed your file, and conducted preliminary

research to learn the pertinent facts with respect to your current problems and drafted a letter of protest for you to protect your rights. For those and additional services to be rendered, you have paid me a retainer of Five Hundred Dollars ($500.00) which is my minimum fee in this matter.

I will now contact the above in the attempt to negotiate a favorable settlement to collect salary, severance pay, and commissions allegedly owed for an additional period of time beyond the company's unilateral decision to pay you only until (date). For my efforts, it is agreed that I shall be paid a contingency fee of One Third (33%) of all gross monies collected on your behalf exceeding the company's prior offer, less the $500.00 previously paid, if a settlement can be effectuated.

All settlements will require your approval before I conclude same. Additionally, the aforementioned contingency-fee arrangement is for legal work performed in *negotiations* only and does not cover work rendered in connection with a lawsuit. In the event you desire this office to assist you in formal litigation, both of us will discuss and agree upon a suitable fee arrangement in writing at a later date.

Finally, you are aware of the hazards of negotiations and that, despite my efforts on your behalf, there is no assurance or guarantee of the success or outcome of this matter.

As always, I look forward to serving you and will keep you posted with all developments as they occur.

Very truly yours,
Steven Mitchell Sack

SMS/nc
Enc.

Law Office of Steven Mitchell Sack
135 East 57th Street, 12th Floor
New York, NY 10022
Telephone (212) 702-9000, ext. 34
Telecopier (212) 702-9702

Date

Name of Client
Address

Re: Name of Employer

Dear Susan,

This will confirm our agreement whereby you have retained this office to represent your rep firm in a lawsuit in the Supreme Court, New York County, to collect commissions allegedly earned and due from the above conceivably worth in excess of One Hundred Thirty Thousand Dollars ($130,000.00).

In that regard, you have forwarded a retainer of Three Thousand Five Hundred Dollars ($3,500.00) which is my minimum fee in this matter. This retainer shall be applied against, and deducted from, a contingency fee of Thirty-Three Percent (33%) of all money collected in settlement, judgment, or otherwise. In the event your matter proceeds to trial and an actual trial occurs, you also agree to pay an additional trial fee of Five Hundred Dollars ($500.00) per day or any part of a day thereof, which will be a separate fee and not deducted from the above contingency-fee arrangement.

All settlements will require your approval before I conclude same. Additionally, the above fee arrangement only covers work rendered in connection with this lawsuit and does not cover any work in appellate courts, other actions or proceedings, or out-of-pocket disbursements. Out-of-pocket disbursements include, but are not limited to, costs of filing papers, court fees, process servers' fees, witness fees, court reporters' stenographic fees, and out-of-state travel and lodging expenses, which disbursements shall be paid for or reimbursed to me immediately upon my request. It is noted that you have forwarded the sum of Three Hundred Dollars ($300.00) for me to hold in my escrow account for such initial costs and disbursements.

Finally, I have advised you and you are aware of the hazards of litigation and that, despite my efforts on your behalf, there is no assurance or guarantee of the outcome of this matter, particularly with respect to your claim for reorders through the end of the selling season (since there was no written agreement confirming your right to receive such post-termination compensation). Also, you have assured me that there is no counterclaim exposure and no detrimental acts were committed on (name of employer), such as slander or breach of your fiduciary duty of loyalty or good faith while representing the line, and I have only agreed to represent you in this matter based on those assurances.

Kindly indicate your understanding and acceptance of the above by signing this letter below where indicated and returning the signed original to this office, keeping the copy for your files.

As always, I look forward to serving you.

Very truly yours,
Steven Mitchell Sack

I, (name of client), have read the above letter, understand and agree with all of its terms, and have received a copy:

Name of Client

SMS/nc

Enc.

422 / THE EMPLOYEE RIGHTS HANDBOOK

Be aware that there are distinct advantages and disadvantages in using different fee arrangements. For example, when you pay a flat fee, you know how much will be charged, but you do not know how much care and attention will be spent on your matter. The hourly rate might be cheaper than a flat fee for simple matters, but some dishonest lawyers "pad" time sheets to increase their fees. And although contingency-fee arrangements are beneficial to clients with weak cases or clients who cannot afford counsel's hourly rates, such arrangements often encourage lawyers to settle winning cases for less money rather than go to court. That is why no matter what type of fee is agreed upon, it is essential to hire a lawyer who is honest and has your best interests in mind at all times.

It is wise to ask for a monthly statement of services rendered, particularly if you are being charged by the hour. Request that billing statements be supported by detailed and complete time records including the date service was rendered, the time, type of service provided, and names of people contacted. Some lawyers are reluctant to do this, but by receiving these statements on a regular basis, you will be able to question inconsistencies and errors before they get out of hand and keep billing mistakes to a minimum.

The following is an example of an hourly billing statement sent by my office to a client. Note that the client is only billed for a five-minute telephone call where warranted. Some lawyers bill in minimum increments of fifteen minutes. *Avoid* this arrangement, because if the lawyer is charging a high hourly rate (i.e., more than $200 per hour), the additional ten minutes can be very expensive.

## Sample Monthly Billing Statement

Date

Name of Client
Company
Address

Current statement for all services rendered in the matter of the contract negotiation between (name of client) and (name of employer) at the rate of $200.00 per hour per agreement:

| | | |
|---|---|---|
| 1. 1/05/2001 | Tel. conv. with Employer's Attorney | |
| | 9:40–9:45 a.m. | 5 min. |
| | Tel. conv. with Client | |
| | 9:15–9:20 a.m. | 5 min. |
| | Tel. conv. with Client | |
| | 12:10–12:15 p.m. | 5 min. |
| 2. 1/04/2001 | Draft of Revised Agreement including | |
| | Tel. conv. with Client | |
| | 6:50 a.m. –8:05 a.m. | 75 min. |
| 3. 1/03/2001 | Meeting with Client | |
| | 1:40–2:50 p.m. | 70 min. |
| 4. 12/19/2000 | Review of initial proposed Agreement | |
| | 7:30 a.m. –7:55 a.m. | 25 min. |
| | Tel. conv. with Client | |
| | 9:35–9:40 a.m.; 3:40–3:45 p.m. | 10 min. |

Total time spent on Matter from December 19, 2000, through January 5, 2001, at standard rate of $200.00 per hour:

195 min. or 3.25 hours

Amount earned: $650.00

At the hiring interview you should also ask if the lawyer you are speaking to will handle the matter. When dealing with law firms, clients may think they are hiring one lawyer but their case is then assigned to another. To avoid this problem, specify in writing which lawyer will handle your case.

Also specify in writing that the lawyer will return phone calls within twenty-four hours and will promptly pursue your rights. Some lawyers procrastinate once they are retained. The legal system is often a slow process. Don't stall it further by hiring a procrastinating lawyer. And to avoid problems down the road, be sure there are no conflicts of interest (such as that the law firm represented your employer several years ago). You should ask the lawyer up front if there are any such potential conflicts.

---

**STRATEGY:** *If applicable, request an opinion letter, which spells out the pros and cons of a matter and how much money may be spent to accomplish your objectives. Even if you are charged for the time it takes to draft the letter, an opinion letter can minimize future misunderstandings between you and your lawyer and help decide whether or not to proceed with a lawsuit or legal intervention.*

---

Discuss the lawyer's escrow account arrangements. Escrow accounts are separate bank accounts that lawyers must maintain on the client's behalf. A lawyer must notify you immediately when funds are received on your behalf, and these funds must be deposited in a special account, separate from the firm's general business account. Insist on nothing less. Also insist that all funds be deposited in an interest-bearing account and be sure you receive the interest together with your share of the settlement proceeds. Some lawyers fail to remit interest to the client.

*Ask for a receipt if you pay for the initial retainer in cash.* If a retainer is required, inquire whether the retainer is to become part of the entire fee and whether it is refundable. The retainer guarantees the availability of the lawyer to represent you and is an advance paid to demonstrate your desire to resolve a problem via legal recourse. Ask if the retainer and other fees can be paid by credit card. Be sure interest will not be added if you are late in paying fees. Request that all fees be billed periodically.

---

**STRATEGY:** *Request that the attorney send you copies of all incoming and outgoing correspondence so you will be able to follow the progress of the case.*

---

Understand what legal fees are deductible. Legal fees are tax-deductible provided they are ordinary and necessary business expenses. This means that the costs of legal fees paid or incurred for the "collection, maintenance, or conservation of income" or property used in producing income can be deducted. Deductions are also allowed for legal fees paid to collect, determine, or refund any tax that is owed. Ask the attorney whether fees paid are deductible. Structure the fee arrangement to maximize tax deductions and ask for a written statement that justifies the bill on the basis of time spent or some other allocation to support the claim. Keep the statement in a safe place until tax time and show it to your tax preparers. Accountants and other professionals often clip copies of the statements directly to the return so the IRS won't question the deduction. The following is a summary of deductible legal fees:

- Attorney fees paid to negotiate severance pay and other post-termination benefits
- Attorney fees paid to obtain a tax ruling
- Attorney fees paid to negotiate an employment agreement
- Attorney fees paid to fight the enforcement of a restrictive covenant precluding you from earning a living
- Attorney fees paid to file a lawsuit to collect wages, commissions, or other compensation
- Attorney fees paid to oppose a suspension or disbarment of a professional license

## Problems Encountered After a Lawyer Is Hired

If a settlement appears imminent, don't allow yourself to be intimidated by your lawyer into accepting it unless you are satisfied. Always remember that the lawyer works for you, not vice versa. If the lawyer believes a settlement is in your best interests, be sure you receive logical reasons why. Only accept his or her opinion if it makes sense.

You have the right to change lawyers at any time if there is a valid reason. Valid reasons include improper or unethical conduct, conflicts of interest, and malpractice by the lawyer. If you are dissatisfied with the lawyer's conduct or the way the matter is progressing, consult another lawyer for an opinion. Do this before taking action, because you need a professional opinion to tell whether the lawyer acted correctly or incorrectly.

Never fire the lawyer until a replacement is hired, because you may be unrepresented and the case could be prejudiced or dismissed. If you fire the lawyer, you may be required to pay for the value of work rendered. You may also have to go to court to settle the issue of legal fees and the return of your papers, since some lawyers assert a lien on the file. However, these potential problems should never impede you from taking action if warranted.

If you have evidence that the attorney misused funds for personal gain or committed fraud, you may file a complaint with the state grievance committee or local bar association. Don't be afraid to do this. All complaints are confidential. You cannot be sued for filing a complaint if it is later determined that the lawyer did nothing wrong.

Another alternative is to commence a malpractice lawsuit against the lawyer. Legal malpractice arises when an attorney fails to use "such skill or prudence as lawyers of ordinary skill commonly possess and experience in the performance of the tasks they undertake." This doesn't mean you can sue if your lawyer gets beaten by a better attorney. You can sue only if he or she renders work or assistance of minimal competence and you are damaged as a result. You can also sue for malpractice when there is a breach of ethics (like the failure to remit funds belonging to a client) in addition to suing for breach of contract and/or civil fraud. The following are examples of lawyer malpractice:

- Settling a case without your consent
- Procrastinating work on a matter (e.g., neglecting to prepare a will after being paid and before the client dies)
- Charging grossly improper fees and failing to provide detailed, accurate time sheets to compute fees
- Failing to file a claim within the requisite time period (the statute of limitations)
- Failing to keep you advised of major developments in a matter to your detriment
- Failing to disclose that a conflict of interest exists (such as neglecting to inform you that the lawyer or someone from his law firm previously represented your opponent)

Consult another lawyer before embarking on any of these courses of action to learn if you have a valid claim. An honest and unbiased lawyer will also tell you what steps should be taken to protect your rights.

---

**STRATEGY:** *More lawyers are now willing to testify against each other. If your complaint to a state's disciplinary board is viable, it will be investigated (the process may take months). An investigative committee will decide whether the case should be given a hearing. After a thorough investigation the board may make recommendations for disciplinary action against the professional, including a formal reprimand, suspension from practice, or revocation of the lawyer's license (which is rare). You may file a private lawsuit against the professional in addition to requesting that such an investigation ensue. In such a lawsuit the lawyer will generally carry malpractice insurance and be de-*

*fended by lawyers from his or her insurance carrier. Deciding whether or not malpractice has actually occurred is a question of fact to be decided by a judge or jury. Due to the complexity of most malpractice cases, and the fact that the lawsuit will typically be vigorously defended, it is critical to seek advice from a skilled lawyer.*

## Summary of Steps to Take to Use a Lawyer Effectively

1. Speak to a lawyer before action is contemplated to determine if one is needed.

2. Schedule an interview if necessary; inquire if you will be charged for it.

3. Bring relevant documents to the interview.

4. Do not be overly impressed by plush surroundings.

5. Be sure the lawyer of your choice will be handling the matter.

6. Hire an experienced practitioner who devotes at least 50 percent of his or her working time to your type of problem.

7. Look for honesty and integrity in a lawyer.

8. Insist on signing a retainer agreement to reduce misunderstandings.

9. Have the agreement read and explained to you before signing, and save a copy for your files.

10. If the lawyer cannot state exactly how much you will be charged, get minimum and maximum estimates. Include this in the agreement.

11. Be certain you understand how additional costs are calculated and who will pay for them.

12. If an hourly rate is agreed on, negotiate that you will not be charged for a few telephone calls to your lawyer.

13. Inquire if you can pay the bill by credit card.

14. Structure the fee arrangement to maximize tax deductions and savings.

15. Insist on receiving copies of incoming and outgoing correspondence and monthly, detailed time records.

16. Be sure the lawyer will be available, that he or she will immediately commence work on your matter, and that there are no potential conflicts of interest.

17. Insist that all funds received by the lawyer be deposited into an interest-bearing escrow account. Don't forget to ask for the interest later on.

18. Never allow the lawyer to pressure you into settling a case or making a rushed, uninformed decision.

19. Consult another lawyer before deciding to fire the present one, file a complaint with the grievance committee, or commence a malpractice lawsuit.

20. Do not expect miracles.

## Conclusion

If you have read this book carefully and thoughtfully, you now have a hands-on guide to avoiding many of the employment termination problems you may face, and for those you cannot avoid, you have a guide on how to detect employer improprieties to protect your rights. Many of the items we have discussed in these pages encompass simple rules of common sense and reason.

The body of employment law has been created to further fairness and justice. It is there to protect you, but it will not help you unless you participate in your own defense. Before you make a major move, reread the appropriate portions of this book. Know the law. Discuss your situation with an attorney who specializes in labor and employment law. And, above all, good luck.

Steven Mitchell Sack, Esq.

# GLOSSARY OF TERMS

**Abuse of process:** A cause of action that arises when one party misuses the legal process to injure another.

**Accord and satisfaction:** An agreement between two parties, such as the employee and his or her company, to compromise disputes concerning outstanding debts, compensation, or terms of employment. Satisfaction occurs when the terms of the compromise are fully performed.

**Action in accounting:** A cause of action in which one party seeks a determination of the amount of money owed by another.

**Admissible:** Capable of being introduced in court as evidence.

**Advance:** A sum of money that is applied against money to be earned. Sometimes referred to as draw.

**Affidavit:** A written statement signed under oath.

**Allegations:** Written statements of a party to a lawsuit that charge the other party with wrongdoing. In order to be successful, allegations must be proved.

**Answer:** The defendant's reply to the plaintiff's allegations in a complaint.

**Anticipatory breach:** A breach of contract that occurs when one party, e.g., the employee, states in advance of performance that he or she will definitely not perform under the terms of his or her contract.

**Appeal:** A proceeding whereby the losing party to a lawsuit requests that a higher court determine the correctness of the decision.

**Arbitration:** A proceeding whereby both sides to a lawsuit agree to submit their dispute to arbitrators, rather than judges. The arbitration proceeding is expeditious and is legally binding on all parties.

**Assignment:** The transfer of a right or interest by one party to another.

**Attorney in fact:** A person appointed by another to transact business on his or her behalf; the person does not have to be a lawyer.

**At-will employment:** *See* Employment at will.

**Award:** A decision made by a judicial body to compensate the winning party in a lawsuit.

**Bill of particulars:** A document used in a lawsuit that specifically details the loss alleged by the plaintiff.

**Breach of contract:** A legal cause of action for the unjustified failure to perform a duty or obligation specified in an agreement.

**Brief:** A concise statement of the main contents of a lawsuit.

**Burden of proof:** The responsibility of a party to a lawsuit to provide sufficient evidence to prove or disprove a claim.

**Business deduction:** A legitimate expense that can be used to decrease the amount of income subject to tax.

**Business slander:** A legal wrong committed when a party orally makes false statements that impugn the business reputation of another (e.g., imply that the person is dishonest, incompetent, or financially unreliable).

**Calendar:** A list of cases to be heard each day in court.

**Cause of action:** The legal theory on which a plaintiff seeks to recover damages.

**Caveat emptor:** A Latin expression frequently applied to consumer transactions; translated as "Let the buyer beware."

**Cease and desist letter:** A letter, usually sent by lawyer, that notifies an individual to stop engaging in a particular type of activity, behavior, or conduct that infringes on the rights of another.

**Check:** A negotiable instrument; the depositor's written order requesting his or her bank to pay a definite sum of money to a named individual, entity, or to the bearer.

**Civil court:** Generally, any court that presides over noncriminal matters.

**Claims court:** A particular court that hears tax disputes.

**Clerk of the court:** A person who determines whether court papers are properly filed and court procedures followed.

**Collateral estoppel:** *See* Estoppel. Collateral estoppel happens when a prior but different legal action is conclusive in a way to bring about estoppel in a current legal action.

**Common law:** Law that evolves from reported case decisions that are relied on for their precedential value.

**Compensatory damages:** A sum of money, awarded to a party, that represents the actual harm suffered or loss incurred.

**Complaint:** A legal document that commences a lawsuit; it alleges facts and causes of action that a plaintiff relies on to collect damages.

**Conflict of interest:** The ethical inability of a lawyer to represent a client because of competing loyalties, e.g., representing both employer and employee in a labor dispute.

**Consideration:** An essential element of an enforceable contract; something of value given or promised by one party in exchange for an act or promise of another.

**Contempt:** A legal sanction imposed when a rule or order of a judicial body is disobeyed.

**Contingency fee:** A type of fee arrangement whereby a lawyer is paid a percentage of the money recovered. If unsuccessful, the client is responsible only for costs already paid by the lawyer.

**Continuance:** The postponement of a legal proceeding to another date.

**Contract:** An enforceable agreement, either written, oral, or implied by the actions or intentions of the parties.

**Contract modification:** The alteration of contract terms.

**Counterclaim:** A claim asserted by a defendant in a lawsuit.

**Covenant:** A promise.

**Credibility:** The believability of a witness as perceived by a judge or jury.

**Creditor:** The party to whom money is owed.

**Cross-examination:** The questioning of a witness by the opposing lawyer.

**Damage:** An award, usually money, given to the winning party in a lawsuit as compensation for the wrongful acts of another.

**Debtor:** The party who owes money.

**Decision:** The determination of a case or matter by a judicial body.

**Deductible:** The unrecoverable portion of insurance proceeds.

**Defamation:** An oral or written statement communicated to a third party that impugns a person's reputation in the community.

**Default judgment:** An award rendered after one party fails to appear in a lawsuit.

**Defendant:** The person or entity who is sued in a lawsuit.

**Defense:** The defendant's justification for relieving himself or herself of fault.

**Definite term of employment:** Employment of a fixed period of time.

**Deposition:** A pretrial proceeding in which one party is questioned, usually under oath, by the opposing party's lawyer.

**Disclaimer:** A clause in a sales, service, or other contract that attempts to limit or exonerate one party from liability in the event of a lawsuit.

**Discovery:** A general term used to describe several pretrial devices (e.g., depositions and interrogatories) that enable lawyers to elicit information from the opposing side.

**Dual capacity:** A legal theory, used to circumvent workers' compensation laws, that allows an injured employee to sue his or her employer directly in court.

**Due process:** Constitutional protections that guarantee that a person's life, liberty, or property cannot be taken away without the opportunity to be heard in a judicial proceeding.

**Duress:** Unlawful threats, pressure, or force that induces a person to act contrary to his or her intentions; if proved, it allows a party to disavow a contract.

**Employee:** A person who works and is subject to an employer's scope, direction, and control.

**Employment at will:** Employment by which an employee has no job security.

**Employment discrimination:** Conduct directed at employees and job applicants that is prohibited by law.

**Equity:** Fairness; usually applied when a judicial body awards a suitable remedy other than money to a party (e.g., an injunction).

**Escrow account:** A separate fund where lawyers or others are obligated to deposit money received from or on behalf of a client.

**Estoppel:** A legal bar to prevent a party from asserting a fact or claim inconsistent with that party's prior position that has been relied on or acted on by another party.

**Evidence:** Information in the form of oral testimony, exhibits, affidavits, etc., used to prove a party's claim.

**Examination before trial:** A pretrial legal device; also called a deposition.

**Exhibit:** Tangible evidence used to prove a party's claim.

**Exit agreement:** An agreement sometimes signed between an employer and an employee on resignation or termination of an employee's services.

**Express contract:** An agreement whose terms are manifested by clear and definite language, as distinguished from agreements inferred from conduct.

**False imprisonment:** The unlawful detention of a person who is held against his or her will without authority or justification.

**Filing fee:** Money paid to start a lawsuit.

**Final decree:** A court order or directive of a permanent nature.

**Financial statement:** A document, usually prepared by an accountant, that reflects a business's (or individual's) assets, liabilities, and financial condition.

**Flat fee:** A sum of money paid to a lawyer as compensation for services.

**Flat fee plus time:** A form of payment in which a lawyer receives one sum for services and also receives additional money calculated on an hourly basis.

**Fraud:** A false statement that is relied on and causes damages to the defrauded party.

**General denial:** A reply contained in the defendant's answer.

**Ground:** The basis for an action or an argument.

**Guaranty:** A contract in which one party agrees to answer for or satisfy the debt of another.

**Hearsay evidence:** Unsubstantiated evidence that is often excluded by a court.

**Hourly fee:** Money paid to a lawyer for services, computed on an hourly basis.

**Implied contract:** An agreement that is tacit rather than expressed in clear and definite language; an agreement inferred from the conduct of the parties.

**Indemnification:** Protection or reimbursement against damage or loss. The indemnified party is protected against liabilities or penalties from that party's actions; the indemnifying party provides the protection or reimbursement.

**Infliction of emotional distress:** A legal cause of action in which one party seeks to recover damages for mental pain and suffering caused by another.

**Injunction:** A court order restraining one party from doing or refusing to do an act.

**Integration:** The act of making a contract whole by integrating its elements into a coherent single entity. An agreement is considered integrated when the parties involved accept the final version as a complete expression of their agreement.

**Interrogatories:** A pretrial device used to elicit information; written questions are sent to an opponent to be answered under oath.

**Invasion of privacy:** The violation of a person's constitutionally protected right to privacy.

**Judgment:** A verdict rendered by a judicial body; if money is awarded, the winning party is the "judgment creditor" and the losing party is the "judgment debtor."

**Jurisdiction:** The authority of a court to hear a particular matter.

**Legal duty:** The responsibility of a party to perform a certain act.

**Letter of agreement:** An enforceable contract in the form of a letter.

**Letter of protest:** A letter sent to document a party's dissatisfaction.

**Liable:** Legally in the wrong or legally responsible for.

**Lien:** A claim made against the property of another in order to satisfy a judgment.

**Lifetime contract:** An employment agreement of infinite duration that is often unenforceable.

**Liquidated damages:** An amount of money agreed on in advance by parties to a contract to be paid in the event of a breach or dispute.

**Malicious interference with contractual rights:** A legal cause of action in which one party seeks to recover damages against an individual who has induced or caused another party to terminate a valid contract.

**Malicious prosecution:** A legal cause of action in which one party seeks to recover damages after another party instigates or institutes a frivolous judicial proceeding (usually criminal) that is dismissed.

**Mediation:** A voluntary dispute resolution process in which both sides attempt to settle their differences without resorting to formal litigation.

**Misappropriation:** A legal cause of action that arises when one party makes untrue statements of fact that induce another party to act and be damaged as a result.

**Mitigation of damages:** A legal principle that requires a party seeking damages to make reasonable efforts to reduce damages as much as possible, e.g., to seek new employment after being unfairly discharged.

**Motion:** A written request made to a court by one party during a lawsuit.

**Negligence:** A party's failure to exercise a sufficient degree of care owed to another by law.

**Nominal damages:** A small sum of money awarded by a court.

**Noncompetition clause:** A restrictive provision in a contract that limits an employee's right to work in that particular industry after he or she ceases to be associated with his or her present employer.

**Notary public:** A person authorized under state law to administer an oath or verify a signature.

**Notice to show cause:** A written document in a lawsuit asking a court to expeditiously rule on a matter.

**Objection:** A formal protest made by a lawyer in a lawsuit.

**Offer:** The presentment of terms, which, if accepted, may lead to the formation of a contract.

**Opinion letter:** A written analysis of a client's case, prepared by a lawyer.

**Option:** An agreement giving one party the right to choose a certain course of action.

**Oral contract:** An enforceable verbal agreement.

**Parol evidence:** Oral evidence introduced at a trial to alter or explain the terms of a written agreement.

**Partnership:** A voluntary association between two or more competent persons engaged in a business as co-owners for profit.

**Party:** A plaintiff or defendant in a lawsuit.

**Perjury:** Committing false testimony while under oath.

**Petition:** A request filed in court by one party.

**Plaintiff:** The party who commences a lawsuit.

**Pleading:** A written document that states the facts or arguments put forth by a party in a lawsuit.

**Power of attorney:** A document executed by one party allowing another to act on his or her behalf in specified situations.

**Pretrial discovery:** A legal procedure used to gather information from an opponent before the trial.

**Process server:** An individual who delivers the summons and/or complaint to the defendant.

**Promissory note:** A written acknowledgment of a debt whereby one party agrees to pay a specified sum on a specified date.

**Proof:** Evidence presented at a trial and used by a judge or jury to fashion an award.

**Punitive damages:** Money awarded as punishment for a party's wrongful acts.

**Quantum meruit:** A legal principle whereby a court awards reasonable compensation to a party who performs work, labor, or services at another party's request.

**Rebuttal:** The opportunity for a lawyer at a trial to ask a client or witness additional questions to clarify points elicited by the opposing lawyer during cross-examination.

**Release:** A written document that, when signed, relinquishes a party's rights to enforce a claim against another.

**Remedy:** The means by which a right is enforced or protected.

**Reply:** A written document in a lawsuit conveying the contentions of a party in response to a motion.

**Restrictive covenant:** A provision in a contract that forbids one party from doing a certain act, e.g., working for another, soliciting customers.

**Retainer:** A sum of money paid to a lawyer for services to be rendered.

**Service letter statutes:** Laws in some states that require an employer to furnish an employee with written reasons for his or her discharge.

**Sexual harassment:** Prohibited conduct of a sexual nature that occurs in the workplace.

**Shop rights:** The rights of an employer to use within the employer's facility a device or method developed by an employee.

**Slander:** Oral defamation of a party's reputation.

**Small-claims court:** A particular court that presides over small disputes (e.g., those involving sums of less than $3,500).

**Sole proprietorship:** An unincorporated business.

**Statement of fact:** Remarks or comments of a specific nature that have a legal effect.

**Statute:** A law created by a legislative body.

**Statute of frauds:** A legal principle requiring that certain contracts be in writing in order to be enforceable.

**Statute of limitations:** A legal principle requiring a party to commence a lawsuit within a certain period of time.

**Stipulation:** An agreement between the parties.

**Submission agreement:** A signed agreement whereby both parties agree to submit a present dispute to binding arbitration.

**Subpoena:** A written order requiring a party or witness to appear at a legal proceeding; a *subpoena duces tecum* is a written order requiring a party to bring books and records to the legal proceeding.

**Summation:** The last part of the trial wherein both lawyers recap the respective positions of their clients.

**Summons:** A written document served on a defendant giving notification of a lawsuit.

**Temporary decree:** A court order or directive of a temporary nature, capable of being modified or changed.

**Testimony:** Oral evidence presented by a witness under oath.

**"Time is of the essence":** A legal expression often included in agreements to specify the requirements of timeliness.

**Tort:** A civil wrong.

**Unfair and deceptive practice:** Illegal business and trade acts prohibited by various federal and state laws.

**Unfair discharge:** An employee's termination without legal justification.

**Verdict:** The decision of a judge or jury.

**Verification:** A written statement signed under oath.

**Waiver:** A written document that, when signed, relinquishes a party's rights.

**Whistle-blowing:** Protected conduct where one party complains about the illegal acts of another.

**Witness:** A person who testifies at a judicial proceeding.

**Workers' compensation:** A process in which an employee receives compensation for injuries sustained in the course of employment.

# APPENDIX

**American Arbitration Regional Offices**

**ARIZONA**
333 East Osborn Road, Suite
    310
Phoenix, AZ 85012-2365
(602) 234-0950/230-2151 (fax)

**CALIFORNIA**
2030 Main Street, Suite 1650
Irvine, CA 92714-7240
(714) 474-5090/474-5087 (fax)

3055 Wilshire Boulevard, 7th
    Floor
Los Angeles, CA 90010-1108
(213) 383-6516/386-2251 (fax)

600 B Street, Suite 1450
San Diego, CA 92101-4586
(619) 239-3051/239-3807 (fax)

417 Montgomery Street
San Francisco, CA 94104-1113
(415) 981-3901/781-8426 (fax)

**COLORADO**
1660 Lincoln Street, Suite 2150
Denver, CO 80264-2101
(303) 831-0823/832-3626 (fax)

**CONNECTICUT**
111 Founders Plaza, 17th Floor
East Hartford, CT 06108-3256
(860) 289-3993/282-0459 (fax)

**DISTRICT OF COLUMBIA**
1150 Connecticut Avenue NW,
    6th Floor
Washington, DC 20036-4104
(202) 296-8510/872-9574 (fax)

**FLORIDA**
799 Brickell Plaza, Suite 600
Miami, FL 33131-2800
(305) 358-7777/358-4931 (fax)

201 East Pine Street, Suite 800
Orlando, FL 32801-2742
(407) 648-1185/649-8668 (fax)

**GEORGIA**
1975 Century Boulevard NE,
    Suite 1
Atlanta, GA 30334-3203
(404) 325-0101/325-8034 (fax)

**HAWAII**
810 Richards Street, Suite 641
Honolulu, HI 96813-4714
(808) 531-0541/533-2306 (fax)
In Guam, (671) 477-1845/477-3178 (fax)

**ILLINOIS**
225 North Michigan Avenue,
Suite 2527
Chicago, IL 60601-7601
(312) 616-6560/819-0404 (fax)

**LOUISIANA**
2810 Energy Centre
1100 Poydras Street
New Orleans, LA 70163-2810
(504) 522-8781/561-8041 (fax)

**MARYLAND**
10 Hopkins Plaza
Baltimore, MD 21201-2930
(410) 837-0087/783-2797 (fax)

**MASSACHUSETTS**
133 Federal Street
Boston, MA 02110-1703
(617) 451-6600/451-0763 (fax)

**MICHIGAN**
One Towne Square, Suite 1600
Southfield, MI 48076-3728
(810) 352-5500/352-3147 (fax)

**MINNESOTA**
514 Nicollet Mall, 6th Floor
Minneapolis, MN 55402-1092
(612) 332-6545/342-2334 (fax)

**MISSOURI**
1101 Walnut Street, Suite 903
Kansas City, MO 64106-2110
(816) 221-6401/471-5264 (fax)

One Mercantile Center, Suite 2512
St. Louis, MO 63101-1614
(314) 621-7175/621-3730 (fax)

**NEVADA**
4425 Spring Mountain Road,
Suite 310
Las Vegas, NV 89102-8719
(702) 364-8009/364-8084 (fax)
From Reno, (702) 786-6688

**NEW JERSEY**
265 Davidson Avenue, Suite 140
Somerset, NJ 08873-4120
(908) 560-9560/560-8850 (fax)

**NEW YORK**
666 Old Country Road, Suite 603
Garden City, NY 11530-2004
(516) 222-1660/745-6447 (fax)

140 West 51st Street
New York, NY 10020-1203
(212) 484-3266/307-4387 (fax)

205 South Salina Street
Syracuse, NY 13202-1376
(315) 472-5483/472-0966 (fax)

399 Knollwood Road, Suite 116
White Plains, NY 10603-1916
(914) 946-1119/946-2661 (fax)

**NORTH CAROLINA**
428 East 4th Street, Suite 300
Charlotte, NC 28202-2431
(704) 347-0200/347-2804 (fax)

**OHIO**
441 Vine Street, Suite 3308
Cincinnati, OH 45202-2973
(513) 241-8434/241-8437 (fax)

17900 Jefferson Park, Suite 101
Cleveland, OH 44130-3490
(216) 891-4741/891-4740 (fax)

**PENNSYLVANIA**
230 South Broad Street, 6th
    Floor
Philadelphia, PA 19102-4106
(215) 732-5260/732-5002 (fax)

4 Gateway Center, Room 419
Pittsburgh, PA 15222-1207
(412) 261-3617/261-6055 (fax)

**TENNESSEE**
211 7th Avenue North, Suite 300
Nashville, TN 37219-1823
(615) 256-5857/244-8570 (fax)

**TEXAS**
13455 Noel Road, Suite 1440
Dallas, TX 75240-6620
(214) 702-8222/490-9008 (fax)

1001 Fannin Street, Suite 1005
Houston, TX 77002-6708
(713) 739-1302/739-1702 (fax)

**UTAH**
645 South 200 East, Suite 203
Salt Lake City, UT 84111-3834
(801) 531-9748/323-9624 (fax)

**VIRGINIA**
707 East Main Street, Suite
    1610
Richmond, VA 23219-2803
(804) 649-4838/643-6340 (fax)

**WASHINGTON**
1325 4th Avenue, Suite 1414
Seattle, WA 98101-2511
(206) 622-6435/343-5679 (fax)

## EEOC Field Offices

Albuquerque
505 Marquette NW, Suite 900
Albuquerque, NM 87102-2189
(505) 766-2061

Atlanta
75 Piedmont Avenue NE, Suite
    1100
Atlanta, GA 30335
(404) 331-0604

Baltimore
City Crescent Building
10 South Howard Street, 3rd
    Floor
Baltimore, MD 21201
(410) 962-3932

Birmingham
1900 3rd Avenue North, Suite
    101

Birmingham, AL 35203-2397
(205) 731-0082

Boston
1 Congress Street, 10th Floor
Boston, MA 02114
(617) 565-3200

Buffalo
6 Fountain Plaza, Suite 350
Buffalo, NY 14203
(716) 846-4441

Charlotte
5500 Central Avenue
Charlotte, NC 28212-2708
(704) 567-7100

Chicago
500 West Madison Street, Room
  2800
Chicago, IL 60661
(312) 353-2713

Cincinnati
Ameritrust Building
525 Vine Street, Suite 810
Cincinnati, OH 45202-3122
(513) 684-2851

Cleveland
Tower City, Skylight Office
  Tower
1660 West Second Street, Suite
  850
Cleveland, OH 44113-1454
(216) 522-2001

Dallas
207 South Houston Street, 3rd
  Floor

Dallas, TX 75202-4726
(214) 655-3355

Denver
303 East 17th Avenue, Suite 510
Denver, CO 80203-9634
(303) 866-1300

Detroit
477 Michigan Avenue, Room
  1540
Detroit, MI 48226-9704
(313) 226-7636

District of Columbia
1400 L Street NW, Suite 200
Washington, DC 20507
(202) 275-7377

El Paso
The Commons, Building C,
  Suite 100
4171 North Mesa Street
El Paso, TX 79902
(915) 534-6550

Fresno
1265 West Shaw Avenue, Suite
  103
Fresno, CA 93711
(209) 487-5793

Greensboro
801 Summit Avenue
Greensboro, NC 27405-7813
(919) 333-5174

Greenville
SCN Building
15 South Main Street, Suite 530
Greenville, SC 29601
(803) 241-4400

Honolulu
677 Ala Moana Boulevard, Suite
 404
PO Box 50082
Honolulu, HI 96813
(808) 541-3120

Houston
1919 Smith Street, 7th Floor
Houston, TX 77002
(713) 653-3377

Indianapolis
101 West Ohio Street, Suite
 1900
Indianapolis, IN 46204-4203
(317) 226-7212

Jackson
Cross Roads Building Complex
207 West Amite Street
Jackson, MS 39201
(601) 965-4537

Kansas City
911 Walnut, 10th Floor
Kansas City, MO 64106
(816) 426-5773

Little Rock
425 West Capitol Avenue, 6th
 Floor
Little Rock, AR 72201
(501) 324-5060

Los Angeles
255 East Temple Street, 4th
 Floor
Los Angeles, CA 90012
(213) 251-7278

Louisville
600 M. L. King Jr. Place, Room
 268
Louisville, KY 40202
(502) 582-6082

Memphis
1407 Union Avenue, Suite 621
Memphis, TN 38104
(901) 722-2617

Miami
One Northeast First Street, 6th
 Floor
Miami, FL 33132-2491
(305) 536-4491

Milwaukee
310 West Wisconsin Avenue,
 Suite 800
Milwaukee, WI 53203-2292
(414) 297-1111

Minneapolis
330 South Second Avenue,
 Room 430
Minneapolis, MN 55401-2224
(612) 335-4040

Nashville
50 Vintage Way, Suite 202
Nashville, TN 37228
(615) 736-5820

Newark
One Newark Center, 21st Floor
Newark, NJ 07102-5233
(201) 645-6383

New Orleans
701 Loyola, Suite 600

New Orleans, LA 70113-9936
(504) 589-2329

New York
7 World Trade Center, 18th
    Floor
New York, NY 10048
(212) 748-8500

Norfolk
252 Monticello Avenue, 1st
    Floor
Norfolk, VA 23510
(804) 441-3470

Oakland
Oakland Federal Building,
    North Tower
1301 Clay Street
Oakland, CA 94612-5217
(510) 637-3230

Oklahoma City
531 Couch Drive
Oklahoma City, OK 73102
(405) 231-4911

Philadelphia
1421 Cherry Street, 10th Floor
Philadelphia, PA 19102
(215) 656-7000

Phoenix
4520 North Central Avenue,
    Suite 300
Phoenix, AZ 85012-1848
(602) 640-5000

Pittsburgh
1000 Liberty Avenue, Room
    2038A

Pittsburgh, PA 15222
(412) 644-3444

Raleigh
1309 Annapolis Drive
Raleigh, NC 27608-2129
(919) 856-4064

Richmond
3600 West Broad Street, Room
    229
Richmond, VA 23230
(804) 771-2692

St. Louis
625 North Euclid Street, 5th
    Floor
St. Louis, MO 63108
(314) 425-6585

San Antonio
5410 Fredericksburg Road,
    Suite 200
San Antonio, TX 78229-9934
(210) 229-4810

San Diego
401 B Street, Suite 1550
San Diego, CA 92101
(619) 557-7235

San Francisco
901 Market Street, Suite 500
San Francisco, CA 94103
(415) 744-6500

San Jose
96 North 3rd Street, Suite 200
San Jose, CA 95112
(408) 291-7352

Savannah
410 Mall Boulevard, Suite G
Savannah, GA 31406
(912) 652-4234

Seattle
909 First Avenue, Suite 400
Seattle, WA 98104-1061
(206) 220-6883

Tampa
Timberlake Federal Building
  Annex
501 East Polk Street, 10th Floor
Tampa, FL 33602
(813) 228-2310

## State Human Rights Commissions

Alabama
Civil Rights & EEO Office
649 Monroe Street
Montgomery, AL 36131
(334) 242-8496

Alaska
Human Rights Commission
800 A Street, Suite 202
Anchorage, AK 99501-3628
(907) 276-7474

Arizona
Civil Rights Division
1275 West Washington
Phoenix, AZ 85007
(602) 542-5263

California
Fair Employment & Housing
  Commission
1390 Market Street, Room 410
San Francisco, CA 94102-5377
(415) 557-2325

Colorado
Civil Rights Division
1560 Broadway, Suite 1050

Denver, CO 80202
(303) 894-2997

Connecticut
Human Rights & Opportunities
  Commission
90 Washington Street
Hartford, CT 05106
(203) 566-3350

Delaware
Human Relations Division
820 North French Street
Wilmington, DE 19801
(302) 577-3485

District of Columbia
Human Rights Commission
51 N Street NE, 6th Floor
Washington, DC 20002
(202) 724-0656

Florida
Civil Rights Division
303 Hartman Building
2021 Capitol Circle SE
Tallahassee, FL 32399-2152
(904) 488-5905

Georgia
Fair Employment Practices
   Office
156 Trinity Avenue SW, Room
   208
Atlanta, GA 30303
(404) 656-1736

Hawaii
Labor & Industrial Relations
   Department
EEO Officer
830 Punchbowl Street
Honolulu, HI 96813
(808) 548-4533

Idaho
Human Rights Commission
PO Box 83720
Boise, ID 83720-0040
(208) 334-2873

Illinois
Human Rights Department
100 West Randolph Street, Suite
   10-100
Chicago, IL 60601
(312) 814-6245

Indiana
Civil Rights Commission
100 North Senate Avenue,
   Room N-103
Indianapolis, IN 46204
(317) 232-2600

Iowa
Human Rights Department
Lucas State Office Building
321 East 12th Street

Des Moines, Iowa 50319
(515) 281-7300

Kansas
Civil Rights Commission
900 Southwest Jackson Street,
   Suite 851-S
Topeka, KS 66612-1252
(913) 296-3206

Kentucky
Human Rights Commission
Heyburn Building, 7th Floor
332 West Broadway
Louisville, KY 40202
(502) 595-4024

Louisiana
Civil Rights
PO Box 3776
Baton Rouge, LA 70821
(504) 342-2700

Maine
Human Rights Commission
State House, Station 51
Augusta, ME 04333
(207) 624-6050

Maryland
Human Relations Commission
6 St. Paul Street, 9th Floor
Baltimore, MD 21202
(410) 767-8600

Massachusetts
Commission Against
   Discrimination
John W. McCormack State
   Office Building, Room 601
One Ashburton Place

Boston, MA 02108
(617) 727-3990

Michigan
Civil Rights Department
Victor Office Building
201 North Washington Square
Lansing, MI 48913
(517) 335-3165

Minnesota
Human Rights Department
500 Bremer Tower
7th Place & Minnesota Street
St. Paul, MN 55101
(612) 296-5665

Mississippi
Appeals Board
301 North Lamar Street, Room
    100
Jackson, MS 39201
(601) 359-1406

Missouri
Human Rights Commission
3315 West Truman Boulevard
Jefferson City, MO 65102-1129
(573) 751-3325

Montana
Human Rights Division
PO Box 1728
Helena, MT 59624
(406) 444-3870

Nebraska
Equal Opportunity Commission
PO Box 94934
Lincoln, NE 68509
(402) 471-2024

Nevada
Equal Rights Commission
1515 East Tropicana Avenue,
    Suite 590
Las Vegas, NV 89158
(702) 486-7161

New Hampshire
Human Rights Commission
163 Louden Road
Concord, NH 03301
(603) 271-2767

New Jersey
Civil Rights Division
383 West State Street, CN089
Trenton, NJ 08625
(609) 984-3100

New Mexico
Human Rights Division
1596 Pacheco Street
Santa Fe, NM 87502
(505) 827-6823

New York
Human Rights Division
55 West 125th Street
New York, NY 10027
(212) 870-8790

North Carolina
Human Relations Commission
217 West Jones Street
Raleigh, NC 27603
(919) 733-7996

North Dakota
Equal Employment Opportunity
600 East Boulevard Avenue
Bismarck, ND 58505
(701) 328-2660

Ohio
Civil Rights Commission
220 Parsons Avenue
Columbus, OH 43215
(614) 466-2785

Oklahoma
Human Rights Commission
2101 North Lincoln Boulevard,
  Room 480
Oklahoma City, OK 73105
(405) 521-3441

Oregon
Civil Rights Division
State Office Building, Suite 1045
800 Northeast Oregon Street,
  #32
Portland, OR 97232
(503) 731-4873

Pennsylvania
Human Relations Commission
PO Box 3145
Harrisburg, PA 17105
(717) 787-4410

Rhode Island
Human Rights Commission
10 Abbott Park Place
Providence, RI 02903
(401) 277-2661

South Carolina
Human Affairs Commission
PO Box 4490
Columbia, SC 29240
(803) 253-6336

South Dakota
Human Rights Division
State Capitol
910 East Sioux
Pierre, SD 57501
(605) 773-4493

Tennessee
Human Rights Commission
400 Cornerstone Square
  Building
Nashville, TN 37243
(615) 741-4940

Texas
Human Rights Commission
8100 Cameron Road, Building
  B, Suite 525
Austin, TX 78754
(512) 837-8534

Utah
Labor Division & Anti-
Discrimination Division
160 East 300 South, 3rd Floor
Salt Lake City, UT 84114
(801) 530-6921

Vermont
Public Protection Division
109 State Street
Montpelier, VT 05602
(802) 828-3171

Virginia
Human Rights Council
PO Box 717
Richmond, VA 23206
(804) 225-2292

Washington
Human Rights Commission
711 South Capitol Way, Suite 402
Olympia, WA 98504
(360) 753-6770

West Virginia
Human Rights Commission
1321 Plaza East, Room 104-106
Charleston, WV 25301-1400
(304) 558-2616

Wisconsin
Equal Rights Division
PO Box 8928
Madison, WI 53708
(608) 266-0946

Wyoming
Labor Standards & Fair
  Employment Division
Herschler Building, 2nd Floor
  East
Cheyenne, WY 82002
(307) 777-6381

# INDEX

# ABOUT THE AUTHOR

STEVEN MITCHELL SACK maintains a private law practice in New York City devoted to severance negotiations of terminated workers and executives, discrimination lawsuits, contract negotiations, representation of salespeople and employees in breach of contract and commission disputes, and general labor law. He is a Phi Beta Kappa graduate of the State University of New York at Stony Brook and Boston College Law School.

Mr. Sack hosts a live national radio show every Sunday called *Steven Sack, The Employee's Lawyer* through i.e. america radio network and is the author of seventeen legal books for the American public. His views on employment law have been reported in the *Wall Street Journal*, the *New York Times, Fortune* magazine, and dozens of other publications. He has appeared on *The Oprah Winfrey Show, Jenny Jones,* and *The Sally Jessy Raphael Show* (three times discussing unjust firings and sexual harassment) and has made numerous appearances on CNBC's *Smart Money* and *Steals and Deals*. Mr. Sack also serves as a consultant to FindLaw.com.

Mr. Sack is the president of Legal Strategies Inc., a publishing firm. He is a member of the American Bar Association Labor and Employment Sections and is admitted to practice before the U.S. Tax Court. He also serves as a commercial and labor arbitrator for the American Arbitration Association and as general labor counsel for many trade organizations. In addition to regularly conducting seminars on employment issues for both employee and employer groups, he is engaged by law firms throughout the United States to strategize cases and testify as an expert witness.

Mr. Sack is married and has two sons. He enjoys boating and sports in his spare time.